# Loving God through the Truth

# Loving God through the Truth

An Introduction to Systematic Theology

<small>SECOND EDITION</small>

# Mark Kim

WIPF & STOCK · Eugene, Oregon

LOVING GOD THROUGH THE TRUTH
An Introduction to Systematic Theology

Wipf & Stock

An Imprint of Wipf and Stock Publishers

199 W. 8th Ave., Suite 3

Eugene, OR 97401

www.wipfandstock.com

PAPERBACK ISBN: 978-1-6667-6950-0

HARDCOVER ISBN: 978-1-6667-6951-7

EBOOK ISBN: 978-1-6667-6952-4

VERSION NUMBER 052323

For Ken Thomas Kim

(2014–)

*"Behold, children are a gift of the LORD"* (Ps 127:3, NASB)

# Contents

# Preface to the First Edition

THIS PROJECT BEGAN IN the fall of 2007 when I commenced my studies in the doctoral program at Wycliffe College, University of Toronto. By that time I had already read several systematic theology works from different theological perspectives to gain a better understanding of what was out there in the field. At the time when this project was started, systematic theology was already in vogue in evangelical academic circles as numerous works were published just before and right after the turn of the century. Some notable titles that come to mind include Millard J. Erickson's *Christian Theology*, Gordon R. Lewis and Bruce A. Demarest's *Integrative Theology*, Wayne A. Grudem's *Systematic Theology*, and Robert L. Reymond's *A New Systematic Theology of the Christian Faith*. Professors, students, and Christian laypeople were starting to realize more and more the importance of studying systematic theology, not only in the context of Christian academia but for the life and mission of the church.

One may ask why I wrote a systematic theology considering that the Christian academic market is currently inundated with a plethora of systematic theology works written by authors from various theological traditions. In fact, one could make a case that writing another systematic theology work at the present time is more or less not a constructive use of one's time. However, I believe that the evangelical church today can never be too short on producing edifying systematic theology works that attempt to faithfully proclaim God's word for those active in Christ's church. It goes without saying that every believer in Christ needs to continually feast on the teachings and dogmas of Scripture if he or she desires to grow spiritually and be sanctified by the word of God.

Finally, this work is principally geared towards seminary students who are studying to become ministers or laypeople who desire to understand the basics of evangelical Christian doctrines for their own knowledge and spiritual growth. As one can surmise by the length of this book (unlike the works I mentioned above which are quite lengthy), this work is not meant to be an exhaustive study on Christian doctrine. Although some professional theologians may find this book useful, I did not have them in mind primarily when I wrote the manuscripts for eventual submission. However, if any individual benefits from this work in any way (regardless of where they are at in their spiritual pilgrimage) then I have accomplished what I intended to do when I first started writing this book.

Mark Kim
Toronto, Canada
April 2021

# Introduction

IN MATTHEW 22:37–38, JESUS states, in response to a question posed by a Jewish teacher of the law regarding the greatest commandment, that the first and greatest commandment is to love God with all of one's heart, soul, and mind. One of the ways we can love God is by endeavoring to know who he is, what he has done for us in Christ, and what he requires of us as his covenant people. In other words, loving God requires not only that we do the things that he requires of us but that we rightly understand the truths he has revealed to us through his inspired prophets and apostles. As a result, the study of *theology* (or the doctrines of our apostolic faith) holds a pivotal and necessary place in the life of Christ's church and the individual believer. However, we must also clearly define what theology is.

The word *theology* is derived from two Greek words: *theos* (meaning God) and *logos* (meaning word or discourse). Thus, we can say that theology is a "discourse about God." In academic circles throughout history theology has been called the "Queen of the Sciences." Although real or life sciences have their share of importance because they relate to the earthly existence of human beings, Christian theology demonstrates its higher importance not only for its real applicability on earthly matters but also because it deals with the eternal destinies of human beings. Therefore, one can define theology as an *organized system of beliefs based on Scripture that seeks to know what is true about God, his works, and human beings so that it may impact the way the Christian lives out his or her divine calling.* Theology, then, must not only be biblical and internally coherent but also experientially practical in order for it be meaningful to the life of the believer. True Christian theology cannot be merely an academic exercise that stimulates the intellect but something that will impact the daily life of the believer.

As Stanley J. Grenz states, "Theology fulfills a role in the life of the people of God. Its purpose is ultimately 'practical'; it is related to Christian life and practice."[1] Although we will be keenly aware throughout this work that theology is a highly academic enterprise, we will also recognize that it is foremost practical in its results and application.

One of the core difficulties in this modern age within Christian scholarship is determining what is true and accurate from a biblical point of view. With the rise of historical criticism and the triumph of modernity in Western academic circles, the Bible and its divine origin have come under sharp criticism not only from outside the circle of Christian scholarship but also from within. For example, in regards to the infallibility and inspiration of Scripture, the liberal Protestant theologian Peter C. Hodgson remarks: "Such claims on behalf of scripture and tradition have been severely tested and largely discredited during the past two centuries on both critical and theological grounds. It is clear that these documents are very human products, sharing the insights and limitations of the cultures that produced them."[2] One still wonders how one can properly do *Christian* theology when one holds such a skeptical view of Scripture.

One of the hazards of following this typical path of modern theological liberalism is quite obvious: it relativizes and makes incoherent the task of theology. Such a course leads to the point where Scripture ceases to be the ultimate authority in shaping the believer's life and thinking during his or her pilgrimage in the faith. Other authoritative sources will then need to supplement Scripture: humanistic sciences, critical-historical studies, secular social theories, and even one's own psychological tendencies. The rise of liberation and other radical social-interest theologies in recent decades are some examples of what happens when Scripture is replaced as the Christian's normative authority. Theology, therefore, must essentially be about finding the authorial intent of the biblical writers and organizing the vast array of biblical information into a coherent whole. In order for a Christian systematic theology to be *truly Christian* we must resist the temptation to superimpose our own personal agendas, interests, and anxieties on the Bible when engaging with it. This is one of the essential problems with contemporary context-driven theologies where the aim of formulating a Christian theology is governed more by socio-political concerns or questions of existential alienation than scriptural truth.

1. Grenz, *Theology for the Community of God*, 7.
2. Hodgson, *Winds of the Spirit*, 19–20.

Since it is clear that a proper Christian theology must have Scripture as the ultimate authoritative source regarding matters of life and faith it is also very important that we interpret Scripture correctly. Many false doctrines have sprung up throughout the history of the church due to irresponsible and flawed ways of reading Scripture. The key in clearing up all the confusion that exists in biblical scholarly circles today regarding hermeneutics is that we employ the grammatical-historical principle consistently unless *a particular passage demands otherwise.* Scripture is clear enough—although written many centuries earlier—that even the average Christian sitting in the pew today can understand what it is trying to tell him or her on matters of faith and salvation.[3] The biblical writers did not write in esoteric ways to confuse the reader (and any confusion that does exist is due to the spiritual blindness of the reader because of the noetic effects of sin) but sufficiently clear enough so that their readers can understand the contents of Scripture.[4] However, as we will point out in the first chapter of this work, Scripture must also be read within the context of the Great Tradition handed down to us by our spiritual forefathers in order that safeguards may be put in place against unorthodox ways of handling the inspired text.

What we are proposing, therefore, in this work is a distinctly *evangelical* theology. The doctrines that we present in the subsequent chapters of this work will be from an explicitly evangelical theological perspective. This means that the work holds to the key Protestant principles like *sola Scriptura*, the free justification of the sinner through faith alone in Christ alone, the priesthood of all believers, and the necessity of sharing the gospel to unbelievers for their salvation. This also means that the work uncompromisingly holds to the verbal and plenary inspiration of Scripture. That is, what is revealed in Scripture—historically, doctrinally, and ethically—is all true and accurate based on the Spirit's work of inspiration upon the biblical prophets and writers. In other words, nothing in Scripture will be taken as being inaccurate or false. Finally, although the work is written from an evangelical perspective and geared towards evangelicals of all denominational backgrounds, it is also written with a distinctly Reformed soteriological orientation.

---

3. We will discuss the perspicuity of Scripture in chapter 1 below.

4. Some good works on hermeneutics from an evangelical perspective include Osborne, *Hermeneutical Spiral*; Kaiser and Silva, *Introduction to Biblical Hermeneutics;* and Stein, *Basic Guide to Interpreting the Bible.*

Although some may find the approach taken in this work to be too biblicist, dogmatic, or conservative, we write this book primarily to help believers grow in their knowledge of God and the Christian faith. Its purpose is not to develop some creative theology for the modern person with no faith commitment or to put forth a certain socio-ethical religious outlook, but to aid believers to have a better understanding of what Scripture says on key doctrines of the Christian faith and to cultivate in them a more obedient heart towards the Triune God. As mentioned above, theology must ultimately be practical, and to be *effectively* practical we must know what the truth is first. It is the hope of this writer that this work will stimulate believers to ponder more about what the Christian faith has to teach them and how they can become more effective ministers of the gospel in a world alienated from God due to sin.

# CHAPTER 1

# The Sources of Theology, General Revelation, and Scripture

## 1. The Sources of Theology

ONE TOPIC THAT IS regularly discussed in Christian theological discourse today is the subject of the sources of theology. This pertains to what sources we draw upon to formulate and develop our theological convictions (individually and corporately), and what are the necessary foundations for an internally coherent and biblical theology. These are the types of issues that are often raised when Christians discuss the foundational grounds of theology for the church's witnessing task.

In the eighteenth century, John Wesley (1703–91), the father of Methodism, provided a methodological framework, now commonly known as the Wesleyan Quadrilateral, to develop a distinctly Christian theology. Wesley posited that to have a proper knowledge of God and his works one must not only rely on Scripture as a source but also tradition, reason, and experience.[1] Of course, to be fair to Wesley, he did not argue that tradition, reason, and experience are all equal to Scripture in terms of authoritative sources in the development of the church's theology; he merely posited that these extra-biblical sources can be illuminating guides to Scripture (which

1. For a good discussion of Wesley's Quadrilateral schema see Don Thorsen's work *Wesleyan Quadrilateral*.

is the ultimate authoritative source) in the church's theological formation and task.

The question we must ask, therefore, is whether Wesley's eclectic view of the sources of theology is an adequate approach in formulating an explicitly evangelical systematic theology. Since we will devote a separate section below on the doctrine of Scripture, we will only discuss the other three sources of theology in this section—tradition, reason, and experience—and determine if they are also acceptable authoritative sources for formulating an evangelical theology today.

## Tradition

The first proposed source of theology after Scripture, according to Wesley, is tradition. Roman Catholic theologians have historically argued that the ethics and dogmas of the Catholic faith are largely based on the traditions of the church. Of course, Scripture's role in the formation of doctrine is a fundamental one, but it is one that is set *alongside* tradition. Since it is tradition alongside Scripture that kept (and keeps) the church alive and faithful, according to Roman Catholic teaching, we must view the traditions of the church as a key authoritative voice when constructing the church's dogmas. As the *Dei Verbum* (one of the principal documents of the Second Vatican Council) puts it, "Sacred Tradition and Sacred Scripture . . . are bound closely together, and communicate one with the other. For both of them, flowing out from the same divine well-spring, come together in some fashion to form one thing, and move towards the same goal."[2] Thus, the rationale for this view is that the church's tradition is necessary, along with Scripture, to keep the apostolic tradition secure and free from all theological deviations and error.

It is not only the Roman Catholic Church that views tradition as having a high level of authority in the formulation of ecclesiastical beliefs, but certain Protestant traditions have also elevated their own confessional standards to a normative status. Although Protestants do not view traditions and confessions as having the same level of authority as in the Roman Catholic Church, many Protestant groups maintain that their own confessional standards offer some form of normative authority to protect the theological and ecclesiastical identities of their respective denominations. For instance, in certain conservative Presbyterian and Reformed

2. Quoted in *Catechism of the Catholic Church*, 31.

denominations, the Westminster Confession of Faith (1646) is viewed as a secondary authority just below Scripture on matters of faith and doctrine. While Scripture is seen as the "supreme judge" on all matters of theology and faith (WCF, I.10), certain Presbyterian and Reformed denominations require that an ordinand subscribe to all (if not, most) of the points in the Westminster Standards to be eligible to preach from their pulpits. Therefore, even Protestants view confessions as having a certain type of normative authority for the explication of doctrines and shaping of the church's practice.

How do we, therefore, respond to this idea that tradition must have a highly authoritative place in the theological task? First, we must not reject tradition *in toto* because we fear undermining Scripture's unique authoritative role in the church. Traditions and confessions can guide and assist believers to understand the teachings of Scripture with more clarity. However, even though traditions and confessions do have their place in theological reflection, they must not be elevated to the point that what was written in the past must be permanently fixed for future generations.

Second, traditions and confessions must be reshaped when necessary to conform to new interpretations of Scripture via new findings by contemporary biblical scholars. In the sixteenth century, Martin Luther's theological "breakthrough" in rediscovering the biblical doctrine of justification through faith alone was due to a fresh re-reading of Paul's letter to the Romans. As a result, this sparked a revolution in Western Christendom where old ideas had to be reshaped to adjust to more accurate ways of reading Scripture.

Third, traditions and creeds are formulated by fallible human beings. Since all of us are not immune to mistakes and personal agendas we must view all past declarations by the church as a set of decrees that were subject to some degree of corruption, error, and falsity. Even evangelical biblical scholars throughout history had varying interpretations on a specific biblical passage—which reveals the fallibility of the fallen human mind. On the other hand, one's interpretation of Scripture must also be *shaped by* the apostolic tradition (formulated in the early ecumenical creeds) passed down to later generations of believers through the centuries. This means that Christians must also read Scripture within the context of the Great Tradition and not formulate their own private interpretations of a given passage. Therefore, tradition does have a proper place in the theological task and does set appropriate boundaries for what the church can consider doctrinally sound and orthodox. But as stated earlier, tradition should never take over Scripture's unique place of authority even though it can guide a Christian's reading of Scripture and his or her theological interpretations.

## Reason

The next proposed source of theology to consider is *reason*. Human reason has been used at various times throughout the history of the church in the development of theological convictions and certain doctrinal affirmations. In fact, modern evangelical hermeneutical methods must employ reason to make sure that biblical interpretation is logical, consistent, and coherent. Any hermeneutical approach that pits two biblical passages in contradiction to each other must be judged as being internally unsustainable and, therefore, discarded. Hence, even contemporary biblical scholarship has been prompted by the use of human reason. In addition, biblical ethics is also in some way in submission to reason. One example of this is when we make an inference that a certain activity is sinful because we draw that out from a more explicit commandment from Scripture. For instance, because Scripture explicitly commands us not to steal (Exod 20:15), we use that command to infer that it is a sin to waste an employer's time at work when we engage in frivolous activities that do not contribute to the overall productivity of the company during work hours.

Is reason, therefore, a legitimate source in regards to the formulation of the church's theology? Again, we must make qualifications here before we provide a positive or negative answer in the absolute. Reason, like tradition, does have its proper place in the theological task. God gave human beings a mind to use, and being able to formulate concepts and ideas is one of the fundamental ways humans use their God-given intellectual faculties. Reason, therefore, is one way Christians can organize theological concepts into an orderly, coherent, and manageable whole. A biblically-based theology, therefore, cannot be irrational or internally incoherent. It must make sense for the average Christian so that the teachings revealed in Scripture are clear and useful for his or her understanding of the faith. As Millard J. Erickson states, "We must employ the best methods of interpretation or hermeneutics. And then we must decide whether the Christian belief system is true by rationally examining and evaluating the evidences."[3] Reason,

---

3. Erickson, *Christian Theology*, 283.

therefore, does have a place in the articulation of Christian beliefs organized systematically.

We must, however, insist that reason, like tradition, cannot be elevated to such a high level of authority that Scripture's unique authoritative place is compromised. The excessive use of reason in the organizing of certain theological concepts has produced idiosyncratic ideas that are not consistent with teachings taught by the biblical writers. For example, liberal scholars today who have accepted the historical-critical method, modern ideas of morality, and secular worldviews have elevated human reason to such heights in the theological task that they have begun to espouse doctrinally flawed ideas not supported in Scripture. For example, some liberal scholars cannot accept that a good and loving God can (and will) pour out his divine wrath against impenitent human beings, and therefore, insist that the Bible's teaching on divine judgment must be wholly discarded as something theologically untenable for the modern person.[4] One can see here how reason has its limitations if one seeks to formulate a thoroughly biblically-based theology. Like tradition, reason is under the influence of a fallen human psyche. It soon becomes apparent that when human reason is given far too much reign in the theological task it results in a skewing of the witness of Scripture.

Therefore, although reason has its rightful place in the church's theological formation and task it cannot be relied upon too excessively or given a place comparable to that of Scripture. Many serious theological mistakes of the past could have been avoided if reason was given a more modest role in the discipline.

## Experience

Finally, another probable source to consider in the discipline of theology is experience. As mentioned above, some groups (e.g., some modern-day charismatic groups) use experience as a normative source for Christian theology. This is understandable since experience is such a powerful phenomenon due to its highly personal nature. Its existential orientation gives people great impetus to interpret situations, the world, and meanings based on it. In the task of theology experience is a valued source of authority for some groups. Certain Pentecostal and Charismatic groups rely heavily on experience as a hermeneutical tool in interpreting Scripture. Many in the

---

4. Cf. Robinson, *In the End, God . . .*, 99–121.

Pentecostal or Charismatic movement will argue that since they have at one time or another "spoken in tongues" then tongue-speaking must be a normative phenomenon today that is available to all Christians.[5] Accordingly, they will interpret various passages (especially in the book of Acts) in a manner that corresponds to their own personal experiences. Another example is the way in which the Wesleyan-Holiness movement understands sanctification. For instance, despite the fact that Scripture clearly teaches that sin still exists in the lives of Christians (1 John 1:8–9—2:1), many believers in this movement argue that "entire sanctification" (or "Christian perfectionism") is possible because they maintain that they went through extended periods of time when they were entirely free from "deliberate" sin.

As the examples above demonstrate, experience must be looked upon only as a marginal source in terms of its function in the formation of the church's theology. If one's Christian experience does not conform to what is explicitly taught in Scripture, we must then discard it as a pseudo-Christian phenomenon with no spiritually edifying content. Also, experiences are highly subjective and varied. If one forms theological convictions primarily on so-called spiritual experiences then there is a myriad of conclusions that can be drawn up to develop a particular belief. This cannot be acceptable if one seeks to formulate a biblically faithful and doctrinally sound theology. However, even though relying too heavily on experience does have its obvious limitations for theology, we must not totally discard it as a source since all human beings live under real circumstances and life situations. Grant R. Osborne makes this insightful comment on this issue: "One's experiences are interpreted on the basis of the community's teachings; both are heavily influenced by traditional beliefs; and all are informed by the Word of God."[6] Even the most staunch "biblicists" are not immune from the circumstances of their personal lives (in both their private and ecclesiastical dimensions) in terms of impacting the way they interpret the world around them and how they will form their own theological opinions as a result. Therefore, a believer's life experiences cannot be completely removed out of the equation in terms of the development of his or her theological belief system no matter how hard he or she tries to extricate it out of the process.

Like tradition and reason, experience does have its proper place in the theological task. Personal reflection and actual living out of the faith can aid believers in understanding their divinely given vocations. It also helps

5. We will elaborate more on this topic in chapter 10.

6. Osborne, *Hermeneutical Spiral*, 296.

them to see more clearly why they think and act in certain ways. Thus, experience has an *informative* role in the discipline of theology. As Stanley J. Grenz avers, "Our experience is informative, for it helps us clarify the human relationship to God."[7] Therefore, Christians should not completely discard experience as a source in their theological reflections. In fact, experience can help us understand certain aspects of theological thinking more clearly.

## What Does This All Mean?

It goes without saying that Scripture must be the ultimate authority and source for a sound evangelical theology. Although tradition, reason, and experience have their proper places in the discipline of theology, they must all be subsumed *under* Scripture and critically interpreted *through* it. However, we must also never go to the other extreme and assert (like certain sectarian groups do) that tradition, reason, and experience play absolutely no role in the church's theological reflection. There are significant differences between the Reformation principle of *sola Scriptura* and the modern fundamentalist principle of *solo Scriptura*.

The Christian tradition requires rules for the correct interpretation of Scripture and theology requires proper methodological strategies. Theology cannot be adequately done if one throws out all other sources and attempts to draw out a theology from the Scriptures in a closed system apart from proper hermeneutical methods, responsible use of reason, and the faithful witness of the church derived from the teachings of past saints. A biblically faithful systematic theology, therefore, requires that even though we put Scripture at the forefront we are not to discard the other three sources in this unique academic task that is in service to God's kingdom.

## 2. General Revelation

General revelation deals with how God is known apart from Scripture and the Incarnate Word. Theologians sometimes call this "natural revelation" since it is through the created order that God reveals himself to all of humanity[8] (although the former terminology is broader in scope than the

---

7. Grenz, *Theology for the Community of God*, 16.

8. Moore, "Natural Theology," 67–101.

latter). For the Christian theologian, the limitations of general revelation are quite obvious. Most importantly, this revelation given in the created order is inadequate to meet the salvific needs of the human race, which can only come about through conscious faith in Jesus Christ. Secondly, general or natural revelation fails to provide a complete and accurate knowledge of who God is and what he does. This is why Paul clarified on Mars Hill to the Athenians that an altar they dedicated to an "unknown god" (Acts 17:23) is actually the God of heaven and earth who created the whole human race from one man (v. 26), and who gives life, breath, and every good thing to all people (v. 25). We can see here that even though the Athenians had some faint idea of who the Almighty God is they did not have a clear, full, or intimate knowledge of him. In fact, as we will discuss later at the conclusion of this section, general revelation does not only provide an inadequate knowledge of God and his redemptive work but also causes sinners to be exposed and under God's divine wrath (Rom 1:19–23).

We will now discuss the various theories of general revelation offered up by some notable theologians of the past and then attempt to provide a biblical perspective on the subject matter.

## Theories of General Revelation

### Thomas Aquinas

Thomas Aquinas proposed what is now famously called the "five proofs" of how human beings can have knowledge of God. These five proofs are: 1) things being put in motion by an initial mover; 2) efficient cause (there needs to be a first cause for the effect); 3) existence being from an already existing source; 4) gradation of good and beauty (which entails a perfect standard of goodness and beauty); and 5) the fact of design and order in the universe (which points to an ultimate Designer).[9] We can see by these proofs that Thomas depended heavily on philosophy and human reasoning to postulate the existence of God. Knowledge of God, according to Thomas, can be deduced from basic philosophical premises.

We can see here how Thomas's methodology can be criticized at various points. The heavily philosophical nature of these proofs reveals that Thomas did not rely on Scripture as the ultimate revelation for his knowledge of God. The most that can be said about Thomas's proofs is that they

---

9. Aquinas, *Summa Theologica* 1.2.3.

merely *confirm* what Scripture already reveals about God, his works, and his character. Also, it is impossible for sinners who are alienated from God to salvifically know him and have a personal relationship with him through this method. Thomas's scheme appears to suggest that personally knowing God in a way Christians know him through the gospel of Christ can also be achieved by sinners through rationalistic deductions and propositions. As Russell D. Moore aptly writes about Thomas's method, "All of this was built on a view of epistemology that believed even fallen humanity could still perceive and make use of the evidences for God built in the created order."[10]

A more realistic understanding of humanity will demonstrate (as mentioned above) that human beings in their unredeemed state will use any proofs given to them to form a god of their own making for their own corrupt purposes (Rom 1:21–23, 25). The failure of Thomas's paradigm is the underlying anthropological optimism and the assumption that fallen human reasoning can be an adequate way to postulate for the existence of God.

## John Calvin

For John Calvin personal knowledge of God and his redemptive work can only be found in the Scriptures. Seeking God through other means will only lead people to seek some uncertain deity.[11] For sinners to have true and saving religion shine upon them, according to Calvin, they "ought to hold that it must take its beginning from heavenly doctrine and that no one can get even the slightest taste of right and sound doctrine unless he be a pupil of Scripture."[12] Therefore, it is only in Scripture that there is fuller knowledge and greater clarity about who God is and what he has done for humankind's salvation.

Calvin, however, did not altogether deny natural revelation. In fact, there are two ways human beings can get a glimpse of God's glory: through 1) the magnificence of the created order; and 2) the implanted knowledge of God in the human mind. In regards to revelation through the created order, he writes: "But upon his individual works he has engraved unmistakable marks of his glory, so clear and so prominent that even unlettered

---

10. Moore, "Natural Theology," 84.

11. Calvin, *Inst.* 1.6.1.

12. Calvin, *Inst.* 1.6.2.

and stupid folk cannot plead the excuse of ignorance."[13] No matter what intellectual level a person is at, God cannot be unknown to that person. In regards to the second mode of natural revelation, he declares: "To prevent anyone from taking refuge in the pretense of ignorance, God himself has implanted in all men a certain understanding of his divine majesty."[14] This is demonstrated by the fact that the invention of non-Christian religions is in some way sparked by the innate knowledge of the triune God in the human. To put it another way, religion is no arbitrary invention.[15] Both types of revelation, however, do not lead to redemption: they only show that sinners are without excuse before God when they are judged at the end. Therefore, for Calvin, knowledge of God comes in two forms: special and natural (or saving and non-saving, respectively).

The soundness of Calvin's understanding of revelation comes in its primacy on Scripture. Scripture, for Calvin, is viewed as the only source for a saving knowledge of God. However, he does not just stop there. In order for sinners to savingly appropriate the knowledge that is available in Scripture they must be regenerated and enlightened by the Holy Spirit.[16] Without this internal work of the Holy Spirit in their hearts Scripture only remains a dead letter to the unredeemed. Even having said all this, Calvin was still no fervent biblicist that discounted all other means of revelation. Also, his emphasis on the regenerating work of the Holy Spirit to properly understand Scripture protected him from committing any type of bibliolatry. Calvin, thus, avoids both the extremes of relying too heavily on non-scriptural means for knowing God and seeing the "bare Scriptures" as the only means of knowing God.

## Karl Barth

The renowned twentieth-century Swiss Reformed theologian, Karl Barth, proposed a unique understanding of revelation that was also in some way the logical extension of the views of the Reformed scholars before him. For Barth, revelation of God can only come about by God's self-revealing act. He writes: "*God* reveals Himself. He reveals Himself *through Himself.*

13. Calvin, *Inst.* 1.5.1. Calvin even calls creation the "most beautiful theatre" of the glory of God (*Inst.* 1.14.20).

14. Calvin, *Inst.* 1.3.1.

15. Calvin, *Inst.* 1.3.2.

16. Calvin, *Inst.* 1.7.5.

He reveals *Himself.*"[17] This self-disclosure is specifically located in the life, death, and resurrection of Jesus Christ (the "Christ-event"). As he states: "'God reveals Himself'—if the statement is made in respect of the revelation attested in Holy Scripture, it is made in view of the actually *miraculous event*, the special new direct act of God in the breaking in of new time into the midst of the old."[18] For Barth, human beings cannot know God by any other means—whether through the created order or human philosophy. When human beings attempt to know God through other means than the self-revealing act of Jesus Christ, they develop a theology (or religion) that is grounded in unbelief and idolatry.[19] God's self-disclosure, therefore, must be a sheer gift that comes down from above.[20]

Although one can commend Barth for his endeavor in formulating a view of revelation that attempted to elevate Christ and be consistent with the Reformation principle of *sola gratia*, we must demur that his understanding fails to be adequate on a number of fronts. First, Barth's highly christocentric view of revelation is a rejection of the clear testimony of Scripture. Paul makes it plain in Rom 1:19–23 and 2:14–15 that *all* humans have some sort of knowledge of God through the created order and an innate knowledge of his law, respectively.[21] This is also demonstrated, as mentioned above, in Paul's Mars Hill address to the Athenians in Acts 17:22–34. Although

17. Barth, *Church Dogmatics*, 1/1:296.

18. Barth, *Church Dogmatics*, I/2:63.

19. Barth, *Church Dogmatics*, I/2:297–325.

20. Barth's rejection of natural revelation met with severe criticism from his fellow contemporary neo-orthodox theologian, Emil Brunner. Though Brunner was against any type of Thomistic view of natural theology he argued that humans have a certain level of knowledge of God based on the created order and the retention of the *imago Dei* (cf. Barth and Brunner, *Natural Theology*). Barth, of course, responded in his famous pamphlet *No!* that natural theology was the culprit behind the support for the Nazi regime by the *Deutsche Christen* ("German Christians") in Germany.

21. In regards to Rom 1:18–32, Barth argues that one cannot use this passage to support the notion that heathens receive natural revelation of God through the created order because Paul is really talking about the person who has been confronted by God's *apokalypsis* in Jesus Christ (*Church Dogmatics*, II/1:119). The problem with this interpretation is that Paul nowhere mentions the gospel between verses 18 to 32. Instead, the people described here are those who are condemned not because they reject the gospel message but because they continue to follow their sinful ways even though God has given them enough light for them to know the difference between righteousness and wickedness. Also, he talks about the condemnation of unbelieving gentiles in these verses in order to prepare his readers for the truth that only by having faith in Jesus Christ can they be saved from God's wrath to come (Rom 3–5).

unregenerate humans are "idol factory making machines" (Calvin's terminology) that does not mean that *absolutely* no knowledge of the triune God exists in them.[22] Second, we cannot escape the fact that to a *certain extent* Thomas was correct in his understanding of revelation. Not only is the created order an adequate testimony of the existence of God but our own conceptions of eternity, morality, beauty, etc. provide us with a glimpse of what has been imparted into our souls from above. Evangelical Christians would agree with Barth that saving knowledge of God only comes through the special revelation found in Scripture and the Incarnate Word, but we cannot agree with him that God cannot be known at all *except* through the Incarnate Word. Third, Barth's view of revelation is a rejection of two thousand years of church tradition. No notable theologian has advocated such a view before him. This demonstrates to the novelty of such an approach where revelation is solely located in Jesus Christ.[23]

## Peter C. Hodgson

The view of revelation put forward by the liberal Protestant theologian Peter C. Hodgson is quite different from the three more "conservative" positions delineated above. For Hodgson, revelation is not about "a body of truths from another world," but an "event of unconcealment—of opening, healing, communication, liberation—in this world, in the process of which God is disclosed indirectly."[24] God can even be "met" in the face of another human being, although it is a mediated disclosure.[25] In this way, God is known indirectly through our interaction with the world and other people around us.[26]

---

22. Herman Bavinck makes the interesting comment that "Christianity is not only positioned antithetically toward paganism; it is also paganism's fulfillment. Christianity is the true religion, therefore also the highest and purest; it is the truth of all religions. What in paganism is the caricature, the living original is here" (*Reformed Dogmatics*, 1:319–20).

23. One can understand, after the German Christians' support for Nazism, why Barth rejected natural theology. Despite this, Erickson is right to point out that his rejection of natural theology was an overreaction to the negative experiences he had with it (cf. *Christian Theology*, 190).

24. Hodgson, *Winds of the Spirit*, 128.

25. Hodgson, *Winds of the Spirit*, 129.

26. Hodgson even states that it is "the whole world, natural as well as human, that is God's 'back' or 'body,' and that discloses God's glory even as it shelters us from it" (*Winds*

Hodgson's understanding of revelation is intended to be more practical in its aims. He does eschew any view of revelation that is *merely* about having some sort of special knowledge of the divine. In fact, he states that God is "revealed as liberating power by the way in which God's word works in the world."[27] This liberating power is supposed to create "new meaning and new possibilities of being" in the form of "communicative rationality" and "communicative freedom."[28] The goal of this communicative rationality is that all hierarchies are leveled, privileges dissolved, provincialisms transcended, and distortions and concealments overcome.[29] The goal of communicative freedom, on the other hand, is the establishment of a "free and liberated human community, based on unrestrained dialogue, mutuality, solidarity, and equality."[30] Thus, the ultimate goal of revelation, according to Hodgson, is the creation of a type of religious utopia that encompasses the whole world and everything in it.

Although we must commend Hodgson for attempting to make the doctrine of revelation practical and existentially meaningful, we must still aver that his view of revelation has some serious flaws in it. First, it borders on panentheism.[31] The distinction between the Creator and the creation/creature is blurred. Divine transcendence, in essence, is swallowed up by a radical view of immanence. This is against the scriptural testimony that God is clearly distinct from the created order (cf. Ps 113:5–6; Isa 55:8–9; Acts 17:24). Second, the distinction between the sacred and sinful is blurred. God is holy, righteous, and good (Lev 11:44; Jer 9:24; Matt 5:48); human beings are sinful, fallen, and corrupt (Rom 3:9–18). Although God works for the eventual redemption of the cosmos and all those who have trusted in Jesus Christ (Rom 8:19–21), the world system as a whole during the present age is in enmity towards God (Jas 4:4; 1 John 2:15–17). Thus, to say that God can be "met" in the sinful human community undermines one of the basic characteristics of God—his holiness. Third, Hodgson's view borders on universalism. Although it is true that God desires all human beings to be saved (2 Peter 3:9), his work of redemption is only effectual for those who have trusted in the risen Christ (John 3:18). Also, salvation is not

---

*of the Spirit*, 130).

27. Hodgson, *Winds of the Spirit*, 128.

28. Hodgson, *Winds of the Spirit*, 130–32.

29. Hodgson, *Winds of the Spirit*, 130.

30. Hodgson, *Winds of the Spirit*, 131.

31. Hodgson prefers the label "holism" (*Winds of the Spirit*, 166).

about the universal restructuring of society towards some utopian ideal in the present age, but about the eventual deliverance of the cosmos from the effects of sin and the eternal redemption of sinners through the death and resurrection of Jesus Christ.

## A Biblical Perspective

Although we have looked at some of the views on general revelation from some notable theologians from the past, we must ask ourselves what Scripture ultimately says about this subject. When looking at some relevant passages in Scripture we can see that it speaks quite clearly about the fact of God's general revelation to all his creatures (contra Barth). The three passages that are often invoked to support the idea of general revelation are Psalm 19, Romans 1:18, and 2:14–15. The first two passages talk about how people know God through the created order and the third discusses how people know God due to an innate knowledge of what he requires of them (i.e., the law). Acts 14:17 also demonstrates the truth of general revelation: God leaves a testimony of himself to all humankind through his kindness and earthly gifts. Therefore, God has given all human beings enough knowledge of himself through the created order and the moral impulses that lie within them. No one on the day of judgment can plead ignorance before God.

What benefit, then, does upholding the truth of general revelation have in Christian life and thinking? First, it shows that God has left some imprints in the created order for humankind to be *not* ignorant of him. Though general revelation cannot lead to saving knowledge, it still reveals to humankind that God exists and that he is holy, just, and good. Thus, at the last judgment, all humans will be without excuse when they stand before him (cf. Rom 1:20). Second, it demonstrates that believers and unbelievers share the same common ground. It shows us that *all* human beings are accountable to God, are created by him, and receive the same basic benefits from him (what Reformed theologians typically call "common grace"). Third, general revelation points to the fact that all human societies are structured by a morality that is divinely given to them from above. Human beings did not develop morality out of their own ingenuity and whim but by God's impartation to them of what is good and just.

## 3. Scripture

The Bible is seen as the most authoritative and normative source for Christian life and doctrine by many Christians today—whether Roman Catholic, Orthodox, or Protestant. Although there is a myriad of opinions among Christians today regarding what degree of authority Scripture has, all of them agree that Scripture can never be excised from the entire theological enterprise. This means that the importance of Scripture cannot be minimized if we are going to do honest theological reflection for our own lives and the community of faith. In this section, therefore, we will discuss the various theories of inspiration, the inerrancy of Scripture, the clarity of Scripture, and the sufficiency of Scripture.

### Theories of Inspiration

#### The Intuitive Theory

According to this theory biblical inspiration is not a supernatural act but merely an incredible insight achieved by a human being. The biblical writers were not supernaturally inspired by the Holy Spirit to write the biblical books but rather possessed enhanced mental abilities that gave them the ability to write such remarkable literary materials. Thus, the Bible is like any other book written by people with remarkable literary skills. This view tends to be highly naturalistic in perspective. Major proponents of this view include liberal higher critics.

#### The Illumination Theory

This theory, in contrast to the one above, does claim that the Holy Spirit played a role in the composition of the biblical texts. However, the Holy Spirit merely intensified the spiritual awareness of the human biblical writers. The only difference between the biblical writers and all other believers is that the Spirit worked quantitatively greater (but not in kind) in the former than the latter.[32] A major proponent of this view is the liberal Reformed theologian Friedrich Schleiermacher (1768–1834).

---

32. Gulley, *Systematic Theology*, 1:303.

## The Dynamic Theory

This theory also accounts for the fact that the Holy Spirit inspired the writers of the Scriptures. According to this view, the biblical writers maintained their unique personalities and writing styles when the Holy Spirit superintended them. In essence, it strongly maintains the individuality of the biblical writers.[33] Therefore, the writers expressed the thoughts given to them by the Holy Spirit through their own unique characteristics and qualities.[34] However, even though the thoughts are inspired, the actual *words* of the Scriptures are not. Proponents of this view include Augustus H. Strong (1836–1921) and G. C. Berkouwer (1904–96).

## The Dictation Theory

According to this theory, the Holy Spirit directly dictated the actual words of Scripture in the original manuscripts. The biblical writers were mere channels or "type writers" for the Holy Spirit. The unique personalities and distinctive styles of the writers had no influence whatsoever in the composition of the Scriptures. All the words that appear in Scripture are the exact words that God used to convey his thoughts. This theory, in a way, is the direct opposite of the dynamic theory discussed above. Some forms of modern fundamentalism hold this view.

## The Verbal-Plenary Theory

This view states that the Holy Spirit inspired the biblical writers in such an intensified way that the words used in Scripture were chosen by the Holy Spirit himself. This view is different from the dictation theory because it maintains that the biblical writers wrote down the Spirit-inspired thoughts with their own unique personalities and styles intact. However, it differs from the dynamic theory because it maintains that the Holy Spirit also gave the inspired writers which words to use and how to use them (thus the words are also inspired). Therefore, *all* of the sixty-six books of the Bible are *fully* inspired by God. This view is the most common view among conservative Protestants. It is also congruent with the evangelical understanding of biblical inerrancy. We believe this to be the correct view of inspiration.

33. Gulley, *Systematic Theology*, 1:304.
34. Erickson, *Christian Theology*, 232.

## The Inerrancy of Scripture

The inerrancy of Scripture has been a very contentious subject matter between mainline and evangelical Christians in the last two hundred years. Mainline Christians claim that biblical inerrancy is a doctrine rationally deduced from the doctrine of inspiration and an invention that came out of modern conservative ideas in North American Christianity. Evangelicals, on the other hand, argue that this doctrine is pivotal in maintaining the integrity of God's word and maintaining a solid basis for a distinctly Christian theology. Aside from this debate, however, coming up with a definition of inerrancy is not a simple task as it appears. Many definitions have been proposed, some being more precise and satisfactory than others. However, we believe that the best definition of inerrancy is provided by Millard J. Erickson: "The Bible, when correctly interpreted in light of the level to which culture and the means of communication had developed at the time it was written, and in view of the purposes for which it was given, is fully truthful in all that it affirms."[35] Although, of course, when Erickson talks about "the Bible," he means the original autographs. Some may, however, argue that inerrancy cannot be empirically proven and, therefore, has no solid basis in fact. This is where we must look to the nature of inspiration and the testimony of Scripture for answers.

The verbal-plenary inspiration of Scripture provides the backbone for the doctrine of inerrancy. Although one can still believe that all sixty-six books of the canon are inspired and *not* inerrant at the same time, this view is in some way inconsistent. If the Holy Spirit inspired *all* of the books of the Bible how is it possible to find errors in any of them? Some will argue that even if all sixty-six books are inspired there are parts within each individual book that are not inspired and contain errors. This leads to the problem of deciding which parts contain error and which do not. We can only, therefore, use modern empirical criteria to decide what is erroneous or what is not: Does it conform to modern understandings of science? Is it historically accurate based on recent archaeological findings? This approach, as it will become obvious, will only lead to more problems in regards to the internal coherency and infallibility of Scripture. Rather, we argue that the foundation for inerrancy is based on the reality that *all* of Scripture is inspired by God. As Jack Cottrell points out, "If inspiration does not result in inerrancy,

---

35. Erickson, *Christian Theology*, 259. Wayne Grudem offers a more simplistic definition: "*The inerrancy of Scripture means that Scripture in the original manuscripts does not affirm anything that is contrary to fact*" (*Systematic Theology*, 90).

then it has no purpose; if there are errors in Scripture, then inspiration is irrelevant and futile."[36] Now that we know the basis for the Bible's inerrancy, what is Scripture's testimony on this matter?

Although Erickson is correct to point out that inerrancy cannot be inductively proven nor is it explicitly taught in Scripture (rather it is a corollary of the doctrine of plenary inspiration), the biblical writers, nevertheless, believed in the complete truthfulness of Scripture.[37] Some passages that evangelicals have used to defend inerrancy include Psalms 12:6; 18:30; 119:160; Matthew 4:4; and John 17:17. Moreover, the classic text used by evangelicals to defend the notion of verbal and plenary inspiration—2 Timothy 3:16—indicates that all of Scripture (from Paul's view, the entire Old Testament) is true and flawless because it is "breathed out by God" (Gk. *theopneustos*). Also, 2 Peter 1:21 also suggests that all of Scripture is true because "men spoke from God as they were carried along by the Holy Spirit." Since we know that God cannot lie or promote falsehood[38] all of those inspired individuals who spoke prophecy and wrote the books of the Bible could not have proclaimed untruths or errors. Again, we will say that although the scriptural verses provided above do not present an ironclad case for inerrancy they are certainly suggested.

One question may be asked: Does accepting or rejecting inerrancy have any impact on the way Christians live and think? Many believe today that the issue of inerrancy has no real bearing on the life of the church or the individual believer. This we strongly disagree. What are some of the problems associated with the denial of the inerrancy of Scripture? First, we begin to wonder what is true or false in the Scriptures. Not only is this problematic for the discipline of theology but also problematic for Christian faith and practice. If what is written in the Bible is not totally reliable how can we know what is morally right or wrong, or doctrinally true or false? If the Bible cannot be completely trusted we cannot live out our Christian calling effectively knowing that some things that God has said to us in Scripture may be untrue. Second, we start to construct our own ideas of what is true and right. The Bible stops being our highest authority on matters of doctrine and ethics. We will start to pick and choose which parts of the Bible have relevance for our lives and which do not. Third, it conveys the idea that God is untruthful and untrustworthy. Even if the majority of

36. Cottrell, *Faith Once For All,* 59.

37. Erickson, *Christian Theology,* 255.

38. We will discuss the divine attributes in more detail in the next chapter.

the Bible is true, factual, and free from error we will still have to deal with those parts that are not. This means that at certain times God has not been totally truthful to us. This is contrary to the Bible's portrayal of God as being completely trustworthy and free from all deceit (Num 23:19; Heb 6:18).

Therefore, we can see that the doctrine of inerrancy is not something that is merely of great theological importance to the church but also has great practical significance for individual believers as well. One can see how the beliefs of the church and the life of the Christian are deeply anchored on this doctrine.

## The Clarity of Scripture

Evangelical theologians often call this the *perspicuity of Scripture*. What this means is that even though there are parts of Scripture that are puzzling or difficult to understand, yet

> those things which are necessary to be known, believed, and observed, for salvation, are so clearly propounded and opened in some place of Scripture or other, that not only the learned, but the unlearned, in a due use of the ordinary means, may attain unto a sufficient understanding of them.[39]

The Scripture's perspicuity, therefore, pertains to those things that are crucial on matters of salvation. Although we may not be completely certain on this side of eternity who the "sons of God" are in Genesis 6:2 we certainly have a clear knowledge of what God has accomplished through Christ for our salvation and what he requires of us in order to escape his wrath (John 3:16, 18; Acts 16:31; Rom 3:28; Gal 2:16; Eph 2:8–9). This means that once we open the Bible and refer to the passages mentioned above we should be able to read them without confusion or ambiguity. Even during his earthly ministry, Jesus proclaimed his gospel message clearly but some did not believe not because his words were ambiguous but because they had hardened hearts due to the noetic effects of sin (Matt 13:14–15). Therefore, when we encounter unbelievers in the world and the gospel does not penetrate into their hearts we should realize that it is not due to vagueness on the part of Scripture but due to their hearts being naturally resistant to God and his truth. We can trust that the Bible is very clear on matters of salvation and that no one has any excuse before God.

39. *Westminster Confession of Faith*, I/7.

The clarity of Scripture has been one of the cries of the Protestant Reformers against the Medieval Church at the time of the Reformation. The Roman Catholic Church at that time viewed Scripture as requiring interpretation by a select group of individuals in the church—the bishops or learned clergy. Only through these officers of the Roman Catholic Church can the laity understand what is spoken of in Scripture. Even in modern times, the Roman Catholic Church has not essentially stepped away from this position. In the *Catechism of the Catholic Church* (1994) it states (following the *Dei Verbum*) that the "task of interpretation has been entrusted to the bishops in communion with the successor of Peter, the Bishop of Rome" (no. 85). Thus, personal interpretation by a layperson needs to be guided by bishops who are successors of the apostle Peter. We can see here the practical importance, in contrast to Rome, of affirming perspicuity. If we follow the biblical and evangelical view of Scripture we do not need to be guided by ordained bishops or clergy to understand what God has done for us and what he requires of us for our salvation.[40] Even a young child can understand the basics of the gospel from the Scriptures and be saved. Scripture is not something that is held under hostage in the hands of an elite class of ordained officers. All human beings have access to this special revelation from God, and therefore, all can potentially benefit from the spiritual treasures contained in it.[41]

## The Sufficiency of Scripture

The notion that Scripture is sufficient on all matters pertaining to salvation, faith, and ethics has been one of the key touchstones of evangelicalism. It means that we do not require any other source outside of Scripture to know how sinners are saved and how believers are to live out their God-given calling. As discussed above, we argued that Scripture is the supreme and normative authority on matters of doctrine and faith. The sufficiency of Scripture is the corollary of Scripture's authority. This means that the truth of the sufficiency of Scripture fights against two fronts: 1) the Roman

40. What we do not mean here is that lay Christians do not need to make use of commentaries or theological texts to understand Scripture clearly. What we are saying is that Scripture is clear on matters of salvation and this clarity is not reserved for a special class of believers.

41. Of course, when we say "all" we do not mean it in the absolute sense. Only those who have had their spiritual eyes opened by the Holy Spirit can spiritually benefit from this divine revelation. The apostle Paul makes this clear in 2 Cor 3:14–16.

Catholic Church's claim that its confessional tradition is just as authoritative as Scripture; and 2) the claims of some modern charismatic mystics that divine revelation can also be found in present-day "prophecies."

In the first case, the Roman Catholic Church's assertion that its tradition has equal status with Scripture creates a problem. If this is true, how can Scripture rightly govern the contents of that tradition? How can we know that a particular tradition has moved beyond the limits of the testimony of Scripture?[42] In the Roman Catholic position, therefore, Scripture, by de facto, loses its normative authority and sufficiency.

In the second case, if we hold that the charismatic mystic is correct, that the modern-day phenomenon of "prophecies" has revelatory authority almost comparable to that of Scripture, we have then found a very subjective source of authority to shape the practices and beliefs of the church. There can be an infinite number of possibilities that can arise regarding what is true and right in regards to what the church must believe and how Christians should live. The natural consequence of this is a type of spiritual and hermeneutical chaos where "anything pretty much goes." The charismatic might respond that only prophecies that are in accord with the explicit teachings of Scripture are only acceptable and true, but that view leads us back logically to the principle that Scripture is the ultimate authority and completely sufficient for all things pertaining to doctrine and life.

## Excurses: The Relationship Between Exegesis and Systematic Theology

One of the more polemical issues in the last several decades in Christian academia is the relationship between exegesis and systematic theology. The debate regarding the relationship between these two fields, however, was not unknown before the middle of the twentieth century. For instance, the well-known conservative Princeton theologian B. B. Warfield (1851–1921) had much to say about the relationship between "exegetical theology" and systematic theology—acknowledging that systematic theology gleans from the conclusions that result from exegetical work.[43] In the years following, many biblical scholars argued that systematic theology should have no role to play when it comes to interpreting the Scriptures, since the Scriptures should be understood in their own historical, linguistic, and

---

42. Reymond, *New Systematic Theology*, 85–86.
43. Cf. Zaspel, *Theology of B. B. Warfield*, 80–81.

sociological contexts. Scripture, these scholars argue, should be studied "scientifically" with theological commitments having no role in exegesis and interpretation.[44]

In reaction to this almost naïve way of understanding the relationship between exegesis and systematic theology, we argue that both disciplines need each other if a biblically sound theology is to be explicated for the church's life and vocation. It is granted that systematic theologians need to recognize that organized theological constructs are grounded upon the fruitful labors of rigorous exegesis; however, biblical scholars also need to recognize that there are no such things as presuppositionless exegeses of Scripture. In fact, biblical scholars need theologians (just as much as theologians need them) in order for the conclusions of the hard work of exegesis to be set forth in an organized and coherent whole (since Scripture is God's word given to us in fundamental unity). On the other hand, biblical scholars can remind theologians not to allow their rigid dogmatic commitments to influence their interpretation of the Scriptures to the level that it misconstrues the intentions of the biblical authors. As Craig L. Blomberg helpfully points out:

> If one danger in exegesis is to read foreign theology into a text too quickly—whether from an overall system that has some problems, or from another biblical author's different use of concepts or terms, or simply from the exegete not paying careful enough attention to all of the factors already discussed for analyzing a given text—there is an opposite danger as well. Exegetes may stop their work, even after a flawless articulation of a text's meaning, and not reflect on the import of that meaning when it is integrated into the theology of the entire Bible, systematically arranged.[45]

What can we conclude from all of this? We conclude that the relationship between exegesis and systematic theology must always be a dynamic "two-way street." Biblical scholars need to recognize that Scripture, despite its diversity, is a fundamental unity and that the teachings found there must be expressed in an organized manner so that the contemporary audience can understand them. Theologians, on the other hand, need to acknowledge that their theological commitments can negatively affect the way they

44. George Eldon Ladd mentions the likes of C. C. McCown, H. J. Cadbury, and Millar Burrows who take this approach to the interpretation of Scripture (cf. *Theology of the New Testament*, 12).

45. Blomberg and Markley, *Handbook of New Testament Exegesis*, 224.

read certain parts of Scripture *and* that they need to rely on the labors of biblical scholars to keep them from interpreting Scripture superficially and artificially.[46]

## Summary of the Doctrine of Scripture

The inerrancy, clarity, and sufficiency of Scripture are doctrinal affirmations that believers must fervently hold on to in this age of relativism and skepticism. Scripture is what provides believers with a sure foundation when it comes to understanding their divinely given calling and adhering to a biblically sound evangelical theology. Although secular worldviews pass away as each successive age turns to a new ideological fad, the words and teachings of Scripture will always remain true even after the kingdom of God arrives in its fullness (cf. Matt 5:18).

The approach taken here is decisively antithetical to the view of contemporary liberal theology which questions the doctrinal and ethical expressions of Scripture as having any authoritative role for the church today.[47] For evangelical Christians the contemporary liberal option is an unacceptable one. Scripture, we maintain, will always be an authoritative source when it comes to directing the lives of God's people and providing them with knowledge of who God is and what he has done for them. As David K. Clark states, "It is the Bible that authorizes the theological teaching and moral guidance of the church because the Bible itself is God's own self-witness. If I am committed to following the Lord, I am committed to following his Word. So what the Bible declares and (authorizes by that) what the church teaches, I should believe."[48] With this statement we say a hearty "Amen," and pray that the church will always fervently embrace Scripture as God's sure word for believers on all matters pertaining to faith and life.

---

46. Silva, *Interpreting Galatians*, 204–10; cf. also Carson, "Role of Exegesis in Systematic Theology," 39–76.

47. Cf. Smart and Konstantine, *Christian Systematic Theology*, 47.

48. Clark, *To Know and Love God*, 98.

# CHAPTER 2

# God and the Trinity

## 1. God

Does God exist? If he does exist, who or what is he? These are questions often posed by skeptics when challenging believers about a key component of the Christian faith: the reality and existence of God. Having the right answers to these questions is crucial if we desire to faithfully live out our Christian calling and be effective ministers of the gospel. Of course, God has revealed enough about himself so that Christians do know the God they love and worship. As Gerald Bray states, to be "a Christian is to believe that it is possible to know God. More than that, it is to believe that God has made it possible for us to know him by revealing himself to us."[1] On the other hand, articulating a doctrine of God that is most faithful to the biblical witness, according to Robert L. Reymond, is "surely one of the most demanding intellectual enterprises man will ever undertake."[2] Although it will be a great challenge to talk about God in a way that is faithful to the testimony of Scripture we will still endeavor to provide a satisfactory answer to the questions posed above in our discussion below.

1. Bray, *Doctrine of God*, 14.
2. Reymond, *New Systematic Theology*, 129.

## The Existence of God

How do we know that God exists? For the believer the answer to this question is quite simple: through the testimony of Scripture and our personal knowledge of him through Jesus Christ our Lord. As discussed in the previous chapter, Scripture provides us with enough evidence that God exists and that he works actively in the created order. We also discussed that God can be known to a certain extent through creation and by the innate knowledge of his law written in our hearts. Although believers know God in a more intimate and distinct way (Rom 8:15–16), unbelievers still have a knowledge of God to a certain degree, although they try to suppress this knowledge (Ps 14:1; Rom 1:21). Various arguments, however, have been put forth throughout the history of the church—some better than others—to prove that God exists. We will now go over the more common arguments below.

### The Ontological Argument

This argument states that God's existence can be proven by the fact that human beings have an idea of a perfect being called "God." Since we can envisage a being that is far superior to us in many ways—an "Ultimate Being"—then God somehow must, by necessity, exist. In other words, why would human beings have *an idea of God* if he cannot or does not exist in reality? The problem with the ontological argument, however, is that it presumes that the *concept* of God can be logically deduced through human reasoning and abstract formulations. Furthermore, formulating an abstract *idea* of a deity-like being is not the same as setting forth the truth of what Scripture reveals regarding the Almighty God who exists in the heavens and is personal and who, through the incarnation of the Second Person of the Godhead, has revealed himself to humankind in the flesh. The ontological argument was first put forward by Anselm (1033–1109)[3] and later defended by René Descartes (1596–1650).

---

3. Anselm states: "Now we believe that thou art a being than which none greater can be thought" ("An Address (Proslogian)," 73).

## The Cosmological Argument

This argument posits that since everything in the universe has a cause, therefore, there must be an Ultimate Cause (God) for all things. In other words, according to this view, one can demonstrate the existence of God by looking at the way the universe first came into existence. The problem with the cosmological argument is that it does not prove that a single being is the prime cause of the universe and everything in it. In addition, and more seriously, the argument runs into difficulties when it has to answer the question: "Who caused God to exist?" If everything in the universe has a cause, then even God has to be caused by something or someone (which is impossible according to orthodox Christianity). Therefore, when taken to its logical conclusion, this argument ultimately fails to prove God's existence. This view was put forth in its classical form by Thomas Aquinas in his "Five Ways" (as discussed in the first chapter).

## The Teleological Argument

This argument seeks to prove the existence of God by looking at the way the universe works. The order and design of the universe proves that there must be an Intelligent Designer who organized the universe for a particular purpose. Only God has the power and capacity to carry this out. Therefore, God must exist because the orderliness of the universe proves it. Although the teleological argument is in some ways superior to the cosmological argument, it fails to demonstrate the existence of God due to the fact that not everything in creation is orderly and well-functioning. There are some aspects of the created order that do not correspond to a perfect "clockwork" understanding of the universe. One can immediately think of deadly germs and natural disasters. If the teleological argument is taken to its logical end, one might conclude that whoever designed this universe is not perfect or omnipotent, and therefore, not God. The modern version of this argument was put forth by the British philosopher William Paley (1743–1805).

## The Moral Argument

This argument begins with the assertion that human beings are born with an innate ability to know right from wrong. The only way human beings can know right from wrong is due to a moral source that is outside and above them. This source, therefore, must be God. Romans 2:14–15 is often appealed to in support of this argument. However, just because human beings possess a moral compass (or conscience) does not mean that this ultimately proves the existence of God. Some critics could argue that human beings developed "moral codes" or "normative ethics" as a survival mechanism to keep societies from descending into chaos and perpetual conflict. Also, ethical norms sometimes differ among various cultures. Therefore, the failure of the moral argument is that it simply cannot prove the existence of God in a convincing way.

Although the philosophical arguments surveyed above *can* demonstrate the existence of God on an *intellectual* plane, they cannot change the sinner from a hater of God to a lover of God. Only through the saving work of Christ and the regenerating work of the Holy Spirit can sinners be converted from the way of ignorance and darkness to the way of truth and obedience.

## Who Is God?

Knowing God requires that we know what he is like. Christians do not believe in an abstract and impersonal concept called "God", but a genuine person who relates to his creatures and works actively within the created order. Christians, in other words, believe in a God who has all the characteristics and qualities that define a person. Theologians have typically called God's characteristics and qualities as the *attributes of God*. Normally, in Christian theology, God's attributes are divided into two categories: incommunicable and communicable. However, instead of using the more traditional categories we will, following John S. Feinberg, divide God's attributes into *non-moral* and *moral* categories.[4]

### Non-Moral Attributes of God

*Omnipotence.* When people think about God's omnipotence they often think about the almighty-nature of God or his ability to do anything that pleases him. Various biblical passages affirm that God is omnipotent: Genesis 18:14; Psalm 147:5; Isaiah 14:27; Jeremiah 32:17; and Mark 10:27. The biblical writers and prophets clearly understood that God's power is

4. Feinberg, *No One Like Him*, 233–374.

unlimited. However, when we talk about God's omnipotence we must be careful that we do not mean that God can do *absolutely anything*. For example, God cannot make a square-circle or create a rock too heavy for him to lift. The first one is a logical contradiction that cannot exist in any universe and the second is a negation of God's omnipotence and, thus, a theological absurdity. Also, there are certain things that God cannot do in the moral sphere because it would contradict his divine nature. These include: the ability to lie (Heb 6:18), renege on a promise made earlier (Rom 11:29), or be unfaithful to his own word (2 Tim 2:13). These are all acts that go against who he is as a holy and righteous God. Therefore, it is better to understand God's omnipotence as the ability to do whatever pleases him *as long as it is not logically impossible or contradictory to his own nature*. That God is omnipotent should give Christians comfort knowing that he has the ability to carry through with his promises to the end without difficulty.

*Omniscience*. That God is omniscient means that God's knowledge of the universe is all-encompassing. Not only does he know what is happening in Alpha Centauri and our own solar system at the same time he also knows everything that is happening in a person's life in every detail. Also, he knows everything that has happened in the past, what is happening in the present, and *what is going to happen in the future*. Although there are certain passages in Scripture that seem puzzling and appear to contradict God's omniscient power (Gen 22:12), there are various passages in Scripture that affirm that God has exhaustive knowledge of things that have happened and *will* happen (Ps 139:1–4; Isa 46:10; Rom 11:33; Heb 4:13). His knowledge, therefore, fully extends horizontally (time) and vertically (space). As a result, Christians should have complete trust in God knowing that nothing in the universe escapes his "divine radar."[5]

5. In recent years, a small but vociferous group of evangelical theologians have put forth a position called the Openness of God theology. Theologians like Clark Pinnock, John Sanders, and Greg Boyd have advocated this position through their various works. Basically, the theory, according to Roger E. Olson, asserts that "God does not know with absolute certainty all that the future holds, but he is able to predict events and respond in such a way that his ultimate and final will for the future is never thwarted" (*Mosaic of Christian Belief*, 195). The problem with this view is that it tends to a rigid reductionistic rationalism where the relationship between God's comprehensive omniscience and human responsibility is a zero-sum game. However, when looking at Scripture as a whole, the interplay between God's comprehensive omniscience and human responsibility is more complex and dynamic. Scripture affirms *both* God's comprehensive omniscience and human responsibility. One example of this is Paul's sea voyage to Rome narrated in

*Omnipresence.* That God is omnipresent means that he is present everywhere and at all times. This means that nothing in the created order escapes God's watchful eye. God's omnipresence is also clearly made known in Scripture (cf. 1 Kgs 8:27; Ps 139:7–10). Omnipresence also relates to his immanence. While omnipresence describes God's *presence throughout* the created order; immanence describes his *presence in* the created order. Both, however, cannot be confused with the ideas of pantheism and panentheism. Pantheism maintains that God and the created order are synonymous, while panentheism asserts that the created order is part of God. Both are outside the boundaries of orthodox Christianity and cannot be considered a legitimate evangelical option. The biblical and orthodox position is that God is *both* transcendent and immanent in relation to his creation (cf. Eph 4:6).

*Eternity.* The eternity of God means that he is not subject to the limitations of time as his creatures are. Scripture is clear that God is eternal: Deuteronomy 33:27; Psalm 90:2; Isaiah 57:15; and 1 Timothy 1:17. One can see from these passages that God has always existed and will exist forever. That is why the question "Who made God?" is an absurdity in regards to this discussion of God's timeless existence. Since God is the creator of all and eternal in being he cannot have a beginning or end. This, however, does not mean that God does not work chronologically with the sequence of time. Although God is above time and sees all (Isa 46:10), he also sovereignly interacts with his creatures in time as redemptive history moves forward. This is demonstrated by the fact that God interacts with human beings throughout history as mentioned numerous times in Scripture (although God is not limited by time, as human beings are, because of his transcendence). Even though "one day is as a thousand years, and a thousand years as one day" (2 Pet 3:8) for God, this does not mean he is ignorant of the sequential order of time. God is eternal but he also works with the ordinary means of the created order—in this case, time.

---

Acts 27. Paul tells the sailors in verses 23–25 that God, through an angel, told him that he and the sailors will reach their destination alive. However, he later tells the centurion and soldiers that the sailors must stay on board the ship in order to be saved (v. 31). The passage shows that human responsibility did not contravene God's omniscience (and vice versa).

*Infinity.* Related to God's eternity is his infinity. The infinity of God means that he is not subject to the limitations that are a part of creaturely existence—or, to put it in another way, he is *un*limited. That God is not limited is one of the key non-moral attributes of God according to classical Christianity. This is what makes God truly unique. Even elements in the universe that we often perceive as having no limitations do have limits (light, energy, etc.). God's infinity is also recognized in various passages. For example, in Jeremiah 23:23, God declares through the prophet, "Am I a God at hand . . . and not a God far away?" Another example is when Paul tells the Athenians that the God who made everything "does not live in temples made by man" (Acts 17:24). We can see from these verses that God is not bound by the limits of space. Although human beings can only be at one place at a particular time, God has access to every part of the created order at *any* time.

*Immutability.* The immutability of God basically means that he is unchanging.[6] Several passages in Scripture affirm this about God: Numbers 23:19; Psalms 33:11; 102:27; Hebrews 6:17; and James 1:17. However, when we talk about the immutability of God we must also be careful that we do not misunderstand what it means. Immutability does not mean that God is static, inactive, or unresponsive. In fact, the God revealed in Scripture is dynamic, active, and responsive. He works mightily in the created order for its redemption (Rom 8:20–21) and actively responds to human beings depending on whether they obey or disobey him (Exod 32:14, Joel 2:13). Recognizing that God is the same today as he was in eternity past—and, more importantly, does not change in regards to his promises—should motivate believers to trust and obey him more. In fact, because of this truth about God's character, believers should have a greater motivation to live in obedience to him.

6. Process theologians, following the ideas of Alfred North Whitehead (1861–1947) and Charles Hartshorne (1897–2000), argue that God is always changing because the whole created order is constantly changing. The problem with this view is that it severely undermines who God is—foremost, that he is perfect. If God can change, then it means that God needed improvement because he was imperfect before the change took place. This goes against the scriptural testimony that God is perfect and complete in and of himself (Rom 11:35; Heb 1:10–12). As Henry Clarence Thiessen states, "All change must be to the better or the worse, but God cannot change to the better, since he is absolutely perfect; neither can he change to the worse, for the same reason" (*Lectures in Systematic Theology*, 83). For an introductory work on process theology, see Cobb and Griffin, *Process Theology.*

*Aseity.* Finally, the most important non-moral attribute of God is his aseity. The word *aseity* is from the Latin phrase *a se* which means "from or by himself."[7] God's aseity means that God is self-existent and does not depend on other things or beings to exist (Acts 17:24–25). Unlike human beings, God does not require nourishment, rest, or an external power source to live (since he is life himself). He is who he is ("I AM WHO I AM" [Exod 3:14]). Also, God's aseity means that he is independent and does not need the counsel of others before he carries out his perfect will (Rom 9:15–16; Eph 1:5; Rev 4:11). Contrary to the situation of human beings who need knowledge and guidance from others so that they can make appropriate decisions in order to survive, God, on the other hand, is so self-sufficiently wise and infinitely intelligent that he does not need to depend on others to make right decisions. The aseity of God is a key non-moral attribute of the triune God who created all things and rules everything from the heavens. If God is not self-sufficient, self-determining, and self-existing then he cannot be the same God that the Christian church has always worshiped. God's total independence from all things is what also makes him a God of grace. Since God does not need anything from human beings (Acts 17:24–25) and he owes nothing to them (Rom 11:35–36), every good gift that we receive from him is an expression of his inexpressible grace grounded on his self-determination and independence.

## Moral Attributes of God

*Holiness.* One of the key moral attributes of God is his holiness. It is one of the attributes that essentially defines who God is. The Hebrew verb *qādaš* in the Qal stem means "to *be* holy" (as a state), while in the Piel and Hiphil stems it means "to *make* holy" (as an action). It essentially means to be separate or set apart. In the Greek, the adjective is *hagios* and the verb is *hagiazō*. It basically carries the same meaning as the Hebrew term.[8] The holiness of God, therefore, means that he is distinct and separate from the common and profane. There are several biblical passages that discuss the magnitude of God's holiness: Exodus 15:11; Leviticus 11:44; Psalm 22:3; Isaiah 6:3; 1 Peter 1:15; Revelation 4:8. The biblical writers acknowledged that God's holiness is infinite and incomparable. That is why the demands

---

7. Frame, *Doctrine of God*, 600.

8. Mounce, *Analytical Lexicon to the Greek New Testament*, 49–50.

of God's law are very strict and uncompromising (Matt 5:20; Gal 5:3; Jas 2:10). Knowing how holy God is should spur believers to greater holiness in their own lives. Although believers will never reach the level of holiness that God possesses, they are still commanded to be holy because they themselves are the children of a holy God (Matt 5:48).

*Love.* Another key attribute of God is love. Although we should never synonymize God with love (or vice versa), we should point out clearly that love is one of the essential characteristics of the God that Christians worship. One well-known German theologian states: "Love is based on God, because apparently he alone can start the event of love, initiate it, because he alone can *begin* to love without any reason, and always has begun to love."[9] As the Scriptures testify, God's love is not like human love—it is freely given and initiated by him (John 3:16; 1 John 4:19). Also, Scripture often speaks about the greatness of God's love: Psalm 42:8; Jeremiah 31:3; Romans 5:8; Ephesians 2:4–5; 1 John 4:10. We must note, however, that the way Scripture speaks of God's love is not in some abstract and impersonal way. It is a love that is redemptive and very personal. It is a "down-to-earth" kind of love that truly affects the lives of individuals. It is a holy love that has always existed among the members of the Trinity and is now being passed onto human beings. That God genuinely loves his creatures is demonstrated by the fact that he provides good things for them even if they do not deserve his kindness (Matt 5:45; Acts 14:17; 17:25). His love, more importantly, is supremely demonstrated in sending the Son to die on the cross for the sins of rebellious human beings (John 3:16; Rom 5:8; Eph 5:2).

How does knowing that God is love affect us in a practical way? Again, like his holiness, we should love God (Matt 22:37; Rom 8:28) and others (Matt 5:44; 19:19; John 15:12; 1 John 2:9–11) because God is love and demonstrated this love to us by sending his Son to die for us while we were still sinners (1 John 4:19). That is why Paul could say in 1 Corinthians 13:13 that out of the triad of faith, hope, and love, that love is the greatest among them all.

*Grace.* Another attribute that is often discussed in Christian theological discourse is the grace of God. That God is gracious is demonstrated by the fact that even though we are enemies of God due to sin he still sent his Son to die on the cross to bring peace between himself and us (Rom 5:10).

9. Jüngel, *God as the Mystery of the World*, 327.

Contrary to popular opinions that the Old Testament depicts God as chiefly a God of vengeance and wrath, the Old Testament writers understood fully that the God they fear and worship is a very gracious God. That is why Nehemiah, David, and Jonah could say what they said about him—that he is a very merciful and gracious God (cf. Neh 9:17; Ps 103:8; and Jonah 4:2). In the Hebrew the word for "grace" is *chesed*. The word denotes enablement, guidance, forgiveness, preservation, and deliverance from enemies and calamity.[10] In the New Testament the same word is *charis*. However, in the New Testament, the word is more narrowly focused on God's provision of salvation in Jesus Christ.[11] Thus, the gracious nature of God was fully known by the inspired writers of *both* Testaments. Knowing that God is utterly gracious should provide believers great impetus to be thankful to God for everything they have and, in turn, to demonstrate grace to those around them.

*Righteousness.* That God is righteous is affirmed many times throughout Scripture (Deut 32:4; Job 37:23; Pss 7:11; 36:6; Isa 30:18; Acts 17:31; Rom 3:25–26; 2 Thess 1:5–7; Rev 16:5–7). It is, in fact, closely connected with his holiness. That God is righteous is the grounds for the coming judgment against all those who die in unbelief and rebellion against him. If God were not righteous there would be no standard of righteousness (the law) in creation and those who do evil will receive no punishment at the end. That is why even sinful human beings have an innate knowledge of what is right and wrong (Rom 2:14–15). One can even say that God *cannot help but be righteous* in his dealings with people. That is why his righteousness is often correlated with his justice: they are essentially two sides of the same coin.

The righteousness of God, therefore, should comfort believers knowing that one day all the impenitent wicked will be punished for their sins (2 Thess 1:6), that the saints will be rewarded for the good deeds they have done in this life (Matt 6:4), and that God will establish justice fully in the age to come (Isa 42:3–4). As Robert Duncan Culver puts it, "If at times we have difficulty in seeing the justice of God in the way He temporarily allows evil to prosper, we may nevertheless trust His justice to triumph at last (Ps. 73; Hab. 2; Jer. 12:1–4)."[12]

---

10. Enns, *Moody Handbook of Theology*, 202–3.

11. Enns, *Moody Handbook of Theology*, 203.

12. Culver, *Systematic Theology*, 100.

*Faithfulness.* Faithfulness is a trait of God that is connected with his immutable nature. Although immutability is an absolute, non-moral, and incommunicable attribute of God, faithfulness is an attribute that has to do with God's covenantal perseverance with his people. That God is faithful is clearly affirmed in passages like Deuteronomy 7:9; Romans 11:29; 1 Corinthians 10:13; 1 Thessalonians 5:23–24; 2 Timothy 2:13; and Hebrews 10:23. God's faithfulness is also demonstrated in key events in redemptive history like his promise to Adam and Eve to bring forth a Redeemer (Gen 3:15) and to Abraham to provide him with offspring (Gen 15:4). All these promises were fulfilled and God's word will always remain true. It is this faithfulness of God that allows believers to remain in God's love even though they still fall into sin time to time (1 John 1:9–2:1). It is also this same faithfulness that demands that we accept his words revealed in Scripture as being entirely true (some theologians have called this the *trustworthiness* of God).[13]

The faithfulness of God should give immense comfort to believers. It is the source of God's persevering love towards them even though they may morally fail him at times (Rom 8:38–39; 2 Tim 2:13). This, however, does not permit believers to be indifferent to God's will. In fact, this truth should spur them on to continually live in integrity and righteousness in a world permeated with falsehood and sin. They should not make cavalier promises to others they cannot fulfill or break promises they have already made. They should always be faithful and trustworthy when dealing with others because God, who is faithful and trustworthy in all things, is the source of their faithfulness and trustworthiness.

## Conclusion

Knowing God's attributes and character is an essential aspect of the Christian faith. We must either believe in the true God or a fabrication of our imagination (which is idolatry). God has given us enough information about himself through his revealed word and the Incarnate Son that we cannot excuse ourselves out of culpability when we worship something that is false. It is also important to point out that anything that is revealed to us about God (again, whether through Scripture or the Incarnate Son) is a sheer gift given to us from above. As John Calvin correctly points out, "God himself is the sole and proper witness of himself."[14] Therefore, we

13. Bavinck, *Reformed Dogmatics*, 2:207–10.
14. Calvin, *Inst.* 1.11.1.

cannot make a portrait of God based on our own philosophical convictions or intellectual faculties. For this we should always give thanks to the One who has not concealed himself from us.

## 2. The Trinity

The doctrine of the Trinity is considered one of the key doctrines of the Christian faith. It is a doctrine that distinguishes biblical Christianity from other religions and pseudo-Christian cults. Over the years, however, many self-proclaimed Christians have downplayed the importance of this doctrine or denied it altogether. The main reasons, they argue, is that it is incomprehensible to the average layperson, not "explicitly" taught in Scripture, or of no real practical significance for the Christian in his or her daily walk. Of course, those in the church who are faithful to the teachings of Scripture and historic Christianity will strongly disagree with these assertions. The main reason why this doctrine is extremely important is because it deals with the identity of the God who created all things and who has revealed himself to us in grace. Christians cannot worship and follow a false god and, therefore, they must safeguard the doctrine of the Trinity against all assaults with the utmost fervency. As Paul C. McGlasson writes, "What is at stake in the doctrine of the Trinity is the reality of divine self-revelation, and what is at stake in the reality of divine self-revelation is the very identity of the God we worship."[15] Therefore, the safeguarding of the doctrine of the Trinity is vitally important to the Christian faith because it deals with the believers' knowledge of this one true God whom they worship and have a personal relationship with.

### The Biblical Basis for the Doctrine of the Trinity

Although the word "Trinity" does not appear anywhere in Scripture, the doctrine is implicitly taught in several passages. In fact, one can even say that the whole of Scripture is both monotheistic *and* trinitarian in perspective. As John Frame puts it, "Scripture testifies from beginning to end that God is one, but it also presents three persons who are God: the Father,

---

15. McGlasson, *Invitation to Dogmatic Theology*, 187.

the Son, and the Holy Spirit."[16] We will now examine the passages that are regularly cited by Christians to support the triune nature of God.

> Genesis 1:26 (cf. also 3:22 and 11:7). "Then God said, 'Let *us* make man in *our* image, after *our* likeness. And let them have dominion over the fish of the sea and over the birds of the heavens and over the livestock and over all the earth and over every creeping thing that creeps on the earth.'"

- This verse is often cited by evangelical scholars to argue that even in the first book of the Old Testament there is evidence of an understanding of God as being triune in nature. Some, however, have taken the plural forms of this verse to mean that either 1) God was addressing a heavenly court of angels, or 2) that it refers to the plurality of God's majesty in relation to creation. The problem with the first view is that nowhere in the immediate context is it suggested that human beings are created in the image or likeness of angels. Human beings are made *only* in the image of God. The second view is also exegetically problematic: If the plurality of majesty is referred to here, why is there a shift from the singular to the plural in the first and third of the examples? In fact, according to Millard J. Erickson, the "Scripture writer does not use a plural (of majesty) verb with *elohim,* but God is quoted as using a plural verb with reference to himself."[17] Also, the fact that in verse 27 it states that human beings are created both male *and* female (i.e., plural) implies that the image of God consists in a plurality of sorts.[18] Thus, even in the first book of the Old Testament, the image of God as being triune is implied.[19]

> Psalm 110:1. "The LORD says to my Lord: 'Sit at my right hand, until I make your enemies your footstool.'"

- This verse is also commonly used by orthodox Christian scholars to point out that a plurality within the Godhead is inferred in the Old

16. Frame, *Doctrine of God,* 621.

17. Erickson, *Christian Theology,* 354.

18. It is suggested that in the Old Testament the word *elohim* is a plural form of the noun of God—which implies a trinitarian understanding of God.

19. Also, the passages in the book of Genesis that make reference to the "angel of the Lord" (cf. 16:7–13; 18:1–21; 19:1–28; 32:24–30) is sometimes brought up by evangelical scholars to point out that there exists a plurality in the Godhead.

Testament. They argue that David is referring to two separate persons here. This interpretation seems likely based on what Jesus says in Matthew 22:41–46. Jesus used this verse (v. 44) in his debate with the Pharisees to show them who the true Messiah is. He wanted to demonstrate to the Pharisees that they had a limited understanding of this Messiah and wanted them to understand who *he* is (as King and Redeemer of Israel). Thus, the verse, based on the way Jesus uses it, certainly suggests that David knew in rudimentary form of a plurality within the Godhead. As Wayne Grudem notes, "Jesus rightly understands that David is referring to two separate persons as 'Lord' (Matt. 22:41–46), but who is David's 'Lord' if not God himself? And who could be saying to God, 'Sit at my right hand' except someone else who is also fully God?"[20]

> Matthew 28:19. "Go therefore and make disciples of all nations, baptizing them in the name of the Father and of the Son and of the Holy Spirit."

- In this verse Jesus commissions the disciples to spread the gospel and baptize others in the name (singular) of all three persons of the Trinity. The fact that the three persons are referred to in the singular and are equally mentioned in Jesus' Great Commission proves that they all share the same divine nature.[21]

> 2 Corinthians 13:14. "The grace of the Lord Jesus Christ and the love of God and the fellowship of the Holy Spirit be with you all."

- Paul's benediction here to the Corinthians includes all three members of the Trinity. The fact that all three members of the Trinity are mentioned in unison demonstrates that Paul firmly believed that Jesus Christ and the Holy Spirit, like God the Father, are fully divine.

> 1 Peter 1:1–2. "Peter, an apostle of Jesus Christ, To those who are elect exiles of the Dispersion in Pontus, Galatia, Cappadocia, Asia, and Bithynia, according to the foreknowledge of God the Father, in the sanctification of the Spirit, for obedience to Jesus Christ and

20. Grudem, *Systematic Theology*, 228.

21. We will discuss the divinity of Jesus Christ and the Holy Spirit in more detail in the chapters on Christology (chapter 8) and Pneumatology (chapter 10), respectively.

for sprinkling with his blood: May grace and peace be multiplied to you."

- Here we can see that Peter uses the triadic formula to remind his readers that their salvation is a combined work of the Father, the Son, and the Holy Spirit. This shows that all three share the same divine nature because only God can redeem people from their sins. As Edwin A. Blum writes, "Here he reminds his readers of their Triune faith and of the Triune work of God. While Peter does not go into the developed theological form of the Trinitarian faith, the triadic pattern of the Christian faith is already evident in his words."[22]

Although orthodox Christianity has always affirmed the triune nature of the true God there have always been dissenting voices that have deviated from this doctrine throughout the history of the church. We will now discuss the three most common trinitarian heresies in the history of the church below.

## The Three Common Trinitarian Heresies in the History of the Church

### Tritheism

Tritheism was a trinitarian heresy that arose in the early church that asserted that not only are the three persons of the Godhead distinct in personhood but that they are also three separate, independent, and autonomous divine beings. The best analogy for this view is imagining three separate human beings who independently exist within themselves. Although they share the same human nature, they are three separate beings with their own unique personalities and characteristics.

The problem with this view is that it compromises the unitary understanding of God as revealed in the Scriptures (Deut 6:4; Rom 3:30; Jas 2:19) and results in the notion that there exists three independent gods. Of course, this understanding of God is untenable from an orthodox Christian perspective. The God that Christians worship is one and unified. Therefore, even though all three members of the Trinity are distinct persons, they all share the same divine essence (Gk. *homoousios*) which ties them together.

22. Blum, "1 Peter," 219.

## Modalism

Another trinitarian heresy that has beguiled the church at various times throughout history is modalism (or Sabellianism). Although this view avoids the charge of advocating three separate Gods (tritheism) it swings too far in the opposite direction by rejecting the distinct personhoods within the Godhead. The first person to advocate this heresy was Sabellius, a third-century theologian who was excommunicated by Pope St. Calixtus. Sabellius argued that the three members of the Godhead are simply three different modes or manifestations of God.

The problem with this understanding is that Scripture identifies all three members of the Trinity as being distinct and having their own personhood (cf. Matt 28:18; 1 Cor 2:10–11; 6:19; 15:24; Eph 1:22; 4:30; Heb 9:14). Also, this view makes God truly unknown. If Father, Son, and Holy Spirit are merely three "manifestations" of God this would mean that there is a fourth divine entity, above these three "modes," that is hidden and unknown to us. Finally, this view results in the work of Christ becoming superfluous. If Christ is merely one of the modes of God, how could he truly make a propitiatory sacrifice to the Father on behalf of the human race? As Kerry D. McRoberts states, "All of the basic Christian convictions centering on the work of the Cross presuppose the personal distinction of the three members of the Trinity."[23] A modern version of this heresy is found in the various "Jesus Only" or Oneness Pentecostal groups.[24]

## Arianism

The heresy known as Arianism was first set forth by Arius, a presbyter in Alexandria who lived during the third and fourth centuries. Arius maintained that the Logos or Son was the first created being of the Father. Although the Son is considered a heavenly being far greater than anything in creation, he does not share the same divine essence as the Father. (The Holy Spirit is also a created being—the Father creating him after *through* the Son.) Arius's rationale for his understanding is that God could not share his essence with anyone, which is invisible and changeless, unlike his creatures.

---

23. McRoberts, "Holy Trinity," 168.

24. For a good overview and critique of this movement see Greg A. Boyd's work *Oneness Pentecostals and the Trinity.*

Also, followers of Arius pointed out that Colossians 1:15 supported their position because Paul states that the Son is "the firstborn over all creation."[25]

The problem with the Arian view is that it clearly goes against numerous statements found in Scripture affirming the full divinity of the Son. Passages like Isaiah 9:6; John 1:1, 14; Philippians 2:5–7; Titus 2:13; 2 Peter 1:1; and Revelation 22:13 make it clear that the Son shares the same divine attributes as the Father. Also, if Arianism is true, the Son could not make an effectual atonement for the sins of humankind because a mere creature cannot redeem another mere creature.[26] Finally, as revealed in the scriptural witness, the early believers worshiped Jesus as God (Matt 28:16–17; John 20:28). If Jesus was another creation of the Father, the disciples would have been guilty of idolatry (which would clearly go against the monotheism of the Old Testament faith they grew up in). Due to being contrary to the clear statements of Scripture, making the work of Christ superfluous, and its polytheistic implications, the Council of Nicaea (325) and the Council of Constantinople I (381) rightly condemned Arianism as a heresy.[27] A modern version of this heresy is advocated by the Jehovah's Witnesses.

## How Should We Understand God's Three-in-Oneness?

If the views discussed above are unacceptable models for an orthodox Christian understanding of the Godhead how are we to correctly understand the relationships among the three persons of the Trinity? When we

---

25. Although this verse appears to support the position of the Arians, it does not on closer examination. The phrase "the firstborn over all creation" is likely a reference to the Son's rank in relation to creation. Although a chronological ordering is not denied (he is, of course, before creation) it appears that the passage is primarily talking about the Son's supremacy over all creation (cf. Vaughan, "Colossians," 11:182).

26. Athanasius (293–373) used this argument against Arius and his followers.

27. In the Nicene Creed, it states that Jesus Christ was "begotten, not made, *being of one substance with the Father,* by whom all things were made" (emphasis added). There was some debate among the early church theologians at the time of the Council of Nicaea on whether to use the Greek word *homoiousios* ("of a similar substance") or *homoousios* ("of the same substance") when it came to understanding the Son's divine nature in relation to the Father. Some (like Arius) preferred the former understanding to safeguard the distinction between the Father and the Son; others, however, advanced the latter understanding arguing that the word *homoiousios* did not go far enough in making it patently clear that the Son and the Father share the same divine essence. To remain faithful to the biblical understanding of the Trinity, the Council of Nicaea opted for the *homoousios* view. This was affirmed again at the Council of Constantinople in 381.

attempt to properly articulate the doctrine of the Trinity we must keep in mind, as Frame notes, that much "that the Bible teaches about the Trinity is very mysterious, and we must bow in humility as we enter into this holy realm."[28] However, this hardly means that Christian theologians should immediately give up on this endeavor. In fact, to the contrary: we should do our best to formulate a doctrine of the Trinity that carefully corresponds to what has been revealed to us in the inspired Scriptures. This is what we will now attempt to do below.

### The Proper Understanding of God's Three-in-Onenesss

It is clear from the scriptural witness, as discussed above, that the God we worship—the God of Israel in the Old Testament and the God who became flesh in the New Testament—is One. Deuteronomy 6:4–9, called the *Shema*, was invoked by the Jews to teach their children of the oneness of God so that they could be distinguished from their polytheistic neighbors. In fact, the very first commandment of the Decalogue was a command against any worship of any gods except Yahweh (Exod 20:3). Thus, the oneness of God was strongly affirmed by the Israelites of the Old Testament and was carried over into the belief system of Jewish and gentile Christians in the New Testament (Rom 3:30; 1 Cor 8:4–6; 1 Tim 2:5–6; Jas 2:19).

The truth of the oneness of God is not something that is difficult to grasp by most who embrace the Christian faith. The difficulty lies in trying to understand how this one God can be understood as being three eternally distinct persons. The Nicene Creed (which was expanded at the First Council of Constantinople in 381 AD) established this truth when the formulators stated that Jesus Christ is "the only-begotten Son of God, begotten of the Father before all worlds, God of God, Light of Light, Very God of Very God, begotten, not made, being of one substance with the Father by whom all things were made," and that the Holy Spirit is "the Lord and Giver of Life, who proceedeth from the Father and the Son,[29] who with the Father and the Son together is worshiped and glorified, who spoke by the prophets."

Although the formulators of the creed provided the basic statement of the identities of the Son and the Holy Spirit and their relationships to the Father they did not put forward a systematic formulation of how the

---

28. Frame, *Salvation Belongs to the Lord*, 30.

29. We will deal with the *filioque* clause below.

three persons can share the same essence. However, the Cappadocian Fathers regularly used two Greek words to describe how the three persons of the Trinity share the one divine essence. The two words they used were *ousia* (which describes the "substance" or "essence" of a thing) and *hypostasis* (which describes the individual reality or the "who"). Thus, to clarify the orthodox position against their opponents, the Cappadocian Fathers declared that God is "three *hypostases* in One *ousia*." Or in other words, God is one "substance" or "essence" in his divine Being but three *hypostases* or Persons in their particular existence. Also, although there may be differences in terms of roles within the triune Godhead, all three persons of the Trinity *equally* share this one divine essence. (We must also emphasize again, against Modalism, that all three persons are distinct and have their own personhoods. Therefore, the Father is not the Son or the Holy Spirit, the Son is not the Father or the Holy Spirit, and the Holy Spirit is not the Father or the Son.)

Since we have drawn out a clearer understanding of the doctrine of the Trinity above, we must still ask if there are any analogies from the natural world to help the average Christian understand the doctrine of the Trinity in a more comprehensible manner. Throughout the history of the church Christians have advocated various analogies from the real world to illustrate how the Father, Son, and Holy Spirit can still be of one divine essence. The most popular analogy people have used is water and its three states. People who use this analogy say that the Trinity is like water: water can still retain its chemical composition even if it is in a solid (ice), liquid, or gas form. Thus, the Trinity is like the properties of water: ice (Father), Son (liquid), and gas (Holy Spirit). The problem with this analogy is that the three forms of water are merely "modes" of the same substance. If we use this analogy to its logical end it will only lead to a type of modalism. This also applies if we use the sun as another analogy. Illustrations, therefore, from the natural world are severely limiting because none of them can truly capture the mystery and nature of the triunity of God. The best way to make the doctrine of the Trinity understandable is to provide a substantial but concise definition of it. The best, so far, we believe, is offered by the Princeton Reformed theologian B. B. Warfield: "There is one only and true God, but in the unity of the Godhead there are three coeternal and coequal Persons, the same in substance but distinct in subsistence."[30]

---

30. Warfield, "Trinity," 5:3012.

*An Economic Trinity?*

In recent years there have been discussions among theologians regarding an *economic* understanding of the Trinity (or the economic Trinity). In contrast to the ontological understanding of the Trinity (which deals with the personal properties of each persons of the Trinity and the relationships among them), the economic understanding of the Trinity sought to reveal how each member of the Trinity works—especially in relation to creation and humanity's redemption. The economic understanding of the Trinity has been advanced by various theologians throughout history to combat a non-personal and sterile understanding of the Trinity (thought to be inherent in the ontological understanding).[31] They desired to make the doctrine of the Trinity alive and meaningful to Christians who struggled daily trying to live out their faith in a spiritually hostile and skeptical world.

Although we laud the intentions behind the advocacy of this particular understanding of the Trinity we must insist that its attempt to restrict the doctrine of the Trinity only by the way God reveals himself to the world through his acts as being theologically and biblically inadequate.[32]

*The Filioque Clause*

That the Holy Spirit proceeded from *both* the Father and the Son is the common consensus among the Western churches throughout history. Theologians throughout the centuries have called this the *filioque* clause (the word *filioque* meaning, "and [from] the son" in Latin). During the early period of the church there was a severe disagreement between the churches of the East and West regarding the Holy Spirit's procession as coming *only* "from the Father" (found in the original Nicene Creed). Gradually, however, the Western churches began to insert the word *filioque* in the Creed as a result of being persuaded by Augustine's view that the Holy Spirit is the "love bond" between the Father and Son[33] and in response to the growing threat of Arianism.

By the ninth century, the *filioque* clause officially became part of the Western churches' understanding of the processionary relationships among the members of the Trinity. The Eastern churches, however, objected to

31. Cf. Rahner, *Trinity*.

32. Weber, *Foundations of Dogmatics*, 1:388.

33. Cf. Augustine, *On the Trinity*, 199.

this language arguing that to insert the *filioque* clause tampers with the original statement of the creed, compromises the unitary nature of God (according to them, only the Father can be the sole source of divinity), and puts undue emphasis on the Son which can undermine the role of the Holy Spirit in redemption. In fact, one renowned Russian Orthodox theologian went further by insisting that the *filioque* clause is erroneous because it is intrinsically contradictory to the doctrine of the Trinity. He writes:

> The nature [the *ousia*] . . . is one and identical in the consubstanti-
> ality of the three hypostases, but it is also thoroughly hypostatized,
> Trinity in unity or unity in Trinity, by the *one* trihypostatic subject,
> by the three persons of the Holy Trinity. That is why the Filioque
> postulate, the postulate of *from the Father and the Son as one prin-*
> *ciple* in Their hypostatic nondifferentiation, contradicts the very
> essence of the trinitarian dogma.[34]

On the other hand, the churches in the West countered that there are indications in Scripture that suggest that the Holy Spirit proceeds not only from the Father but also from the Son (John 15:26; 16:7; Acts 2:33; Gal 4:6). They argue that one must seriously deal with these passages and not pass over them because they do not agree with the statements of the earlier Nicene Creed. Also, they argue that if you do not include this clause in the creed there would be no clear distinction between the Son and the Holy Spirit within the Godhead—which could lead to a type of modalism. Finally, one evangelical theologian writes that without the clause an agnosticism of sorts can result regarding our knowledge of who the triune God is:

> It is not an unimportant consideration that without the *Filioque*
> we have knowledge of the Father's *ontological* as well as *economic*
> relationship to the Son and the Spirit, but knowledge only of the
> *economic* relationship between the Son and the Spirit. This would
> leave a *prima facie* lacuna in our knowledge of God as he is in him-
> self, and an area of knowledge of God in which the principle that
> he is as he reveals himself to be would not pertain. An agnosticism
> in relationship to God's actual being results.[35]

If we have to decide which side has more scriptural support for their respective positions we would have to conclude that the Western churches have the decided advantage here. The key passage that Western Christians often refer to in their defense of the *filioque* clause is John 15:26. Jesus states

34. Bulgakov, *Comforter*, 127.

35. Ferguson, *Holy Spirit*, 77.

there that "when the Helper comes, *whom I will send to you from the Father*, the Spirit of truth, who proceeds from the Father, he will bear witness about me." Jesus makes it clear here that it is not only the Father who will send the Spirit to the disciples but that *he* will also send the Spirit to them to bear witness about him. This procession from the Son is also indicated in other passages in John's Gospel (cf. 14:16, 26; 16:7, 13–15). Also, the fact that the Spirit also proceeds from the Son does not necessarily imply that a division of deity within the triune Godhead will result, as Orthodox Christians have maintained. In fact, one can argue that the *filioque* clause actually safeguards the unitary nature of God by insisting that the Spirit who proceeds not only from the Father but also from the Son *equally* shares the same divine essence as the first two persons of the Trinity.

Despite the stronger position of the Western churches on this subject we must also say that a degree of charity must be exercised when discussions of the *filioque* clause are brought up. It is not so crucial a point that a denial of the clause results in the denial of the faith. As Sergius Bulgakov states, "Dogmatically, the 'question' of the procession must yet be a subject of further investigation. But in and of itself the divergence expressed by the two traditions, Filioque and *dia tou Huiou*, is not a heresy or even a dogmatic error. It is a difference of theological opinions which was dogmatized prematurely and erroneously."[36]

## The Importance of the Doctrine of the Trinity

Does having a correct understanding of the Trinity make a difference in church practice and how individual Christians live out their faith? It certainly does. Many will demur that it does not matter how we understand the relationships among the members of the Godhead as long as we live in obedience to God's will and maintain unity among the churches. This type of thinking, although laudable to a certain degree, is not only naïve but also spiritually detrimental. The doctrine of the Trinity is not a self-contained doctrine that does not impact other doctrines—it has significant bearing on other aspects of Christian theology, especially soteriology.[37] As McRoberts states, "The doctrine of salvation (including reconciliation, propitiation, ransom, justification, and expiation) is contingent upon the cooperation of the distinctive members of the triune God (e.g., Eph. 1:3–14). Therefore,

36. Bulgakov, *Comforter*, 148.

37. *Soteriology* is the technical term for the study of the doctrine of salvation.

a conscious renouncing of the Trinity doctrine seriously jeopardizes the hope of one's personal salvation."[38] To reject the doctrine of the Trinity, in other words, reveals that one does not truly know the God revealed in the Scriptures and the salvation he offers us through the Incarnate Son, Jesus Christ.

38. McRoberts, "Holy Trinity," 168.

# CHAPTER 3

# Creation and Providence

## 1. Creation

It CANNOT BE SAID enough that the doctrine of creation is a doctrine that must never be relegated to the sidelines in any Christian theological discussion. Regrettably, some evangelical Christians today view the doctrine of creation with some apathy or indifference. They argue that the doctrine only fuels controversy and disunity among Christians. Instead, they opine, we should pass by this doctrine and discuss more important subjects like soteriology (the doctrine of salvation) or ecclesiology (the doctrine of the church). This attitude towards the doctrine, however, is contrary to the way the biblical writers understood God's work of creation. In fact, if one surveys the whole of Scripture, one will notice that the biblical writers attached great importance to understanding the purpose of God's creational work. Also, we must recognize that the whole created order reveals something about the God we know and worship. All the wonders and beauties of creation give witness to God's character, love, and holiness. Therefore, those who profess to follow Christ should pay careful attention to this doctrine and have a clear understanding of God's creative work throughout the cosmos.

In the first section of this chapter we will discuss three key issues surrounding the doctrine of creation: 1) the biblical view of creation; 2) the relationship between creation and modern science; and 3) the ultimate goal of creation.

## The Biblical View of Creation

### God Created Out of Nothing (creatio ex nihilo)

In Genesis 1:1, according to the English Standard Version, it states: "In the beginning, God created the heavens and the earth." The very first verse of the Bible suggests that God created the heavens and the earth out of nothing (what is traditionally known as *creatio ex nihilo* [from the Latin phrase "creation out of nothing"]).[1] The Apostles' Creed, the most basic confession for most Christian denominations today, reaffirms this when it declares on the very first line: "I believe in God, the Father Almighty, Creator of heaven and earth." One can see that from the earliest days of the church the doctrine of *creatio ex nihilo* was accepted as the unanimous position.

Having said that, we must be careful how we articulate this doctrine to avoid any misunderstanding. When we talk about God creating *ex nihilo* we are not saying that God did not work in chronological sequence to complete his work of creation. All we mean by the terminology is that God not only fashioned the heavens and the earth, but also created the necessary building blocks for their existence. Also, when we use the word "nothing" we do not mean that in times past something called "nothingness" existed before God created (as some ancient philosophers believed). As John S. Feinberg astutely points out, "When Christian thinkers speak of creation out of nothing, they are not talking of nothing as though it is a something out of which God made things. Creation out of nothing means creation despite the absolute absence of anything."[2]

Among the vast majority of Christians today the *creatio ex nihilo* view is still the commonly accepted one. Recently, however, this view has been challenged not only by secular academicians but also scholars who profess

---

1. The key is the Hebrew word *bara*. Does it suggest that God created with no pre-existing materials at hand? Or does it merely signify the temporal sequence of creation ("When God began to create," found in the footnote of the Revised Standard Version)? Although the word *bara* does not absolutely decide the issue either way, it is preferable to opt for the first view considering the context of the passage and statements in other parts of Scripture. This view has been defended quite ably by John H. Sailhamer (cf. Sailhamer, "Genesis," 2:21–23).

2. Feinberg, *No One Like Him*, 552.

to embrace the Christian faith. For example, Ninian Smart and Steven Konstantine write: "The notion that God creates the world out of nothing is designed to signify that God's purposes are not limited or frustrated by *the preexisting properties of matter*."[3] For them, there could have been no creation *ex nihilo* because the cosmos is already the body of God.[4] Process theologians have also joined this trend against the traditional *creatio ex nihilo* doctrine. For instance, John B. Cobb and David R. Griffin write: "Process theology rejects the notion of *creatio ex nihilo*, if that means creation out of *absolute* nothingness."[5] Since God and creation are both in the process of development (making them both virtually synonymous), according to these scholars, creation and God had to exist in unison since eternity past. The rationale these theologians give in rejecting the classic *creatio ex nihilo* doctrine is not so much for scientific reasons as theological. Finally, in the New Jewish Version of the Old Testament, the wording of the first three verses of Genesis has been translated in a way to move away from the traditional *creatio ex nihilo* position, as Robert L. Reymond has pointed out.[6]

There are a number of problematic implications that result from denying the *creatio ex nihilo* doctrine. First, it goes against the numerous statements in Scripture that God created the heavens and the earth *out of nothing*: Nehemiah 9:5–6; Psalm 33:6; 90:2; Proverbs 3:19; Isaiah 44:24; Jeremiah 32:17; John 1:3; Romans 4:17; Colossians 1:16; Hebrews 1:2; 11:3; and Revelation 4:11. If one accepts the Scriptures as divine testimony of what is true one cannot escape the conclusion that the prophets and biblical writers held to the belief that God created everything with no preexisting materials to work with. Second, to say that matter existed in eternity before God's creative act is to suggest that God is not self-sufficient, independent, and unique (his aseity is compromised). It infers that something was already in existence from eternity past that competed with or rivaled God (a type of cosmological dualism). We would, therefore, have to say that creation is somehow part of God and, thus, an object of worship also. The testimony of Scripture, however, makes it clear that creation is dependent on God and not in some way eternally co-existent with him. Third, the denial of this doctrine undermines the sovereignty of God. As discussed

3. Smart and Konstantine, *Christian Systematic Theology*, 207 (emphasis added).

4. Smart and Konstantine, *Christian Systematic Theology*, 207

5. Cobb and Griffin, *Process Theology*, 65.

6. Reymond, *New Systematic Theology*, 385.

in the previous chapter, God has the right and power to do as he pleases. To acknowledge that God created *ex nihilo* is to acknowledge that God is supreme over the whole created order.

## God Created Everything in the Universe

Not only did the Christian tradition unanimously believe that God created the universe out of no preexisting materials, it also maintained that *all things* in the universe were created by him. All the stars, nebulas, quasars, planets, oceans, and living things in the universe came from the creative hand of God. Scripture makes this clear in a number of passages. The three passages that are often invoked by Christian thinkers to highlight this truth are Ephesians 3:9; Colossians 1:16; and Revelation 4:11. All of them use the Greek phrase *ta panta* ("all things") to describe the all-encompassing nature of God's creative act. Other passages like Acts 4:24; 14:15; 17:24; and Revelation 10:6 also state that God created all things. This is important to point out because it reveals that all things have no independent existence and owe their existence to God alone. It also demonstrates again the supremacy of God over all things—marking out the Creator/creature distinction firmly in place.

## Everything Created by God Is Good

The fact that God created everything in the universe also leads to another important truth about creation: that it is good. The fact that everything has its source from the creative hand of God automatically presupposes its goodness. This truth is readily affirmed in the first chapter of Genesis. In Genesis 1:25, after God created all non-human entities and surveyed everything he created, it states that God "saw that it [creation] was good." This is also reaffirmed in Genesis 1:31 *after* God created human beings. Scripture's clear affirmation of the goodness of creation is in stark contrast to the view of some ancient Greek philosophers who viewed creation as inherently evil. Also, the rejection of creation's goodness, according to Paul, is one of the signs of apostasy and spiritual deception (1 Tim 4:1–3). Although we are not to worship creation, we are to acknowledge its goodness and enjoy it in proper measure (Gen 1:29; 2:16; 1 Tim 4:4). Finally, the fact that creation comes from the hand of God provides us with an obligation to take good care of it. In fact, this command to be responsible stewards of creation was one of the first ordinances given by God to human beings (Gen 1:28). This command, contrary to what many modern Christians believe, has not been abolished today. If human beings fully obeyed God's command to be responsible stewards of his creation we would not experience the problems of resource exploitation, mass over-consumption, and ecological morass that are prevalent today. Christians of all eras must set a godly example for the world by properly fulfilling their God-given calling to take care of creation and to live in harmony with it.

*Creation Demonstrates God's Love*

As mentioned above, the reason why the doctrine of creation should be discussed in Christian theological reflection is due to the fact that it reveals the character of God. Creation is a reflection of God's goodness and love. That is why Paul can say to the Lycaonians that the God who made "the heaven and the earth and the sea and all that is in them" (Acts 14:15) showed "kindness" (NIV, Gk. *agaphourgon*, meaning "to do good") to them by giving them "rains from heaven and fruitful seasons" and providing them with food so that their hearts will be filled with joy (v. 17). As one can see here, God's goodness and love prompted him to create the universe and give good things to his living creatures (cf. Matt 6:26, 28–29). Karl Barth puts it well when he states that creation "is the presupposition of the realisation of the divine purpose of love in relation to the creature. Creation is the indispensable presupposition because it is a question of the realisation of the *divine* intention of love."[7] God did not create the universe because he was bored or felt unsatisfied with himself. He created because he wanted to express his goodness and love to his creatures. One can even say that creation is the culmination of the mutually interdependent love that has always existed among the three persons of the Trinity. This should give believers pause when reflecting on the majesty, goodness, and love of God—which should motivate them to glorify him more as they interact with the material world on a daily basis.

7. Barth, *Church Dogmatics*, III/1:96.

*God Did Not Have to Create the Universe*

We have demonstrated above that God's love is reflected in creation (and we will demonstrate below that his glory is the ultimate goal of creation). However, we should not surmise that God created the heavens and the earth *out of necessity*. No external *or* internal force compelled God to create. Although creation is the expression of the intra-trinitarian love that has existed since eternity, God created the universe by the free act of his will. As Stanley J. Grenz writes, "God's creation of the universe is a free act, a non-necessary act. God is not driven to create, not forced by some sense of compulsion to bring the universe into existence."[8] Therefore, we can conclude that God created the universe as an outgrowth of his love and desire to bring glory to himself, but not in a way as if he were compelled to do so.

## The Relationship Between the Doctrine of Creation and Science

The relationship between the biblical understanding of creation and natural science has always been conflictual in nature. One always recalls the clashes between the Roman Catholic Church and Galileo for the latter's support of Copernicus's heliocentric cosmology, overturning many centuries of what the church believed about the cosmos. In more recent times, Charles Darwin's work *On the Origin of the Species* (1859) always stirs up controversy among more conservative members of Christ's universal church. The idea that human beings were not directly created by God at one moment but evolved over a very long time from more simple organisms scrapes hard against evangelical sensibilities, since the inerrancy of Scripture and the doctrine of humanity's uniqueness as God's image-bearers are thought to be compromised by these modern scientific ideas.

The question then is: can the biblical view of creation be harmonized with the findings of modern science? Some evangelical theologians believe that this is an impossible goal to achieve. For them, if modern scientific discoveries are accepted by the church it will compromise the authority and inspiration of Scripture. For instance, Floyd H. Barackman writes that "any attempt to harmonize God's inerrant account with changing scientific opinion not only requires an unnatural explanation of the creation record but also subjects God's true, authoritative Word to man's fallible

---

8. Grenz, *Theology for the Community of God*, 99.

reasoning."[9] Science, therefore, must always give way to biblical revelation. Others, however, argue that Christian faith and science can be harmonized. Daniel L. Migliore, a proponent of this view, writes that we "can explore the congruence of scientific and theological understandings of the world without insisting on a proof or disproof of the one by the other."[10] This is needed urgently, he insists, because of the ecological crisis we face in our age.[11] Although we can never truly solve the conundrum between Christian faith and science there does not need to be a total incongruence between a high view of Scripture and that of modern science. However, as Christians, we must always maintain that the witness of Scripture always takes precedence over any scientific discoveries made by human beings based on modern (and *imperfect!*) scientific methods.

## When Did God Create the Universe?

One of the more contentious issues between Christianity and science has been the age of creation. In the past, there have been various attempts by Christian thinkers to calculate the age of creation based on the internal testimony of Scripture. One well-known example is Archbishop James Ussher's (1581–1656) attempt at coming up with the age of creation based on the genealogies given in the Bible. Through his calculations Ussher concluded that God created everything in 4004 BC. Therefore, creation is around six thousand years old. In recent times, there have been attempts by Christian scholars to come up with a more adequate way of determining the time of creation without contradicting the claims of modern science. Several proposals have been offered by Christian scholars in an attempt to reconcile the apparent disharmony that exists between the biblical view of creation and modern scientific findings. We will go over these proposals now.

*The Gap Theory.* This theory holds that there was a gap (Gen 1:2) between the original and unformed creation (1:1) and the re-created earth (1:3–27) in which God teemed the latter with various types of plant and animal life. This explains, according to those who hold this theory, why there exists an apparent dissonance between fossil records and the way

9. Barackman, *Practical Christian Theology*, 78.

10. Migliore, *Faith Seeking Understanding*, 115.

11. Migliore, *Faith Seeking Understanding*, 116.

God's creative work is narrated in the early chapters of Genesis. The incongruity, they argue, can be explained by the fact that a gap of many billions of years existed between the first and second creation events. Also, the ruin and chaos of the first creation is attributed to the fall of Satan—in which case, God had to restore creation to order. This is the view set forth by C. I. Scofield (1843–1921) in his *Scofield Reference Bible*.

*The Day-Age Theory.* Those who hold this theory argue that the Hebrew word *yom* used throughout Genesis 1 means long periods of time (which, otherwise, normally means a twenty-four-hour period). Basically, God created everything in long successive epochs. This would explain why geological findings place the earth as having been in existence for over four billion years. For instance, after arguing that the word "day" does not mean a literal twenty-four-hour period,[12] J. Rodman Williams, a proponent of this view, states shortly after:

> Here we may look again in the scientific direction, and note that geological and biological data say much the same thing. It is now generally recognized that prior to man's arrival on the scene there were lengthy periods of time. For example, vegetable life appeared long before animal life, and animal life long before human life. Each of these "days" could have been thousands or multiples of thousand years (recall 2 Peter); the exact length is unimportant. The important thing is that God completed a work during that period. Its completion therefore is the completion of a day.[13]

Williams's argument is typical of those who state that the Day-Age theory is best able to account for the apparent discrepancy between the creation narrative of Genesis 1–2 and modern science. Therefore, one of the strengths of this position is that it does not contradict the findings of modern geological research in regards to the age of the earth. Some prominent Christian scholars of the past who held this view include Charles Hodge, James Oliver Buswell, and Bernard Ramm.

*The Flood Theory.* This theory maintains that the world is only a few thousand years old but maintains an appearance of being very old because of the tremendous impact of the flood on the earth during Noah's time (Gen 6–9). The flood caused an extremely high pressure on the earth resulting

12. Williams, *Renewal Theology*, 1:108.
13. Williams, *Renewal Theology*, 1:108–9.

in the creation of fossil fuels in a relatively short time (due to life forms being deposited in various rock strata). This would explain, according to this theory, why fossil records show the earth to have the appearance of age.

*The Literary-Framework Theory.* Those who hold this theory argue that the days of creation recorded in Genesis 1 are more matters of "literary-framework" rather than a record of a chronological sequence of events. This is demonstrated by the fact that parallelisms can be seen in the author's account of the six days of creation: day 4 (creation of the luminaries) with day 1 (light and darkness); day 5 (creation of sea creatures and birds) with day 2 (water and sky); and day 6 (creation of land animals and humans) with day 3 (dry land).[14]

Although the author, according to proponents of this view, does not discount any chronological sequencing in the creation account, his primary purpose, using a literary device, is to underscore the fact that God created everything with a theological message behind it—that the whole of creation is fulfilled on the Sabbath Day when God and humans commune.[15] One of the advantages of this position is that there are other parts in Genesis that also use artistic literary devices to get theological messages across. Another advantage of this view is that it can provide an answer to the apparent chronological discrepancies between the two creation accounts (in Genesis chapters 1 and 2)[16] in relation to the time of Adam's creation and the appearance of vegetation. Meredith G. Kline was a well-known proponent of this view.

## The Case for a Young Earth/Twenty-Four-Hour-Day Creationist Position

Although all the views surveyed above have their own particular strengths, we believe that a form of the twenty-four-hour-day creation view is most faithful to the testimony of Scripture. We will now go over the reasons as to why we believe this.

First, it has been shown that radiocarbon dating and fossil records are not completely reliable, and sometimes even suspect. It is possible that God

14. Hiebert, "Create, Creation," 134.

15. Hiebert, "Create, Creation," 134.

16. In Genesis chapter 1, it is narrated that Adam is created (vv. 26–27) after the appearance of vegetation (v. 24); in chapter 2, he is said to be created (vv. 5–7) before the appearance of vegetation (v 9).

created the world less than ten thousand years ago with the appearance of age (just like God created Adam directly as a fully grown human being). Second, the argument that the Hebrew word *yom* can be translated as lengthy periods of time is not convincing. There appears to be no evidence within the context of Genesis 1–2 to argue that *yom* can have a meaning other than the standard twenty-four-hour-day span. Also, when the Scriptures in other places talk about the "the day of the Lord" (cf. Isa 7:18–25; Zeph 1:7) or "the day of destruction" when God brings down his wrath (cf. Joel 1:15; 2:2), they are referring to an actual twenty-four-hour-day period. Third, in regards to understanding the creation account in Genesis as a literary-framework, there seems to be some ambiguity in regards to when it is appropriate to read things figuratively and when it is appropriate to understand things literally within Genesis 1–3, as Feinberg perceptively points out. If the days are figurative, should we understand Adam and Eve, Satan, the animals, and the plant life as figures of speech too?[17] Fourth, the gap and flood theories do not satisfy since they attempt to accommodate too easily with the so-called facts of modern scientific research.

The strength of the young earth/twenty-four-hour-day creation view is principally based on the fact that it preserves the integrity of Scripture's language. If Scripture states that God created the world in six literal twenty-four-hour-days then we can trust that God did create the world within that specific time span. Also, Wayne Grudem helpfully points out some of the strengths of the young-earth/literal days approach when he writes:

> At present, considerations of the power of God's creative word and the immediacy with which it seems to bring response, the fact that "evening and morning" and the numbering of days still suggest twenty-four-hour days, and the fact that God would seem to have no purpose for delaying the creation of man for thousands or even millions of years, seem to me to be strong considerations in favor of the twenty-four-hour day position.[18]

However, as Frame points out this issue should not be one that should cause divisions among evangelical Christians. He writes: "Personally, I see no reason why the days could not have been twenty-four-hour days. But I don't believe we should fight battles over this issue."[19] Although we agree with Frame that this issue does not necessarily determine who is considered

17. Feinberg, *No One Like Him*, 613.

18. Grudem, *Systematic Theology*, 297.

19. Frame, *Salvation Belongs to the Lord*, 20.

orthodox or heretical, we believe that it is still an important enough issue that Christians of differing convictions should maintain healthy discussions on this subject for the foreseeable future.

*Excurses: Is Evolutionary Theory Compatible with Biblical Creationism?*

There are some evangelical theologians in recent decades who believe that evolutionary theory does not conflict with the Scripture's account of how God created the universe. One well-known proponent of this view is the Baptist theologian Augustus H. Strong. He writes: "Evolution does not make the idea of a Creator superfluous, because evolution is only the method of God."[20] Howard J. Van Till, a contemporary Christian scientist who also holds to this position, avows that Scripture and natural science should never be at odds when it comes to the subject of creation. For instance, he states that "the *scientific* concept of evolution, properly defined, does not entail any idea that conflicts with the historic Christian doctrine of creation."[21] Therefore, for Strong, Till, and others who hold to theistic evolution, the evolutionary process is the means by which God creates the world and every living organism in it. Although this view can account for the fact that scientific research demonstrates that the world is very old, it is difficult to reconcile with Scripture's account of creation.

Those who hold to theistic evolution, however, will argue that in the animal world there are a variety of species of a given genus, which demonstrates that creation has been in an evolutionary process for many millions of years. On the other side, those who believe in a relatively young creation will argue that the existence of a variety of species within a genus is due to the God-given process of adaptation to adjust to new environments for the survival of the species. In other words, although God directly made different kinds of plant and animal life, he also included in their DNA certain physiological mechanisms so that their descendants can adapt and survive in new environments. One example that comes to mind is the polar bear. The polar bear has thicker blubber and fur compared to other bear species because it needs to be insulated against the extreme cold temperatures within the Arctic Circle. This, however, is not due to some macro-evolutionary process but through the physiological adaptation by an earlier bear species over a stretch of many centuries to protect itself from the extreme

20. Strong, *Systematic Theology*, 466.
21. Till, "Fully Gifted Creation ('Theistic Evolution')," 172.

cold. This also explains why the human race is varied in terms of color, shape, height, facial characteristics, and adaptive qualities. Although all human beings descend from the first couple, each so-called racial group developed its own unique biological characteristics over a long period of time to adapt to the respective conditions of the environment their recent ancestors were living in.

Therefore, we can maintain that there was a progressive sequence in God's creation of the world but not in the way theistic evolutionists maintain.[22]

## The Ultimate Goal of Creation: God's Glory

Although God's love, as mentioned above, is revealed in creation, God's glory is the ultimate *goal* of creation. That the goal of creation is God's glory is witness to in various passages of Scripture. For instance, in Psalm 19:1–2, David declares: "The heavens declare the glory of God, and the sky above proclaims his handiwork. Day to day pours out speech, and night to night reveals knowledge." We can see here that for David everything that is created in the heavenly realms testifies to God's glory. Also, in Isaiah 43:6–7, God, speaking through the prophet, announces: "bring my sons from afar and my daughters from the end of the earth, everyone who is called by my name, whom I created *for my glory,* whom I formed and made." This passage states clearly that God did not create human beings because he was lonely and needed companionship; he created them because he wanted to glorify himself through those who bear his image. Finally, in the last book of the Bible, John describes an awesome scene where angelic creatures praise God and shout: "Worthy are you, our Lord and God, to receive glory and honor and power, for you created all things, and by your will they existed and were created" (Rev 4:11).

One does not have to search through the Scriptures alone to know that creation testifies to the glory of God. The sun, the moon, the stars, the mighty oceans, the high mountains, and every living creature that dwells on this planet attest to the glory of God. The harmony and intricacy of the world indicates beyond a shadow of a doubt that a mighty, wise, and glorious Being created everything that moves and exists in the world. As John Calvin puts it, "Yet, in the first place, wherever you cast your eyes, there is no spot in the universe wherein you cannot discern at least some sparks

22. Erickson, *Christian Theology*, 409.

of his glory."[23] This should provide believers with a greater appreciation of God's glory and a greater impetus to shape their lives according to this profound truth. God's glory is fully revealed in creation and, therefore, we have no excuse when we withhold the praise that God rightfully deserves.

## 2. Providence

Although the doctrine of creation deals with God's initial work of bringing forth the universe, the doctrine of providence deals with God's *continuing* work in the universe. It specifically deals with God's preserving and governing activities within the created order. It is important to mention that a correct understanding of providence prevents us from falling into two significant errors: 1) *deism* (the belief that God lets the universe run on its own after creating it), and 2) *pantheism* (the belief that the created order and God are identical). We also have to point out that providence is not the same as fate or determinism (where events occur as a result of impersonal forces). Providence deals with a *personal* God who oversees and governs every facet of the universe with his infinite and caring power.

In this section of the chapter we will discuss: 1) God's preserving activity in the universe, 2) God's governing activity in the universe, 3) the relationship between providence and prayer, 4) the relationship between providence and miracles, 5) and the relationship between providence and evil. We will then conclude by stating why the doctrine of divine providence matters for the Christian life.

### God's Preserving Activity in the Universe

What does it mean when theologians talk about God's preserving activity in the universe? At its core it means that God works actively not only to sustain the created order so that it does not spiral into destruction but to provide everything for its benefit. That God continues to preserve the universe after its creation is testified in numerous places throughout Scripture. For instance, Job declares: "he gives rain on the earth and sends waters on the fields" (Job 5:10). Even in his anguished state, Job recognizes that God is still the sustainer and provider of the universe. Another example is Jeremiah 10:13, when the prophet states: "When he utters his voice, there is

---

23. Calvin, *Inst.* 1.5.1.

a tumult of waters in the heavens, and he makes the mist rise from the ends of the earth. He makes lightning for the rain, and he brings forth the wind from his storehouses." According to the prophet, all the natural processes of the world that makes it function properly come from God's mighty hand. In the New Testament, the apostle Paul writes that "all things hold together" in Christ Jesus (Col 1:17). This demonstrates to the trinitarian nature of the work of preservation—all three persons of the Trinity are involved.[24] Other biblical passages that discuss God's work of preservation include: Nehemiah 9:6; Psalm 65:9–10; 104:14; 147:8–9; Matthew 5:45; 6:26; Acts 14:17; and Hebrews 1:3. We can demonstrate from these passages that God continues to work mightily to nurture, nourish, and flourish the earth. Whether it is sending rain clouds over a field to water it or bringing the sun's rays down onto the earth so that it will not be enveloped in darkness, God continues to work within creation so that everything will work together in harmony and in order.

In addition, God's work of preservation in creation is comprehensive. Not only does God care for and sustain human beings by providing them with food and other earthly gifts (Acts 14:17), he nourishes and cares for non-human life forms like flowers (Matt 6:28–29) and birds (Matt 6:26) as well. This means that his work of preservation encompasses *all* life forms and includes *every* part of the created order—no aspect of the universe is left alone. As Calvin writes:

> But faith ought to penetrate more deeply, namely, having found him Creator of all, forthwith to conclude he is also everlasting Governor and Preserver—not only in that he drives the celestial frame as well as its several parts by a universal motion, but also in that he sustains, nourishes, and cares for, everything he has made, even to the least sparrow [cf. Matt. 10:29].[25]

Also, not only is God's preserving activity comprehensive, it is also extensive: even the amount of rain that will fall on a particular field is determined by God. In this way, God's continuing work of preservation is a reflection of God's love. God could have created the universe and then left it to run on its own (like a clockmaker). However, this would not be consistent

---

24. Reymond rightly maintains that "one must never sever any aspect of God's providence away from the ἐν Χριστῷ, *en Christō*, relationship that exists between God and his creation, since all of God's dealings with his creation are mediated through the Christ" (*New Systematic Theology*, 400.).

25. Calvin, *Inst.* 1.16.1.

with God's character. The God who created out of his infinite love also sustains everything as a result of that same love. For this, we should take great comfort knowing that the universe is not run by blind fate or chance but by a personal God who deeply cares for his creatures.

## God's Governing Activity in the Universe

When theologians talk about God's governing activity in creation they are talking about his *purposive* will in it. This includes much more than just preservation since it deals specifically with God's directing of history to fulfill his overall purpose planned out since eternity. This aspect of God's providential work is closely connected with his eternal decrees (thus, God is also *sovereign* in his governing activities).[26] Like preservation, there are a number of places in Scripture that discuss the manner in which God governs everything to achieve his purpose. One passage that comes immediately to mind is Romans 8:28: "And we know that for those who love God all things work together for good, for those who are called according to his purpose." Here, Paul makes it clear that in *all things* God will work for the good (salvation) of all believers who love him (cf. Eph 1:11).

Another classic passage often referred to in regards to God's governing activity is Genesis 50:20. In this verse Joseph tells his brothers: "As for you, you meant evil against me, but God meant it for good, to bring it about that many people should be kept alive, as they are today." We can see here that the plan to do harm against Joseph by his brothers was used by God for a greater purpose—to save many lives. Job 12:23–24 is another passage that demonstrates that God is actively governing the world: "He makes nations great, and he destroys them; he enlarges nations, and leads them away. He takes away understanding from the chiefs of the people of the earth and makes them wander in a trackless waste." Job here points out a sobering truth about the way God deals with the world: it is ultimately God who raises nations up or brings them down. This reveals that God's governing activity pertains to both individuals and nations.

A question that often comes up when discussing the subject of God's governing activity is the issue of its relationship to human responsibility. If God governs everything sovereignly in the universe for his perfect end what is the role of human choice in all of this? What we must point out here

26. In contrast to providence, God's eternal decree deals with the plans that he has established before the creation of the universe that *will* take place in the world.

is that God's governing activity is not mutually exclusive with the choices that humans make (theologians often call this *concurrence).* God uses the choices made by humans to achieve his ends—or, in other words, they are the appointed *means* to that end. One good example of this is the crucifixion of Jesus Christ. Although God had already decreed that the Son would be crucified for the sins of his people (Isa 53:4–6) he still used the various human players (the Jewish religious leaders, the Roman authorities, Judas Iscariot, etc.) to carry out this decreed plan. This should remind us that although God's purpose for all of creation *will* come to fulfillment one day, this is no excuse for us to become lazy and careless in our Christian walk. God has decreed that our decisions and activities play a meaningful role in building up the body of Christ (Eph 4:12) and bringing about the redemption of sinners living throughout the whole world (Matt 28:19–20).

Knowing that it is God who ultimately controls the destiny of individuals and nations this understanding should humble us as we take stock of our lives and watch the evening news regarding events that are happening around us. One day, all things (including death) will be under the complete power and authority of God in Jesus Christ (1 Cor 15:23–28). Knowing that nothing escapes God's governing hand as he directs everything toward his perfect goal this revelation should bring Christians great comfort as they reflect on the way he works in the world for their redemption.

## The Relationship Between Providence and Prayer

Related to the issue of concurrence is the matter of the relationship between God's providence and our petitionary prayers. Many Christians have wondered how it is possible to harmonize the apparent conflict that exists between God's providence and the efficacy of our prayers. What is the point of prayer if God is in charge of everything that happens in our lives? This is a vital matter to reflect upon because it pertains to how and why we pray to the triune God. Christians often pray about various matters that are important to their lives: which career path to choose, whom to marry, where to live, etc. Oftentimes, when Christians reach a critical juncture in their lives, they resort to prayer as a last "stop gap" to finally decide which path to take. Prayer, then, becomes the last solution after all of our evaluative options have been exhausted. Scripture, however, exhorts us to "pray without ceasing" (1 Thess 5:17; cf. Matt 6:5–13; Eph 6:18; Phil 4:6; Jas 5:13–18). This statement by Paul demonstrates that God *does* listen to our prayers and they *do* matter to him.

Despite the biblical exhortations to pray continually, the relationship between providence and prayer is still an issue that we should bring to the table in our theological discussions. A proper understanding of providence will enable us to have a better understanding of prayer and a richer prayer life. As Terrance Tiessen writes, "How we understand God's action in the world will determine how and when and why and for what we pray."[27] Prayer should never be abandoned because we believe that God's ultimate purpose for creation and his people will come to fulfillment despite human intransigence and rebellion. The biblical writers did not deal with this issue like a philosophical problem like some modern Christian thinkers do. For them, God's sovereign providential work to bring his purposes to fulfillment *and* the efficacy of our prayers are both true. James 5:14–15 is a good example of this. James does not discuss whether it is in God's sovereign plan to heal *all* sick people in the church through prayer, although he does affirm that this is the likely outcome. All he does say is that believers should get the elders in the church to pray for the sick. This shows that God uses our prayers as a *means* to accomplish his purposes. It does not alter his purposes but it is required if the desired outcome is to be achieved.[28]

## The Relationship Between Providence and Miracles

Another interesting subject to discuss in regards to the doctrine of providence is the issue of miracles. How do miracles relate to God's providential work? Are miracles aberrations in God's work of preservation and governance? Considering the technological boom of the last one hundred years and a greater reliance on science to solve the problems of the world the issue of miracles has become increasingly irrelevant to modern people. In fact, belief in miracles is seen as a sign of unenlightened irrationality (or, even worse, utter foolishness) by many today. However, we cannot ignore the fact that Scripture often speaks of the reality of miracles (cf. Exod 14:22;

27. Tiessen, *Providence and Prayer*, 20.

28. Of course, even if we fervently pray for something it does not mean we will get the results we desire. Paul is a case in point. He prayed three times to get the "thorn" removed out of his flesh (2 Cor 12:8). However, God did not grant his request because he had a greater purpose in mind—the strengthening of Paul's faith in Christ (vv. 9–10). This shows that God does not always answer the prayers of his people the way they expect because he has a greater purpose in mind for them.

17:5, 7; Josh 10:12–14; 2 Kings 6:5–6; Matt 4:23–24; 8:16–17; Mark 6:45–52; John 6:1–24; 9:1–12; 11:38–44). Even those of more liberal theological convictions acknowledge that miracles are possible even in our scientific age.[29] The more pressing issue here, however, is not whether miracles do occur but how they can be harmonized with God's providential work of governing the created order.

Some have argued that the existence of miracles is a problem because it is incongruent with how God works within creation. Since God has already established the physical laws of the universe then it is not possible, they argue, for him to contradict those laws by certain disruptive acts (i.e., "miracles"). This argument was posed by the Scottish philosopher David Hume (1711–76) in his well-known work *An Enquiry Concerning Human Understanding* (section 10, part 1). Many in the past have attempted to "legitimize" these miracles described in Scripture by arguing that they either must have a scientific explanation for their occurrences or were basically extraordinary phenomena that did not violate the physical laws of the universe.[30] Although this is a valiant attempt at reconciling the apparent disharmony that exists between the reality of miracles and the established laws of the universe, we believe that this view is ultimately unsatisfactory. For example, how does this view explain the phenomenon of the floating ax head as mentioned in 2 Kings 6:5–6? Or the healing of the man who had been born blind so that he can see for the first time (John 9:1–12)? Any attempt to give a scientific explanation for these occurrences will lead to failure. When Scripture states that these events actually occurred we must accept them as plain facts. In other words, these miraculous events *really did* happen in our space-time world even though we may not have a scientific explanation for them.

What we must assert here is that miracles do not violate the ordinary ways God providential works in the created order. Miracles can often be attributed to natural occurrences that do not take place very often. However, they are on more rare occasions actual supernatural events that have no scientific explanation. When these inexplicable events do occur we must recognize that God can use any means he desires (ordinary or extraordinary) to achieve his ends (cf. John 14:11). Also, when we talk about miracles we must be aware that it does not mean that God can do something that is logically impossible. For instance, God's parting of the Red Sea (Exod

29. Smart and Konstantine, *Christian Systematic Theology*, 224–25.
30. Cf. Jenson, *Systematic Theology*, 2:42–45.

14:21–22) is not the same as him creating a square circle. The former is something that God *can* do and the latter is something he *cannot* do (because it is an impossible conceptuality). Finally, as believers, we must not be preoccupied with miracles in and of themselves (a preoccupation that is common among modern Charismatic Christians). We must recognize that miracles are only a *means* to a greater end—specifically, to reveal God's redemptive purpose and sheer glory.

## The Relationship Between Providence and Evil

One of the more vexing questions pertaining to the doctrine of providence is the existence of evil in the world. Even though it is a question that raises difficulties for all theologians, it is an issue that cannot be set aside nonchalantly for those who are convinced of the veracity of the Christian faith. One of the reasons why this issue is so difficult to ignore is due to the fact that it often challenges the way Christians normally believe about God. If God is good, why does he allow evil and suffering to exist? If God is almighty, why does he not use his power to remove all evil and suffering from the world? It appears that the existence of evil and suffering challenges at least one of the basic premises that Christians have always believed about who God is. As James Montgomery Boice writes, "How evil could even enter a good world created by a good God is puzzling. Why God permits evil to exist even temporarily as he obviously does is also beyond our full comprehension."[31] Boice is correct to maintain that it is beyond our full comprehension to know why a good and almighty God allows evil to exist in the world. However, various theologians have attempted to solve the problem by offering differing solutions to this puzzling question (what is typically called *theodicy*). We will now go over some of these solutions proposed by various theologians of the past and present, and then offer our own perspective based on the testimony of Scripture.

### Irenaeus

The early church theologian Irenaeus of Lyon offered a unique solution to the difficult problem of God's providence and the existence of evil. According to Irenaeus, the existence of evil serves a divine purpose: to develop the

---

31. Boice, *Foundations of the Christian Faith*, 195.

human race from spiritual "childhood" to "adulthood" (typically called the "soul-making" theodicy). He writes:

> This . . . was the [object of the] the long-suffering of God, that man, passing through all things, and acquiring the knowledge of moral discipline, then attaining to the resurrection from the dead, and learning by experience what is the source of his deliverance, may always live in a state of gratitude to the Lord, having obtained from Him the gift of incorruptibility, that he might love Him the more.[32]

The existence of evil, according to Irenaeus, was ordained by God so that the human race would become more spiritually awakened and develop a deeper love for God because of his redemptive work. Without evil there would be no need for human perseverance and work of redemption. Therefore, according to Irenaeus, evil had to come into existence for this to become a reality.[33]

Although the strength of this argument posits that God can actively use evil to develop the human race spiritually, the problem with this view is that it veers towards venerating evil and suffering. This is in stark contrast to the view offered in Scripture. For example, in Isaiah 5:20, the prophet declares: "Woe to those who call evil good and good evil, who put darkness for light and light for darkness, who put bitter for sweet and sweet for bitter!" Here we can see that there is a stark contrast between good and evil. Both are mutually exclusive to each other and have no common ground in God's created order. Another example is James 1:13: "Let no one say when he is tempted, 'I am being tempted by God,' for God cannot be tempted with evil, and he himself tempts no one." We can see in this passage that James makes it emphatically clear that God cannot be tempted by evil *nor* does he tempt people with evil because God and evil are opposed to each other—both cannot work together.

Also, how can we justify the Irenaean approach to someone who is undergoing a significant degree of suffering in this life? How can we explain to a parent who loses a child due to the recklessness of a drunk driver that the tragedy is actually a good thing? As Alister E. McGrath rightly points out, this approach "seems merely to encourage acquiescence in the presence of

---

32. Irenaeus, *Against Heresies*, 3.20.2.

33. A modern exponent of this view is John Hick (see his *Evil and the God of Love*).

evil in the world, without giving any moral direction or stimulus to resist and overcome it."[34]

### Augustine

In reaction to the errors of the gnostics (who considered all matter as evil, and thus, the root of the existence of evil in the world), Augustine viewed the existence of evil as a result of the misuse of freedom by human beings. He explains:

> If man is good, and cannot act rightly unless he wills to do so, then he must have free will, without which he can not act rightly. We must not believe that God gave us free will so that we might sin, just because sin is committed through free will. It is sufficient for our question, why free will should have been given to man, to know that without it man cannot live rightly. That it was given for this reason can be understood from the following: if anyone uses free will for sinning, he incurs divine punishment. . . . Both punishment and reward would be unjust if man did not have free will.[35]

Augustine's view is a version of the "human freedom" theodicy. Augustine's defense of the reality of human free will is grounded in his understanding of divine justice. Human beings must have free will in order for God to demonstrate his justice to them perfectly. Therefore, the existence of evil in our world is due to the fact that human beings use their freedom to choose evil rather than good.

The problem with Augustine's approach is that it does not solve the ultimate origin of evil. If the first couple were created sinless and morally upright (Gen 2:25; Eccl 7:29), where did the temptation to sin come from? For Augustine, this temptation had its origin in Satan. Then, of course, one will ask: how could Satan be tempted to sin since he was also created morally upright (cf. Isa 14:12)? One can see here the problem with Augustine's free-will approach to theodicy.[36] Another problem with this approach is that it tends to see human responsibility as an independent agent that has power over God's work of providence in human affairs and the created

---

34. McGrath, *Christian Theology*, 264.

35. Augustine, *On Free Choice of the Will*, 2.1.36.

36. This criticism can also be directed against theologians of the Arminian persuasion who emphasize the freedom of the human will.

order. In a way it implies that God is not totally omnipotent and omni-science (the irony being that Calvinist Christians throughout history have looked to Augustine to defend their particular view of divine sovereignty). Finally, this approach fails to adequately address evils that are not directly caused by human sin. For instance, how can Augustine's perspective an-swer the problem of the suffering of people caused by natural disasters (i.e., earthquakes, tsunamis, etc.)? It seems that Augustine's approach has its limitations.

*Karl Barth*

Although generally standing in the Reformed tradition, Karl Barth at-tempted to solve the apparent tension between God's providence and the existence of evil in a way that was somewhat at variance with the staunch Calvinist view of Reformed orthodoxy. According to Barth, the typical Reformed understanding of the relationship between providence and evil was based on logical deductions made by the Reformed Scholastics starting from the premise that God is supreme in all that he does and that anything he does is holy, just, and good.[37] This, for him, led to a "tragic" understand-ing of God's providence because it led to a "Stoic resignation."[38] For Barth, the solution to this problem was to view evil as "nothingness." In other words, it is "that which God does not will. It lives only by the fact that it is that which God does not will. But it does live by this fact. For not only what God wills, but what He does not will, is potent, and must have a real correspondence."[39] This view is in stark contrast to the classic Reformed view where God from eternity did decree that evil will come into existence. Furthermore, according to Barth, this "nothingness" is overcome by God's grace manifested in the person and work of Jesus Christ. Through the Son's death and resurrection, "nothingness" has been exposed and defeated to its utmost depths by the gracious and almighty God.[40]

Although Barth's attempt at explaining the relationship between divine providence and evil is commendable for its non-speculative and eschatological orientation, it is still problematic in some respects. One serious problem is calling evil "nothingness." It seems that Barth is quite

37. Barth, *Church Dogmatics*, III/3:115.
38. Barth, *Church Dogmatics*, III/3:115–16.
39. Barth, *Church Dogmatics*, III/3:352.
40. Barth, *Church Dogmatics*, III/3:311–12.

arbitrary when it comes to describing the nature of evil. Evil is not nothingness but the *opposite* of that which is good (Rom 12:9). Therefore, to call evil "nothingness" takes away from the seriousness and diabolical character of evil (cf. Hab 1:13; Matt 6:13; 12:35; John 17:15; Eph 6:16).

## Bruce Reichenbach

Not satisfied with the way traditional theological systems have attempted to justify the ways of God, Bruce Reichenbach attempts to solve the problem of evil by arguing that God limits his power by giving his creatures the freedom of choice.[41] He writes that

> God deems it more valuable for there to be free persons who can do good and respond to him in love than for there to be no morally good (or bad) actions and no love responses . . . .But granting us freedom not only makes it possible for us to do good and respond to God and others in love, it also allows us to do evil and respond in greedy, selfish and exploitive fashion to one another.[42]

Since humans are conscious, rational, and free beings there is always the risk of evil existing in this world. God's power to remove evil is, thus, limited by the existence of human freedom, according to Reichenbach.

The problem with this view is quite obvious: the compromising of God's omnipotence in favor of human freedom to explain the existence of evil. Any theory of theodicy that undermines any of the core attributes of God cannot be viewed as an acceptable solution within orthodox Christianity. Christians who adhere fully to the inspired witness of Scripture must reject this option outright.

## Four Proposals

Although any attempt at harmonizing the providence of God with the existence of evil will be a difficult endeavor for any theologian it is still an important subject to discuss since evil and suffering are continually around us. Just turning on the news will reveal that evil is a regular occurrence around the world: unjustified killings of civilians during war, young children dying from malnutrition every day around the world, earthquakes

41. Reichenbach, "God Limits His Power," 99–124.
42. Reichenbach, "God Limits His Power," 121.

killing hundreds and disrupting the lives of many, etc. As Christians, the problem of evil cannot simply be ignored and swept aside to sooth our consciences and make life more bearable. If the problem of evil cannot be ignored, are there any theologically adequate ways to understand this issue?

First, we affirm with the classic Reformed tradition that God is in full control of everything that happens in the world. Whether it concerns nature (Ps 65:9–10; Matt 6:26), nations (Ps 22:28; Dan 4:17), or individuals (Job 14:5; Ps 139:16; Rom 8:28), God is in complete control over everything and his eternal decrees will be fulfilled unopposed (Isa 14:26–27; Acts 4:28; Rom 8:29; Eph 1:4). Therefore, Reformed theologians like Gordon H. Clark are correct in *some sense* when they maintain that even tragic and evil events are part of God's decretive will, since Scripture states clearly that God has ordained *everything* for a specific purpose (Prov 16:4; Isa 45:7; 1 Pet 2:8; Jude 4).[43] This is vitally important to maintain as we will demonstrate in our second point below.

Second, the fact that God has sovereignly decreed everything that has come to pass (and will come to pass) shows us that we can be comfortingly assured that he also *has complete power over everything that has happened (and will happen) in our world—including evil events.* Although those outside the Calvinist or Reformed tradition may take issue with this understanding of God's providential control over creation, this truth should actually give us great comfort instead of being a cause for great consternation. If God did not ordain that evil and sin should enter his good creation how can we affirm that God has ultimate control over them? The fact that God has allowed evil and sin to enter the created order by his divine ordinance demonstrates that *nothing* escapes his almighty hand.

Third, taking a cue from Barth, just because God is in control over everything that happens in the world does not mean believers should have an attitude of "Stoic resignation." We are called to constantly fight against evil (Ps 34:14; Rom 12:9, 17; 1 Thess 5:22), and to continually promote justice, mercy, and righteousness (Exod 23:6; Prov 1:3; Amos 5:15; Mic 6:8; Matt 5:9; 23:23). Knowing that God is sovereign over everything should

---

43. Clark, *God and Evil*, 30. Even Calvin shares this outlook when he writes: "Let us imagine, for example, a merchant who, entering a wood with a company of faithful men, unwisely wanders away from his companions, and in his wandering comes upon a robber's den, falls among thieves, and is slain. His death was not only foreseen by God's eye, *but also determined by his decree.* For it is not said that he foresaw how long the life of each man would extend, *but that he determined and fixed the bounds that men cannot pass [Job 14:5]*" (*Inst.* 1.16.9 [emphases added]).

spur Christians on to do the things that he requires of them continually. In fact, what we do in this world and the choices we make in this life truly do matter in God's redemptive-historical purpose. We are not automatons that passively "go along" with the flow of history. God's purposeful decree from eternity and his goal of the redemption of the cosmos involves the activities of human beings.[44] As Paul Helm writes, "Certainly one's view of divine providence *conditions* one's personal response to evil, and in this way divine providence and human spirituality come together."[45]

Fourth, even if there are some evils in the world that cannot be explained on this side of eternity, believers should always keep in mind that this life is not the final goal of God's perfect plan. There will always be evil and suffering in this world until Christ returns and removes all the destructive effects of sin. Until that day comes, however, we are to wait and hope patiently because, as Paul states, our "sufferings of this present time are not worth comparing with the glory that is to be revealed to us" (Rom 8:18), and "we know that for those who love God all things work together for good, for those who are called according to his purpose" (Rom 8:28). One day God will set all things right when he establishes the new heaven and earth (Rev 21) and judges all those who have done evil and have refused to repent (Rev 21:8; 22:15). An eschatological perspective on this matter will enable us to joyfully live our lives as Christians even in the midst of suffering because we know that this life is only a temporary pilgrimage before the ultimate Sabbath rest to come.

## Why God's Providence Matters

The providence of God is a doctrine that should provide us with great joy and comfort in the midst of our difficult pilgrimage to the eschatological

44. Although space constraints will limit how much we can discuss this matter here, we believe that God does possess "hypothetical" counterfactual knowledge in regards to what choices humans make in history. For example, when David was in Keilah after defeating the Philistines (1 Sam 23:1–5) he was warned by God that if he stayed in the city the citizens of the city will hand him over to Saul (1 Sam 23:10–12). God knew if David stayed in Keilah that he would be given up to Saul by the inhabitants of the city. Even though God had decreed that David would leave the city and escape the hands of Saul, God also knew what would happen to him if he stayed. Even though this possibility cannot be genuinely real in the sense of it coming to actualization in history, God does truly possess this "hypothetical" divine knowledge of the counterfactual possibilities (in this case, if David stayed in Keilah) (cf. Frame, *Doctrine of God*, 153).

45. Helm, *Providence of God*, 215.

city. Even though Christians can take great comfort knowing that God is preserving and governing everything towards a perfect end, this provides no excuse for spiritual complacency among Christ's followers. In fact, we are called to continuously press on to the higher calling that God has given us which is expressed in our faithfulness to God and love for our neighbors. Even though in the meantime we will never fully understand why evil exists in the world, we are still called to fight the good fight of faith (1 Tim 6:12) and "to do justice, and to love kindness, and to walk humbly" with our God (Mic 6:8).

## CHAPTER 4

# Angels and Demons

## 1. Angels

ANY DISCUSSION OF ANGELS in this scientific age is liable to bring reproach among modern people. Many today believe that belief in angels is evidence of an irrational mind that is trapped in the primitivism of earlier times. Even some forms of contemporary theology, especially in the West, insist that discussions regarding angelic beings should be discarded since it cannot speak with relevance to modern people. As Bruce D. Marshall amusingly states, "Among the guild of professional theologians in America today, serious talk about angels is roughly as common as serious talk about Santa Claus or the tooth fairy."[1] Ironically, it is also in today's scientific age that the fascination with angels has reached a new peak. With many people in recent years getting involved with the New Age movement this heightened fascination is not surprising. However, when Christians talk about who and what angels are it must be based on the witness of Scripture and not on fanciful interpretations given by those with active imaginations.

Theologians have traditionally called the doctrine of angels *angelology*. In the first half of this chapter, we will discuss the nature of angels, the purpose of angels, and our relationship to angels.

---

1. Marshall, "Are There Angels?," 69.

## The Nature of Angels

### Angels Are Spirit Beings

That angels are spirit beings is clearly attested to in Hebrews 1:14: "Are they [angels] not all ministering *spirits* sent out to serve for the sake of those who are to inherit salvation?" Consistent with their spirit nature angels cannot be normally seen by people (Num 22:31; Luke 2:13) unless God gives them the ability to see them. Paul writes in Colossians 1:16 that God through Jesus Christ created all things in "heaven and on earth, visible and *invisible,* whether thrones or dominions or rulers or authorities—all things were created through him and for him." This verse demonstrates that invisible things, including angels, also exist in the created order. However, angels can also take on corporeal form when it is deemed necessary in order to complete a task set for them by God (Gen 19:1–20; Heb 13:2).

### Angels Are Personal Beings

That angels are personal beings with emotions and wills is clearly attested to in passages like Job 38:7; Psalm 148:2; Luke 1:13–17; 1 Corinthians 6:3; Jude 9; and Revelation 4:6–9. They are not automatons that merely take orders from God and carry them out; they express their inner thoughts just like the way human beings do. As Robert P. Lightner states:

> Angels are not "its," powers, forces, figments of human imagination, or personifications of good and evil. They possess the essential elements of personality—intellect, emotion, and will, and the power of self-consciousness and self-determination. This means angels are aware of themselves. This is more than mere consciousness. Angels are able to objectify themselves, just as people are able to do so.[2]

The fact that some of these angels fell from their glorious position to follow Satan and do evil (2 Pet 2:4; Jude 6) demonstrate that they have the ability to make moral choices on their own. Therefore, angels, like human beings, are personal beings with unique personalities and self-identities.

---

2. Lightner, "Angels, Satan, and Demons," 552.

*Angels Possess Extraordinary Powers*

That angels have abilities that normally go beyond what human beings possess is testified clearly in Scripture. Jesus provides some indication of this when he states: "But concerning that day and hour no one knows, *not even the angels of heaven,* nor the Son, but the Father only" (Matt 24:36). This verse suggests that angels possess superhuman powers that allow them to know certain things that are not normally accessible to human beings. Other biblical passages also affirm that angels possess great powers above that of any normal human being (cf. Ps 103:20–22; Col 1:16; Heb 2:7; and 2 Pet 2:11).

The fact that angels need to carry out special ordinances of God that require extraordinary abilities (cf. Matt 25:31–32; Luke 1:11–19; 2:9–15) demonstrate that, although limited, they have powers far superior to that of human beings. However, it must be emphasized that these powers come from God alone and can only be exercised according to his will and permission. John Theodore Mueller states: "The power of the angels is very great, Ps. 103:20; 2 Thess. 1:7; 2 Kings 19:35; yet it is a finite power, completely under the control of God, Job 1:12. While their power is superhuman, Ps. 91:11–12, or greater than that of man, Luke 11:21–22, they are not omnipotent, but subject to God, who rules over them, Dan. 7:10."[3]

*Angels Do Not Marry*

The fact that angels do not marry is clearly attested to in Matthew 22:30 (cf. Luke 20:34–36). There, Jesus tells the Sadducees: "For in the resurrection they [human beings] neither marry nor are given in marriage, *but are like angels in heaven.*" This shows that angels do not have the same type of physical relationships that human beings have in the created order. Also, the fact that angels do not marry reveals that *all* of them were created by God *before* the creation of the world.[4] J. Rodman Williams states: "Angels were nonsexual from the beginning, for God did not create them as a couple to fill the earth but as a vast number to dwell in heaven. They did not—and do not—form a race that continues to multiply by birthing but a company that

---

3. Mueller, *Christian Dogmatics*, 198.

4. Although Scripture does not reveal when exactly angels were created, the best possible hypothesis is that they were created at least by the sixth day.

has totally existed since their original creation."[5] Since all the angels were created at one time before the world came into existence they, therefore, do not require reproductive organs for the purpose of procreation.

## Different Types of Angels

### The Cherubim

Although all angels possess extraordinary powers, they are not all of the same class. One type of angel mentioned in Scripture is the *cherubim* (pl. *cherub*). Popular imagination often depicts these angels as cute, childlike, and chubby entities with small wings. However, Scripture portrays these angels as anything but cute, childlike, and chubby. When the first couple was expelled from the Garden of Eden, God placed a cherubim to guard the way to the tree of life (Gen 3:24). The carved figures on each ends of the cover of the Ark of the Covenant in the Old Testament tabernacle (Exod 25:17–22) and in the inner sanctuary of Solomon's temple (1 Kgs 6:23–28) were modeled after the cherubim. Also, according to Scripture, God is depicted as being enthroned between or above the cherubim (1 Sam 4:4; Ps 80:1) and even riding on one of them (2 Sam 22:11; Ps 18:10).

### The Seraphim

Another class of angels that Scripture mentions is the *seraphim* (singular *seraph*). These angels are only mentioned in Isaiah 6:1–7 in the prophet's vision of God. In Isaiah's vision, the seraphim were standing above God (v. 2) and were seen to be worshiping him by proclaiming: "Holy, holy, holy is the LORD of hosts; the whole earth is full of his glory!" (v. 3). The seraphim may also have been witnessed by the prophet Ezekiel when he spoke in detail of the "four living creatures" (Ezekiel 1:5–25) and by John when he saw the "four living creatures" with six wings and eyes covered all around (Rev 4:6–8).

---

5. Williams, *Renewal Theology*, 1:178.

*The Archangel*

Although the cherubim and seraphim can be viewed as different types of angels, the *archangel* is not exactly a type or class of angel but a *lead* angel that has authority over other angels. In 1 Thessalonians 4:16, Paul talks about an archangel who will announce with his voice the return of Christ. In Jude 9, Michael is described as an archangel, and in Revelation 12:7, he is seen waging war against Satan and his angels in heaven. Finally, whether there are ranks within the race of angels we do not know. Scripture does not give us enough information that shows that there is some hierarchical ordering among the angels, and due to this lack of scriptural evidence on this issue it is best not to speculate.

## The Purpose of Angels

*Angels Primarily Exist to Glorify God*

The primary purpose of angels is to glorify God. Because angels have emotions and wills like human beings they have the capacity to glorify God. This is demonstrated in passages like Psalm 103:20; Isaiah 6:2–3; and Revelation 4:8 where the heavenly hosts praise God for his glory and holiness. Also, when Jesus Christ was born, a great number of angels glorified God for his gracious work of redemption (Luke 2:14). Therefore, the primary purpose of angels is to glorify God and to reveal his glory when they carry out his purposes among the human community.

*Angels Exist to Minister to Believers*

Aside from glorifying God, angels also exist to minister to believers. Scripture clearly attests to this fact. In Acts 5:19 and 12:6–11, we see that the angels rescued the apostles and Peter, respectively, when they were imprisoned. In Genesis 19:1–29, we see that two of God's angels helped Lot and his family escape from the coming destruction on Sodom. Also, in Exodus 14:19–20, we see that the angel of the Lord stood between the people of Israel and the Egyptians, resulting in the deliverance of the former. However, the majority of the ministry of the angels to believers are of a spiritual nature. This is demonstrated by the fact that angels minister to believers by serving them (Heb 1:14), communicating God's messages to them (Luke

1:13–20, 26–38; Acts 8:26; 11:13; 12:7–11; 27:23), overseeing what goes on in the church (1 Cor 11:10), and delivering deceased believers to the place of blessedness (Luke 16:22).

Despite these roles that angels play in the lives of believers, we must not conclude that every believer has a "guardian angel." The Scriptures do not teach in any way that all believers have a personal guardian angel that watches over them continuously. Although Acts 12:15 is sometimes used to argue that every believer has a personal guardian angel, it is precarious to draw such a conclusive statement based on one passage of Scripture. The fact that even true believers die of terminal illnesses, car accidents, and other hazards of this fallen world demonstrate that the notion of guardian angels being assigned to every believer is suspect at best.

### Angels Help Execute Judgment

Finally, angels exist to help execute judgment in the world. This judgment can either be temporal: when the angel of the Lord killed 185,000 Assyrians (2 Kgs 19:35) or struck down Herod for his irreverence (Acts 12:23); or eternal: when they will separate the good crop from the weeds at the Great Assize (Matt 13:40–43) and administer judgment against the unbelieving world during the future tribulation period (Rev 8:6–9:21; 16:1–17). Also, that angels will play a pivotal role when Christ returns to earth is attested to in passages like Matthew 25:31; 1 Thessalonians 4:16–17; and Revelation 19:14.

## Conclusion

Christians should be aware that God not only created the physical world but also the spiritual world. Recognizing this, Christians should rejoice knowing that there are angelic hosts who are in service to God, and who exist to minister to their spiritual needs and aid them in times of trouble. Despite these truths about angels and their relationship to believers, Christians should always remind themselves that angels, like the rest of creation, are *created* beings and, thus, not to be worshiped or venerated (Col 2:18; Rev 19:10).

## 2. Demons

Any discussion of demons in the modern age must be treaded upon judiciously. Although discussions of angels might peak some interest among some moderns, an overwhelming majority of them will find any discussion of demons as childishly outdated or superstitious. However, Christians in the modern age must not give in to these sentiments and ignore the reality of a spiritual realm that opposes God and his people. To ignore the enemy is the first step in allowing him to gain a foothold on the spiritual battlefield. Having said that, Christians should not be unduly preoccupied with these spirit beings who oppose God. To have an excessive preoccupation with demons can stifle personal ministry and sanctification due to inappropriate use of time, resources, and energy in "fighting off" demons in one's personal life. At the same time, we must know our enemies in order to know how we can resist them and claim victory over them whenever we are put in a position to wage a spiritual struggle against them.

### Origin of Demons

Although Scripture does not provide us with a detailed and explicit presentation of where demons originated from, there are some passages in Scripture that give us a clue to their original station in the created order. In 2 Peter 2:4, the apostle writes that "God did not spare angels when they sinned, but cast them into hell and committed them to chains of gloomy darkness to be kept until the judgment." Also, Jude tells us that those "angels who did not stay within their own position of authority, but left their proper dwelling," God has "kept in eternal chains under gloomy darkness until the judgment of the great day" (v. 6).[6] From these two scriptural references we see that demons were once holy angels who sinned against God and fell from their glorious estate. According to Peter and Jude, their sin appears to be that of pride—which led to their refusal to accept their assigned place in God's creation.[7]

---

6. Although Peter and Jude state that the angels who fell are now bound in dungeons and chains, this does not mean that the demonic forces in general have no influence in the world whatsoever. We see in other passages of Scripture that some demons roam around free in the world causing mayhem and spiritual harm in their wake (cf. Mark 5:6–13; 1 Cor 10:19–20; 2 Cor 4:4).

7. Grudem, *Systematic Theology*, 413.

Some biblical scholars also argue that Isaiah 14:12–15 and Ezekiel 28:11–19 have the fall of Satan in view. The language used in both passages appears to go beyond the description of an ordinary human ruler. In the Isaianic passage, the prophet describes the individual in question as the "Day Star, son of Dawn" and how he has been cast out of heaven to the earth (v. 12). The sin in question appears to have been his desire to take the place of God (vv. 13–14). Though the passage is directly pointing to the king of Babylon in its immediate context, it also has an indirect reference to Satan.[8] The passage in Ezekiel also gives us a vivid description of Satan and his origins. Again, the passage is directly referring to a human ruler (in this case, the king of Tyre), but it can also have an indirect reference to Satan. The fact that the prophet mentions that the subject in question was once "an anointed guardian cherub" who was "on the holy mountain of God" (v. 14) and was once "blameless" in his ways from the day he was created (v. 15) seems to describe a personality that goes beyond any human ruler.[9]

We see from these passages that Satan and his demonic hosts were once holy angels in the service of God. This is consistent with the declaration in Genesis 1:31 that God saw that everything he had made "was very good." Therefore, Satan and his hosts were once created good but rebelled against God and fell from their holy estate to oppose God and all that he stands for.

## The Activities of Demons

The Scriptures give us ample information regarding the nature of the activities of Satan and his demonic hosts. We must know what these activities are in order to effectively resist these spiritual forces that oppose God and his people.

### Sin Originated from Satan

In Genesis 3:1–6, we see that Satan (in the form of a serpent) tempts Eve to eat the fruit from the forbidden tree. As a result of Eve's failure to resist the temptation of Satan and Adam's failure to obey the directives of God, the human race and the rest of the created order have existed under the

---

8. Grogan, "Isaiah," 105.
9. Ryrie, *Basic Theology*, 162.

bondage of sin and death ever since (Gen 3:14–19; Rom 5:12; 8:20–22). Also, what Satan did in the garden of Eden is in line with his character as "a murderer from the beginning" and "a liar" (John 8:44). John tells us that Satan "has been sinning from the beginning" (1 John 3:8). Satan also tried to tempt the Son of Man to sin and turn away from God (Matt 4:1–11). We can see from these passages that Satan, ultimately, is the one who is responsible for bringing sin into the world and putting the world under its bondage. This fact frees God from any accusation that he is the originator of sin, since God cannot sin or tempt people to sin, unlike the devil (cf. Jas 1:13).

### Demons Bring Havoc into the Created Order

We see in Mark 5:1–20 how a legion of demons possessed a man and subjected him to physical agony (v. 5). They can also inflict various ailments like muteness (Matt 9:32), blindness (Matt 12:22), seizures (Matt 17:15–18), and mental disorders (Mark 5:4–5; 9:22; Luke 8:27–29). Satan, although limited by God's power and decree, brought physical and personal disasters on Job (Job 1–2). Near the end of this age, demons will be involved in bringing the leaders of various nations together to wage war against God and his people (Rev 16:13–16). Although not all catastrophes and evils can be attributed to demons (cf. John 9:3), we can say that a significant portion of the sufferings that occur in this world can be attributed to demonic activity.

### Demons Oppose the Work of the Gospel

Not only do demons bring physical calamities in the world, they also use their powers to draw people away from the gospel. In 2 Corinthians 4:4, Paul states that the "god of this world has blinded the minds of the unbelievers, to keep them from seeing the light of the gospel of the glory of Christ, who is the image of God." And in Galatians 4:8, Paul tells the believers at the church of Galatia: "Formerly, when you did not know God, you were enslaved to those that by nature are not gods." Also, when professing believers partake of idolatrous activities they are actually participating in the worship of demons (1 Cor 10:19–21), and arouse the jealousy of God and fall under his judgment (v. 22). Therefore, we see that demons do whatever they can in their power to turn people away from the gospel and, consequently, bring about the eternal destruction of their souls.

## The Nature of Demons

Scripture reveals to us that demons, like their angelic counterparts, are intelligent beings. This is revealed by the fact that they have an orthodox confession of the existence of God (Jas 2:19) and promote false doctrines to deceive many (1 Tim 4:1; Rev 2:20–22). Therefore, believers in Jesus Christ must recognize that they are not struggling against mere impersonal powers or "mindless" creatures popularly portrayed by the modern media, but against beings that are intelligent, crafty, and have a set purpose in mind. Knowing this should equip believers properly in how they should deal with these spirit beings that oppose God and his saints.

## Conclusion

Satan and his demons exist for one purpose: to draw people away from the gospel, and ultimately, to the true and living God. Although Satan prowls around like a "roaring lion" to devour anyone he can find (1 Pet 5:8), and believers are constantly engaged in a spiritual battle against him (1 Pet 5:9), we can have the assurance that one day God, in Christ, will finally deliver believers from the wiles of Satan. Furthermore, right before the new heaven and earth arrives (Rev 21), Satan and his demonic hosts will finally be judged and cast into the lake of fire (Matt 25:41; Rev 20:10) where they will no longer be able to oppose God and his people and wreak havoc throughout creation.

# CHAPTER 5

# Humanity

THE DOCTRINE OF HUMANITY (or anthropology) is a vital component of Christian theological discourse because of the fact that humankind is the object of God's redeeming act in Jesus Christ. Without properly knowing who we are in light of the revelation of Scripture we will never be able to fully understand how and why God redeems us in Christ. Not only is this doctrine important in discussions of theology but also important in matters of pastoral ministry. Pastors minister to embodied human beings who have intellects, emotions, and wills, and whose destinies are eternal. In other words, ministry is not done towards soulless robots but towards those who are made in the image of God. Hence, we can see the great importance attached to the doctrine of humanity in any discussion that is theological in nature.

This chapter will be devoted to how we can biblically understand who and what human beings are. To accomplish this we will discuss in detail in this chapter: 1) the origin of human beings, 2) the image of God (*imago Dei*) in human beings, and 3) the essential nature of human beings.

## The Origin of Human Beings

### The View of Naturalistic Science

Natural scientists today posit that *Homo sapiens* have existed on our planet for over 200,000 years. They argue that the origins of modern human beings can be traced back to a small group who lived in Africa thousands of years ago. The same scientists argue that before the arrival of *Homo sapiens* there also existed various hominid species that roamed various parts of the earth. Some of these hominids (like the *Homo heidelbergensis* and *Homo erectus*) evolved over many millennia into what we know as modern human beings. This is the typical evolutionary view of the origins of humankind often espoused in modern scientific textbooks.[1] This view also maintains that there was no personal deity involved when it comes to the origins and the evolutionary development of the human race. Human beings appeared on the earth through the random processes of molecules, motions, and time working together. This view is obviously incompatible with the historic Christian view of the origins of humankind because it excludes the idea that a divine being created the earth and all living things in it. In fact, one of the key beliefs of historic Christianity is that a personal God created human beings and gave them life.[2]

*Theistic Evolution*

Those who hold to the theistic evolution view of the origin of human beings maintain that the human race evolved from more simple organisms but that the whole process of evolutionary development was superintended by God (this view is different from the deistic evolutionary position where God initiates the creative process but then withdraws from any further involvement in it). As mentioned in chapter 3 a major proponent of this view is Augustus H. Strong. In terms of how God supervised the evolutionary development of the human race, Strong writes:

> We are compelled . . . to believe that God's 'breathing into man's nostrils the breath of life' (Gen 2:7), though it was a mediate creation as presupposing existing material in the shape of animal forms, was yet an immediate creation in the sense that only a divine reinforcement of the process of life turned the animal into man. In other words, man came not *from* the brute, but *through* the brute, and the same immanent God who had previously created the brute created also the man.[3]

1. Charles Darwin was the first to put forth this revolutionary viewpoint in a scientific way in his *The Origin of Species* (first published in 1859).

2. Millard J. Erickson states, "Surely, if the opening chapters of Genesis say anything at all, they affirm that a personal being was involved in the origin of humans" (*Christian Theology*, 503).

3. Strong, *Systematic Theology*, 466–67.

In other words, though God is the one who created the immaterial part of humans directly (and in a special way) the material part of humans was the product of evolutionary development. God created the human soul and infused it into higher primates. Those who hold this view usually maintain that there were no historical persons named Adam and Eve and that the first three chapters of Genesis are mythic (or "a saga") to teach us lessons about God, humanity, innocence, and sin.[4]

Although theistic evolution can provide an answer to the findings of modern science and is not necessarily incompatible with historic Christian beliefs, there are difficulties with this view when examined in the light of Scripture. First, when Paul contrasts Jesus Christ with Adam in the history of redemption (Rom 5:12–21) he naturally assumes that the latter is just as much a historical person as the former. Since Jesus Christ is a historical person who once lived on earth at a particular time and place it would be highly incongruent to argue that Paul was contrasting a historical individual with a symbolic or mythic one (cf. also 1 Cor 15:22, 45). Second, if Adam was not a historical person there would be no solidarity among the human race in terms of a common origin. This would also imply that sin did not originate from the first man who, thereby, corrupts the whole human race by his single transgression (Rom 5:12, 18–19; cf. 1 Cor 15:22). Rather, one would have to conclude that sin springs forth from the self-willed decisions of every individual (which is a form of Pelagianism).[5] Although one can commend this view for attempting to reconcile the findings of modern science with the witness of Scripture, it still falls short as a satisfactory view of the origins of the human race from a Christian perspective.

## Direct Creationism

In contrast to the views discussed above, direct creationism maintains that God created the first human pair directly without any intermediate evolutionary processes (fiat creationism). This view is commonly embraced by those who hold to a high view of Scripture and follow the grammatical-historical-normative hermeneutical method. Also, this view appears to

---

4. Cf. Barth, *Church Dogmatics*, 3/1:42–94.

5. Emil Brunner asserts that any view of the origin of man that attempts to reach a compromise between modern science and the biblical revelation leads "us into a 'platonizing' view of Creation as a whole, which must have a disastrous effect on the doctrine of Sin and the Fall" (*Christian Doctrine of Creation and Redemption*, 51).

accord well with the creation account of Genesis 1–2. According to Paul Enns, there are four key factors that make this view the most consistent with the biblical witness (these are direct statements from his work while leaving some parts out):

> 1. God created man directly (Gen. 1:27; 27; 5:1; Deut. 4:32). Genesis 1:27 is the general statement, while 2:7 provides additional detail concerning how God created man.

> 2. God created the male and female genders (Gen. 1:27). According to this account man and woman were both created directly by God; they did not evolve from lower forms of life.

> 3. God created in six twenty-four-hour days.

> 4. God created man as a unique being. If man evolved, he is only a higher form of animal, without moral sensibility or accountability.[6]

We believe that Scripture supports the direct creationist view of the origins of human beings. Some will contend that this view is not in congruence with the conclusions of modern scientific research. However, as we have pointed out in chapter 3, scientific findings are not completely reliable or flawless. Therefore, we must not allow fallible scientific findings produced by fallen human beings to have the final word against the clear testimony of Scripture on this subject.

## The Image of God in Human Beings

The precise nature of the image of God (*imago Dei*) in human beings has been one of the more enigmatic teachings of Scripture. The image is first described in the creation narrative of Genesis 1–2. In Genesis 1:26–27, the passage reads:

> Then God said, "Let us make man in our image, after our likeness, and let them have dominion over the fish of the sea and over the birds of the heavens and over the livestock and over all the earth and over every creeping thing that creeps on the earth."
> So God created man in his own image, in the image of God he created him; male and female he created them.

The key Hebrew words in the opening section of the passage are *tselem* ("image") and *demût* ("likeness"). The words convey the meaning of

6. Enns, *Moody Handbook of Theology*, 317.

an object being similar to another without indicating exact replication or sameness. To put it another way, the words signify similarity or representation but not identicalness.[7]

Having said that, determining exactly what the nature of this "image" is has aroused lively debate among theologians over the years. In this section we will discuss the various suggestions offered in the past and then offer our own proposal as to what the *imago Dei* is.

*The Relational View*

One view that has gained some following in recent years regarding the *imago Dei* is the *relational* view. Those who advocate this view argue that the image involves the human being's capacity to experience personal relationships. Like the functional view discussed below, the relational view asserts that the image of God is not something that is intrinsic to humans. Rather, God's image is revealed in the human person by the way he or she relates to God and others. As Daniel L. Migliore writes:

> Thus the image of God is not to be construed primarily as a set of human faculties, possessions, or endowments. It expresses self-transcending life in relationship with others—with the "wholly other" we call God, and with all those different "others" who need our help and whose help we also need in order to be the human creatures God intends us to be.[8]

In addition, those who argue for this position insist that since the three members of the Trinity have always existed in communal fellowship amongst themselves, human beings also exemplify the relationships among the persons of the Trinity in their own way in this world.[9]

A more idiosyncratic version of the relational view was advocated by the well-known Swiss Reformed theologian Karl Barth. He argued that "Man is no more solitary than God. But as God is One, and He alone is God, so man as man is one and alone, and two only in the duality of his kind, i.e., in the duality of man and woman. In this way he is a copy and imitation of God."[10] Furthermore, he states: "Man can and will always be

---

7. Cf. Grudem, *Systematic Theology*, 442–43.

8. Migliore, *Faith Seeking Understanding*, 141.

9. Grenz, *Theology for the Community of God*, 179.

10. Barth, *Church Dogmatics*, III/1:186.

man before God and among his fellows only as he is man in relationship to woman and woman in relationship to man."[11] Thus, for Barth, the image is about human beings being both male and female in an "I" and "Thou" relationship.[12]

## The Functional View

Another view which has had some strong advocates throughout the church's history is the *functional* view. This view asserts that the image of God consists of man's authority to have dominion over the earth (Gen 2:15). The image is not something that is inherent to the human being but is a result of his or her authoritative position, given by God, in relation to the rest of the created order. As one exponent of this view writes, "biblically speaking, the phrase 'image of God' has nothing to do with morals or any sort of ideals; it refers only to man's domination of the world and everything that is in it. It says nothing about the nature of God, but everything concerning the function of man."[13] Therefore, the reason why human beings are said to be made in the divine image, according to the advocates of this view, is because they have a unique mandate from God to rule over the earth.

The rationale for this view of the image is that since God has ultimate authority, dominion, and lordship over the universe, human beings also have this authority in the created order but in a lesser form. One can argue that the dominion view of the image can be demonstrated in Scripture by the close connection between God's declaration, "Let us make man in our image," followed by "let them have dominion over the fish of the sea and over the birds of the heavens and over the livestock and over all the earth and over every creeping thing that creeps on the earth" in Genesis 1:26 (the close connection can also be found in verses 27 and 28). Also, Psalm 8:5–8 seems to suggest that human beings have this divinely-given prerogative to have dominion over other creatures in God's created order.

---

11. Barth, *Church Dogmatics*, III/1:186.

12. Barth, *Church Dogmatics*, III/1:185.

13. Snaith, "Image of God," 24.

## The Substantive View

Finally, a view that has always had a sizeable number of adherents through-out the history of the church is the *substantive* view.[14] This view argues that the image of God is something that is inherent in every human being. In contrast to the functional view above, this view posits that the image has more to do with what human beings *are* rather than what they *do*. In other words, it has more to do with some defining characteristic of the human being rather than what his or her role is in the created order.

Various suggestions have been offered by Christian thinkers through-out history on what the substantive nature of the divine image is. Some have argued that the image consists of the human being's ability to reason or think rationally. Others have argued that the image consists of a person's ability to make moral judgments—to discern what is right or wrong (which, however, is severely compromised by sin). Still others have argued that the image consists of a person's ability to make free choices—that he or she is a being with a freedom of the will.

Although this view sets forth various proposals on what the image actually consists of, all those who hold to a variation of the substantive view agree on this: the image is something that is intrinsic to the human being.[15]

## A Proposal

Although all three views presented above have some discernible merits and shortcomings, we believe that the image of God involves all three of the views discussed above in varying ways. However, we believe that the image is first and foremost something that is intrinsic to the human being (the substantive view). It is these inherent qualities in the human being that allows him or her to have a relationship with God and other human beings and to have responsible stewardship over the rest of creation. To say that the image relates to only *one* of the three views presented above is to understand the image of God in a very restrictive manner. God is far more complex than we can ever imagine—and it is to grossly misunderstand who

---

14. Two major proponents of this view include Thomas Aquinas (*Summa Theologiae*, Ia, Q. 93) and John Calvin (*Institutes*, 1.15.3).

15. Mormonism goes beyond the scriptural evidence by insisting that the physical body of the human being *is* the image of God (Mormonism also insists that God has a physical body).

he is by asserting that he is *merely* a being who has rational faculties or supreme power over the universe.

In the same way, human beings, who are made in God's image, are also complex beings who have diverse qualities, characteristics, and roles. As a result of being able to think in complex ways, make moral judgments, and experience emotions like joy and grief, human beings, therefore, can relate to one another in highly intricate ways and are able to exercise dominion over the rest of creation. Therefore, the image encompasses all that human beings *are* and *do*.

### Some Conclusions about the Imago Dei

Having discussed the three most common understandings offered by various Christian thinkers on what the image of God is, what are some conclusions we can offer about this doctrine? Here, we can provide three:

1.  Although sin has corrupted and tainted the human race, the image is not totally lost in human beings because of sin (contrary to the traditional Lutheran view).[16] This means that the image is not something that is externally infused into human beings but is something that is intrinsic to who they are.

2.  The image is present in *all* human beings—no matter the ethnicity, sex, intelligence level, age, marital status, or religious conviction. The universality of the image is demonstrated in passages like Genesis 9:6 (the prohibition against murder) and James 3:9–10 (the command against cursing another human being). Therefore, because all human beings are made in God's image, all human beings must be treated with the appropriate respect and dignity corresponding to that reality.

3.  The redeemed grow more in likeness to Christ as they are progressively sanctified by the grace of God. That is why Paul can say that all believers who are "beholding the glory of the Lord, are being transformed into the same image from one degree of glory to another" (2 Cor 3:18; cf. Rom 8:29; Col 3:10). At the eschaton, God's image will be completely restored in all believers and they will be fully conformed to Christ's image when they are raised to glory (1 Cor 15:49; 1 John 3:2).

---

16. Cf. Mueller, *Christian Dogmatics*, 207.

## The Essential Nature of Human Beings

Since we have already discussed the origin of human beings and the nature of God's image in them we still need to answer the question: what is a human being? Throughout history secular and Christian thinkers have attempted to answer this question in some depth. As Emil Brunner writes, "Knowledge of Man is the common theme and the common concern both of secular and of Christian (theological) wisdom."[17] Many secular thinkers today insist that human beings are merely elevated animals who have advanced cognitive functions. According to these thinkers, all of our complex mental functions are merely the product of highly developed neurochemical reactions going on in the brain.

Christian thinkers of a more evangelical persuasion, however, will demur and argue that human beings are much more than just elevated animals with higher intellectual capabilities: they are spiritual beings who were created in God's image to enjoy, serve, and glorify God. With an evangelical anthropology being the perspective we will work with, we will proceed to discuss what human beings are and what purpose they serve in God's created order.

### Human Beings Are Both Material and Immaterial

*The Biblical Evidence.* In contrast to the secularist views of the human person, Scripture states that human beings not only possess a material component but also an immaterial component. Even in the Old Testament—where human beings are viewed as an intricate unity—it speaks of human beings as having both material and immaterial parts. In Genesis 2:7, the verse states that the "LORD God formed the man of dust from the ground and breathed into his nostrils the *breath of life* [Heb. *nephesh*], and the man became a living creature." In Genesis 35:18, we read that at the time of Rachel's death her "soul was departing." In Ecclesiastes 3:21, the teacher states that no one knows "whether the spirit of man goes upward." In the New Testament Jesus tells his disciples not to "fear those who kill the body but cannot kill the soul," but rather to "fear him who can destroy both soul and body in hell" (Matt 10:28). According to Acts 7:59, Stephen cried out right before his death, "Lord Jesus, receive my spirit." In 1 Corinthians 5:5, Paul commands the Corinthians to expel the incestuous man out of the church

17. Brunner, *Christian Doctrine of Creation and Redemption*, 46.

and to deliver him to Satan "for the destruction of the flesh, so that his spirit may be saved in the day of the Lord." In 2 Corinthians 7:1, Paul admonishes the Corinthians to cleanse themselves from "every defilement of body and spirit, bringing holiness to completion in the fear of God." James also tells us that "the body apart from the spirit is dead" (Jas 2:26). Finally, in the book of Revelation, John narrates a scene where he sees under the altar "the souls of those who had been slain for the word of God" for their witness (6:9), and the souls "of those who had been beheaded for the testimony of Jesus and for the word of God" (20:4). These biblical references clearly show that human beings have an immaterial component to them (what we normally call *souls* or *spirits*).[18]

*The Trichotomist View.* If we agree that the biblical evidence shows that human beings are both material and immaterial, how are we to understand this relationship properly? Some Christian thinkers have argued that the human soul and the human spirit are two distinct aspects of the immaterial part of man. They argue that a human being is not only composed of body and soul, but also a third part—the spirit.[19] This view is typically called the *trichotomist* view of the human being. They argue that Scripture sometimes speaks of human beings as composed of three parts. One example is 1 Thessalonians 5:23 when Paul tells the Thessalonian believers: "Now may the God of peace himself sanctify you completely, and may your whole *spirit and soul and body* be kept blameless at the coming of our Lord Jesus Christ." Another passage appealed to by trichotomists is Hebrews 4:12: "For the word of God is living and active, sharper than any two-edged sword, piercing to the *division of soul and of spirit*, of joints and of marrow, and discerning the thoughts and intentions of the heart."

Trichotomists also argue that if the soul and spirit are not separate parts within the human being then it is not possible for human beings to be distinguishable from animals (who also, they claim, have souls). This also leads to the problem, according to the proponents of this view, of human beings not being able to worship God *in spirit*. Without a distinct spirit, human beings are unable to perceive God spiritually—which is distinct from their everyday emotions and thought-patterns (which belongs to the *soul*).

18. In contrast to the view above, the view that human beings are unitary with no dual aspects to them is called *monism*. One notable proponent of this view is the Lutheran theologian Robert W. Jenson (*Systematic Theology*, 2:108–11). This is also the official position of the Seventh-Day Adventist Church and the Watchtower Society.

19. This is advocated by Franz Delitzsch in his *System of Biblical Psychology*.

Although it is not the majority opinion within Christianity, this view does have a strong following in certain sectors of evangelicalism.

*The Dichotomist View.* The dichotomist view is probably the most widely held view in the Christian tradition. This position states that human beings are composed of both the body (the material aspect) and the soul/spirit (the immaterial aspect). Arguments advanced for the dichotomist position are often arguments against the trichotomist position.[20] Although both positions agree that human beings are composed of both material and immaterial aspects, they differ on how they understand the relationship between the soul and the spirit.

Dichotomists often point out that referring to 1 Thessalonians 5:23 to argue for the trichotomist position becomes untenable when other passages in Scripture come into view—for instance, Luke 10:27, when Jesus declared: "You shall love the Lord your God with all your *heart* and with all your *soul* and with all your *strength* and with all your *mind*, and your neighbor as yourself" (cf. also Mark 12:30). Since Jesus talks about four components in the human being instead of three, dichotomists argue that one cannot use passages like 1 Thessalonians 5:23 or Hebrews 4:12 to put forward the idea that human beings are composed of three parts—body, soul, and spirit. Also, dichotomists argue that Ecclesiastes 3:21 does not distinguish between spirit and soul (the Hebrew word used in this verse is *ruach*) in the animal. In addition, Mary, the mother of Jesus, in Luke 1:46–47 sings: "My *soul* magnifies the Lord, and my *spirit* rejoices in God my Savior" (indicating that both terms are interchangeable).

According to the dichotomist position, human beings are a dichotomy in the truest sense of the term—they have a material body and a spiritual (or "soulish") component. However, although they are composed of both aspects, they are not complete human beings unless both aspects are conjoined together in this life and in the life to come. Therefore, the ultimate hope that Christians have is not just the escape of the soul from hell but the resurrection of the body suited for the new heaven and earth.

*The "Conditional Unity" View.* Millard J. Erickson offers a unique understanding of the human being that differs from both the trichotomist and dichotomist positions. He calls this understanding the "conditional unity"

---

20. Erickson, *Christian Theology*, 540.

position.[21] He argues that while "body and soul are sometimes contrasted (as in Jesus' statement in Matt. 10:28), they are not always so clearly distinguished. Furthermore, the pictures of humans in Scripture seem to regard them for the most part as unitary beings."[22] However, further on he states that "Scripture indicates that there is an intermediate state involving personal conscious existence between death and resurrection."[23]

Erickson seeks to avoid the rigid dualism that the dichotomist position is at risk of falling into while at the same time trying to avoid the pitfalls of naturalistic monism (that humans are *only* complex physical organisms). Thus, Erickson's position is not a rejection of either dichotomism or monism but a combination of some aspects of both.[24] The strength of Erickson's position is that it avoids the dualistic tendencies of dichotomism, while at the same time allowing for the possibility that the personal consciousness of the human being survives after death (Luke 23:43; 2 Cor 5:6–8; Phil 1:23).

Also, this position explains why the neuro-physical makeup of a person's brain plays such an integral role in the development of his or her unique personality and identity. It essentially avoids a dualistic anthropology where body and soul are so radically distinguished that the biological makeup of the person is downplayed in favor of the immaterial or "spiritual" aspect. Thus, according to this view, the human being is truly a unity in this life where the material and immaterial aspects are intricately connected and work closely together as one.

Finally, this view emphasizes the importance of the physical aspect of the human person. Human beings are physical beings who live in physical environments, and thus, the physical aspect of their lives is not something that should be downplayed. This recognition should influence the way we evangelize and minister towards people—as *whole* human beings.[25] As

21. Erickson, *Christian Theology*, 554–57.

22. Erickson, *Christian Theology*, 554.

23. Erickson, *Christian Theology*, 555.

24. However, this view should be contrasted with the *Christian monistic* view in that the latter sees the human being in his or her entirety as being extinguished at physical death with no intermediate state of conscious existence (cf. Berkouwer, *Man*, 194–233).

25. The importance of this truth is clearly evident in the area of pastoral ministry towards people with psychological disorders. To assume that psychological disorders are merely problems of the "heart" or "soul" is not only to ignore the fact that human beings are physical beings but to dangerously view medical science as being of no use for people who are suffering from psychological disorders. Thus, when necessary, the minister

Charles Sherlock states, "To be human . . . means being embodied, material creatures, yet made for life in more than material ways."[26]

In comparison to the trichotomist and dichotomist views, therefore, we believe that the *conditional unity* position best explains the relationship between the material and immaterial aspects of the human being and as being the most consistent with what is revealed in Scripture.

## The Origin of Human Souls: Traducianism or Creationism?

Throughout the history of the church the two most commonly held views on the origin of human souls are *creationism* and *traducianism*. Since Scripture does not teach *reincarnation* (the idea that the immaterial part of the human being is later reborn in another body) or *pre-existentianism* (the idea that the souls of human beings existed long before conception) we are left to decide only between creationism and traducianism.

*Creationism.* This view maintains that human souls are created by God and directly placed into the human being at the moment of conception. This view is typically held by Roman Catholics and Reformed Christians. Although Scripture does not give us definite answers regarding where our souls come from, there are some indications in Scripture that reveal that God directly creates souls and puts them into human beings when they are conceived in the mother's womb. For example, in Psalm 139:13 David declares to the Lord, "For you formed my inward parts; you knitted me together in my mother's womb." Also, Zechariah declares that it is God who "formed the spirit of man within him" (Zech 12:1). Finally, the author of Hebrews writes that it is God who is "the Father of spirits" (Heb 12:9). Therefore, these passages seem to suggest that God is the one who directly creates the souls of people at conception.

*Traducianism.* In contrast to the creationist view, traducianism states that human bodies *and* souls are inherited from the individual's father and

---

should refer a person who is suffering from a mental health issue to a psychiatrist who is qualified to administer appropriate prescriptive medication that may help alleviate the symptoms of the disorder. For a balanced perspective on this issue that recognizes that psychological disorders have both spiritual and physical causes see Edward T. Welch's work *Blame It on the Brain?*

26. Sherlock, *Doctrine of Humanity*, 226–27.

mother at the moment of conception. This is the view held by the Reformer Martin Luther (and Lutherans throughout history have generally followed suit on this matter). Proponents of traducianism argue that Scripture does indeed speak of the soul being inherited from the parents. One example is Genesis 5:3, which reads: "When Adam had lived 130 years, he fathered a son in his own likeness, after his image, and named him Seth." In this passage Seth is viewed as being in the same likeness as Adam, and thus, as having also inherited Adam's soul. Another passage often used by defenders of traducianism is Hebrews 7:9–10, where the author writes: "One might even say that Levi himself, who receives tithes, paid tithes through Abraham, *for he was still in the loins of his ancestor* when Melchizedek met him." This passage appears to suggest that Levi's soul was still in his ancestor Abraham. Also, advocates of traducianism claim that since all human beings are sinful from birth it is most natural to claim that it is not only the sinful body that is inherited from the parents but also the sinful soul. Thus, this avoids the problem of viewing the transmission of original sin as merely a matter of biological processes.[27]

*The Solution?* Although the various biblical references do not give us a clear answer to where human souls originate, the biblical evidence seems to lean towards creationism. That God creates souls directly and places them into human beings at the time of their conception seems to be less theologically and biblically problematic than the idea that souls are somehow inherited from the parents. If souls are inherited from the parents, as supporters of traducianism claim, then we must conclude that souls are *somehow* preexistent before the time human beings are conceived in the womb—an idea not found in Scripture. This, however, does not mean children do not inherit their parents' mental or personal characteristics—which is a result of biological factors (e.g., genes) being passed down to the children. In addition, creationism best explains why souls can continue to exist even after the physical death of the human being. If God is the one directly creating the immaterial part of human beings then it is reasonable to conclude that God gave it a particular quality so that it can continue to exist even apart from the body.

27. Reymond, *New Systematic Theology*, 425.

*Human Beings as Male and Female*

One of the fundamental aspects of the human race is that it is both male and female. Scripture affirms this when it states that "God created man in his own image, in the image of God he created him; male and female he created them" (Gen 1:27; cf. 5:1–2). God, in his perfect wisdom, did not just create a male Adam but created a female Eve to complete the human race. This is made plain in Genesis 2:18 when God declared: "It is not good that the man should be alone; I will make him a helper fit for him." One can even say that without the differentiation between the sexes the human race would have been something less than good in the eyes of God.[28] Also, though there are differences in roles between the sexes (especially within the marriage covenant [Eph 5:22–33; Col 3:18–19; 1 Pet 3:1–7]), both sexes are equal in personhood before God. In other words, one sex is not viewed as being more valuable than the other in God's eyes. This is demonstrated by the way Jesus conversationally engaged the Samaritan women at the well (John 4:1–26) and the way he responded to the hemorrhagic woman when she touched his cloak for healing (Matt 9:20–22). Considering the socio-cultural context of the New Testament period where women were generally seen as second-class citizens, the way Jesus viewed and interacted with women would have been understood as being quite radical by many of Jesus' contemporaries.

Especially in God's new covenant family both males and females are *equally* considered as spiritual children of God (Gal 3:28). Paul even gives positive acknowledgements to female members of the household of God who diligently worked for the advancement of the gospel (Rom 16:1, 3–6, 12). Although this is considered revolutionary among many groups and cultures throughout history (and even in some cultures today), Scripture is clear that males and females are equally important to God whether just as human beings or as participants in his work of redemption. The way Scripture portrays women greatly impacts the way they are to be treated and ministered to, and history is evidence of that. As James Leo Garrett writes, "Across the centuries Christianity has served to elevate, even if slowly, the recognized worth and status of womanhood in contrast to woman's quite inferior and almost servile role in many primitive and non-Christian

---

28 Although at first glance Genesis 2:18 appears to say that God ordained that women be subordinate to men in the created order, the word "helper" (Heb. *'ezer*) in that verse actually means a *helpmate* who helps the male bring forth children and not about a woman taking on the role of a servant or lackey (cf. Sailhamer, "Genesis," 2:46).

societies. This long-term elevation of womanly worth and status is an extension of, if at times altogether unconsciously, of the 'neither male nor female' of Gal. 3:28."[29]

### The Purpose of Human Beings According to Scripture

The true purpose of human existence is one that has inundated the minds of secular philosophers, political theorists, and sociologists throughout history. The question is both difficult and profound especially in a time when secularization is on the rise and many modern people, personally and philosophically, see no real purpose of why human beings are here on earth. Despite these trends, Scripture gives us ample information on why human beings were created and what purpose they serve in God's created order. It is here we now end this chapter on the doctrine of humanity by discussing the biblical view of the purpose of human beings.

In Genesis 1:28, God gives a clear mandate for human beings when he declares to them: "Be fruitful and multiply and fill the earth and subdue it, and have dominion over the fish of the sea and over the birds of the heavens and over every living thing that moves on the earth." In this one verse alone we can see that God's purpose for human beings is that they 1) reproduce and fill the earth with their own kind, 2) subdue the earth, and 3) have dominion over all other living creatures on earth. However, the second and third parts of the mandate should not be restricted to just taking stewardship over the earth and having dominion over animals—it includes everything else that involves human activity and ingenuity: art, politics, science, work, etc. This means that the spiritual and physical activities of human beings are closely intertwined. This understanding should greatly impact the way Christians take care of their families, carry out their professions, pursue their studies, and enjoy their hobbies in this life. Also, as a result of sin, Christians have a special duty to carry the gospel to all nations and to teach them all that Christ has commanded (Matt 28:19–20). This Great Commission, however, is a consequence of the fall and is not something that was ordained by God at the time of creation. In fact, this commission is something that is exclusively given to Christians to carry out for a *fallen* world.

In conclusion, by fulfilling what God has purposed for human beings, Christians bring glory to God, make his name known to unbelievers, and

29. Garrett, *Systematic Theology*, 1:494–95.

bring blessing upon themselves. However, of the three just mentioned, the first is the primary reason why Christians live and carry out their particular vocations. As Paul tells the Corinthian believers, "So, whether you eat or drink, or whatever you do, do all to the glory of God" (1 Cor 10:31). This, ultimately, is the reason why God created human beings in the first place: to bring glory to himself. As the Westminster Shorter Catechism puts it, "Man's chief end is to glorify God, and to enjoy him forever" (Q. and A. 1).

# CHAPTER 6

# Sin

IN THE BEGINNING, GOD created everything good and upright but due to human disobedience in the garden of Eden (Gen 2:16–17; 3:6) humanity and the rest of creation are now under the captivity of something that opposes God and his will. This "something" is called *sin* in Christian theological discourse. The well-known Reformed theologian John Murray once stated that the "Christian estimate of sin is that it is wrong, that it ought not to be. It is not only undesirable; it is damnable in the strongest sense of the word."[1] Contrary to this biblical understanding of sin, secular modernists ignore this awful reality in the lives of individuals and societies at large. For many modern secular people, "sin" is merely seen as an "act" resulting from a person's negative life experiences or some inherent defect in the person's neuro-biological makeup. It is not seen, therefore, as something that is utterly offensive to God and contrary to his divine purpose for creation. However, as the evangelical Baptist theologian Stanley J. Grenz rightfully comments:

> Despite the unpopularity of this topic in a society which seeks to set aside the concept of sin, we must unabashedly assert the truth of the human tragedy. We must boldly declare this dimension of our Christian affirmation, because the concept of sin belongs to the biblical *kerygma*, it is a non-negotiable thesis of our theological heritage, and the category retains its ability to cast light on human self-awareness and experience in every generation.[2]

1. Murray, *Collected Writings of John Murray*, 2:81.
2. Grenz, *Theology for the Community of God*, 182.

Along with Grenz, we boldly maintain, as with those who uphold the beliefs of the historic Christian faith, that sin is not something to be ignored or downplayed but a tragic truth that must be strongly acknowledged for the sake of the integrity of the gospel and God's redemptive purpose for sinners.

In this chapter, we will discuss the nature of sin, the origin of sin, and the results of sin.

## The Nature of Sin

What is sin? Though the question for many Christians may appear trite, it is a legitimate question to ask in Christian theological discourse because how we understand sin affects the way we understand other doctrines like humanity, Christology, and the atonement. Without a proper and biblical understanding of sin we will fall into serious error on other important doctrines of the faith (e.g., the doctrine of salvation). Hence, it is important that we present a satisfactory and biblical understanding of sin here.

### The Biblical Words Used for Sin

The most commonly used word for "sin" in the Old Testament is *chatha*.[3] According to Grenz, the word basically means "to miss the right point" or "to deviate from the norm."[4] Like the Old Testament, the New Testament uses a variety of words to define sin,[5] but the most commonly used word is *hamartia*. Like its Old Testament counterpart it means to "miss the mark" (cf. Rom 3:23). However, it also goes beyond the Old Testament meaning when the New Testament writers assert that *hamartia* is also a force

---

3. Other words used for sin in the Old Testament are *'avah* (meaning "to bend" [cf. Isa 21:3; 24:1]), *'aval* (which generally means "iniquity" or lack of integrity [cf. Lev 19:15]), *'avar* (transgression), *ra'* (treachery), *ma'al* (the breaching of trust), *pasha'* (to revolt against a rightful authority), and *shiqquts* and *to'ebah* ("abomination") (cf. Girdlestone, *Synonyms of the Old Testament*, 76–86).

4 Grenz, *Theology for the Community of God*, 183.

5. These are *parabasis* (transgressing of a boundary), *parakoe* (disobeying a voice or command), *paraptoma* (failing to be upright at the time one should have been), *agnoema* (being ignorant of a knowledge that ought to have been known by the person), *hettema* (diminishing of what should have been rendered fully), *anomia* (not observing a law), and *plemmeleia* (discord in God's harmonious universe) (cf. Trench, *Synonyms of the New Testament*, 240).

or power operating in the human being.[6] *Hamartia*, therefore, is not only sinful acts committed by human beings but also an internal power that has control over them.

## The Essence of Sin

Although we have briefly discussed above how Scripture fundamentally understands what sin is, we still need to discuss what its *essence* is. Though sin is essentially understood as "missing the mark" in Scripture, as mentioned above, it is also understood as "lawlessness" (1 John 3:4). The context for understanding the essence of sin *is the law of God*. This is demonstrated in the Sermon on the Mount when Jesus refers to the law (cf. Matt 5:17–18) to reveal to his listeners what sin truly is (for example, like the sins of murder [5:21–26] or adultery [5:27–30]). Paul also demonstrates this truth about sin in Romans 2:17–29 when he talks about the culpability of the Jews because of their failure to observe the law. In fact, he states elsewhere that sin can only be known through the law (cf. Rom 3:20; 7:7). Also, James in his letter states that those who show favoritism towards the rich are sinning and "are convicted by the law as lawbreakers" (2:9, NIV). In addition, the Ten Commandments given to the Israelites at Sinai reveal what the standard of righteousness is from God's perspective (Exod 20:2–17), and that a failure to obey these commandments is what constitutes sin (cf. Exod 32:21, 30–34). Therefore, we see that Scripture views the essence of sin as any act, word, or thought that goes against the law of God. As the Westminster Shorter Catechism states, "Sin is any want of conformity unto, or transgression of, the law of God" (Q. and A. 14).

Some Christian thinkers in the past, however, have argued that *selfishness* is what constitutes the essence of sin. The Baptist theologian Augustus H. Strong, for example, argues for this position.[7] Although it is true that some types of self-interest are considered sinful (2 Tim 3:2; Jas 3:14), not all self-interest is (1 Cor 9:27; Phil 3:12–14). Also, not all sinful acts are grounded in selfishness as the term is ordinarily understood today. Some examples of these "unselfish" sinful acts include: devoting one's life to modern ideologies that are opposed to the principles of God's kingdom, sacrificing one's life for an ungodly cause, or loving someone more than God (which is idolatry) (cf. Ex 20:3; Gal 4:8).

6. Stählin, "ἁμαρτάνω," 1:295–96.

7. Strong, *Systematic Theology*, 567–73.

Therefore, we maintain that the essence of sin is the transgression of God's law, whether that law is revealed on tablets of stone or written on the hearts of people (Rom 2:12–16).

## Sin Is Both an Outward Act and an Inward Attitude

Although many in our modern age consider "wrongdoings" as concrete evil acts that result in concrete consequences, Scripture views sin as not only those acts committed outwardly that transgress God's law (e.g., murder, stealing, or lying) but inward attitudes that also transgress that same law (e.g., coveting, lusting, or being envious). For instance, in the Decalogue one of the commandments has to do with a person's attitude ("You shall not covet" [Exod 20:17]). In the Sermon on the Mount, Jesus makes it clear that one's attitude is just as important as one's actions. That is why he tells the crowd that "anyone who is angry with his brother will be subject to judgment" (Matt 5:22, NIV), and that "anyone who looks at a woman lustfully has already committed adultery with her in his heart" (Matt 5:28, NIV). Paul warns his readers in Galatia that it is not only outward sins like drunkenness, orgies, and sexual immorality that bar one from the kingdom of God but also attitudinal sins like "hatred, discord, jealousy, fits of rage, selfish ambition, dissensions, factions and envy" (Gal 5:20–21, NIV). In the letter to the Ephesians, Paul exhorts his readers to get rid of attitudinal sins like bitterness, wrath, anger, clamor, and slander because these things "grieve the Holy Spirit of God" (4:30–31). Furthermore, in his letter to the Colossians, he commands his readers to get rid of "anger, rage, malice, slander, and filthy language" (3:8, NIV), and instead to clothe themselves with "compassion, kindness, humility, gentleness and patience" (3:12, NIV).

Scripture is clear that God finds "inward" sins just as reprehensible as "outward" sins. We must never fool ourselves thinking that God will let us get away with attitudinal sins like bitterness, lust, and envy as long as we do not actually take a person's life, physically commit adultery, or steal a person's belongings. God will judge *all* sins and *no* sin is hidden from his view. That is why Christians must even turn away from sins that are often deemed "respectable" or those that are frequently tolerated by our culture.[8] God demands that his children be righteous in *all* that he requires of them,

---

8. For a very good book on this subject see Jerry Bridges's work *Respectable Sins*.

and when they refuse to do so they bring forth his divine displeasure and painful chastening.[9]

### Sin Is Also the Failure or Refusal to Do What We Are Supposed to

Too often we think of sin only as something that we *actively* commit against another person. It is easy to identify outward acts like murder, adultery, and theft as sins because these acts are more-or-less observable and actively done against another human being (typically called "sins of commission"). However, Scripture also speaks of sin as not only something that is actively done against another but also *not* doing what is right when the opportunity arises: in other words, failing or refusing to do what is explicitly command-ed by God when the occasion warrants it (typically called "sins of omis-sion"). James makes this plain to his readers when he writes: "Anyone, then, who knows the good he ought to do and doesn't do it, sins" (Jas 4:17, NIV).

Also, awful punishments are meted out against those who fail to do what is commanded by God. For instance, Paul declares an anathema against those who do not love God (1 Cor 16:22), and Jesus eternally con-demns those people who fail to physically minister to his disciples (Matt 25:45–46). These passages show that God is not only concerned about what we are not supposed to do but also *what we are supposed to do.* This truth should impact the way we live our lives in a society that largely cares less about doing what is right and more on not doing what is wrong (often to avoid judicial punishment and other negative consequences). Therefore, failure to do what is right when we ought to displeases God and this truth should make Christians more proactive when fighting against sin and in-justice in the world.

### Although All Sins Bring the Penalty of Eternal Death, Sin Has Degrees of Severity

Scripture declares that *all* sin brings the penalty of eternal death (Rom 1:32; 2:12; 5:16; 6:23; Gal 3:10), whether that sin is murder, lying, or coveting a neighbor's goods. However, Scripture is also clear that some sins are more

---

9. Although true believers can never forfeit their legal standing before God in Jesus Christ, they can bring forth his divine discipline in their lives for disobeying his com-mandments (1 Cor 11:30; Heb 12:5–11). We will discuss this matter in more detail when we discuss the doctrine of justification in chapter 14.

heinous than others because they bring more destructive consequences. For instance, in Numbers 15:30, God tells Moses that the "person who does anything with a high hand, whether he is native or a sojourner, reviles the LORD, and that person shall be cut off from among his people." In other words, those who commit sins with a "high hand" (sins with wilful intent) must be cut off from the people of Israel, which is contrasted with the punishment of the person who commits a sin unintentionally (Num 15:27–29). In the various laws presented in Leviticus some sins bring greater punishment than others. For instance, a person who commits adultery is subject to the death penalty (Lev 20:10), while the man who has sexual relations with a woman who is not betrothed to another man only has to pay the girl's father fifty shekels of silver and marry her (Deut 22:28–29).

In the Sermon on the Mount, Jesus declares that "whoever relaxes one of the least of these commandments and teaches others to do the same will be called least in the kingdom of heaven, but whoever does them and teaches them will be called great in the kingdom of heaven" (Matt 5:19). In Matthew 23:23, Jesus pronounces woes on the Pharisees for neglecting the *weightier* matters of the law like justice, mercy, and faithfulness. In John 19:11, Jesus, standing before Pilate, tells him, "Therefore he who delivered me over to you has the greater sin" (indicating that Judas' sin of betrayal was of much greater severity than Pilate's). In 1 John 5:16–17, John makes a distinction between the sin that leads to death and sins that do not—indicating that there is a type of sin that brings worse consequences than others.[10] This truth is also demonstrated in everyday life. For example, a person who physically murders another person out of anger will bring more devastating consequences on himself (a lengthy prison sentence), the victim (the loss of life), and the families of the victim (the loss of a loved one) than if that same person expressed his anger with only unkind words.

However, we must recognize that the acknowledgment of varying degrees of severity of sins is not an endorsement of the Roman Catholic teaching that sins can be classified as either *venial* (sins that do not necessarily separate one from God, and can be forgiven through penance) or *mortal* (sins that separate a person from God and result in spiritual death). Scripture, on the other hand, teaches that *all* sins are mortal and result in spiritual death (Rom 1:18–32; Gal 5:19–21). James declares that failure to keep one point of the law makes one guilty of breaking all of it (Jas 2:11–12;

---

10. All indications suggest that those who commit the "sin that leads to death" are not true believers (cf. Stott, *Letters of John*, 188–93).

cf. Gal 3:10), which reveals that the distinction between venial and mortal sins is scripturally unfounded.[11] On the other hand, all sins are considered venial (except the blasphemy against the Holy Spirit [Matt 12:31–32]) in the sense that they are forgivable if one humbly repents and trusts in Jesus Christ for forgiveness. This truth is clearly demonstrated in 1 Corinthians 6:9–11 when Paul declares that some of the Corinthian believers who were once habitually engaged in grossly immoral sins are now washed, sanctified, and justified in the name of Jesus Christ and by the power of the Holy Spirit (v. 11).

Therefore, we can conclude that even though all sins lead to spiritual death, some sins are of greater severity and bring forth graver consequences than others.

### Sin Is Universal

Scripture makes it clear that *all* human beings are sinners. The universality of sin is something that Scripture affirms without ambiguity. In Romans 3:23 (cf. 3:10, 12; 5:12, 19), Paul makes this truth clearly known: "for *all* have sinned and fall short of the glory of God." That is why Paul also states that no human being will be righteous before God through the law because it only brings knowledge of sin and a curse (Rom 3:20; Gal 3:10). In Psalm 143:2, David also acknowledges the universality of sin when he declares: "Enter not into judgment with your servant, *for no one living is righteous before you.*" King Solomon too recognizes this truth when he tells God: "If they sin against you—*for there is no one who does not sin*" (1 Kings 8:46). In Ecclesiastes 7:20, the teacher writes: "There is not a righteous man on earth who does what is right and never sins" (NIV). The fact that even genuine believers in Christ continue to struggle with sin in this life (1 John 1:8, 10; 2:1) demonstrates to the universality of sin. These passages reveal that sin is a tragic truth that all human beings participate in and are affected by. Therefore, sin is an awful reality that no one escapes from in this life.

---

11. John Calvin writes: "Let the children of God hold that all sin is mortal. For it is rebellion against the will of God, which of necessity provokes God's wrath, and it is a violation of the law, upon which God's judgment is pronounced without exception" (*Inst.* 2.8.59).

*Excurses: What Is the Blasphemy Against the Holy Spirit?*

In Matthew 12:31–32 (also in Mark 3:28–30 and Luke 12:10) Jesus gives this very solemn warning to the Pharisees who were with him: "Therefore I tell you, every sin and blasphemy will be forgiven people, but the blasphemy against the Spirit will not be forgiven. And whoever speaks a word against the Son of Man will be forgiven, but whoever speaks against the Holy Spirit will not be forgiven, either in this age or in the age to come." Many Christians have at one time or another worried whether they have committed the "unforgivable sin" and are headed to spend eternity in hell without the opportunity for forgiveness. Over the years, misguided Christians have conjured up fanciful ideas regarding the meaning of Jesus' words in this passage: some of these include 1) committing some heinous transgression like murder, adultery, or idol worship; 2) desecrating some "holy" object in a church; 3) using a profane word after God's name; or 4) refusing to believe that the "miracles" performed by some televangelist is from the Holy Spirit.

Contrary to these erroneous assumptions, the unforgivable sin, as the context of Matthew 12:22–32 demands, is wilfully refusing to believe that Jesus' miraculous works are from the Holy Spirit. Furthermore, it is not only refusing to believe that the miracles performed by Jesus are from the Holy Spirit but also attributing them to the works of Satan (v. 24). Despite the Pharisees having witnessed on numerous occasions the supernatural works of Jesus during his earthly ministry, they still refused to believe that his works originated from the Holy Spirit. Instead, they saw his works as having their source from the evil one (vv. 26–27).[12] We can conclude, therefore, that the blasphemy against the Holy Spirit is wilful and persistent rejection of Jesus Christ and attributing his works to the devil. It is not a particular act but a hardened state of unbelief despite all the evidence presented (cf. John 3:18).

---

12. Some conclude, however, that this sin could only be committed during the time Christ was present on the earth (cf. Stanley, *Eternal Security*, 131–33). However, this is not certain. Jesus would not have given such a general warning ("every sin and blasphemy will be forgiven people" [v. 31]) if that had been the case (Heb 10:26–27 and 1 John 5:16–17 appear to suggest that it is possible to commit this sin even after Christ's ascension).

## The Origin of Sin

Christian theology has traditionally maintained that though human beings were originally created upright and sinless they have failed to live according to the righteous standard of God through rebellion and unfaithfulness. As a result of this tragic decision by the first couple to disbelieve God and seek after their own way (traditionally known as "original sin"), the entire human race was plunged into sin along with the devastating physical and spiritual consequences that come with it. Although the doctrine of original sin is commonly viewed as absurd or obsolete by moderns it is a truth that is clearly revealed in Scripture. As mentioned above, sin is an awful reality that every descendant of Adam (aside from Christ) is infected with and affected by. Sin does have an original source and to ignore that fact will lead to a deficient understanding of the human situation and the nature of Christ's work of redemption.

### The Nature of the First Sin

The first human sin ever committed is narrated in Genesis 3. Despite the fact that God placed Adam and Eve in an idyllic place (Gen 1:31; 2:8–16, 19–20, 25), sin remained a real possibility that they could succumb to (Gen 2:17). The explicit command that God gives Adam is that though he could eat fruit from any tree of the garden (Gen 2:16), he could not eat from "the tree of the knowledge of good and evil," with the consequence being that on that day he would die (Gen 2:17). The command given was uncomplicated and clear, and all Adam had to do was trust God and refrain from eating from the forbidden tree while he took care of the garden (Gen 2:15) and enjoyed all its bounty (Gen 2:9, 16).

Reformed theologians have traditionally argued that the command given in Genesis 2 was an arrangement called a "covenant of works." In this view, the first couple were not in a position of active obedience to God and did not possess eternal life in its fullness. Instead, in order for the first couple to obtain eternal life to the fullest extent they had to fulfill their side of the covenantal arrangement by simply obeying God.[13] Although the concept of a covenant of works is exegetically and theologically questionable,[14]

---

13. Berkhof, *Systematic Theology*, 216.

14. We will discuss the feasibility of the Reformed doctrine of the covenant of works in more detail in the next chapter.

Reformed theologians have pointed out something important with this doctrine that is often overlooked by many Christians: although created upright and sinless, *Adam and Eve knew the difference between obedience and disobedience* (Gen 3:3). However, we must point out that the first couple were not *fully* cognizant of the difference between good and evil when they were still in a state of innocence. This came about after they ate the fruit from the forbidden tree (Gen 3:7, 22). As a result of their disobedience, the first couple were not only expelled from the garden (Gen 3:23) but forfeited eternal life (Gen 3:19, 24), were estranged from God (Gen 3:8–10), brought enmity within the marriage relationship (Gen 3:16), caused the ground to be cursed (Gen 3:17), and made work toilsome for humankind (Gen 3:17, 19). The sin of the first couple was passed down to all of their offspring and the consequences of this have been felt throughout humankind's history.

This naturally leads us to the discussion of how the first sin of Adam is transmitted to the rest of humanity.

### How the Sin of Adam Affects the Rest of Humanity

Having established that the sin of Adam has affected the rest of the human race, the way this is understood, though, has been a matter of debate among Christian theologians throughout history. All Christian thinkers agree that the consequences of Adam's sin were not confined to him alone. In some way Adam's sin has had far-reaching effects on the human race ever since. How we understand this, however, is entirely a different matter and not as simple as it appears as history has shown us.

We will now survey the various views held by Christians throughout history regarding how Adam's sin has affected the human race.

*The Pelagian View.* According to the British monk Pelagius (b. 354), the sin of Adam has no spiritual or genetic connection to his descendants in any way. Adam's sin did not transmit naturally down to his children nor did he become a legal representative of sinful humanity. The only connection that the sin of Adam has with the sins of his descendants is that Adam's children merely *imitate* what Adam did in the garden of Eden. For Pelagius and his followers, Adam was created in a neutral state, neither righteous nor sinful. In the same way, all those who are descended from him are born in that same condition. Therefore, people sin not because their natures have been corrupted by Adam's sin but because they decide, out of their own free will, to follow Adam's example and disobey God's law.

*The Augustinian View.* In opposition to Pelagius, Augustine of Hippo (354–430) argued that Adam's original sin had a much greater impact and influence to the rest of the human race than what Pelagius and his followers permitted. According to Augustine, before the fall human beings had the freedom not to sin (*posse non peccare*) but after the fall all human beings lost that freedom not to sin (*non posse non peccare*). As a result, all those who are infected by the sin of Adam are bound to its power and cannot be delivered out of it by their own will.[15] Only by the gracious initiative of God can sinners be converted and transformed to live new lives that enable them to overcome sin and obey God.[16] Therefore, while Pelagius maintained the moral neutrality and freedom of the will for all human beings, Augustine went in the opposite direction and asserted that all human beings after the fall are bound by the power of sin dwelling in them.

*The Semi-Pelagian View.* In reaction against the perceived excesses of the Augustinian view, there arose a position that became a mediating position between that of Augustine and Pelagius. Although the label first appeared in the Lutheran *Formula of Concord* (1577) and became associated with Luis Molina's theology (1535–1600), this view was in existence during the time of Augustine. In the fifth century, two men John Cassian (d. 435) and Vincent of Lérins (d. ca. 450), objected to the strict deterministic view of grace put forward by Augustine.

According to the semi-Pelagian view of humanity, human beings 1) are responsible for the preparatory acts like prayer for the beginning of faith and receiving of divine grace; and 2) by means of their own will, must persevere in faith and good deeds in order to obtain final salvation. By taking this course, semi-Pelagianism, by implication, rejects Augustine's doctrine of predestination and his radical view of human depravity. However, in opposition to Pelagius, semi-Pelagianism also argues that Adam's sin did in fact corrupt the human race and that God's grace is necessary in order for human beings to obtain salvation. During the sixth century, semi-Pelagianism was denounced as a heresy at the Second Council of Orange (529).

15. Cf. González, *Story of Christianity*, 1:214–15.
16. Cf. McGrath, *Christian Theology*, 430.

*The Arminian View.* A view that has gained popularity in recent years in some sectors of evangelicalism is the Arminian view (named after the well-known Dutch Reformed theologian Jacobus Arminius [1560–1609]). The Arminian view of original sin, like Augustinianism and semi-Pelagianism, argues that all human beings are corrupted by the sin of Adam. For instance, the Nazarene theologian H. Orton Wiley states: "Not only are all men born under the penalty of death, as a consequence of Adam's sin, but they are born with a depraved nature also, which in contradistinction to the legal aspect of penalty, is generally termed inbred sin or inherited depravity."[17] However, this does not mean that a sinner becomes incapable of receiving the grace offered through the vicarious death of Christ. Though grace is required, all human beings, by their own will, can turn to Christ in faith. Again, Wiley writes: "Arminianism holds that salvation is all of grace, in that every movement of the soul toward God is initiated by divine grace; but it recognizes also in a true sense, the co-operation of the human will, because in the last stage, it remains with the free agent, as to whether the grace thus proffered is accepted or rejected"[18]

Therefore, the Arminian view of original sin asserts that though human beings inherit a corrupt nature from Adam that does not mean that human freedom is totally eradicated. All human beings, by the prevenient grace of God, have the ability to trust in Christ and receive salvation.

*The Calvinist/Reformed View.* Another popular view among evangelicals is the Calvinist/Reformed view. Calvinists or Reformed Christians argue that the sin of the first parents has so tainted the human race that no unregenerate human being (in contrast to the semi-Pelagian and Arminian views) can exercise saving faith in Christ apart from the sovereign work of God's grace in the heart. According to this view, the human being is so thoroughly corrupted by sin that his or her whole being (which includes the mind, heart, and will) is under the bondage and sway of sin.[19] This is typified in a statement found in the Westminster Confession of Faith: "From this original corruption, whereby we are utterly indisposed, disabled, and made opposite to all good, and wholly inclined to all evil, do proceed all actual transgressions" (VI/4).

---

17. Wiley, *Christian Theology*, 2:98.

18. Wiley, *Christian Theology*, 2:356.

19. Bavinck, *Reformed Dogmatics*, 3:119.

Calvinists have traditionally called this *total depravity*.[20] Also, even the "good deeds" done by unregenerate people are considered morally defective in God's eyes because they are not done out of love for him.[21] As a result, unregenerate human beings cannot come to faith in Christ unless God, by his sovereign grace, regenerates them by the Holy Spirit and effectually draws them to himself. However, *only the elect* receive this effectual call by the Holy Spirit and are, thus, able to respond through saving faith to receive all the benefits of the work of Christ.

*The View of Karl Barth.* Despite standing generally in the Reformed tradition, Karl Barth had great reservations regarding how his own tradition typically understood this issue. He makes this obviously plain when he states that the idea of "hereditary sin which has come to man by propagation" is an "extremely unfortunate and mistaken one."[22] He even asserts that the traditional Reformed view has a "hopelessly naturalistic, deterministic and even fatalistic ring."[23] What he prefers is that Christian theologians only speak of "original sin" without the connotations of inherited transmission of Adam's sin to the rest of the human race. Even the way he understands original sin is radically different from the way Reformed theologians have traditionally understood it. For Barth, original sin means

> the voluntary and responsible life of every man—in a connexion
> with Adam that we have yet to show—which by virtue of the judi-
> cial sentence passed on it in and with his reconciliation with God
> is the sin of every man, the corruption which he brings on himself
> so that as the one who does so—and again in that connexion—he
> is necessarily and inevitably corrupt.[24]

Therefore, human beings sin not as a result of having a sinful nature passed down to them by the primordial man but as a result of following the first man's example of disobedience. The only connection, in regards to sin, that exists between Adam and his descendants is that all those who sin after him are represented by him because they do what he did in the face of

20. This is based on the first article of the five points of Calvinism often referred to by the acronym TULIP: 1. Total Depravity; 2. Unconditional Election; 3. Limited Atonement; 4. Irresistible Grace; and 5. Perseverance of the Saints.

21. Berkhof, *Systematic Theology*, 247.

22. Barth, *Church Dogmatics*, IV/1:500.

23. Barth, *Church Dogmatics*, IV/1:501.

24. Barth, *Church Dogmatics*, IV/1:501

God's command.[25] In other words, for Barth, Adam shows us who we are as sinners before God.

Acknowledging the difficulty of the subject matter we are discussing, drawing up a satisfactory answer to this question must still be based ultimately on the scriptural evidence and not on what we observe in the world around us or our own personal beliefs about human beings. Scripture must be the ultimate source of knowledge when we attempt to understand this phenomenon called inherited sin. We will, therefore, examine the relevant biblical passages that speak of this matter and then provide an answer based on what those passages say.

*What the Scriptures Say about How Adam's Sin Affects Humanity.* According to Genesis 6 there was a time when humanity was in a state of extreme moral chaos and on the brink of self-destruction. According to the passage, the world at the time "was filled with violence" (v. 11) and people were given over to every manner of corruption (v. 12). As a result, the biblical testimony declares that God was grieved to have created human beings (v. 6) because he "saw that *the wickedness of man was great* in the earth, and that *every intention of the thoughts of his heart* was only evil continually" (v. 5). As we observe in this passage, even in the early stages of human history, people were bent towards sin and their hearts filled with corruption. Further along in the Old Testament, King David, after being confronted by Nathan for adultery and murder, confesses to God for his own sinfulness—a sinfulness he had before he was even born: "Behold, I was brought forth in iniquity, and in sin did my mother conceive me" (Ps 51:5). Also, in Psalm 58:3, he makes this statement regarding the sorry condition of the human race when he proclaims: "Even from birth the wicked go astray; from the womb they are wayward and speak lies" (NIV). Not only did David recognize this sad truth, Jeremiah the prophet proclaims that the "heart is deceitful above all things, and desperately sick; who can understand it?" (Jer 17:9). David and Jeremiah, being inspired by God to say those things, proclaim a piercing truth that many modern people would not like to hear: all human beings are naturally sinful, morally defiled, and ethically corrupt since the time of their conception.

In the New Testament this truth comes out more forcefully. In Matthew 7:11, Jesus makes the point that even though human fathers give good

25. Barth, *Church Dogmatics*, IV/1:510–11.

gifts to their children they are still naturally evil. In John 8:34, Jesus states that unbelievers are slaves to sin because they do what naturally comes to them—which is to sin. The Pauline corpus has several instances discussing the inherent sinfulness of human beings. In Romans 1:18–32, Paul states that God's wrath is being revealed to all ungodliness and wickedness of human beings because they suppress the truth and do (and endorse) the things that are contrary to his will. In Ephesians 2:3, Paul states that before his readers became followers of Christ they were "by nature children of wrath, *like the rest of mankind.*" Later in the same epistle, he writes that the gentiles (another term for unregenerate humanity) are "darkened in their understanding, alienated from the life of God because of the ignorance that is in them, due to their hardness of heart" (Eph 4:18), which he reiterates in Titus 1:15 when he states that for unbelievers "nothing is pure; but both their minds and their consciences are defiled." Also, in Colossians 3:7 Paul reminds his readers that they used to walk in the sinful ways of the unbelieving world (i.e., sexual immorality, impurity, etc.) before coming to Christ through faith (cf. Titus 3:3). Paul even admits, like David did long before him, that "nothing good dwells in me, that is, in my flesh" (Rom 7:18). The passages cited above overwhelmingly demonstrate that all human beings are naturally and thoroughly sinful since the time they were formed in their mothers' wombs.

After examining the pertinent passages, we believe that the Calvinist or Reformed understanding of how original sin affects the human race comes closest to what Scripture teaches. The passages examined above clearly show that human beings, in their natural state, are bound to sin and unable to exercise faith in Christ by their own will. Despite the more positive anthropological views of modern secular humanism (that view human beings as being essentially good), Scripture portrays humanity apart from Christ as thoroughly corrupted by sin and having no spiritual inclination towards the things of God. The sordid history of humankind with its wars, violence, and injustices merely confirms the biblical witness of the sad condition of humanity outside of Christ. Only through the effectual call of the Holy Spirit are sinners able to believe in Christ, turn away from sin, and overcome progressively the fallen nature that dwells within them (cf. Titus 3:3–5).

*How the Sin of Adam Is Transmitted to the Rest of Humanity*

Having discussed the various views on how Adam's sin affects the whole human race, there have also been various theories throughout the history of the church regarding how the sin of Adam is *transmitted* to his offspring. Although many Christians will find no great significance in how we understand this matter, the importance of this question has to do with the fact that how we understand this issue greatly influences the way we understand humanity's condition before God and how redemption is accomplished for sinners in Jesus Christ. We will first discuss the various theories of the transmission of sin in the Christian tradition and then offer our own perspective on this matter.

*The Federal View.* Reformed theologians have traditionally maintained that the first sin of Adam not only corrupted the human race in all spheres of life but that his sin was *imputed* to all of those descended after him (except Jesus Christ). As a consequence, Adam became a "federal head" of the entire human race. Their rationale for this "federal imputative" view is based on the assertion that God established a so-called covenant of works with Adam and his descendants. This covenant of works would entitle human beings to eternal life *if* they successfully obey *all* that God has stipulated to them within the terms of the covenant (the flip side being that they would suffer earthly decay, physical and spiritual death, and eternal condemnation if they disobey).[26] This covenant, according to classic Reformed theology, is still somehow normative throughout all the periods of redemptive history and every human being is bound to its conditions.[27] Consequently, however, all human beings (except Jesus Christ) have broken the stipulations of this covenant through Adam's transgression and must bear the *legal* consequences for being "covenant violators." As Robert L. Dabney writes, "If Adam came under the covenant of works as a public person, and acted there, not for himself alone, but for his posterity federally, this implies the imputation of the legal consequences of his act to them."[28] That is why, according to this theory, all human beings by default are reckoned sinners in God's sight.

26. Frame, *Salvation Belongs to the Lord*, 119.

27. Robert L. Reymond gives four reasons why the "covenant of works," though no longer in force as "a probationary framework for mankind," is still normative even after the fall in his *New Systematic Theology of the Christian Faith*, 439–40.

28. Dabney, *Systematic Theology*, 329.

*The Realist View.* The Realist view (or the Augustinian view) asserts that all human beings committed sin when Adam sinned in the garden because of a "common human nature" they share with him. In other words, the human race is seen as a unified whole as a result of this common human nature and, therefore, the whole human race is also guilty and experiences the dire consequences of Adam's original sin. W. G. T. Shedd, a nineteenth-century Reformed theologian who espouses this view, helpfully summarizes this position when he writes: "The human species existing in them [Adam and Eve] at that time acted in their act and sinned in their sin, similarly as the hand or eye acts and sins in the murderous or lustful act of the individual soul."[29] Some even maintain that John Calvin held this view.[30]

*The Mediate Imputation View.* The Mediate Imputation view was first advocated during the post-Reformation period by the French Reformed theologian Josué de la Place (or Placaeus) (1596–1665). According to Herman Bavinck: "Placaeus taught that Adam's disobedience was only imputed to his descendants mediately, that is, only insofar as, and on the basis of the fact that, they were already born of him in a state of impurity."[31] Thus, the depravity of human beings is the *medium* through which Adam's guilt is imputed to them. The inherent corruption of fallen human beings, in this view, becomes "the vehicle" in which this guilt is reckoned to all of Adam's physical offspring. This is in contrast to the Federal view of classic Reformed orthodoxy where Adam's guilt is *immediately* imputed to his descendants. This view was also advocated by some New England theologians during the eighteenth and nineteenth centuries.[32]

*The Arminian Non-Imputation View.* In contrast to the views surveyed above, Arminian theologians traditionally argue that though original sin is a doctrine that is clearly taught in Scripture, Adam's first sin is *not* something that is legally imputed to his descendants. Instead, human beings *voluntarily* and *consciously* appropriate the depravity caused by sin by their

29. Shedd, *Dogmatic Theology*, 564.

30. Enns, *Moody Handbook of Theology*, 326.

31. Bavinck, *Reformed Dogmatics*, 3:99.

32. For a good exposition and historical survey of this view see John Murray's *The Imputation of Adam's Sin*, 42–64.

own acts of transgression against God, and thus, bring condemnation upon themselves in that way.[33] The argument is made by those who hold this position that the various "representational" theories of the transmission of Adam's guilt severely undercuts the seriousness of individual responsibility for the sins personally committed and unjustly reckons the innocent as being guilty for a sin they were not personally involved in.[34]

*A Resolution?* The position taken in this book is a combination of the Federal view found in classic Reformed theology and the Realist/Augustinian view. The key biblical passage that is often referred to by traditional Reformed theologians to defend the notion that Adam's sin is immediately imputed to his descendants is Romans 5:12–19. Those who advocate this position argue that Paul's use of legal language in the passage (though it is not the only language used) to depict the condemned state of those still in Adam (e.g., vv. 16, 18) demonstrates that the apostle affirmed that all human beings were immediately imputed with Adam's guilt. Although some may argue that such a notion makes a mockery of the way God deals with human beings,[35] this view does have something to be said for based on the passage in question. In verse 16, when Paul parallels Adam's transgression and its consequences with the "free gift" bought by Christ's righteousness, he uses the legal terms "condemnation" and "justification," respectively, to define them. If Christ's righteousness brought about the *forensic* declaration of righteousness to those who believe, it is only logical to assume that Paul is also talking about a *forensic* judgment against all those who are still under the dominion of sin (i.e., those still under Adam's federal headship). This is further supported in verse 18 when Paul talks about how the "one trespass" of Adam led to the "condemnation of all men," but that the "one act of righteousness" of Jesus Christ leads "to justification and life for all men" (once more, a legal pronouncement of righteousness). Again, we see that Paul is talking about a *forensic reckoning* of sin *or* righteousness, depending on whether the person is under Adam's headship or in union with Christ, respectively.[36] Therefore, Reformed theologians are correct to assert that a *representational* parallelism is being described in Romans 5:12–19 when

33. Garrett, *Systematic Theology*, 1:566.

34. Miley, *Systematic Theology*, 1:503–4.

35. Cf. Wiley, *Christian Theology*, 2:116–17.

36. Murray, *Imputation of Adam's Sin*, 64–70.

Paul talks about how Adam's sin and Christ's righteousness are imputed to those they represent under their respective headships.

Having demonstrated that Adam's sin is immediately imputed to his descendants we must not, however, just stop there and assert that the relationship between Adam's sin and his descendants is merely one of an accounting of a *peccatum alienum*. We must also insist that all those under Adam are *truly* responsible and culpable for the sins they personally commit in their lives. If the direct imputing of Adam's sin is viewed as the *only* cause for the condemnation of the human race then a case could be made that such a notion leads to a "legal fiction" of sorts. However, Scripture is replete with passages that state that all human beings are personally responsible for their own sins (cf. Gen 4:10–12; Rom 1:18–32; Jas 1:14–15) and that they will be eschatologically judged based on what they do in this life (cf. Ecc 12:14; 2 Cor 5:10; Rev 20:11–15).

One may still ask: does not one's personal responsibility for one's own sin make the representational role of Adam moot? If we are responsible and guilty because of the sins we personally commit why even bother with the idea of immediate imputation of Adam's guilt? One possible resolution to this difficult tension is to say that we appropriate the guilt of Adam when we reach the "age of accountability" and make a conscious and voluntary decision to sin. In other words, the imputation of Adam's guilt to us is conditional upon what we do after we become morally aware.[37] The problem with this view, however, is that nowhere in Romans 5:12–19 is there a conditional statement regarding who is to be under condemnation as a result of Adam's sin. The apostle, however, makes it clear in verse 18 that the "one trespass" by Adam brought condemnation for *all men*. In fact, throughout the whole passage, the apostle talks as if death and condemnation were brought upon the whole human race *without their own input on the matter*.

The only adequate solution, we believe, to this apparent tension is to say that the relationship between Adam's imputed sin and the sins people are personally responsible for is a *dynamic* one. The personal sins that people commit are the result of the depravity that comes about through the imputation of Adam's sin. In other words, the sinner's personal acts of sin *flow from* his or her corrupt nature as a result of Adam's original disobedience, which then adds to their original guilt.[38] The representational view of the transmission of Adam's sin to his posterity only becomes problematic

---

37. Erickson, *Christian Theology*, 656.
38. Horton, *Christian Faith*, 426.

when one views the imputation as merely "hanging above" the heads of those still in Adam. One way to avoid this is to assert that the relationship between Adam and his posterity is a very close one so much so that Adam's sin is intricately tied to the miserable condition of his posterity. Therefore, God can view all human beings as being legally guilty because of Adam's one act of disobedience *and* have the moral justification to condemn them for the personal sins they commit in this life.

*Why Is It Necessary to Affirm the Doctrine of Original Sin?*

As mentioned before, the modern proclivity against the biblical doctrine of original sin is due to an increase in viewing the world through a more naturalistic viewpoint along with a fairly optimistic view of humanity. Not only is this opinion popular among many modern secularists, even many self-proclaimed evangelicals reject the traditional doctrine of original sin, seeing it as being incompatible with human freedom.[39] Although we can provide key scriptural references—like Romans 5:12–19 and Ephesians 2:3—to defend the doctrine of original sin, we can also defend its truthfulness by understanding the nature of sin *and* humanity's relationship to it solely from a theological point of view. As discussed above, sin is an *abnormal* condition of human beings. God created Adam and Eve sinless and upright (cf. Gen 2:25; 3:7; Ecc 7:29) but they wilfully chose to disobey God, and their children now bear the terrible consequences of that choice (Gen 3:16–19). This sordid condition is also demonstrated in the life of the nation of Israel in the Old Testament. Even before entering the promised land there is a pronouncement by God in Deuteronomy 31:16–18 that Israel's apostasy and covenant unfaithfulness will certainly happen. One only has to take a cursory look at the history of Israel throughout the pages of the Old Testament to witness her repeated covenant unfaithfulness to God.

The ramifications of rejecting the doctrine of original sin (although many of those who espouse this position may be unaware of this) is that we then implicitly give acquiescence to the idea that sin is somehow *normal for human beings* or *a natural part of the created order*. The consequence of this unbiblical idea can be profoundly negative in the spiritual, ethical, and pastoral realms. For instance, if we reject the doctrine of original sin we can excuse sinful actions done by human beings as merely acts due to a "divine

---

39. For instance, in his book *The Faith Once For All*, Jack Cottrell spends an entire chapter (chapter 9) criticizing the traditional doctrine of original sin.

imperative." Also, denying this doctrine implicitly gives way to the idea that since human beings are not inherently sinful in their current state they do not need to be supernaturally redeemed from sin. The doctrine of original sin, then, guards the church against the dangerous idea that fallen human beings are naturally good and that they do not need a Savior to stand in their place for their redemption.

We can be rest assured, therefore, that the condition of human beings after the fall—in enmity towards God and other people—is *not* the original divine intention when God created humankind. This should also give believers hope knowing that the original sin of the first parents will be completely undone because of Christ's atoning sacrifice (Rom 3:23–25) and that the devastating consequences of sin will be finally erased in the new heaven and new earth (Rev 21:4).

## The Results of Sin

Having established what sin is and where it originates from we will now discuss what the physical and spiritual consequences of sin are. Sin not only results in a legal condemnation of sinners before God, it also leads to terrible consequences for human beings in this life and, for the unrepentant, the life to come. We will now discuss what these consequences are below.

### The Corruption of Creation

In Genesis 3:17–18, after the fall of humankind, God pronounces a curse on the ground so that Adam and his offspring would have to endure "painful toil" (v. 17, NIV) to eat of the fruits of the earth because it will produce "thorns and thistles" (v. 18). As one can see from this passage sin has immediately caused the alienation between the human race and the rest of creation. This alienation is expressed concretely when human beings exploit the earth for natural resources and when natural disasters take a toll on the lives of humans in return.

The apostle Paul was fully cognizant of how sin has thoroughly corrupted the created order when he writes in Romans 8:20–22: "For the creation was subjected to futility, not willingly, but because of him who subjected it, in hope that the creation itself will be set free from its bondage to corruption and obtain the freedom of the glory of the children of God. For we know that the whole creation has been groaning together in the pains of childbirth until now." Paul makes it clear in the passage that ever since the introduction of sin into the world all of creation has been under the bondage of sin and has been "groaning" to be set free from the corruption caused by it.

Observing the world right now with its ecological disasters, the growing extinction of animal species, and the relentless exploitation of the earth's resources by sinful humans we can clearly see the disastrous effects of sin on this planet. Even in the animal world, the consequences of sin can be seen in the way different animal species interact with one another. Predatory animals hunt down "weaker" prey for food and fierce competition exists among animals for the earth's limited resources (contrast this with the harmonious relations among animals described in Isaiah 11:6–9 in the eschatological kingdom). Clearly, sin has had a devastating effect not only on human beings but on the entire creation.

### Human Pain, Misery, and Suffering in This Life

As mentioned above, sin has not only condemned the human race to perdition after this life but it has also brought pain, misery, and suffering for human beings existentially in this life. One only needs to pick up a newspaper or watch the daily news on television to see the horrible existential effects sin has had on human beings, individually and corporately. Wars, murders, famine, bodily pain due to disease, and death brought about by natural disasters are all the results of sin and the corruption brought on by sin. Scripture is replete with stories of people suffering various kinds of anguish, pain, and hardship due to various kinds of sins—sins either committed by themselves or committed by others against them.

Ever since the fall of the first couple there seems to be a single constant that transcends time, space, and cultures: sin has brought on devastating consequences on the human race and all of us are paying the price in this life for it (cf. Rom 3:16–17). Even the deaths of infants caused by genetic diseases or the injustices suffered by the innocent at the hands of the wicked are tragic realities that the human race as a whole has to reckon with as a consequence of human sin. Human beings in their original state did not experience the tragedies and pains that we are so used to in this fallen world, nor were they expected to. God put Adam and Eve in a completely idyllic situation where they could freely enjoy the bounties of the earth without agonizing in toil, pain, and hardship (Gen 2:8–16). Ever since the fall, however, human beings constantly toil in despair and suffer the various cruelties that sin has brought upon them in this life.

### Disordered Relationships among Human Beings

Not only has sin brought corruption to the created order and devastating existential consequences for human beings it has also resulted in disordered relationships among people. The first pronouncement of this was forecast in Genesis 3:16 when God tells the woman: "Your desire shall be for your husband, and he shall rule over you." As a result of Adam and Eve's sin, the marriage covenant will be tainted by the desire of the wife to rule over her husband.[40] Of course, the disorder in human relationships brought on by sin is not restricted to the marriage covenant. Throughout the pages of Scripture we see story after story of people murdering, cheating, lying, and acting treacherously in order to satisfy some sinful desire. It was no sooner that Cain murdered his brother Abel because of jealousy and rage (Gen 4:5–8).

Modern people, however, must not commend themselves thinking that people in biblical times behaved this way because they were living in an "unenlightened" or "primitive" period of human history. Even in our so-called modern enlightened age we are constantly bombarded with news reports of horrific terrorist attacks on civilians, ethnic-based military conflicts around the world, and millions living in hunger and destitution because of economic mismanagement or exploitation. Even in the church, whether in the past or present, conflict and discord are sad realities. In James 4:1–2, we get a clear understanding of this distressing reality in the early church when James reproves certain individuals in the church: "What causes quarrels and what causes fights among you? Is it not this, that your passions are at war within you? You desire and do not have, so you murder. You covet and cannot obtain, so you fight and quarrel." Even among true believers sin results in disordered fellowship as demonstrated in petty factionalism and

---

40. There have been various interpretations on the possible meaning of Genesis 3:16. Although most scholars argue that this deals with a woman's desire for independence from her husband and headship over him (cf. Foh, "What Is the Woman's Desire?," 376–83), some disagree with this majority interpretation arguing that the word "desire" refers to the woman's sexual longings for the man (cf. Wenham, *Genesis* 1–15, 1:81). Considering that the response to this "desire" will be that the husband "shall rule over [her]," it is highly unlikely that this verse is talking about a woman's sexual longings towards the man.

infighting in the church (as attested to in 1 Corinthians 3:1–4). As Grenz points out, "Sin . . . destroys the community God intends for his creation. And we are the responsible persons. Because of the unmistakable loss of community, we do not fulfill God's design for us. Consequently, we are alienated from our own true selves. We simply are not who we are meant to be."[41] Therefore, as believers transformed by the blood of Jesus Christ, we are called to overcome personal conflicts caused by sin and live in a way that reflects Christ's character in our lives by looking out for the interests of others (Phil 2:4) and serving them in love (Rom 12:9–10, 13).

### Enslavement

Not only does sin bring about existential suffering and disordered relationships it also results in the enslavement or bondage to sin. In John 8:34, Jesus tells the Pharisees that "everyone who practices sin is a slave to sin" (the liberation from this slavery coming as a result of abiding in Christ's word and knowing the truth [v. 31]). Also, in Romans 6:17, the apostle Paul tells his readers that they were "once slaves of sin" before they became obedient to the teachings given to them by the apostles. One can see the truth of this sad reality when we hear and read about people being addicted to material possessions, fame, power, narcotics, alcohol, and illicit sex. Although one of the valued tenets of modernity is that human beings are free and autonomous, an orthodox Christian anthropology asserts that *all* human beings are not truly free and autonomous—they are born under the bondage of sin and make moral choices according to this awful reality. In other words, unredeemed human beings are never neutral when they are faced with moral choices. In addition to this, unredeemed human beings continue to be under the bondage of sin as they are continually caught up in the nexus of sin by choosing the way of the flesh rather than the way of God-pleasing godliness.

### Physical Death

Physical death is a fact of life and death comes to every individual in one form or another. However, this was not the way it was supposed to be when God created the first human couple. This is clearly demonstrated when God

---

41. Grenz, *Theology for the Community of God*, 208.

tells Adam: "You may surely eat of every tree of the garden, but of the tree of the knowledge of good and evil you shall not eat, *for in the day that you eat of it you shall surely die*" (Gen 2:16–17). If Adam did not eat from the tree of the knowledge of good and evil, death (spiritual *and* physical) would not have become a reality for the human race because they would have had continual access to the tree of life (cf. Gen. 3:22).[42] As a result of the sin of the first parents, human beings are barred from this life-giving tree and sadly experience the process of aging and decay which culminates in physical death (cf. 1 Cor 15:21; Heb 9:27).

Hence, physical death was *not* part of God's original design for the human race. We must not assume, however, that physical death is *merely* a natural consequence of sin. Physical death, as Paul reminds us in Romans 1:32,[43] is also a *penalty* incurred as a result of the sins we commit in this life. Therefore, physical death is not only a natural consequence of sin but also a punishment deserved as a result of sin.[44]

---

42. There has been some debate in the history of the church regarding whether Adam and Eve were immortal by nature and sin ended their immortality *or* if they were inherently mortal and required access to the tree of life to live forever. The scriptural evidence appears to side with the latter (cf. Gen 3:22). As Eugene H. Merrill writes: "One gathers from the narrative that eternal human life (a qualitative concept) was not necessarily inherent in man's creation though it was certainly God's ultimate desire and plan for his image. Otherwise the purpose of the probationary tree of the knowledge of good and evil lacks substantive meaning as does the tree of life which presumably was available for human consumption before the temptation but which had no life-giving efficacy until afterward. The tree of life before the fall symbolized the quality of life that man would experience were he to pass the probation. That same tree after the fall possessed the properties of immortality (everlastingness) absent the quality possible only through forgiveness and restoration. Unable to eat of that tree, Adam and Eve died, lacking life in both its qualitative and physically quantitative sense" (*Everlasting Dominion*, 209–10). In addition, for God to allow Adam and Eve to have access to the tree of life *after* the fall would have been an act of infinite divine cruelty. God's decree that human beings *in their sinful condition* would be forever barred from this tree (Gen 3:22–24) was an act of great mercy. To continue to exist in an immortal state while under the bondage of sin would be the ultimate curse rather than a great blessing. As one Old Testament commentator writes: "For immortality in a state of sin is not ζωὴ αἰώνιος, which God designed for man, but endless misery, which the Scriptures call 'the second death' (Rev. 2:11; 20:6, 14; 21:8). The expulsion from paradise, therefore, was a punishment inflicted for man's good, intended, while exposing him to temporal death, to preserve him from eternal death" (Keil and Delitzsch, *Commentary on the Old Testament*, 1:67).

43. Notice the word "deserve" (also in the NIV, HCSB, and NRSV) in the verse (the NASB has "worthy").

44. As Cottrell rightly notes (*Faith Once For All*, 207).

*Spiritual Death*

When Scripture speaks of death as being a consequence of sin we must also recognize that it includes a spiritual element. When the apostle Paul states in Romans 6:23 that the "wages of sin is death" he has primarily spiritual death in mind. This is what God also had in mind when he told Adam in Genesis 2:17 that death would be the consequence of disobedience (because physical death did not *immediately* come upon the first couple). Therefore, when Scripture speaks of death being a consequence of sin it *primarily* has *spiritual* death in mind.

What, therefore, is this "spiritual death"? One theologian succinctly states that it "is the separation of the entire person from God."[45] Although this definition may sound terse it does truly capture the essence of spiritual death: as a separation of the sinner from God and his goodness (a separation that can only be bridged by the sacrificial death of Christ). As long as sinners stubbornly remain in their rebellion against God there can be no hope of them ever having a relationship with God in the same way God had with the first couple before the fall. God cannot tolerate sin, and those who do not turn to Christ in faith to have their sins forgiven will always be considered God's enemies with no hope of fellowship with him in this age or in the age to come.

Also, although we can distinguish between physical and spiritual death when we talk about death as a consequence of sin, we must not put a total disconnect between the two. One can say that physical death is the fruit of spiritual death and is a visible expression of it. One day both physical and spiritual death will be totally eradicated when God establishes the new heaven and new earth where sin, suffering, and death will be no more (Rev 21:4, 27).

*Eternal Death*[46]

As physical death is the physical manifestation of the spiritual death that all human beings receive as a result of sin, eternal death can be seen as the ultimate end of the spiritual death that sinners experience in this life. Because God cannot tolerate sin, as mentioned above, those who do not

---

45. Erickson, *Christian Theology*, 631.
46. We will discuss the doctrine of hell in more detail in chapter 19.

have their sins paid for by Christ's life-giving death must suffer the penalty of their sins *eternally* in hell.

For many modern people the idea of an eternal hell is viewed as being contrary to an "enlightened" sense of justice. One often encounters objections like "How can a loving and just God punish a person forever in hell for sins only committed within a finite length of time on earth?" However, the fact that God is *just* and that his holy law has been violated requires him to punish sin one way or another. If God did allow sin to go unpunished it means that he will be acting against his holy nature, which is impossible for him to do. But one may still ask: why eternal? This question becomes moot when we recognize that God is *infinitely* holy and righteous and that the only *just* punishment for the violation of his law is that the impenitent pay for their sins eternally in hell. The eternal punishment of the impenitent in hell is the only way that the enormity of their sins before God can be demonstrated to all. As John Gill writes, "The reasons of the eternal duration of punishment for sin, are, because it is committed against an infinite and eternal Being, and is objectively infinite, and requires infinite satisfaction, which a finite creature cannot give; and this not being given, punishment must proceed on *ad infinitum,* and so be eternal."[47]

Before we close this discussion, we must still address what the nature of this eternal death is. It would be simplistic to merely assert that eternal death is "consciously existing forever in hell." What needs to be emphasized is that we need to understand eternal death in relation to the sinner's relationship to God. The awfulness of eternal death is not only based on the fact that the unredeemed will forever experience the dreadful pangs of hell, but also that they will exist without ever being able to enjoy the infinite blessing that radiates from the God who is the giver of all that is good. That is why it is so urgent that believers do their utmost to bring the good news of the gospel to unredeemed sinners by sharing with them the love of God in the person and work of Jesus Christ (John 3:16–17).

47. Gill, *Body of Doctrinal Divinity*, 343.

# CHAPTER 7

# The Covenants

BOTH THE OLD AND New Testaments reveal that God has always related to his people through covenant relationships. Although the covenantal arrangements between God and his people come in various forms throughout redemptive history, the basic and underlying concept of the covenant is essentially the same in all of those arrangements. In a typical covenant arrangement between human beings in the ancient world there were certain stipulations contained therein with certain promises attached to it—the realization of these promises depending on the fulfillment of those stipulations. Customarily, therefore, a covenant sets out requirements that both parties must fulfill in order for the promises of the covenant to come to realization or for the covenant relationship to be in force continually.[1] Covenantal arrangements between human parties have existed since antiquity and these pacts regularly were enacted for mutual benefit. In a typical covenant arrangement entered into by two human parties, like a marriage covenant between a husband and wife, certain stipulations were to be fulfilled by both parties in order for the covenant promises to be maintained or to reach fruition.

---

1. Michael Horton points out that within the suzerain-vassal covenants of the ancient near east there were certain obligations that the vassal had to meet in order to receive the protection and care of the suzerain. He writes: "Just as the suzerain graciously and without any inherent obligation pledged to move against those who invaded his vassal territory as if it were his own capital, he would move against the vassal state itself just as ferociously should the terms of the covenant be violated" (*God of Promise*, 27).

In God's covenantal dealings with people, however, the covenant arrangements are slightly altered from the typical covenant treaties enacted among human beings in this significant way: God's covenant relationships with his people are founded upon his unmerited grace, with the terms set forth *by him alone*. Human beings have no claim on God to initiate a covenant relationship. All covenant relationships that God has entered into with human beings throughout history is grounded in his sovereign and gracious initiative.[2] Thus, the word "arrangement" could lead to some misunderstanding when talking about divine-human covenants in Scripture. Although the covenants revealed in Scripture have always been arranged by God's sovereign initiative, there is still the expectation that the people who have entered into a covenant relationship with him will fulfill certain obligatory requirements stipulated in the covenant. As will be shown below, all the covenants between God and human beings throughout salvation history include this promise-stipulation structure. Therefore, although God does reconcile sinners to himself purely by his grace and enters into a covenant relationship with them solely by his divine initiative, he still demands that his redeemed people live by the set stipulations of the covenant.

In this chapter we will discuss: 1) the biblical covenants between God and his people in their redemptive-historical order; 2) the validity of the Reformed "covenant of works" doctrine as examined in light of Scripture; and 3) the controversial issue of "monocovenantalism" in light of recent biblico-theological discussions among some Reformed evangelical scholars.

## The Biblical Covenants between God and His People as Revealed in Scripture

### Noahic Covenant

The first covenant established by God and his people is recorded in Genesis 9:1–17 when God makes a promissory declaration to Noah and his sons (although it is properly established as a covenant in verse 9) that all animals will fear them and be delivered into their hands (which includes the right to use them as food) (vv. 2–3). The promise also includes that all living creatures (i.e., "all flesh") will not "be cut off by the waters of the flood" so that the earth will not be destroyed by water again (vv. 11, 15). Furthermore, God seals this *everlasting* covenant by sending them a sign—a "bow in the

2. Murray, *Covenant of Grace*, 9.

cloud" (v. 13, 16)—which will be an everlasting reminder to God (v. 14) of the covenant he has established with Noah, his offspring, and all other living creatures (vv. 16–17). The terms of this covenant are unilateral and eternal, which means that God will not break this covenant despite the evil inclinations of human beings (8:21). The reason for its perpetuity is well-summarized by John Murray:

> These features of the covenant plainly evince that this covenant is a sovereign, divine administration, that it is such in its conception, determination, disclosure, confirmation, and fulfillment, that it is an administration or dispensation of forbearance and goodness, that it is not conditioned by or dependent upon faith or obedience on the part of men.[3]

Some, however, will contend that if the Noahic covenant is purely unilateral in character then it cannot rightly be called a "covenant" in the proper sense of the term. In other words, if the Noahic covenant is completely promissory, unilateral, and sovereignly established by God, does this not belie the fact that it is a covenant arrangement? One of the common misconceptions regarding the Noahic covenant is that because it is an unconditional and perpetual covenant it must contain *no requirements whatsoever* for human beings to observe. However, even a cursory reading of Genesis 9:1–17 reveals that covenant stipulations are in place for the human beneficiaries of this particular covenant.

First, God commands Noah and his family to be fruitful and fill the earth with their descendants (vv. 1, 7). Although this ordinance may come across as sounding like a suggestion, it is in fact given as a command. It is only by being fruitful and spreading over the earth that the human race can continue to exist and exercise dominion over creation (vv. 2–3). That is why it is *through* Noah and his children that God permits the human race to continue and flourish. Second, Noah and his descendants must not eat meat of an animal with its blood still in it (v. 4). The reason for this is that blood symbolizes life, and this life belongs to God alone. This reveals that God holds blood—the essence of life—as being sacred.[4] Third, God makes it clear that the taking of the life of another human being is strictly

---

3. Murray, *Covenant of Grace*, 14.

4. Another possible reason for this ordinance is given by T. D. Alexander: "Prior to the flood the shedding of innocent blood polluted the ground, decreasing significantly its fertility. In 9:1–7 God issues certain instructions which are intended to prevent the earth from being contaminated in the future" (*From Paradise to the Promised Land*, 135).

forbidden (vv. 5–6). Whether the human life is extinguished by an animal or another human being the consequence for transgressing this command is that the transgressor be put to death also.[5] Human life is precious in the sight of God because human beings are made in his image (v. 6), and any sinful act that physically destroys the image-bearer is an abomination to God.

In summary, although the Noahic covenant is a gracious covenant that was sovereignly established by God with Noah and his descendants it still contains requirements for human beings to observe. As Peter J. Gentry and Stephen J. Wellum state, "The covenant with Noah entails divine promises whose fulfilment cannot be thwarted, yet it also calls the community of animals and humans to answer for their actions and stewardship."[6] The Noahic covenant, therefore, contains a promise-stipulation pattern (even though it is an everlasting covenant) as seen in other future divine-human covenants in biblical history.

## Abrahamic Covenant

The precursor to the Abrahamic covenant is laid out in Genesis 12:2–3 when God tells Abraham:

> And I will make of you a great nation, and I will bless you and make your name great, so that you will be a blessing. I will bless those who bless you, and him who dishonors you I will curse, and in you all the families of the earth shall be blessed.

---

5. The question of whether Christians today should support their respective governments in carrying out the death penalty for murderers is a controversial one. Many Christians today argue that the death penalty cannot be a legitimate form of state-sanctioned punishment for those who commit premeditated murder. They argue that this ordinance belongs only in the Old Testament and that execution of murderers goes against Jesus' command to "turn the other cheek" (Matt 5:39). However, the perpetual and universal nature of the Noahic covenant, which transcends all redemptive-historical periods, is inconsistent with this viewpoint. As O. Palmer Robertson states, the "preservative character of the covenant with Noah plays a central role in the progress of redemptive history. Men today still live under the provisions inaugurated in this covenant. The regularity of the seasons derives directly from God's determination to preserve the earth until deliverance from sin can be accomplished. The institution of the state indicates the purpose of God to restrain the evil inherent in humanity" (*Christ of the Covenants*, 121).

6. Gentry and Wellum, *Kingdom through Covenant*, 174.

In this promissory declaration, God makes it clear that the blessings given here are not only for Abraham and his physical descendants but for the entire world. Although the word "covenant" is not used in this passage it would be difficult to argue that there is no foreshadowing of the covenantal enactment between God and Abraham that will take place later in Genesis. It is in Genesis 15:18–21 that the actual word *covenant* is used:

> On that day the Lord made a *covenant* with Abram, saying, "To your offspring I give this land, from the river of Egypt to the great river, the river Euphrates, the land of the Kenites, the Kenizzites, the Kadmonites, the Hittites, the Perizzites, the Rephaim, the Amorites, the Canaanites, the Girgashites and the Jebusites."

However, it is in Genesis 17:1–14 that we are presented with a full description of the promises and stipulations of the covenant between God and Abraham. So, what are those promises and stipulations contained in the covenant?

The promises contained in this covenant for Abraham are clearly laid out in Genesis 12:2–3; 15:18–19; and 17:2–8. The blessings promised in this covenant are: 1) numerous descendants; 2) a land; and 3) being a blessing to all nations.

1. *Numerous Descendants.* In Genesis 12:2 and 17:2, 4–5, God promises to give Abraham numerous descendants. In fact, not only will he be the father of many nations but he will also be the father of many kings (17:6) and will have a great name (12:2). We should be careful here that we do not restrict the meaning of this promise only to Abraham's *physical* descendants. As a result of the *ultimate* Seed of Abraham, the Lord Jesus Christ (cf. Gal 3:16), all those who are united to him through faith, regardless of ethnicity, are considered Abraham's children (Gal 3:26–29).

2. *A Land.* Not only does God promise that Abraham will have numerous descendants and be the father of many nations, he also promises that his descendants will take possession of "all the land of Canaan" as an "everlasting possession" (17:8; cf. 15:18–19). Although the land promise here seems restrictive in its immediate context, in the New Testament, like the promise of numerous descendants, it will have a broader application. This is seen in Matthew 5:5 when Jesus declares that the "meek" shall "inherit the earth", and when Paul states in

Romans 4:13 that Abraham and his spiritual offspring will be the "heir of the world."

3. *Being a Blessing to All Nations.* The promise here includes that Abraham and his descendants will become mediators of God's blessing to the rest of the world. This aspect of the promise, however, like the promises of numerous descendants and a land, should not be restricted to the Old Testament dispensation and/or material blessings. In the New Testament, as mentioned above, this blessing involves the spiritual redemption of all those in Christ through faith. As Robert L. Saucy states regarding the universality of the Abrahamic covenant, "The nature of the universal blessing consists in spiritual salvation now made available to all through faith in Christ."[7] We should not, however, rashly assume that because gentile believers today are included in the Abrahamic promise through faith that the physical descendants of Abraham no longer have a special place in this covenant (i.e., replacement theology). Expansion of the Abrahamic promise does not necessarily entail replacement or supersession.

With these great promises given by God to Abraham through this covenant arrangement it is appropriate, therefore, to call it a "covenant of promise."[8] Although the Abrahamic covenant can be properly called a promissory covenant, some evangelical theologians in recent years have contended that because of its promissory character the Abrahamic covenant is a *purely unconditional* one. This argument is usually brought forth by theologians who identify themselves as dispensationalists.[9] It is often argued, by those who believe that this covenant is purely unconditional, that it was *only* God who passed between the animal carcasses to ratify the covenant arrangement (Gen 15:9–10, 17). Therefore, the covenant can only be unconditional in character.[10]

Although it is true that it was God alone who established the covenant and walked between the animal pieces to confirm its institution, it is not entirely correct to conclude that the covenant is purely unconditional in character. God (Gen 17:1, 9–14) makes two demands on Abraham within this covenant arrangement. First, Abraham was to walk before him and be

---

7. Saucy, *Case for Progressive Dispensationalism*, 57.

8. Saucy, *Case for Progressive Dispensationalism*, 128.

9. Showers, *There Really Is a Difference!*, 60–68.

10. Johnson, "Covenants in Traditional Dispensationalism," 125.

blameless (v. 1) and, second, he was to circumcise himself and all males in his household (whether born in his house or a foreigner) (vv. 10–13). In fact, any male who is uncircumcised will be "cut off" from God's people because he has broken God's covenant (v. 14). Murray writes:

> Without question the blessings of the covenant and the relation which the covenant entails cannot be enjoyed or maintained apart from the fulfillment of certain conditions on the part of the benefi- ciaries. . . . The obedience of Abraham is represented as the condi- tion upon which the fulfillment of the promise given to him was contingent and the obedience of Abraham's seed is represented as the means through which the promise given to Abraham would be accomplished.[11]

Although this covenant does contain requirements that Abraham and his descendants are to live by, we must be careful that we do not conclude that the covenant arrangement is synergistic in any way. This covenant is a divinely established covenant founded upon God's grace apart from any human merit. Abraham was *sovereignly called by God* (Gen 12:1) to enjoy intimate fellowship with him. We must not mistakenly assume that *condi- tionality* implies synergism. Just like the Noahic covenant, the Abrahamic covenant is a covenant of grace that contains certain stipulations that the beneficiaries are commanded to abide by.

## The Mosaic (or Sinaitic) Covenant

The Mosaic covenant is a covenant that has been misunderstood by many Christians throughout the history of the church. The most common mis- understanding is that this covenant is *exclusively* legal in nature. In other words, many believe that a works-righteousness legalism is what under- girds this covenant between God and Israel that was established at Sinai.[12] This misunderstanding is understandable considering that God gave Israel, through the mediation of Moses, intricate divine commandments to follow

11. Murray, *Covenant of Grace*, 18.

12. This view is most commonly held by both traditional dispensational and Lutheran theologians. However, even some Reformed covenant theologians, who despite having a more positive view of God's law compared to their Lutheran counterparts, have argued that the Mosaic covenant is a type of "covenant of works." For instance, the Reformed theologian Mark W. Karlberg gives somewhat of a nuanced view of this in his *Covenant Theology in Reformed Perspective*, 46–49.

in order for the nation to continually receive the blessings of the Mosaic covenant. It is no wonder that Murray writes that the "Mosaic covenant offers more plausible support to the conception of compact than does any other covenant of God with men."[13] Therefore, it is no surprise that the Mosaic covenant has been misunderstood by many evangelical Christians as being a strictly legal covenant since the Reformation era.

We must challenge, however, this common misunderstanding of the Mosaic covenant as a strictly legal covenant that had no elements of grace contained in it. God gave the Mosaic covenant (with its laws) as a *gift* to the Israelites. The gracious nature of the covenant is indicated in Exodus 20:2 when Yahweh declares, "I am the LORD your God, who brought you out of the land of Egypt, out of the house of slavery." It was not because the Israelites were found more worthy than other nations that God delivered them from the oppressive hand of the Egyptians and established a covenant relationship with them, but rather, God's establishing of a covenant with the Israelites was entirely based on his grace. As Gentry and Wellum write:

> God did not set his love on Israel because they were better or more numerous than the nations (Deut. 7:7). Neither was it for their righteousness that they were given the land of Canaan. The basis for God's calling of Israel was not to be found in them, but instead in God's sovereign choice and his covenant loyalty to Abraham (Ex. 19:4; Deut. 7:8). The old covenant, then, cannot be understood apart from the Abrahamic covenant, since it is *organically* related to it, which in turn must be understood in light of the covenant with creation.[14]

Also, through this covenant Israel became a treasured possession in God's eyes. She would receive the special privilege of carrying out the Messianic line, of becoming a theocracy under divine protection, and of becoming a priestly light to the surrounding nations (cf. Exod 19:3–6). Although strict stipulations were demanded on the Israelites within the covenantal arrangement if they sought to enjoy the blessings of it (Deut 27–30), it was also a gracious covenant enacted by God due to his promise to Abraham, Isaac, and Jacob (Deut 30:20). As Herman Bavinck writes:

> Just as God first freely and graciously gave himself as shield and reward to Abraham, apart from any merits of his, to be a God

13. Murray, *Covenant of Grace*, 20. However, Murray does view the Mosaic covenant as being fundamentally gracious in character (*Covenant of Grace*, 22).

14. Gentry and Wellum, *Kingdom through Covenant*, 636.

to him and his descendants after him, and on that basis called Abraham to a blameless walk before his face, so also it is God who chose the people of Israel, saved it out of Egypt, united himself with that people, and obligated it to be holy and his own people.[15]

Therefore, like the Abrahamic covenant, the Mosaic covenant was presupposed upon divine grace, and the resultant law-keeping expected of the Israelites was only a *response* to the divine initiative grounded upon the sovereign benevolence of God.

## The Davidic Covenant

The Davidic covenant is a covenant that fully exemplifies the promise character of God's covenantal dealings with his people. In this covenant, God makes certain promises to David that he will bring to fulfillment for David and the Israelites in the near and distant future. In terms of fulfillments that will occur in the near future, God promises David, as described in 2 Samuel 7:8–11, that certain blessings will be realized during his lifetime. These include: 1) giving David a great name; 2) reaffirming Israel as God's own treasured possession; and 3) providing David rest from his enemies. One thing to notice here is that there are no stipulations mentioned in the entire passage of 2 Samuel 7 for David to fulfill for these promises to be realized (cf. Ps 89:3–4, 34–35). This unilateral aspect of the covenant is demonstrated in 2 Samuel 8:13–14 when the passage states that David made a name for himself after "striking down 18,000 Edomites in the Valley of Salt" and when "all the Edomites became David's servants." This rest from all enemies continues on into the period of Solomon's reign as indicated in 1 Kings 5:4.

In regards to the promises that will be fulfilled in the distant future, God pledges that David will have an heir that will reign in Israel forever. Although David will have successive heirs in the near future that will temporarily rule from the earthly throne in Jerusalem (1 Chr 3:10–16), the ultimate heir will be the Son of Man who will come in the flesh and rule globally from the eschatological Jerusalem with perfect justice and righteousness forever (2 Sam 7:16; 1 Chr 17:14; Isa 9:6–7; Jer 33:15–17, 20–21). The fulfillment of this promise is described in Luke 1:31–33 when the angel Gabriel tells Mary, "And behold, you will conceive in your womb and bear

15. Bavinck, *Reformed Dogmatics*, 3:220.

a son, and you shall call his name Jesus. He will be great and will be called the Son of the Most High. And the Lord God will *give to him the throne of his father David*, and he will reign over the house of Jacob forever, and of his kingdom there will be no end." Christ is now the kingly heir of David who was crucified on the cross but ascended to heaven to be at the Father's right hand (Acts 2:29–33). His current rule from above is only the inauguration of his ultimate rule on earth after he returns, defeats his enemies, and establishes his earthly kingdom (Rev 19:11—22:5). In this way the promises of the Davidic covenant will be realized in its completeness.

One issue that must be addressed concerning the Davidic covenant is whether it, like the Abrahamic and Mosaic covenants, contains any stipulations. We mentioned above that the Davidic covenant fully exemplifies the promissory character of God's covenant dealings with his people. However, this does not entail that the Davidic covenant contains absolutely no requirements to be fulfilled by the human beneficiary. In 2 Samuel 7:14, it is clearly indicated that God will surely chasten his son "with the stripes of the sons of men" if he "commits iniquity," even if his steadfast love towards him will remain (v. 15). Although the passage typologically refers to Christ, it also refers to Solomon in the immediate context (the direct son of David).[16] Therefore, even if the Davidic covenant contains a sure promise to David that God will raise up a Messianic king who will sit on his throne forever, there is still the obligation on the part of David and his descendants to live according to God's statutes and law.

### The New Covenant

The new covenant is in a sense the fulfillment of the prophetic promises given to the people of Israel under the old covenant. The first explicit mention of a new covenant is found in Jeremiah 31:31–34 (Ezekiel 37:24–28 also describes this covenant, though it is called a "covenant of peace" [v. 26]), which is later repeated in Hebrews 8:8–12 in the New Testament.[17] According to the passage in Jeremiah the new covenant will be characterized by four significant features:

---

16. Youngblood, "1, 2 Samuel," 3:893.

17. It should be kept in mind, however, that the author of Hebrews is quoting from the Septuagint (LXX) version of Jeremiah 31:31–34.

1. *It will be an unbreakable covenant.* Although the Israelites broke the covenant established at Sinai by their constant spiritual adultery ("my covenant that they broke" [v. 32]), the new covenant will be unlike the previous covenant because it will be an inviolable one. Although Jeremiah does not explicitly declare that this covenant will be inviolable, Ezekiel 37:26 describes the "covenant of peace" (another term for the new covenant) as being an everlasting covenant between God and his people. Another place that suggests that the new covenant is everlasting and permanent is found in the Epistle to the Hebrews in the New Testament. The author of the letter writes that by the "means of his own blood," Jesus Christ secures "an eternal redemption" (Heb 9:12), and that he has "appeared once for all at the end of the ages to put away sin by the sacrifice of himself" (Heb 9:26). Therefore, according to the biblical testimony, the new covenant is a covenant that will never fail for those who truly belong to it.

2. *It will be a covenant that will bring genuine transformation of heart.* Although the Mosaic covenant (and its law) was established by God's grace, it did not include in it the power to obey the stipulations of the covenant. Israel as a whole was unfaithful to God and incurred the sanctions of the old covenant. In the new covenant, however, God will write his law in the hearts of his people so that they will faithfully abide by its stipulations and avoid incurring the punishments that fell on the Israelites (v. 33; cf. Rom 11:26; Heb 8:10; 10:16). As D. A. Carson notes: "The new covenant will not be like the tribal covenant associated with Moses' name, when the fathers ate sour grapes and their children's teeth were set on edge. Rather, it is characterized by the removal of the heart of stone among all of God's covenantal people. To use the language of Ezekiel 36, the new covenant will be characterized by cleansing (sprinkling with water) and spiritual renewal (a new heart and a new spirit)."[18] Therefore, the new covenant includes the promise of perseverance in faith and obedience.[19]

3. *It will be a covenant that will bring intimate fellowship between God and his people.* One of the key features of the covenant is that God will truly be the God of his people and his people shall truly belong to him (v. 33). Also, *all* those in the new covenant will know God on

18. Carson, "Reflections on Assurance," 394.

19. A more thorough treatment of the doctrine of the perseverance of the saints will be given in chapter 15.

a personal and intimate level (v. 34; Heb 8:10). Hypocrites and self-deceived confessors within the visible assembly of the Messiah will not be part of this covenant. All those in the new covenant will be genuine believers who have been renewed by the Spirit and have an intimate relationship with the triune God. As David L. Baker states, "One important characteristic of the new covenant, according to Jeremiah 31:34a, is personal knowledge of God."[20]

4. *It will be a covenant that will wipe away all sins and transgressions for those who belong to it.* Those in the new covenant will have *all* their sins forgiven by God so that he will "remember their sin no more" (v. 34; cf. Rom 11:27; Heb 8:12; 10:17). This will become a certain reality because Israel's Messiah—Jesus Christ the Lamb of God—is the ultimate propitiatory sacrifice for those who truly belong to God (cf. Rom 3:25). The animal sacrifices in the Mosaic covenant were merely foreshadowings of the perfect sacrifice of the Son of Man (Heb 9:19–28; 10:4, 11–14) who will do away with all the sins of those who have entrusted themselves to him. Therefore, all those who truly belong to the new covenant will have all their sins paid for *in full* through the sacrificial work of Jesus Christ.

One question that may bring about animated discussion among Christians is the matter of the scope of the new covenant. Does not Jeremiah 31:31 and Ezekiel 37:16–23 state that this covenant shall *only* be given to the physical descendants of Abraham, Isaac, and Jacob? Although the OT prophets envisaged a spiritual renewal for the houses of Israel and Judah, the whole biblical testimony reveals that this covenant is not only restricted to those who belong to the physical lineage of Abraham. It is a covenant for *all* those who entrust themselves to Jesus Christ as their Lord and Savior through faith. The author of Hebrews not only makes this claim (Heb 8) but so do Jesus and the apostle Paul. For instance, on the night before his crucifixion, Jesus, at the table with his disciples, declares to them that the cup which represents his sacrifice "is the new covenant" of his blood (Luke 22:20; Matt 26:28). The institution of the Lord's Supper that Christians partake of today is a memorial sign of the new covenant established by Christ's death. Also, the apostle Paul links the Lord's Supper, that the Corinthian believers were participating in, with the new covenant (1 Cor 11:25). Elsewhere he contrasts the old covenant established at Sinai

20. Baker, *Two Testaments, One Bible*, 259–60.

with the new covenant inaugurated by Christ—which is for all believers, whether Jew or gentile (2 Cor 3:6, 14; Gal 4:21–31). This demonstrates that the new covenant is not restricted to a future time period for a large number of the physical descendants of Abraham when they will be brought into the covenant by embracing their Messiah (cf. Rom 11:25–26),[21] but that it is for all those who come to the Lamb of God for forgiveness and salvation through faith.

Another issue we must discuss pertaining to the new covenant is whether or not it is conditional in character like the covenant established at Sinai. Based on what we have said above about the new covenant, we must affirm that the new covenant is also conditional in character. Although the new covenant is superior in many ways and much more effective in dealing with sin compared to the Mosaic covenant, there is still a conditional element in the new covenant in a *consequential sense*. Even with the sure pronouncement by Ezekiel of the eternal character of this covenant and the declaration by Jeremiah of its effectiveness in removing all sin, it is still conditional in the sense that those who belong to it will obey the stipulations contained in it—not as a way of keeping oneself in the covenant but as the evidence that one truly has responded to God's saving initiative. To put it differently, not only does the new covenant provide complete forgiveness through the atoning sacrifice of Christ, it also guarantees that those who belong to it will persevere in obeying God's law through the power of the Holy Spirit (Jer 31:33; Heb 8:10), albeit imperfectly (cf. James 3:2; 1 John 1:8–10). God's law will be written in the hearts of believers so that their lives will be *characterized* by righteousness rather than sin. As Thomas R. Schreiner writes, "The new covenant fulfils the command to circumcise the heart found in Deuteronomy (10:16; cf. Jer. 4:4; 9:25–26), for in the new covenant God writes his law on the hearts of his people and definitely forgives their sins."[22] Therefore, although the new covenant is a permanent covenantal arrangement, in contrast to the Mosaic covenant which put primacy on the performance of duties for its maintenance (cf. Lev 18:2–5), it is still a covenant that demands obedience on its beneficiaries but only as the *evidence* and *fruit* of being in a covenant relationship with God through Christ's redemptive work.

---

21. We will discuss this subject in more detail in chapter 16 on the church.

22. Schreiner, "Commands of God," 78.

## The Question of the "Covenant of Works"

According to the confessional Reformed tradition, as embodied in the Westminster Standards and the Three Forms of Unity, God established a "covenant of works" with Adam and his posterity in which eternal life is promised on the condition of absolute and flawless obedience to God. According to the Westminster Confession of Faith, the "first covenant made with man was a covenant of works, wherein life was promised to Adam; and in him to his posterity, upon condition of perfect and personal obedience" (VII/2). Thomas Watson, a seventeenth-century Puritan theologian, describes the main characteristics of the covenant this way:

> The covenant of works was very strict. God required of Adam and all mankind, (1.) Perfect obedience. Adam must do all things written in the 'book of the law,' and not fail, either in the matter or manner. Gal iii 10. Adam was to live up to the whole breadth of the moral law, and go exactly according to it, as a well-made dial goes with the sun. One sinful thought would have forfeited the covenant. (2.) Personal Obedience. Adam must not do his work by a proxy, or have any surety bound for him; but it must be done in his own person. (3.) Perpetual obedience. He must continue in all things written in 'the book of the law.' Gal iii 10. *Thus, it was very strict. There was no mercy in case of failure.*[23]

Therefore, the covenant of works was a strictly legal covenant that conferred eternal life to those who perfectly fulfilled the terms of the covenant by flawlessly obeying God's divine law.[24]

Reformed theologians typically argue that the covenant of works is a biblically-based concept grounded upon exegetical and theological factors. The argument from exegesis is largely based on a peculiar reading of Hosea 6:7. The verse in Hosea reads this way in the English Standard Version: "But like Adam they transgressed the covenant; there they dealt faithlessly with me." Other versions, like the New Revised Standard Version, translate the Hebrew *'adam* as a locality ("at Adam"). Although the way one translates *'adam* may not definitively decide whether the idea of the covenant of works is hermeneutically feasible, one can still argue that it is highly questionable to formulate a major theological concept around one verse in the Bible. The verse is ambiguous and can be interpreted to mean a locale, the human race

23. Watson, *Body of Divinity*, 129–30 (emphasis added).

24. There is debate among Reformed theologians on whether the covenant of works is strictly a legal covenant or a covenant that has elements of divine grace in it.

in general, or a person (in this case, the first man Adam). Even if it does re-fer to the historical Adam, the verse does not give clear evidence to suggest that a prelapsarian legal covenant was established between God and Adam in Eden.[25] The verse, however, must be interpreted in the contextual back-ground of the book of Hosea: the covenant unfaithfulness of Israel. The use of Adam in that verse was merely to point out that the Israelites had done something treacherous—like Adam, who disobeyed God's direct command to not eat from the forbidden tree—by turning away from God to follow after idols.[26] Even John Calvin, who is considered by many to be one of the key architects of the Reformed wing of Protestantism, questioned whether Hosea 6:7 can be used as a text to prove the existence of a prelapsarian covenant between God and Adam.[27]

The second argument that Reformed theologians use to argue for the existence of the covenant of works is theological. The argument is based on the notion that Adam and Christ are the respective "federal heads" of the reprobate and elect. In theological circles, this has been called covenant or

25. Even the Reformed theologian Anthony A. Hoekema writes that "there is no in-dication in these early chapters of Genesis of a covenant oath or a covenant ratification ceremony. When we read about the probationary or test command in Genesis 2:16–17, nothing is said about either a covenant oath or a ratification ceremony. Much light has been shed on the nature of covenants in ancient times, including those mentioned in the Bible, by recent research into ancient Near Eastern covenantal treaties. These research-ers found that the covenants of the Old Testament—particularly those described in the later chapters of Genesis (beginning with chap. 15), Exodus, and Deuteronomy—were always ratified by an oath and commonly accompanied by a ceremony, which in some cases involved the cutting up and/or sacrificing of animals. If such confirmatory oaths were characteristic of covenants in those days, as the evidence now indicates, we do not seem to be warranted in concluding that the arrangement God made with Adam and Eve before the Fall was covenantal in nature" (*Created in God's Image*, 120).

26. Robert L. Reymond argues that the elements of the covenant clearly exist in the Genesis 2 narrative. Thus, a covenant must have been enacted between God and Adam before the fall. Even though he acknowledges that the word "covenant" does not oc-cur in Genesis 2, he states that covenantal elements (parties, stipulation, promise, and threat) are present in God's command to Adam in Genesis 2:16–17 (cf. *A New Systematic Theology of the Christian Faith*, 430). However, this is mere conjecture. Just because there are two parties, a stipulation with a promise and threat, does not necessarily mean a covenant arrangement exists.

27. He writes: "Others explain the words thus, 'They have transgressed as Adam the covenant.' But the word, Adam, we know, is taken indefinitely for men. This exposition is frigid and diluted, 'They have transgressed as Adam the covenant;' that is, they have followed or imitated the example of their father Adam, who had immediately at the be-ginning transgressed God's commandment. I do not stop to refute this comment; for we see that it is in itself vapid" (Calvin, *Comm.* Hosea 6:7).

federal theology.[28] This federal theological structure is largely based on a particular interpretation of Romans 5:12–21. Reformed theologians who advocate a federalist understanding of redemptive history argue that just as Adam is the representative head of all those still under the dominion of sin (Rom 5:12, 15, 17–19), Christ is the representative head of all those who have been spiritually made alive by his sacrifice (Rom 5:18–19). To put it another way, those still under the covenant of works (unbelievers) are those still under the federal headship of Adam, while those now under the covenant of grace (believers) are those who are now under the federal headship of Christ. Although there are some strengths in formulating the matter this way, it is improper to call the respective headships of Adam and Christ "federal." Christians of non-Reformed persuasions will agree that there is a dual representational motif occurring in Romans 5:12–21, but disagree that it is a federal headship phenomenon. All Paul could mean is that Adam's transgression has caused the spiritual death and guilt of all humanity outside of Christ, and that only in Christ are the consequences of that transgression reversed. It does not necessarily mean that God made a covenant of works with Adam demanding perfect and perpetual obedience, which all unredeemed human beings are now under also. One can still hold to a representational understanding of Adam's role in relation to the rest of humanity without embracing the Reformed doctrine of the covenant of works.[29]

28. What is popularly known as covenant theology today was systematically developed for the first time (though discussions of the covenant were present in writings of previous Reformed thinkers) by two Reformed theologians: Zacharias Ursinus (1534–83) and Caspar Olevianus (1536–87). According to covenant theology, God made a "covenant of works" with Adam which demanded perfect obedience. However, because Adam failed to fulfill that requirement God made a second covenant called the "covenant of grace"—a covenant that offers life and salvation through Jesus Christ the Mediator (some Reformed theologians add a third covenant called the "covenant of redemption" between God the Father and God the Son). The substance of this covenant is the same in all redemptive periods, though it is administered differently in each period (cf. Osterhaven, "Covenant Theology," 279–80).

29. If a covenant between God and Adam did exist during the prelapsarian state, that covenant has been irrevocably abolished due to Adam's transgression. There is no scriptural support for the existence of a trans-historical covenant of works that all human beings after the fall are under.

## The Question of "Monocovenantalism"

### What Is "Monocovenantalism"?

Another controversial issue in recent years involving the theology of the biblical covenants is the subject of "monocovenantalism."[30] Those who advocate a monocovenantalist understanding of the relationship amongst the divine-human covenants in redemptive history argue that all the redemptive covenants are essentially the same in substance: the promise of eternal blessing for obedience with threats of eternal punishment for disobedience (in its most basic form). Scott J. Hafemann, an advocate of this position, writes: "God's promises (or curses) for the future are therefore dependent upon keeping (or not keeping) his commands in the present, as they flow from what God has done (or not done) in the past and continues to do (or not do) in the present."[31] In essence, therefore, the Mosaic and new covenants are not all that different in *substance*, although the *form* of each covenant may differ in some fashion. Other popular advocates of this perspective include Norman Shepherd,[32] Daniel P. Fuller,[33] and William J. Dumbrell.[34]

Although not identical in every respect when it comes to understanding the role of each covenant in God's salvific purpose in history, all of the authors mentioned above argue that there is a strict continuity between law and gospel, the Mosaic and new covenants. According to them, it is not only the new covenant that genuinely confers eternal life to those who fulfill its stipulations but also the Mosaic covenant. The differences being that the new covenant is wider in scope (not limited to the nation of Israel) and contains within it the promise of the indwelling of the Holy Spirit. For instance, Hafemann writes:

> In the new covenant, *as in the Sinai covenant before it*, keeping the law, made possible by God's prior act of redemption (cf. Jer. 31:1–40), is what maintains the covenantal relationship between God and his people. . . . The contrast between the 'old' and new

30. Jeffrey J. Niehaus calls this the "One Divine Covenant" view ("Argument Against Theologically Constructed Covenants," 264–70); cf. also Horton, *Covenant and Salvation*, 80–101.

31. Hafemann, "Covenant Relationship," 38.

32. Shepherd, *Call of Grace*.

33. Fuller, *Unity of the Bible*.

34. Dumbrell, *Covenant and Creation*.

covenants is not a contrast between a covenant with and without an external law; nor is it a contrast between two different kinds of law. Rather, the contrast between the two covenants *is a contrast between two different conditions of the people* who are brought into these covenants and their correspondingly different responses to the same law.[35]

Therefore, according to the various monocovenantal perspectives, the difference between the Mosaic and new covenants is not a fundamental difference between law and gospel (or works and grace), but a difference between whether or not God gives the enablement (through the Holy Spirit) to the human beneficiaries to fulfill the terms of the covenant (which he does in the latter covenant but did not in the former). In other words, the substance of both covenants remain the same, although those under the new covenant now have the God-given power through the Spirit to persevere in fulfilling the terms of the covenant so that they can obtain salvation at the end.

## A Critique of the Monocovenantal Perspective

Although one can laud this approach for attempting to maintain the unity of Scripture and the salvific work of God throughout the different periods of redemptive history, we must conclude that this approach has several inadequacies from a biblical and theological point of view.

First, the Mosaic covenant (and the law contained within it) was never intended to bestow *eternal* life to those who were under it. Paul makes this clear in 2 Corinthians 3:7 when he calls the Mosaic covenant administration a "ministry of death." Furthermore, in Romans 3:28 (cf. Rom 3:20; Gal 2:16; Phil 3:9) he states that individuals are "justified by faith apart from works of the law." The "works of the law" in this verse (and other Pauline passages) clearly mean the entire Mosaic law and its demands.[36] Notice that Paul here contrasts the "works of the law" with faith when it comes to the justification of believers.

Second, the Mosaic covenant was *national* in character and only pertained to the community of Israel. It was a means not only to make the Israelites distinct from their pagan neighbors (Exod 19:5), but also to establish

35. Hafemann, "Covenant Relationship," 53–54 (emphases added).

36. Moo, "Law of Christ," 329. A more detailed treatment of this issue will be given in chapter 14 on the doctrine of justification.

them as a holy nation of priests (Exod 19:5–6). It was also given as a guardian until the prophecies of the coming Messiah were fulfilled (Gal 3:19, 24), and not as a path to obtain justification and eternal life (Gal 3:21–22).

Third, the promises of the Mosaic covenant were *temporal* and *earthly*. There is no indication that the Mosaic covenant offered *eternal life* to those who followed its demands. In fact, all indications suggest that the Mosaic covenant only promised earthly prosperity and numerous blessings in the land if the Israelites fulfilled their side of the covenant (cf. Deut 28:1–14; 29:9; 30:16). The punishments for failing to keep the terms of the covenant were expulsion from the land and the loss of other earthly blessings (cf. Deut 28:58–68; 29:16–29; 30:18).[37]

Fourth, the demands of the Mosaic covenant were never intended to be faithfully observed by the Israelites (cf. Rom 11:31–32). One of the functions of the Mosaic law, with its strict demands, was to lead sinners away from themselves and to show them how they drastically fall short of God's holy standard (Gal 3:10–11; cf. Rom 9:31–32); which, in turn, would lead them to trust in the coming Messiah alone for forgiveness and redemption (Gal 3:22).

Fifth, embracing a too straightforward continuity between the Mosaic and new covenants poses problems when it comes to making proper distinctions between law and gospel (or works and grace).[38] The faithful

37. The author of Hebrews gives some indication of this when he writes in Hebrews 10:28–29: "Anyone who has set aside the law of Moses dies without mercy on the evidence of two or three witnesses. *How much worse punishment*, do you think, will be deserved by the one who has spurned the Son of God, and has profaned the blood of the covenant by which he was sanctified, and has outraged the Spirit of grace?" The most one can say about this passage is that the penalty for disobedience to the Mosaic covenant only prefigured the eternal damnation of the lost at the final judgment.

38. Jeffrey J. Niehaus rightly recognizes that if Dumbrell's formulation of the biblical covenants is correct then the logical consequence would be the blurring of the differences among the covenants—which also leads perilously close to blurring the lines between law and gospel. He writes: "Dumbrell's observation that the law given at Sinai will be 'reapplied in the same way in the new age' is the logical result of the blurring of covenants which he has accomplished" ("Argument Against Theologically Constructed Covenants," 269). If the Mosaic law is "reapplied" in the same way under the new covenant one must ask why the apostle Paul vigorously attacked those who attempted to maintain the law (with the aid of grace) as a path to salvation (cf. Gal 3:1–18). Paul's vigorous attacks against the view of the Judaizers (that keeping the "works of the law" as still being valid for the new covenant age) appears to be more than just about a redemptive-historical shift that has occurred through the death of Christ. Rather, he seems to be attacking something more fundamental: the error that God's grace must somehow be added by human works in order for salvation to be fully realized.

remnant in Israel under the old covenant were never justified because of their strict adherence to the Mosaic law but on account of their faith in the promised Messiah who would make a perfect atonement for their sins (Heb 10:1–10, 15–17; cf. Rom 9:32; 11:26–27). Therefore, the saints under the old covenant were already saved by the salvific work of the Messiah under the provisions of the new covenant to come (cf. 1 Cor 10:4)[39] apart from their observance of the law.[40]

## Why the Proper Understanding of the Covenants Matter

A proper understanding of the biblical covenants is essential in properly articulating the relationship between law and gospel and, therefore, properly understanding the relationship between works and grace in the whole context of salvation. Hence, this is one of the reasons why we devoted an entire chapter to this topic. The way we understand the covenants in redemptive history shapes the way we understand the gospel message—its promises and demands. The doctrine of the covenant is a largely neglected topic in mainstream evangelicalism today and a revitalization of this subject will help ministers and laypeople alike to have a proper understanding of how God's work of salvation in Christ impacts the way they should live in light of the future coming of Christ's reign in its full glory. May we marvel at God's glory and grace as we seek to live according to the principles of his kingdom made possible by our covenant relationship with him in Jesus Christ.

39. Although the whole passage of 1 Cor 10:1–10 refers to the wilderness generation who displeased God and were judged for their idolatry and immorality, Paul still makes it clear to his readers that the "spiritual rock" that the Israelites drank from was Christ himself (v. 4). Therefore, the Israelites under the old covenant had enough signs of a coming Messiah who would take away their sins by their trusting in his salvific provision.

40. The obedience of the elect Israelite to the requirements of the Mosaic law was *only* the fruit and evidence of his or her salvation—not as a secondary means, alongside faith, to obtain eternal life.

# CHAPTER 8

# Christology

SINCE THE EARLIEST DAYS of the church the doctrine of the person of Christ (Christology) has played a pivotal role in determining the boundaries of Christian orthodoxy. One only needs to survey the theological battles of the early church to know that one of the most animated discussions of theology at the time centered on the person and identity of Jesus Christ. Not only did a proper understanding of the person of Christ provide the church a solid doctrinal foundation against the assaults of the enemies of the church but it also provided a backbone for other essential biblical doctrines as well, most notably the work of Christ.

In this chapter, we will discuss five topics that have commonly been understood as focal points of debate throughout the history of the church regarding the person and identity of Jesus Christ: 1) the preexistence and eternality of Christ; 2) the humanity of Christ; 3) the deity of Christ; 4) the relationship between deity and humanity in Jesus Christ; and 5) the mission of Jesus during his earthly ministry. The view that is espoused in this chapter is the christological position formulated at the Council of Chalcedon (451 AD), which is embraced by all orthodox Christian traditions today.

## The Preexistence and Eternality of Christ

One of the fundamental beliefs of Christian orthodoxy is that the Son of God existed prior to his physical birth from the womb of the virgin Mary. However, Christian orthodoxy also went further and stated that not only did God the Son exist prior to his birth in Bethlehem but that he also existed from *eternity*. As discussed above (chapter 2), in contrast to the beliefs of the Arians, the Son of God was never created at any point—even before the creation of the cosmos. This understanding of Christ's preexistence and eternality was not something the early church theologians logically deduced because of their belief in the triune Godhead or the supernatural nature of the incarnate Son's redemptive action for humankind, but has its basis in the revelation of Scripture.

One well-known passage in Scripture that supports the preexistence and eternality of the Son of God is John 8:58, when Jesus tells the Jews: "Truly, truly, I say to you, before Abraham was, I am." The violent reaction of the Jews towards Jesus because of this statement regarding himself (v. 59) reveals that the Jews fully understood the implications of this statement because it inferred that Jesus was claiming himself to be equal to God and, therefore, eternally preexistent.

Another passage that demonstrates to the truth of Christ's preexistence and eternality is Paul's statement in Colossians 1:16–17 when he writes: "For by him all things were created, in heaven and on earth, visible and invisible, whether thrones or dominions or rulers or authorities—all things were created through him and for him. *And he is before all things*, and in him all things hold together." The fact that through the Son of God "all things were created" and that he is "before all things" demonstrates to the preexistence and eternality of the Son because only someone who is eternally preexistent can bring things into existence. Two other significant passages in the New Testament that can be used to support the preexistence and eternality of the Son of God are Philippians 2:6 and Hebrews 1:2–11.

Even without these explicit statements of Scripture supporting the Son's eternal preexistence, we can conclude with reasonable certainty the truth of Christ's eternal preexistence based on his divine nature and being the second person of the triune Godhead. In chapter 2, we established the triune nature of God based on the revelation of Scripture, and below we will also demonstrate the full deity of the Son using the same Scripture. Since we have demonstrated (and will demonstrate further below) the full deity of the Son, it is only theologically sensible to conclude that the Son is also eternally preexistent because of him possessing all the attributes of deity. Therefore, Jesus Christ was eternally preexistent before his incarnation like God the Father.[1]

1. Some theologians in recent years have concluded that God the Son is eternally subordinate to God the Father within the triune Godhead (cf. Ware, *Father, Son, and the*

## The Humanity of Jesus Christ

*Jesus Christ Had a Fully Human Body, Mind, and Soul*

One of the earliest christological heresies that the primitive church had to face against was the denial of Jesus' full humanity. In the First Epistle of John, the apostle had to affirm again to his readers—against the beliefs of proto-gnostic infiltrators in the church who denied that the Son of God truly came in the flesh—of the full humanity of Christ as witnessed and observed by the apostles themselves ("heard," "seen," and "touched" [1 John 1:1]). John even goes on to declare later in the same epistle that his readers do know the Spirit of God because "every spirit that confesses that Jesus Christ has come in the flesh is from God" (1 John 4:2). A true Christian confession includes the affirmation that the Son of God became incarnate in full human flesh. Negatively, the apostle declares that any spirit that does not acknowledge Jesus Christ as who he truly is comes from the spirit of the antichrist (1 John 4:3)—a serious pronouncement against the gnosticizing false teachers and all who follow them. In other words, the christological heresy that John's opponents were espousing was the belief that the Son of God only *appeared* to come in human flesh—that Jesus' humanity was merely an apparition. The church has traditionally labeled this view Docetism (from the Greek word *dokeō*, which means "to appear"), and it has always been rightfully condemned as a heresy by all the major branches of Christianity. In the epistle, therefore, the apostle John was basically reiterating in stronger words what he wrote at the beginning of his Gospel that described who the Incarnate Son was: "the Word became flesh and dwelt among us" (John 1:14).

Other biblical references also affirm without reservation that Jesus Christ is fully human. In Luke 2:52, after narrating the incident between the boy Jesus and the teachers at the temple in Jerusalem (Luke 2:41–47), Luke tells us that Jesus "increased in wisdom and in stature and in favor with God and man." This verse indicates that despite Christ's full divinity, he grew in wisdom like any other human being. He also grew in stature—meaning that he physically matured over the years unto adulthood like other human beings. Jesus also experienced the daily physical limitations

---

*Holy Spirit*, 21). However, we argue that this view can lead to a disruption in the work of creation and redemption done in harmony among the three persons of the Trinity due to the fact that this understanding leads to a disjunction between the Father and the Son in terms of what was willed for the creation of the world and the redemption of humankind.

of being human. For instance, he became hungry during his fast in the wilderness (Matt 4:2), experienced thirst (John 19:28), became physically tired when he exerted himself (John 4:6), and experienced the need for sleep (Mark 4:38; cf. Matt 26:41). He was also bound to the normal space-time limitations that all human beings experience in this age.

Jesus not only experienced the physical limitations of being human, he also experienced human emotions. Jesus experienced human love, as demonstrated in his love towards a particular disciple (John 13:23), Lazarus (John 11:3), and the rich young man (Mark 10:21). Jesus also had compassion and pity on those who were hungry (Mark 6:34) and sick (Matt 14:14; 20:34). He also experienced other types of human emotions like joy (John 15:11), anger (Mark 3:5; John 2:15–16), indignation (Mark 10:14), distress or trouble (Mark 14:33–36; Luke 12:50; John 12:27), loneliness (Mark 15:34), and even surprise—in a manner that is both positive (Luke 7:9) and negative (Mark 6:6).

In addition to experiencing human emotions, he also displayed intellectual abilities consistent with being fully human. For instance, his questioning of the father who had an epileptic son regarding how long his son had been in that condition reveals that he needed information to assess the situation (Mark 9:21). Also, Jesus told his disciples that no one knows, not even the angels *or himself*, the day and hour of his return (Matt 24:36; Mark 13:32), which clearly demonstrates to his humanity in terms of what kinds of knowledge he was able to possess. The above points indicate that Jesus' humanity not only pertained to the physical aspects of his personhood but also the emotional and intellectual. The Gospels, therefore, provide us with a portrayal of Jesus that is fully human in every way.

The best demonstration of Jesus' humanity, however, is the death he experienced on the cross. Nothing could reveal the complete humanity of Jesus more than what he experienced on that day at Golgotha (Mark 15:22). This fact was never lost to the apostles and the biblical writers. For instance, the author of Hebrews clearly knew that Jesus' death on the cross was a real death not dissimilar to the deaths of other human beings (cf. Heb 2:9). The author also mentions the fact that *he partook of the same flesh and blood of the human race* for the purpose of destroying the works of the devil and delivering those who were held in captivity to the fear of death through his own sacrifice (Heb 2:14–15). In addition, one only needs to read the descriptions of his death in the four Gospel accounts to know that what he experienced on the cross was a true death with no indication at all that it was some other phenomenon (cf. Matt 27:45–56; Mark 15:33–41; Luke 23:44–49; note the graphic description in John 19:32–34). As Wayne Grudem notes, "The culmination of Jesus' limitations in terms of his human body is seen when he died on the cross (Luke 23:46). His human body ceased to have life in it and ceased to function, just as ours does when we die."[2] The reality of Christ's death nullifies, therefore, any notion that his humanity was merely an illusion or an apparition (the heresy of Docetism). Christ truly suffered death on the cross because he was truly human in the flesh.

*Jesus Christ Was Fully Human but Sinless*

The Scriptures make it clear that although Christ was fully human in every respect, he was without sin in every way—whether in actual deeds or inherently. His resistance to the temptations of the devil in the wilderness demonstrate that he was righteous in every regard (Matt 4:1–11; Luke 4:1–13). When Jesus spoke to the Jews he told them: "I am the light of the world" (John 8:12), and when the Jews shortly thereafter confronted him, he answered back: "Which one of you convicts me of sin?" (John 8:46). In John 15:10, he tells his disciples, "If you keep my commandments, you will abide in my love, just as *I have kept my Father's commandments and abide in his love.*" Later on in his trial before the crucifixion, Pilate tells the Jews that he could "find no guilt in him" (John 18:38). In addition, some of the apostle Paul's statements make it clear that Jesus was without sin. In Romans 5:18–19, Paul makes a contrast between the disobedience of Adam that led to the death of the human race and the righteousness of Christ that leads to justification and life for many.

In 2 Corinthians 5:21, Paul tells the believers at Corinth that for our sake God "made him [Christ] to be sin *who knew no sin,* so that in him we might become the righteousness of God." The other apostles also affirm this important truth. Peter declares that Jesus Christ is "like that of a lamb without blemish or spot" (1 Pet 1:19), and that he "committed no sin" and neither "was deceit found in his mouth" (1 Pet 2:22). He also states that his sacrificial death was "the righteous for the unrighteous" so that "he might bring us to God" (1 Pet 3:18). In his first epistle, John calls Jesus Christ "the righteous" (1 John 2:1), and states later on that "in him there is no sin" (1 John 3:5). Finally, the author of Hebrews states: "For we do not have

2. Grudem, *Systematic Theology,* 532.

a high priest who is unable to sympathize with our weaknesses, but one who in every respect has been tempted as we are, *yet without sin*" (Heb 4:15), and goes on to declare furthermore that Christ, as our high priest, is "holy, innocent, unstained, separated from sinners, and exalted above the heavens" (Heb 7:26). The scriptural testimony is very clear that Jesus Christ was completely sinless during his life on earth.

One of the most debated questions in Christian theological discussions regarding the nature of Christ's humanity is whether Christ could have sinned during his state of humiliation. Those who affirm that Christ could have sinned believe in what is called the doctrine of *peccability*. Those who embrace this view argue that Christ endured true human temptations during his earthly ministry and, therefore, the existence of genuine temptations implies that the possibility of sinning was real for him (Hebrews 4:15 is often referenced to defend this view). For example, the Reformed theologian Charles Hodge writes: "Temptation implies the possibility of sin. If from the constitution of his person it was impossible for Christ to sin, then his temptation was unreal and without effect, and He cannot sympathize with his people."[3] On the other hand, those who reject the idea that it was possible for Christ to have sinned believe in what is called the doctrine of *impeccability*. Those who hold this view argue that the divine nature in Christ could not allow for the possibility for Christ to sin, since it is impossible for God to sin. J. van Genderen and W. H. Velema, proponents of this view, state that Christ's "humanity is so united with his divinity that it is unthinkable that he could bring himself to commit sin. He is the holy Son of God, conceived of the Holy Spirit, and always guided by the Spirit. He neither desired to sin nor could sin."[4]

Both sides in this debate have a strong case for their respective positions. The strength of the peccability of view is that it fully recognizes the genuineness of Christ's humanity against the error of Docetism; on the other hand, the strength of the impeccability view is that it does full justice to the deity of Christ against any view that attempts to downplay his divine nature. When examining both of these arguments in this debate, however, it appears that the impeccability position has a much stronger case. The fact that Jesus endured temptations during his time on earth does not imply that he had the capacity—like that of fallen humanity—to transgress God's law. We can argue that Christ's actual sinlessness was in fact a necessary

3. Hodge, *Systematic Theology*, 2:457.
4. Genderen and Velema, *Concise Reformed Dogmatics*, 459.

consequence of his *inability* to sin. His divine nature prevented him from actually committing sin, though in his humanity he experienced the same temptations that any other human being faces.[5] Despite the disagreements among theologians on this subject, all orthodox Christians can agree with Daniel L. Akin when he writes:

> In the end we must affirm the two propositions with which we began: (1) Jesus was genuinely tempted, and (2) Jesus did not sin. Scripture does not address directly the "could he have sinned" question, and we should rest content in what has been revealed to us. Second Corinthians 5:21 and Hebrews 4:15 make clear that Jesus was sinless. This is the nonnegotiable teaching of the Bible.[6]

Although Christians will not agree on the exact details of what it means for Jesus to be the sinless man, all those who uphold the faith of the apostles can agree that Jesus as a fully human being experienced all the common temptations of human beings, yet did not succumb to them as a consequence of being the God-man.

## *The Virgin Birth of Jesus*

Since the time of the primitive church Christians have always maintained that the virgin birth of Christ is a significant aspect of Christ's identity. In one way or another, the virgin birth of Christ always held a pivotal place in the traditional dogmas of the historic Christian faith. For instance, in the Apostles' Creed (one of the earliest ecumenical confessions) it declares that Jesus Christ "was conceived by the Holy Ghost, born of the virgin Mary." This key apostolic belief, however, is confronted with serious skepticism or even outright ridicule in modern times. The questioning of the virgin birth

---

5. Oliver D. Crisp makes this insightful point in defense of the impeccability position: "The defender of the sinlessness [peccability] view cannot claim, as the defender of impeccability may, that Christ has the capacity to sin (*qua* human) but is incapable of ever exercising that capacity, because, say, his divine nature prevents such an outcome or would prevent it, if it became necessary, though such an eventuality never in fact arose. To remain consistent, the defender of the sinlessness view must affirm that Christ (a) had the capacity to sin (*qua* human) and (b) had the capacity to sin (*qua* divine). To affirm the first without the second is to play into the hands of the advocates of Christ's impeccability. In short, if Christ really could have sinned—but did not—then he must have been able to choose to sin *as the God-Man*. The logic of the sinlessness position drives in this direction" (*God Incarnate*, 134).

6. Akin, "Person of Christ," 418.

has not only come from those outside of Christian quarters but also from those within. For example, the Swiss neoorthodox theologian Emil Brunner writes (regarding the church's affirmation of the virgin birth):

> If it be true that Matthew and Luke are simply dealing with the question: how did the Person of the Redeemer come into existence? and not with the Incarnation of the Eternal Son of God, this is a Christological view which the Church cannot accept. In point of fact, the Church never *has* accepted this view, but it has re-interpreted it in a sense which alone could make it acceptable.[7]

Although skepticism towards the virgin birth of Christ has rapidly increased in recent years with the explosion of scientific knowledge and modernity's tendency towards a more naturalistic view of the world, Christians who uphold the apostolic and evangelical faith must remain more committed in defending this essential christological doctrine. One may still, however, understandably inquire what purpose it serves to vigilantly keep this doctrine in the confessions of the church today. Some may object that belief in the virgin birth is merely a relic of a superstitious past which contradicts common sense and the laws of medical science. However, as we will see below, Christians must defend and guard this doctrine because it has significant christological significance for the church's witness today.

One of the reasons why Christians today must do their utmost to uphold this doctrine is because it is a doctrine that is explicitly taught in Scripture. If one does away with the belief in the virgin birth of Christ we undermine Scripture's authority on other matters of faith and doctrine. The accounts given in the Gospels of Matthew and Luke clearly tell us how Jesus Christ was conceived and born. In Luke's account, he tells us that Mary was "a virgin betrothed to a man whose name was Joseph, of the house of David" (Luke 1:27). Mary is greatly surprised by the news given by the angel Gabriel that she will conceive and give birth to a child whom she will name Jesus—the Son of the Most High who will sit on David's throne and reign over the house of Jacob forever (Luke 1:32–33)—due to the fact that she was still a virgin (Luke 1:34). To this, Gabriel replies to Mary: "The Holy Spirit will come upon you, and the power of the Most High will overshadow you; therefore the child to be born will be called holy—the Son of God" (Luke 1:35). It is clear that Gabriel is describing a supernatural conception in Mary's womb not assisted by Joseph or any other male human being. This understanding is strengthened by the fact that shortly after Gabriel

---

7. Brunner, *Christian Doctrine of Creation and Redemption*, 353.

tells of John the Baptist's birth by Elizabeth as not involving the Holy Spirit and the power of the Most High, although it was in some way also a miraculous event (Luke 1:35–36). In the account given by Matthew, however, there is an added detail not given by Luke. In Matthew 1:19, it states that Joseph "resolved" to divorce Mary quietly after he had found out she was with child (Matt 1:18). This was to prevent Mary from being shamed for being pregnant with a child out of wedlock (Matt 1:19).[8] However, in a dream an angel of the Lord tells Joseph not to be afraid to take Mary as his wife because "that which is conceived in her is from the Holy Spirit" (Matt 1:20). Matthew then proceeds to quote a prophecy from Isaiah 7:14 in Matthew 1:23 to let his readers know that Jesus' birth was not an ordinary birth but a supernatural one prophesied in the Scriptures (the Old Testament at that time).[9] Therefore, through these two Gospel accounts, Scripture gives us enough testimony to indicate that Jesus' birth was no ordinary birth through normal reproductive processes but a supernatural one brought about by the Holy Spirit.

Despite the biblical evidence for the virgin birth, one may still ask what the theological significance is to affirm the virgin birth of Christ in our confessional statements. We maintain that there are three significant theological implications that arise out of this doctrine: 1) it proclaims that salvation is ultimately God's sovereign work of grace apart from the merits of human beings; 2) that Jesus Christ is not a result of ordinary human reproductive processes but a result of God supernaturally entering the

8. Millard J. Erickson states that Matthew may have included this account in his Gospel "because a rumor of illegitimacy was in circulation. He may well have been motivated by a desire to preserve both respect for Jesus' parents and the conviction of Jesus' sinlessness" (*Christian Theology*, 764).

9. In the Hebrew version of the Old Testament, the word *'almah* is used to describe the woman who will give birth to the Messiah in Isaiah 7:14. The Hebrew word can ordinarily mean a "young woman" (RSV/NRSV). However, the Septuagint (LXX) translators of Isaiah 7:14 decided to translate *'almah* to the more specific Greek word *parthenos* (which technically means "virgin"). Matthew quotes from this verse and uses the Greek word *parthenos* because he knew that a virgin birth indeed had taken place. Although the translators of the RSV/NRSV translated the word *'almah* as "young woman" to preserve the "non-Christian elements" of the Old Testament, it does not do justice to the whole biblical witness as a *Christian* witness. The fact that Matthew quotes from this verse to demonstrate its fulfillment in the virgin birth of Christ demonstrates that he did not view Isaiah 7:14 as a text that can be interpreted in isolation from Jesus' birth (hence the use of the word *parthenos*). Modern English translations like the ESV, HCSB, NASB, and NIV do better justice to the whole biblical testimony by translating *'almah* as "virgin" in Isaiah 7:14.

space-time continuum of the human world through the union of deity and humanity; and 3) that Jesus Christ is fully human apart from inheriting the sin of Adam.[10] Even if Christians cannot draw any doctrinal or practical significance from the virgin birth doctrine we still must uphold it as true because the biblical witness clearly makes it known to us *as being true*. As Grudem states, "Whether or not we could discern any aspects of doctrinal importance for this teaching, we should believe it first of all simply because Scripture affirms it."[11]

The virgin birth of Christ is not something that should be declared doctrinally irrelevant for the church today. Upholding this doctrine demonstrates that the church still maintains the integrity of the scriptural witness as the final authority on matters of truth and practice today.

## The Resurrection of Christ

Another christological doctrine that has been a significant part of the church's doctrinal confession is the literal resurrection of Christ from the grave. Since the earliest times of the church's history, this doctrine has been viewed as one of the key cornerstones of the confessional statements of the early Christians. As we cite the Apostles' Creed again, it is on the "third day" that Christ "rose again from the dead" and "ascended into heaven" and sits "at the right hand of God the Father Almighty." During the apostolic period, the bodily resurrection of Christ was viewed as a non-negotiable belief among the primitive Christians—demonstrated by the fact that all four Gospel writers provide clear accounts of this event (Matt 28:1–10; Mark 16:1–8; Luke 24:1–12; John 20:1–10). The apostle Paul even goes so far as to say that denying the bodily resurrection of Christ was tantamount to rejecting the Christian faith entirely and overthrowing the truth of the gospel (1 Cor 15:2, 14–18). For Paul, if Christ was not raised, then Christians embrace a false hope which will perish with them at death (1 Cor 15:18). Other biblical passages reveal that Christ is reigning in heaven now beside the Father in victory (cf. Heb 1:3; Eph 1:20–21; 1 Peter 3:22; Rev 3:21) and, thus, fulfilling his role in his *kingly* office (which will be made manifest visibly at the eschaton [Rev 20:4–6; 22:1, 3]).

Without Christ's resurrection and ascension, sin will always have dominion over humankind, Satan's claim over humanity will always remain

10. Grudem, *Systematic Theology*, 529–32.

11. Grudem, *Systematic Theology*, 532.

unchallenged, and those in Jesus Christ will never be able to enjoy the glorious resurrection to come (1 Cor 15:17). The resurrection of Christ, therefore, is also the victory proclamation that Satan, sin, and death have ultimately been defeated at the cross (1 Cor 15:21–22; Col 2:13–15), although they still wreak havoc during the present age. That is why belief in the bodily resurrection of Christ will always be a non-negotiable doctrine and something that can never be set aside by the church to assuage modern sensibilities. In fact, any church that takes the belief in the bodily resurrection of Christ out of its confessional commitments is a church that has rejected the apostolic witness and has placed itself outside the bounds of Christ's universal *ekklēsia*.

One issue that must be clarified when talking about Christ's resurrection and/or ascension is whether or not Christ in his glorified state transcends his human creatureliness. In other words: did the incarnation cause God the Son to be permanently bound to his human condition for eternity? The scriptural evidence seems to indicate that the second person of the Trinity became not only fully human at the incarnation but also permanently human. Although Christ's resurrected body is a body that is perfect and glorious, it is still a human body in every respect. He will live eternally as a human being permanently joined to the human race. The biblical witness attests to this fact when the Gospel writers reveal that the disciples were able to touch and see the risen Jesus in the same way as when he was still walking among them during his pre-glorified state (Matt 28:9; Luke 24:39–40; John 21:19–23). Further evidence of his full humanity after the resurrection is demonstrated by the fact that he could still eat food like before (Luke 24:41–43).

The significance of this is that Christ will always be one of us as a member of the human race—always interceding for us as the sympathetic divine-human Mediator (Heb 7:25; 1 John 2:1) and, thus, fulfilling his *priestly* role. Even in his glorified state he is still bound by the limitations of his humanness. This means that the ascended Christ is not omnipresent like the Father but still bound by the limitations that come with being a full human being. As Robert L. Reymond writes:

> His [Christ's] glorification in no sense altered the essential manness which was his prior to his resurrection into something other or different from that manness which he assumed at the Incarnation. I grant that he entered into that state of glory that comports with the conditions of the postresurrection existence, but his

humanity even in its glorified state did not assume the infinity of God.[12]

The eternal humanity of Christ is the necessary consequence of the Christology of the Chalcedonian Creed. To affirm that Jesus Christ is fully human is also to affirm that his human nature is permanent. To distort or diminish his humanity in any way is a confession of unfaithfulness to the christological confession of the early church, and more importantly, to the biblical witness of the God-man who came to die for the sins of the world.

### Excurses: Is the Kenotic Theory a Valid Explanation of Christ's Human Limitations?

One theory of the incarnation that has been suggested to explain the human limitations experienced by Jesus while on earth is the *Kenotic Theory* (a view advanced by a group of German and British theologians in the nineteenth and early twentieth centuries). Advocates of this view point to Philippians 2:6–7 as a prooftext for this position. The New American Standard Bible (1995) translates the passage from the Greek this way: "who, although He existed in the form of God, did not regard equality with God a thing to be grasped, *but emptied Himself*, taking the form of a bond-servant, and being made in the likeness of men." The phrase "emptied himself" is the translation from the Greek word *kenōsis* (the verb being *kenoō*). The word literally means "self-emptying."[13] Kenoticists argue that the reason why Jesus was unable to exercise some of his divine abilities while on earth (like knowing the exact time of his second coming) was due to the fact that he "gave up" some of his divine attributes at the incarnation.[14]

However, a much better way to understand the phrase "emptied himself" is to understand it as God the Son giving up his own status or privilege as deity.[15] This is demonstrated by the fact that in the same passage it states that Christ "did not regard equality with God a thing to be grasped" (v. 6), and that he took on "the form of a bond-servant" (v. 7, NASB). There is

---

12. Reymond, *New Systematic Theology*, 618.

13. The English Standard Version's translation of *kenoō* ("made himself nothing") is preferred because it does not contain some of the more problematic theological implications that are attached with the more literal phrase "emptied himself."

14. For a good summary of the Kenotic Theory, see S. M. Smith's article "Kenosis, Kenotic Theology," 600–602.

15. Grudem, *Systematic Theology*, 551.

nothing in the passage that suggests that God the Son surrendered some of his divine attributes at the incarnation. Also, if the Son did give up some of his divine attributes while on earth, even temporarily, this would make him less than fully God—which would make him less than a perfect Mediator. The most satisfactory way to understand why the Son of God experienced human limitations while on earth is due to his taking upon himself a whole new nature that was foreign to him before the incarnation. Before the incarnation, the Son of God, as the eternal Logos, was never encumbered by the restrictions that came with being a human being. We should never, however, see this as a defect but a perfect work of God who became *God with us* in Jesus Christ to become the perfect sacrifice and Mediator for our sins.

## The Deity of Jesus Christ

Although many people today have little issue with the argument that Jesus Christ was fully human, many of these same people have great difficulty ascribing any notion of divinity to him. The plethora of books written by skeptics in recent years reveal the kinds of attitudes that are prevalent regarding the historic Christian confession that Jesus Christ is fully God. Even among those who profess to embrace the Christian faith, the notion that Jesus Christ was not only fully human but also fully God is derided as an early Christian fabrication for the purposes of political expediency or due to the influence of pagan ideas.[16] Despite these attacks on Jesus' deity by modern-day skeptics, Christians need to take greater care in defending the truth of Christ's deity or divinity.

In this section of the chapter we will: 1) examine the evidences of Christ's deity as witnessed to by Scripture, and 2) discuss the theological significance of affirming this truth for the church today.

### The Biblical Evidence of Christ's Deity

When Christians are challenged to defend the deity of Christ the first place in the Bible they usually go to is the Prologue found in the Gospel of John, specifically John 1:1. The verse in question reads: "In the beginning was

---

16. Cf. Spong, *New Christianity for the New World*, 129–46. For a complete skeptic's perspective, see Tom Harpur's *The Pagan Christ*.

the Word, and the Word was with God, and the Word was God." The verse is clear that the second person of the Trinity—the Word (or the eternal Logos)—was not only with God but *was* and *is* God.[17] John also makes it clear to his readers shortly after in verse 14 that this "Word became flesh and dwelt among us, and we have seen his glory, glory as of the only Son from the Father, full of grace and truth." Therefore, the eternal Word, who is fully God, became flesh and dwelt among us as Jesus Christ.

Despite the clear evidence of Christ's deity in this verse, some, like the Jehovah's Witnesses, have objected to this rendering of the verse and have argued that the verse does not prove the deity of Christ in the way historic Christianity has understood it. The Jehovah's Witnesses maintain that since the Greek word *theos* in John 1:1 does not have a definite article in front of it the third *theos* in the verse should be rendered as "a god."[18] However, John adeptly avoids using the definite article so that he does not synonymize the Word with God and, therefore, cause any misunderstanding among his readers. Although the Word is fully God, God is much more than the Word. By doing this, John avoids the heresy of modalism or Sabellianism. As Colin G. Kruse writes, "Jesus, the Word incarnate, claims to be one with God, but that involves being in relationship with God. So when the Prologue says 'the Word was God' it is not saying that the Word and God constitute an undifferentiated unity, but rather it is saying, in words aptly coined by [Francis J.] Moloney, 'what God was the Word also was.'"[19] Therefore, according to John, even though the Word is fully God we must still acknowledge the distinction between the Word and God lest we inadvertently break down the real personal distinctions that exist within the triune Godhead.

Although John 1:1–14 is often used as the main text to argue for the deity of Christ, there are other passages in the Johannine literature that demonstrate that Jesus Christ is fully God. In another part of John's Gospel, Jesus tells the Jews who were opposing him that "Abraham rejoiced that he would see my day. He saw it and was glad" (John 8:56). The Jews respond indignantly: "You are not yet fifty years old, and have you seen Abraham?" (John 8:57). Jesus then replies: "Truly, truly, I say to you, before Abraham

17. The New English Translation (NET) helpfully adds the adverb "fully" before the word "God" at the end of the verse. This gives the reader the impression that Jesus Christ, the Word in the flesh, is not partially divine but God in complete fullness.

18. Refer to the brief treatment given by Norman R. Gulley regarding how Jehovah's Witnesses interpret this verse to harmonize with their christological error (*Systematic Theology*, 2:37–39).

19. Kruse, *John*, 62.

was, *I am*" (John 8:58). The "I am" statement is recognized by Jews as an attribution of deity to oneself (Exod 3:14; Isa 41:4). The Jewish opponents readily recognized this self-designation by Jesus as a proclamation of being the one true God (as we discussed earlier in the chapter). By using the designation "I am," Jesus was essentially claiming to be God himself. That is why the Jews "picked up stones to throw at him" (John 8:59) because they perceived his self-proclamation as utter blasphemy.

Also, later in the Gospel, John records an incident between the resurrected Lord and the disciple Thomas. When Jesus told Thomas to put his finger on his hands and to touch his side (John 20:27), Thomas exclaimed "My Lord and My God!" (John 20:28), a declaration confirming that Thomas knew he was the God-man. Finally, in the book of Revelation, God says at the beginning of the book, "I am the Alpha and the Omega" (Rev 1:8), but near the end of Revelation *Jesus* declares, "I am the Alpha and the Omega, the first and the last, the beginning and the end" (Rev 22:13). These two declarations in the same book demonstrate that God and Jesus are equal in deity and that both have no beginning or end. Jesus is the Alpha and the Omega—sharing the same divine essence as the Almighty One who created and rules everything. Although he is not identical with the Father and is dependent upon him within the trinitarian relationship, he is still equal with the Father in deity.[20]

Although many of the biblical references used to support the deity of Christ are found in the Johannine literature, there are scriptural references outside of John's writings that reveal that Christ is God. For example, in the well-known messianic passage found in Isaiah, the prophet declares: "For to us a child is born, to us a son is given; and the government shall be upon his shoulder, and his name shall be called Wonderful Counselor, Mighty God" (Isa 9:6). The prophet here proclaims that the child (Immanuel) will not only be called the Wonderful Counselor but is the Mighty God himself. During Jesus' earthly ministry he often identified himself as "the Son of

---

20. Thomas R. Schreiner writes: "The priority of the Father is maintained in John, since the Father sends and the Son obeys and acts in dependence upon the Father. At the same time the Father and the Son enjoy equal dignity. Indeed, the 'I am' sayings demonstrate Jesus' deity, for the great 'I am' statements regarding the Lord in Exodus and Isaiah are applied to Jesus. He existed as 'I am' before Abraham was born. In the 'I am' sayings we see that Jesus is the bread of life, the light of the world, the door for the sheep, the resurrection and the life, and the true vine. Indeed, Jesus is God's word and message to human beings. As God's Logos, he has existed with God from the beginning and is himself very God, so that he is the revelation of God to human beings and is confessed by Thomas as Lord and God" (*New Testament Theology*, 260).

God" (in the four Gospels combined, this title is used eighty-four times by Jesus to refer to himself). In Philippians 2:6, the apostle Paul states that even though Jesus "was in the form of God," he did not "count equality with God a thing to be grasped." That the apostle believed that Jesus is not only in the "form" of God but is God himself is obvious because he also states in the verse that Jesus did not seek equality with God even though he is fully God by nature. No person can claim to be equal with God unless he is God himself.

Even if we stop with the clear scriptural references that speak of Christ's deity, his actions that are recorded in Scripture demonstrate to his divinity. For example, he was able to change water into wine (John 2:1–11), multiply a few pieces of fish and bread to feed a multitude of people (Mark 8:1–10), and with a word calm a storm at sea (Luke 8:24). Jesus also knew things that ordinary people would not normally know about (Mark 2:8; John 2:25; 4:17–18; 6:64; 16:30). In addition, Jesus' sovereign right to forgive sins (Mark 2:5–7) is a prerogative that belongs to God alone. Finally, and most significantly, Jesus has the authority to demand worship from all (Phil 2:9–11; Heb 1:6; Rev 5:14; 19:10), an authority that only God possesses.[21] These numerous biblical examples and references demonstrate beyond a shadow of a doubt that the earliest Christians believed that Jesus was not only a human being but also the one true God.

## The Theological Significance of Christ's Deity

That the Son of God becoming a man was an event that had profound repercussions for the human race is something no evangelical Christian will contest. The truth of Emmanuel—God with us—cannot be restricted merely to the theoretical aspects of the Christian faith. Rather, it is a profoundly glorious event that God, who is infinitely above his human

21. Richard Bauckham makes this insightful comment about the primitive church's worship of Jesus as being central to the character of its practices: "[T]he worship of Jesus was central to the character of early Christianity throughout the early centuries, beginning in the early Palestinian Christian movement. At the same time as a worshipping response to Jesus was integral to Christian faith, the early church also clung tenaciously to the Jewish understanding of monotheism, according to which belief in the one God was defined in religious practice by the exclusive worship of the one God. In time it became clear that the practice of the worship of Jesus in the context of Jewish monotheism constituted both a christological principle—that Jesus is such that he can be worshipped—and a theological (Trinitarian) principle—that God is such that Jesus can be worshipped" (Jesus and the God of Israel, 151).

creatures, decided to become "one of us" in our space-time continuum. One significant reason why the truth of Christ's deity is important to us is because it reveals to us who God is, especially in regards to his relationship to us. God did not have to become a human being and dwell among us. He was perfectly satisfied existing as God the Father, God the Son, and God the Holy Spirit in complete harmony and love. However, God willed that the Son come down, take up our flesh, and live among us. As a result, the people who encountered Jesus during his earthly ministry got to witness God's true character directly (John 14:9; cf. Heb 1:3) and, thus, heard from the supreme *prophet* of God when he spoke.

Believers today can also get a glimpse of God's true character through the testimony of Scripture by reading about Jesus' actions, words, and emotional responses in the Gospels. In other words, Jesus Christ, the God-man, reveals to us who God truly is in the flesh (cf. Col 1:19; 2:9). That is one reason why upholding the deity of Christ is theologically important for Christians today. Secondly, it is important for the church today to firmly uphold the deity of Christ due to the significant soteriological implications of this truth. Without Jesus being fully God, humanity's problem with sin can never be resolved. Only as the perfect God-man could Jesus be the perfect Mediator that bridges the infinite gulf that exists between God and sinful human beings. Only God can perfectly fulfill the law and satisfy his own justice—which the God-man did on humanity's behalf two thousand years ago. Therefore, the soteriological significance of Christ's deity should never be downplayed when discussions on Christology are involved.[22]

## The Relationship Between Deity and Humanity in Jesus Christ

### The Three Major Errors of the Person of Christ in the Early Church Period

In the early days of the church various christological errors arose that attempted to understand the relationship between Christ's deity and humanity. Although most of those who professed Christianity during the early church period affirmed both Christ's deity and humanity, many of them had difficulty understanding the relationship between these two natures in Christ's one person. Only at the Council of Chalcedon (451) did the

---

22. We will discuss in more detail the salvific significance of Christ's death (i.e., the atonement) in chapter 9.

church satisfactorily come up with a solution regarding how Christ's two natures are united together in one person. Before we discuss how Christ's two natures are united in his person we will first discuss the three most prominent errors that circulated during the early church period regarding Christ's personhood.

*Apollinarianism.* The view advanced by Apollinaris of Laodicea (d. 390) states that although Christ possessed a human body he did not possess a human mind or spirit (Gk. *nous*). In fact, the mind or spirit of Christ was actually divine. In a way this view resulted in a similar problem Docetism faced. Just as Docetism undermined the humanity of Christ by rejecting his physical humanness, apollinarianism undermined the humanity of Christ by rejecting the idea that Christ's mind or spirit was part of his human nature. Thus, the salvific implication of apollinarianism is that it would lead to an incomplete redemption. If Christ did not have a human mind or spirit how could the minds or spirits of believers be redeemed? Apollinarianism was rightly rejected later at the Council of Constantinople in 318.

*Nestorianism.* This view maintains that the deity and humanity of Christ are so separated that there are in reality two persons in the singular person of Jesus Christ. This view is often attributed to Nestorius (386–450), who was the Archbishop of Constantinople at one time. The reason for this commonly-held attribution was due to the fact that Nestorius rejected the popular title *theotokos* ("God-bearer") for the Virgin Mary (because, according to him, it compromised the deity of Christ by asserting that the divine Logos had a human mother). Therefore, his opponents—notably Cyril of Alexandria (376–444)—attacked him fiercely for separating the deity and humanity in the person of Christ too sharply (whether Cyril's accusation against Nestorius is justified is up for historical debate).

Although the motivation of Nestorius—to maintain the integrity of Christ's deity—is laudable, his view falls into the serious error of undercutting the oneness of the person of Christ. Therefore, the problem with Nestorianism is that it contradicts the biblical references that reveal that Christ did everything as a unified person. As the incarnate One, Jesus' deity and humanity were intricately joined together even though his two natures were never confused with each other. In fact, the Scriptures never referred to Jesus as having two personalities in one body or being two persons in one body. Nestorianism, due in large part by the opposition of Cyril, was rejected at the Council of Ephesus in 431.

*Eutychianism.* Another error, which was in some respects a reaction against Nestorianism, was the view set forth by the archimandrite Eutyches (380–456). Eutyches advanced the view that the human nature of Christ was absorbed by his divine nature. In essence, Christ's humanity and divinity were comingled together which resulted in a third new nature being formed. Thus, there is no clear distinction between Christ's humanity and divinity—Christ only had one nature as a result of the mixing of the two. Many in the church condemned this view as undercutting both of Christ's two natures. If Christ was neither truly human nor truly God, how could he redeem his people from their sins? This view was rightly rejected by all the orthodox branches of Christianity for depicting Christ in a way that is contrary to the witness of Scripture.

### How Should We Understand the Relationship Between Christ's Humanity and Divinity?

As mentioned above, the Council of Chalcedon finally resolved the debate regarding how Christ's human and divine natures are united together. The Chalcedonian Definition declared that Christ is "one substance" (*homoousios*) with the Father in the Godhead and also "one substance" (*homoousios*) with us in manhood, which is made known in "two natures" (*physeis*), without confusion, change, division, or separation, while the properties of both natures are preserved and come together in "one person" (*prosōpon*) and "one subsistence" (*hypostasis*). The key phrases in the definition are in quotations with the original Greek words in brackets. The definition quickly makes it clear that Jesus is *homoousios* with the Father (against the Arians). Basically, what the Father is in substance, the Son also is. Christ is also of two natures (*physeis*) which are not confused, changed, divided, or separated. Even in the hypostatic union both natures are preserved and both maintain their unique properties (against Eutychianism). In other words, the Son shares the same divine substance as the Father but also has two natures in him that maintain their distinctive properties in him as a unique individual. Therefore, the orthodox Christian view is that both the divine and human natures are united and preserved in this one Jesus Christ, the Son of God who came in the flesh.

Despite the Chalcedonian Definition's assertion of the distinction between Christ's human and divine natures, this does not permit us to believe that there is absolutely no interaction between the two. As we repeat what was stated above, a biblical and orthodox Christology affirms that Christ's two natures, though preserved and maintained, are united in one person.[23] The implication of this understanding is that Jesus Christ does everything as a singular person. In other words: *all his actions and deeds are done both divinely and humanly.* That is why we can argue that when Christ healed the sick or calmed a storm he did these miraculous acts not only as God but also as a human being. In the same way, when Christ ate, slept, laughed, played in the street as a child, or assembled a wooden table he not only did these things as a human being but also as God Incarnate. When we read about Christ's actions and conversations during his time on earth recorded in the Gospels we see what God truly is like. In fact, when Jesus told Philip, "Whoever has seen me has seen the Father" (John 14:9), there is no indication in that verse that he meant this symbolically or metaphorically. Jesus truly revealed the character of God by all that he did, said, and felt while on earth. As John H. Leith states, "The Christian claim is that this Jesus whom we know from his life among us is the embodiment of God himself, the focused presence of the living God."[24] Therefore, Jesus Christ truly is Emmanuel, God with us.

Having said that, one may inquire whether this means that the human frailties that Jesus experienced on earth somehow involved his divine nature. We would answer that it did not. When Jesus was tired, needed food, and experienced temptation it was solely due to the fact that he was a human being like the rest of us. Just like his miraculous abilities like healing the sick and calming the storm are due to his divine nature—even though he heals the sick and calms the storm *as the unified* God-man—his human limitations are due to his human nature alone. Even though this appears to negate the assertion made in the previous paragraph that Christ's actions

---

23. Having said that, we affirm with historic Christianity that Christ has two wills (Dyothelitism): one based on his deity and the other based on his humanity (against Monothelitism). This seems to be indicated in John 6:38 when Jesus tells the crowd: "For I have come down from heaven, not to do my own will but the will of him [the Father] who sent me." If Jesus only had one will it would lead to the compromising of his full humanity since being a human being entails that one also possesses a human will. Therefore, it is important to emphasize that Jesus not only had a divine will in his personhood but also a human one in our christological doctrinal statements.

24. Leith, *Basic Christian Doctrine*, 135.

on earth were the actions of the unified God-man, this does not necessarily entail an incongruity because we are dealing with the *source* of Christ's supernatural abilities (just like the source of his human frailties are from his human nature). Similarly, we can argue that even though Christ died on the cross as the God-man, it was only his humanity that truly experienced death. This does not mean that his death was in some way incomplete or illusory, but that even though he truly tasted death like other human beings the divine Logos, for obvious reasons, did not succumb to this death. The most we can say about how Christ's death affected his divine nature is to tentatively suggest that the Logos somehow shared in the experience of what death was like as a human being.

## The Mission of Jesus during His Earthly Ministry

Before we close this chapter, we must consider Jesus' ministry during his time on earth before his ascension. This is generally a neglected topic in evangelical dogmatic works but it needs to be addressed before we proceed ahead. The reason why it is important to discuss this topic is due to the fact that it connects the identity and personhood of Jesus Christ with his redemptive work on our behalf (which will be discussed in more detail in the following chapter).

In evangelical theological discussions it is commonplace to talk about Jesus' mission during his earthly ministry as consisting of only living a morally perfect life on earth to "fulfill all righteousness" on our behalf (Matt 3:15) and dying on the cross and rising from the dead to redeem us from the penalty of sin (1 Cor 15:3–4; Gal 3:13). Although this is a very important core truth regarding Jesus' mission on earth, it is only one aspect of his whole earthly ministry. The Son of God became incarnate in the flesh not only to live a morally perfect life (thus, fulfilling God's law on our behalf) and dying on the cross and rising from the dead to atone for the sins of believers (thus, fulfilling his *priestly* role), but also to be the divine-human Prophet and King of the world.

Although Eusebius of Caesarea was the first to discuss the threefold office of Christ in any definitive manner, John Calvin was the one who provided a more elaborate and extensive treatment of the subject in his *Institutes* (2.15). Later Reformed theologians, following Calvin, included this theme in their discussions on Christology in their respective dogmatic works.[25] In fact, both the Heidelberg Catechism (Lord's Day 12, Question and Answer 31) and the Westminster Shorter Catechism (Questions 23–26) provide their own respective treatments on this subject.

The question then becomes: why is it important to briefly discuss Christ's threefold office during his earthly ministry before we conclude this chapter on Christology? We believe it is important because it helps us to avoid a truncated view of Christ's work in his humiliation and exaltation. The incarnate Son was not only a perfect priestly sacrifice for the sins of his people, but the prophet sent from God the Father *par excellence* (cf. Matt 7:28–29) and the Messianic King who will rule (and rules!) the world victoriously (cf. 1 Cor 15:24–25).

The prophetic declaration by Moses that God will raise up a prophet like himself among the people (Deut 18:15) is seen by the apostle Peter as having been fulfilled in Christ (Acts 3:22–23). Therefore, based on this passage alone, it is evident that Christ was appointed by God as the divine-human prophet for Israel during his earthly ministry. Through this particular office, Jesus spoke as a prophet with divine authority (cf. Luke 4:32), taught people the moral will of God (cf. Matt 5–7), revealed who God is through his own person (cf. John 14:9), and announced the arrival of God's kingdom through his teachings (cf. Luke 8:1). Even his healing of the sick and expelling of demonic spirits were expressions of his prophetic ministry since through his miraculous healings and casting out of demons he proclaimed that the kingdom of God was at hand (Mark 1:14–45; Luke 11:20; cf. Matt 11:1–19). The earthly ministry of Jesus, therefore, was not only to prepare for the fulfillment of his priestly role to be a perfect sacrificial Lamb for the sins of the world, but to reveal to Israel (and others) God's will and gospel promises (John 5:24–27; 6:40) for a world ravaged by sin and its consequences.

What about Christ's *kingly* office and its role in his earthly ministry? How does this particular office shape Christ's mission while he was on earth? In the Old Testament a prophetic promise was given to David by God through the prophet Nathan that he will have a descendant who will rule a kingdom forever (as mentioned earlier in chapter 7) (cf. 2 Sam 7:12–16). Other Old Testament passages that mention this prophetic everlasting kingship in a messianic context are Psalm 110; Isaiah 9:6–7; Daniel 7:13–14; and Micah 5:2. After the ascension of Christ, Peter, according to

---

25. Cf. Turretin, *Institutes of Elenctic Theology*, 2:391–499; Bavinck, *Reformed Dogmatics*, 3:364–68.

Acts 2:30–36, makes it clear to the Judeans that Jesus Christ, whom they crucified, fulfills this kingship role promised to David and foretold in the Old Testament.

Christ demonstrating his kingship through this particular office was to show Israel that her messianic hope for a deliverer based on the Old Testament promises was not something that went unfulfilled. The problem was that the vast majority of Israelites at the time misunderstood Jesus' mission and ministry—which was for the whole world (which also included them). They expected something else (of a more material and political nature), but he offered them something far greater: the forgiveness of sins and the gift of eternal life through his sacrificial death (John 3:1–15). However, Christ's death did not detract from or undermine his messianic kingship but highlighted the truth to the Israelites, through his bodily resurrection and ascension, that he truly is the King who overcame all opposition and death—for them *and* for the whole world (cf. Mark 14:62; Eph 1:20–23).

# CHAPTER 9

## The Atonement

THE DOCTRINE OF CHRIST's atoning work on the cross is a crucial article of faith in the Christian tradition because it deals with the heart of the gospel. It is one of the key doctrines of the universal church's confession and a proper understanding of it sets genuine Christianity apart from other religions. The fact that God the Father sent his only begotten Son to the world in the flesh to take away the sins of rebellious human beings is by and large an extraordinary aspect of the Christian religion.

In this chapter we will discuss: 1) the nature of the atonement from a biblical perspective; 2) alternative views of the atonement throughout the history of the church; and 3) special issues concerning the doctrine of the atonement.

### The Nature of the Atonement

*Why the Cross of Christ?*

If one were to take a survey asking people to come up with a visual symbol that is often associated with Christianity many will instinctively come up with the cross in their minds. The cross has been a symbol that has been etched in the minds of many throughout the centuries as the basic symbol of the Christian faith. In the early days of the church, however, the cross was not a symbol of glory that is often thought of by many today, but a sign of horror, suffering, and humiliation. It was a symbol that represented the execution of vile criminals and insurrectionists. Many will wonder why a faith movement that started almost two thousand years ago would want its adherents to associate their religious movement with something that represented shame, defeat, and death (especially if the people involved in the movement sought after converts). As John R. W. Stott writes, "The Christians' choice of a cross as the symbol of their faith is the more surprising when we remember the horror with which crucifixion was regarded in the ancient world."[1] However, it is only when we understand the purpose of Christ's death on the cross do we then start to understand why the early Christians adopted the cross as the key symbol of their faith. The cross represented for these early Christians the profound love of God for his fallen human creatures while at the same time depicting the righteousness of God as the holy Judge of sin.

### God's Love and Justice at the Cross

Although some contemporary theologians have trouble reconciling God's love with his justice when discussions of the atonement come up,[2] the biblical writers did not view God's love and his justice as irreconcilable aspects of his character. For instance, the apostle Paul who told the Christians at Rome in his letter that through the death of Christ "God shows his love for us" (Rom 5:8), also wrote earlier in the letter that Christ's death was to "show God's righteousness" (Rom 3:25). In John's Gospel, in the most well-known verse in the Bible, it states: "For *God so loved the world*, that he gave his only Son, that whoever believes in him should not perish but have eternal life" (John 3:16). However, later on in the Gospel, Jesus tells the Jews who were opposing him that "an hour is coming when all who are in the tombs will hear his voice and come out, those who have done good to the resurrection of life, and *those who have done evil to the resurrection of judgment*" (John 5:28–29). Even though the Father sends the Son to die on the cross for the sins of the world, there will still be a final day of judgment where the unrighteous will stand before the Son of God to be judged for their sins (cf. Rom 2:6–13; Rev 20:11–15). Therefore, there is no irreconcilable tension between God's love and his justice in his work of reconciliation in Jesus Christ.

It is because of sin (inherent and actual) that the Son of God came in the flesh to die on the cross. Sin is a destructive disease that, if not dealt

1. Stott, *Cross of Christ*, 23.
2. Dyk, "How Does Jesus Make a Difference?," 211.

with, will eventually consume the impenitent and will result in judgment and eternal separation from God. As Paul states in Romans 6:23, the "wages of sin is death" (both temporal and eternal). The God of both perfect love and justice, however, sends his Son to die on the cross so that those who believe in him may have their sins paid for and, as a result, enjoy eternal life in him. That is why the cross of Christ was necessary in God's work of redemption in history.

### Sacrificial Images in the Old Testament

As discussed in chapter 7 on the covenants, we posited how believers in the Old Testament were saved on the same basis and terms as believers in the New Testament—by grace alone through faith alone. There is no suggestion whatsoever in Scripture that in the Old Testament God demanded obedience to the law as a means to earn a place in his kingdom but with the coming of Christ the rules changed so that only faith is required. Yet, one may still ask why God required the Israelites to routinely bring sacrifices to him as part of the terms of the covenant. Although there were various kinds of sacrifices God required of his old covenant people, such as gift offerings for thanksgiving (Deut 33:10) and burnt offerings for the whole community (Exod 29:38–43; Num 28), the most significant were the *guilt* offerings where the person sought pardon for an unintentional offence against God by offering these up (Lev 4–5). The most important of which is the annual Day of Atonement sacrifice (Yom Kippur) made by the high priest in the Most Holy Place to atone for the sins of the whole Israelite community.[3] The key aspect of the entire old covenant sacrificial system was the revelation of how sin is such an egregious offence against a holy God that only a substitutionary blood sacrifice will be able to divert his righteous wrath away from the sinner (cf. Heb 9:22).

Despite the fact that these blood sacrifices averted God's judgment against the Israelites, it did not confer on the worshipper(s) complete forgiveness of sin and a place in the eschatological kingdom. The sacrifices revealed God's righteous character, justice, and holiness. It also forestalled judgment upon the transgressor and allowed him or her to enjoy the old covenant blessings of the land momentarily. Even in the Old Testament, there is a clear recognition that sacrifices by themselves cannot atone for sin and bring true reconciliation between the sinner and God (Ps 51:16; Hos

---

3. Milne, *Know the Truth*, 206.

6:6; Mic 6:6–8). In the New Testament, the author of Hebrews makes this more poignantly clear when he writes that "in these [old covenant] sacrifices there is a reminder of sins every year. *For it is impossible for the blood of bulls and goats to take away sins*" (10:3–4; cf. 9:9). Ultimately, these old covenant sacrifices were only mirrors and shadows that pointed to Christ and his perfect sacrifice (cf. Heb 9:13–14, 26, 28; 10:10, 12, 14). Those who were given the gift of faith in the Old Testament knew what those blood sacrifices truly represented, while those with hardened hearts only focused on the externals and the temporary. As J. van Genderen and W. H. Velema write, "There is an inextricable connection between the Old Testament proclamation of atonement through sacrifice and the substitutionary suffering and death of him who was ordained for this by God, and the New Testament gospel of atonement through Christ."[4]

Therefore, believers in both the Old and New Testaments have their sins paid for only through the sacrificial death of Christ. The only difference between the believers living under the old covenant and those living post-Christ's ascension is that the former only saw the shadows of Christ's atoning death through the animal sacrifices, while the latter have a clearer witness through Scripture of what Christ did on their behalf. Altogether, Jesus is the only one who can take away the sins of believers regardless of what period of redemptive history they live under.

### The Nature of Christ's Atoning Work According to Scripture

Although various passages in Scripture can be referenced to when discussing the nature of Christ's atoning work on the cross, the two most prominent passages that are often referred to by Christians are Isaiah 53 and Romans 3:25.

In Isaiah 53:5, the prophet declares that the Suffering Servant[5] was "pierced for our transgressions; he was crushed for our iniquities; upon

---

4. Genderen and Velema, *Concise Reformed Dogmatics*, 515.

5. Although some have argued that the Suffering Servant in Isaiah 52:13–53:12 is the nation of Israel, we conclude that there is no exegetical basis for interpreting the passage in this way from a *Christian canonical* perspective. On the other hand, regarding the problem of using this passage in a christological way, Brevard S. Childs writes: "Some of the difficulty obviously has arisen from the fact that Isaiah 53 appeared to offer the strongest biblical confirmation of Christ's atoning and vicarious death, yet was a passage without any prior tradition of a suffering messianic interpretation within Judaism" (*Biblical Theology of the Old and New Testaments*, 514).

him was the chastisement that brought us peace, and with his wounds we are healed." Later on in the same chapter, he also declares: "Therefore I will divide him a portion with the many, and he shall divide the spoil with the strong, because he poured out his soul to death and was numbered with the transgressors; yet he bore the sin of many, and makes intercession for the transgressors" (Isa 53:12). What is interesting to note here is the strong substitutionary language of the role of the Suffering Servant in respect to his sacrificial death on behalf of his people. The text makes it clear that he "was crushed for our iniquities," that we are healed because of "his wounds," and that peace comes between the sinner and God because of the "chastisement" brought upon him (Isa 53:5). He was also "numbered with the transgressors" because he "poured out his soul to death," and he "bore the sin of many" and, as a result, makes "intercession for the transgressors" (Isa 53:12). All these statements in Isaiah 53 point out that Christ's death on the cross was not merely the result of the hostilities brought against him by his Jewish and Roman enemies, but was a divinely ordained plan to bring the Son of God to come in the flesh and become a substitutionary sacrifice for sinners. That is why when describing Christ's atoning sacrifice on the cross we can rightly conclude that it was not only substitutionary but also *penal*. This is clearly indicated by the fact that the Suffering Servant incurs the *penalty* that was to be brought upon those who sinned against God. Therefore, when reading Isaiah 53, one cannot escape the fact that what Isaiah prophesied was Christ's *penal-substitutionary* death on the cross for the sins of the transgressors.

Another well-known passage that speaks of Christ's death as a penal-substitutionary sacrifice is Romans 3:25. The verse reads in the HCSB translation: "God presented Him as a propitiation through faith in His blood, to demonstrate His righteousness, because in His restraint God passed over the sins previously committed." The word "propitiation" in that verse comes from the Greek word *hilastērion*.[6] The Greek word if translated literally is "mercy seat." However, the Greek word does not mean a symbolic representation of God doing away with people's sins—as in the ritual of Leviticus 16 in which the mercy seat plays a role—but a term that indicates that Christ *truly* does take away the sins of his people so that there will be true and everlasting reconciliation between them and God. Thus, Paul clearly states

---

6. Other English versions translate the word in a more general way by using the phrase "a sacrifice of atonement" (NIV, NRSV). We believe, however, that the translators of the ESV, HCSB, and NASB are correct by translating *hilastērion* as "propitiation."

in this verse that Christ's sacrificial death genuinely removes the sins of his people so that God's wrath is diverted away from them and is instead placed upon the Son. As F. F. Bruce states, "The *hilastērion* which God has provided in Christ not only removes the ungodliness and wickedness, but at the same time averts the retribution which is the inevitable sequel to such attitudes and actions in a moral universe."[7] Hence, the word "propitiation" is the most fitting word to use to translate *hilastērion* because it is the most appropriate way to describe what Christ did on our behalf. God is propitiated through Christ's perfect obedience as a man (which is culminated at the cross) so that divine wrath would not fall on those who appropriate the benefits of the cross through faith.[8] Therefore, Christ's perfect righteousness—via his flawless obedience to the law—completely satisfies God's justice. Furthermore, by his death, not only is the satisfaction of divine justice completely fulfilled but those who belong to Christ are reckoned righteous before God for all time (i.e., justified).[9] In this way God can still maintain his righteousness and justice while justifying sinners who come to Christ through faith.

*Other Significant Passages on Christ's Atonement.* Other significant passages in the New Testament that speak of Christ's death as a penal-substitutionary sacrifice include:

- Romans 8:3–4: "For God has done what the law, weakened by the flesh, could not do. *By sending his own Son in the likeness of sinful flesh and for sin, he condemned sin in the flesh, in order that the righteous requirement of the law might be fulfilled in us,* who walk not according to the flesh but according to the Spirit."

- 2 Corinthians 5:14–15: "For the love of Christ controls us, because we have concluded this: *that one has died for all, therefore all have died; and he died for all,* that those who live might no longer live for themselves but for him who for their sake died and was raised."

- 2 Corinthians 5:21: "For our sake *he made him to be sin who knew no sin,* so that in him we might become the righteousness of God."

- Galatians 3:13–14: "Christ redeemed us from the curse of the law *by becoming a curse for us*—for it is written, 'Cursed is everyone who is

7. Bruce, *Romans*, 100.

8. Morris, *Epistle to the Romans*, 182.

9. We will discuss the doctrine of justification in more detail in chapter 14.

hanged on a tree'—so that in Christ Jesus the blessing of Abraham might come to the Gentiles, so that we might receive the promised Spirit through faith."

- Ephesians 5:2: "And walk in love, *as Christ loved us and gave himself up for us,* a fragrant offering and sacrifice to God."

- 1 Timothy 2:5–6: "For there is one God, and there is one mediator between God and men, the man Christ Jesus, *who gave himself as a ransom for all,* which is the testimony given at the proper time."

- Hebrews 9:26–28: "But as it is, he has appeared once for all at the end of the ages to put away sin by the sacrifice of himself. And just as it is appointed for man to die once, and after that comes judgment, *so Christ, having been offered once to bear the sins of many,* will appear a second time, not to deal with sin but to save those who are eagerly waiting for him."

- Hebrews 10:10, 14: "And by that will we have been sanctified through the offering of the body of Jesus Christ once for all. . . . For by a single offering he has perfected for all time those who are being sanctified."

- 1 Peter 2:22–25: "He committed no sin, neither was deceit found in his mouth. When he was reviled, he did not revile in return; when he suffered, he did not threaten, but continued entrusting himself to him who judges justly. *He himself bore our sins in his body on the tree, that we might die to sin and live to righteousness. By his wounds you have been healed.* For you were straying like sheep, but have now returned to the Shepherd and Overseer of your souls."

- 1 Peter 3:18: "For Christ also suffered once for sins, *the righteous for the unrighteous,* that he might bring us to God, being put to death in the flesh but made alive in the spirit."

- 1 John 2:1–2: "My little children, I am writing these things to you so that you may not sin. But if anyone does sin, we have an advocate with the Father, Jesus Christ the righteous. *He is the propitiation for our sins,* and not for ours only but also for the sins of the whole world."

- 1 John 4:9–10: "In this the love of God was made manifest among us, that God sent his only Son into the world, so that we might live through him. In this is love, not that we have loved God but that he loved us and *sent his Son to be the propitiation for our sins.*"

Based on the passages referenced above, the necessity of a penal and substitutionary atonement is grounded on the fact that all human beings are sinners who have transgressed the divine law (Rom 3:20) and, as a result, are unable to gain a righteous standing before a holy God by their own merits (Gal 3:10). Yet, God in his perfect love and wisdom was able to express his saving love to his creatures, without compromising his justice and righteousness, by sending his Son to die on the cross as a propitiatory sacrifice on their behalf. As Stott masterfully puts it, "By bearing himself in Christ the fearful penalty of our sins, God not only propitiated his wrath, ransomed us from slavery, justified us in his sight, and reconciled us to himself, but thereby also defended and demonstrated his own justice."[10]

Despite the clear teaching of Scripture that Christ's death was both penal and substitutionary, some modern theologians have objected to this view because of some of the unsavory connotations associated with it.[11] They aver that it is not possible for a loving God to require such a gruesome sacrifice as a way of dealing with humanity's sinfulness. In fact, they maintain, this understanding encourages more violence in a period of world history where brutality is quite prevalent. The problem with this objection against the penal-substitutionary view, however, is that it does not do justice to the magnitude of the awfulness of sin. That the Son of God in the flesh died in a gruesome way on the cross reveals the utter horror of sin and its sheer offensiveness to God. Therefore, this objection loses its potency when looked at from the backdrop of why God sent his Son to die on the cross.

Another objection set forth against the traditional penal-substitutionary view is that it pits God's justice and his love in an irreconcilable tension with each other. If God is a loving and gracious God, why does he require a just payment for the sins of the human race? Could not God simply forgive the sins of people without requiring the substitutionary death of his Son? Although this objection is the stronger of the two mentioned here, it also loses its efficacy when we recognize that God's justice and love are not mutually exclusive to each other. In fact, it is due to his love for the world that God took the initiative to send his Son as a sacrificial Lamb for the sins of the human race. As Paul makes clear in Romans 5:8, God "shows his love for us in that while we were still sinners, Christ died for us." It is not because human beings earned God's love, and therefore, God was compelled to

10. Stott, *Cross of Christ*, 211.

11. Cf. Weaver, *Nonviolent Atonement*; Bartlett, *Cross Purposes*.

send his Son to become flesh and die for their sins, but because he wanted to display his sheer grace and mercy toward his fallen creatures.

## Alternative Views of the Atonement Throughout Church History

### The Classical View (or Ransom Theory)

The view that is often labeled as the *classical view* has been argued as being the most prevalent among the early church fathers. Early fathers like Irenaeus, Origen, and Gregory of Nyssa are often referred to as advocates of this theory. In the modern period, Gustaf Aulén (1897–1977) attempted to rehabilitate this view for the church in the twentieth century. He renamed this position as the *Christus Victor* (Christ the Victor) view, which also happens to be the title of his work.[12] In essence, the view maintains that because of humanity's fall into sin Satan is now the ruler over the human race. Since Satan has the right to rule over the human race, God cannot simply force Satan to relinquish his control over fallen humans because this would mean that he would need to employ the same methods as Satan himself, which he cannot do. Thus, according to this theory, the problem of the human race is that they are under the dominion of an unfit ruler (i.e., Satan).

In order to release humanity from this diabolical captivity, Jesus Christ offers his own life to pay the ransom to deliver many from the bondage of the devil (Mark 10:45; Heb 9:15). This ransom, however, was not paid to God (since he cannot pay a ransom to himself) but to Satan. Because of Christ's own sacrifice on the cross, the captives of the devil are released since his death was the just payment for their deliverance. Also, this view is thought to make Christ's death to be totally objective since salvation has no subjective impact on those who benefit from it.

Ironically, it is making Christ's atonement to be wholly objective in this view that raises criticisms against it. If the atonement merely accomplishes deliverance for the human race from the dominion of Satan, then there really is nothing for the beneficiaries of Christ's death to do (not even the exercising of faith) but to just sit back and watch the drama of redemption unfold to completion. Understandably, critics of this view argue that this understanding of the atonement leads to ethical quietism and undermines evangelistic efforts to confront the world with the demands of the gospel.

12. Cf. Aulén, *Christus Victor*.

*The Moral-Influence View*

Another view that has received some degree of acceptance throughout history (and even today)[13] is the view set forth by the French medieval scholar Peter Abelard (1079–1142). Today the view is popularly known as the *moral-influence theory* of the atonement. In contrast to Anselm's satisfaction view (which we will discuss next), Abelard claimed that Christ's death was not a result of God requiring some sort of sacrificial payment to satisfy his honor or justice for humanity's transgression of his law but to demonstrate God's love towards human beings (God's love, in this view, taking primacy over God's justice). As a result of this demonstration of divine love, human beings will begin to change their attitude and behavior as a response to this revelation. Christ's death will influence people to live differently so that they will receive divine pardon on the day of judgment.

The problem with this view is that it has absolutely no place for any concept of Christ's death being a substitutionary sacrifice on behalf of sinners. It basically ignores the copious amounts of scriptural passages that speak of "Christ having died for us" (*Christus pro nobis mortuus*). Also, this view essentially leads to a type of works-righteousness understanding of salvation. If salvation is ultimately accomplished by human beings following Christ's example, then divine grace really has no place in the work of redemption. In essence, what this view ends up doing is putting the work of salvation ultimately in the hands of human sinners rather than in the hands of the sovereign God of grace.[14]

*The Satisfaction Theory*

A view that has received much popularity throughout the history of the church is the *satisfaction theory* of the atonement. Although this view is expressed in undeveloped form in the writings of earlier theologians like Augustine of Hippo and Gregory the Great, it is in Anselm of Canterbury's (1033–1109) well-known work *Cur Deus Homo?* (literally, "Why the God-man?") that this view is presented in a fully developed form. In the work,

---

13. Two modern-day works that advocate this theory are Rashdall, *Idea of Atonement in Christian Theology*, and Fiddes, *Past Event and Present Salvation*.

14. Although the view of Faustus Socinus (1539–1604), typically called the "example theory," is often given a separate treatment in other systematic theology works, we will not give a separate treatment of it because of its similarities with the Abelardian view.

Anselm basically starts the conversation by asking why God took on human flesh to become man (hence, the title of his work).

According to Anselm, the reason why the second person of the Trinity became man is due to the fact that God requires that his honor be satisfied one way or another. Human beings violated God's honor and took what rightfully belongs to him by committing sin. As a result, God must (due to his own righteous nature) uphold his honor and require some payment to satisfy it. According to Anselm, this can take place in either of two ways: by God condemning the sinner to eternal punishment *or* by punishing someone else on behalf of the transgressor to satisfy the honor due him. This is where Christ, the perfect Mediator, comes into play. Since Christ, as the God-man, did not sin and was completely obedient up to his death, his sacrifice went beyond what God required for his honor to be satisfied. As a result, his obedience and death as a human being serves as a true satisfaction for the sins of humanity.

Although Anselm's view is much more supportable scripturally than the other two views discussed above, there are some deficiencies with it. First, Anselm's reasoning for Christ's death was heavily based on logic.[15] Though logic does have a role in theological reasoning, it should not be the overarching tool that shapes biblical doctrines. Second, his view of satisfaction is more grounded on concepts drawn from the medieval feudal system rather than on what is revealed in Scripture. Since he lived in a time when feudal ideas of justice and satisfaction were prevalent, it is no surprise then that he drew from these ideas to shape his understanding of the atonement. Third, there is no place for the resurrection of Christ in Anselm's perspective on the atonement. If Christ's obedience and death satisfies divine honor, what role does Christ's resurrection play in all of this? Although the satisfaction theory helped pave the way for the formulation of a fully developed penal-substitutionary understanding of the atonement, by itself the theory has a number of deficiencies that make it less than satisfactory from a biblical point of view.

### The Governmental View (Hugo Grotius)

Finally, another alternative to the penal-substitutionary view is the theory advanced by Hugo Grotius (1583–1645), which is known today as the *governmental view*. In this view, Grotius argued that God does not require a

15. Erickson, *Christian Theology*, 816.

payment for sin, and that he could have simply forgiven the sins of human beings as a result of his omnipotence. The true purpose of Christ's death was to show the human race that God is a moral Being who has an obligation to uphold the laws he has created. As a result of humanity's rebellion and sin, Christ's death reveals to the human transgressors that a God of law must punish those who break his law. Through Christ's death, God reveals the measures he is willing to take in order to uphold the moral order of his universe. In addition, without the cross, according to this view, there would be no basis for human beings to become morally responsible before God while at the same time receiving his forgiveness for their transgressions. In other words, for Grotius, "the main emphasis of the atonement is subjective: Christ's death motivates sinners to repent of their sins and reform their lives."[16] This view has been associated with some strands of the Arminian tradition.[17]

The problem with this view is that it, like the moral-influence theory, ignores many of the statements found in Scripture that state that Christ died as a substitutionary sacrifice for the sins of his people. It also leads to a form of works-righteousness salvation by making the cross merely a revelation of God's desire to uphold his law so that this will have a morally transforming influence on people. Ultimately, in this view, human beings are the ones who save themselves from eternal judgment while God only influences them along the way. Furthermore, although the governmental view does appear at first glance to view God as being just, when examined more closely it actually undermines God's just character by insisting that the death of Christ was not necessary in order for God to forgive the sins of law-breakers.

## Special Issues Concerning the Doctrine of the Atonement

### The Scope of the Atonement: Particular or Universal?

One of the more contentious issues today pertaining to the atonement within evangelical circles, particularly within the Reformed evangelical community, is the scope of Christ's propitiatory work. To put it another way: is Christ's atonement particular or universal in terms of its extent? Reformed or Calvinistic evangelicals have usually claimed that the extent

16. Lewis and Demarest, *Integrative Theology*, 2:376.
17. Cf. Miley, *Systematic Theology*, 2:65–240.

of the atonement is particular.[18] They base this on the notion that all five points of Calvinism (TULIP), which were formulated at the Synod of Dort (1618–19), either stand or fall together. Remove one of the five points, they argue, and the whole Calvinistic structure collapses. Therefore, one of the reasons why many Reformed evangelicals contend (sometimes vehemently) for the particularity of the atonement is due to the fact that the whole Calvinistic soteriological construction falls apart (they argue) if the atonement becomes universal in scope.

The second reason why many Reformed evangelicals opt for the particularist position is based on the argument that if Christ's atonement is for all human beings it would be unjust for God to send anyone to hell. In other words, if Christ paid for the sins of every human being who has ever lived then those who finally experience judgment in hell are *paying again* for their sins. Thus, they argue, we must either restrict the benefits of Christ's atonement only to the elect or embrace a form of universalism in order to avoid this dilemma.[19]

The third reason many Reformed evangelicals argue for the particularity of the atonement is biblical/exegetical. Some key passages that are often summoned to support the particularist position include: Matthew 1:21; John 6:37–39; 10:11; 17:20; Acts 20:28; and Romans 8:32. Although these passages *can* be interpreted in a way that supports the idea that the benefits of Christ's death are only restricted to the elect, there are other passages in Scripture that seem to indicate that Christ's atonement is universal *in its scope*. We will focus on two key passages that seem to support the universal scope of the atonement: 2 Peter 2:1 and 1 John 2:2.

2 *Peter* 2:1. The apostle Peter writes in the verse: "But false prophets also arose among the people, just as there will be false teachers among you, who will secretly bring in destructive heresies, *even denying the Master who bought them*, bringing upon themselves swift destruction." The key phrase in the verse is: "even denying the Master who bought them." Some Reformed scholars argue that what Peter is saying in this verse is that Christ bought these false prophets through his death in order for him to be their

18. Many Reformed or Calvinistic evangelicals use the word "limited" when discussing the particular extent of the atonement (from the "L" point in the TULIP acronym or the five points of Calvinism). We will use the word "particular" to avoid any wrongful connotations that the word "limited" might imply (e.g., that the atonement was "limited" in effect).

19. Clark, *Atonement*, 138.

ruler or despot (but not their personal Savior). They maintain that the Greek word *agorasanta* ("bought") in the verse is never used in a soteriological sense anywhere in Scripture unless it is connected with the term "price" (Gk. *timēs*) or its equivalent.[20] However, Andrew D. Chang points out that whenever the Greek verb *agorazō* is used with a human being as the object it always has a salvific meaning. He writes: "When the object is a human being, it is always used in the soteriological sense. If this is a correct observation, the word ἀγοράζω in 2 Peter 2:1 is also to be taken in the soteriological sense because the object of purchase is obviously human beings."[21] Although the false teachers finally perish in hell forever, Christ in his death bought them in *some salvific manner* because the benefits of the atonement are genuinely offered to them (signified in their baptisms [cf. 2 Pet 2:22]). However, due to their unbelief, they do not *ultimately* benefit from his sacrificial death.

1 *John* 2:2. John tells his readers in this verse: "He is the propitiation for our sins, and not for ours only but also for the sins of the whole world." Those who support the particularist view argue that when John wrote that Christ's death is also "for the sins of the whole world" he did not mean that it was meant for every single person in the world. Instead, what he meant by this statement is that people from every nation, tribe, and language are "embraced" in this propitiation.[22] Thus, they maintain that John is positing that the atonement is universal only in the sense that it is offered to all *types* of people (whereas in the Old Testament, grace was only given to the Israelites). However, this interpretation will not suffice. John is clearly telling his readers that Christ's propitiatory death is for "the whole world" in the most comprehensive way possible. As Stephen S. Smalley writes:

> The Fourth Evangelist describes Jesus as the "savior of the world" (4:42; cf. 3:16; 1 John 4:14), and here John refers to him as the one whose "atoning sacrifice" relates to the sins of "the whole world." The adjective (περὶ) ὅλου, "(for those of the) whole," is intensive. The sacrificial offering of Christ is effective not just for the sins of the "world" (which could refer to a section of it) and still less for

---

20. Long, *Definite Atonement*, 72.

21. Chang, "Second Peter 2:1 and the Extent of the Atonement," 55.

22. Murray, *Redemption—Accomplished and Applied*, 73.

"our" sins (those of John's immediate circle) alone; it embraces the sins of the *whole* world.[23]

Therefore, when the apostle John declares that Christ's death is for "the whole world," he clearly means that the benefits of Christ's death are made available for *all individuals* (cf. John 1:29).

Other passages in Scripture that can also be summoned to argue for the universal scope of the atonement include: Acts 17:30; 2 Corinthians 5:14–15; 1 Timothy 2:6; 4:10; Titus 2:11; Hebrews 2:9; and 2 Peter 3:9. Although both sides of the debate can readily appeal to Scripture to argue for their respective positions, it must be stated that the most likely position is the position that best fits the *overall* scriptural testimony. We believe that after examining the relevant biblical texts the non-particularist view of the scope of the atonement seems to be the correct one.

Despite having argued for the universal scope of the atonement, we also unreservedly reject the idea that all human beings will be efficaciously covered by Christ's atoning work at the end (and that all will eventually be delivered from eternal perdition). Universal salvation has no support in Scripture and no true Christian confession can entertain the notion that all human beings will eventually be saved in spite of their rebellion and unbelief. In this way, limited atonement advocates are correct in arguing that only those who enter the glorious presence of Christ at the eschaton are the ones who ultimately benefit from Christ's atoning work. Therefore, the most adequate way, we believe, in resolving this dilemma of why Christ's atoning death is available to all yet not all will be saved at the end is to suggest that Christ's death is *sufficient* for all human beings but *effective* only for the elect.[24] This cogently ties together all the biblical passages that speak of the benefits of Christ's death being offered to all people with those that speak of the atonement being effectual only for those who truly belong to Christ.

23. Smalley, 1, 2, 3 *John*, 38.

24. Some may argue that what is proposed here is a modified form of the classic limited atonement view. Be that as it may, the Scriptures are clear that only those who will be glorified are the ones who actually receive the benefits of Christ's atoning work (cf. Rom 8:30).

## *The Atonement and the Situation of the Unevangelized*

A common question raised when discussions of the atonement come up is how we should understand the situation of the unevangelized in relation to Christ's sacrificial work. One of the common criticisms leveled against traditional evangelical Christianity today is that it is too exclusivistic. Many who are troubled by the exclusivistic theology of traditional evangelicalism aver that the tradition puts undue stress on the importance of the individual's faith commitment to Christ as personal Lord, while downplaying the inclusive nature of Christ's role as the Savior of the world. Some scholars in recent years have criticized the evangelical exclusivist position and have proposed a more "inclusivistic" understanding of how the benefits of Christ's death are applied.[25] They argue that it is out of character for a loving God to automatically consign countless numbers of people to hell just by the fact that they have never heard the gospel. As a result, these soteriological inclusivists have come up with an alternative to the traditional exclusivist position. According to them, salvation can be actualized in some of those who never hear the gospel through what is called "the faith principle."[26] Though all will be saved solely on the basis of Christ's redemptive work, those who never hear the gospel are saved by exercising some act of faith towards whatever revelation they receive in their particular situation. For instance, John Sanders writes: "All who are saved are redeemed only because of the work of Christ. On the basis of the atonement of Jesus, God accepts all who exercise faith in him *regardless of the extent of their knowledge.*"[27] Whatever revelation is received, inclusivists aver, will either bring salvation or damnation (depending upon how individuals respond to that revelation).

Evangelical exclusivists have responded by arguing that the evangelical inclusivist positions (like the ones offered by Sanders and Clark Pinnock) can only be accepted if one ignores numerous passages in Scripture of the necessity of personal faith in Christ for salvation (cf. John 3:15, 18; 6:47;

---

25. Two well-known evangelical works that argue for a more inclusivistic understanding of salvation are Sanders, *No Other Name*, and Pinnock, *Wideness in God's Mercy*. From a Roman Catholic perspective, see Rahner, *Theological Investigations*, 5:115–34. For Karl Rahner, those who belong to the redeemed community but have not made an explicit faith commitment to Christ (or visibly become part of the church) are "Anonymous Christians."

26. Pinnock, *Wideness in God's Mercy*, 168.

27. Sanders, "Inclusivism," 55 (emphasis added).

Rom 1:16; 10:14). They also counter that the inclusivist position under-mines the necessity and urgency of evangelism. If people can be saved with-out explicit knowledge of the good news of salvation in Christ then there really is no point in churches sending out missionaries to distant lands to proclaim the gospel, they argue (cf. Matt 28:18–20). Finally, they maintain, if salvation is possible for those who never hear the gospel then we must conclude that the unevangelized are saved in some way by their own works of righteousness grounded on whatever revelation they receive.

Although we empathize with inclusivists like Sanders and Pinnock regarding the destiny of the unevangelized, we must maintain that the in-clusivist view does not stand up under the scrutiny of Scripture.[28] If we hold Scripture, rather than our own sense of justice, as the final authority on matters of faith and doctrine, then we must conclude that only those who explicitly receive the message of the gospel and put their trust in Christ are saved (John 3:16–18; 14:6; Acts 4:12; Rom 10:9–10, 14–15). This then should give Christians even more reason to go out and share the gospel with their fellow human beings who have never heard of the gospel. The mandate for Christians is quite clear because it is *only* through personal faith in Christ that a sinner can be saved from the guilt and penalty of sin. Nothing that sinners do, regardless of what revelation they receive, will merit them a place in God's kingdom.[29] Therefore, although the evangelical exclusivist view does not sound fair to some people, it is what Scripture clearly teaches and, therefore, we must uphold it without compromise.[30]

28. Some inclusivists will argue that their position also answers the question of the salvation of infants and the severely mentally handicapped. However, the situation is different for those who belong in those two categories. Infants have not reached the age where they can be personally accountable for their sins, although they do still inherit the sinful nature of the first parents. Also, Jesus seems to imply that those under the "age of accountability" are destined for a heavenly home (cf. Matt 18:3; Luke 18:16). For those who are severely mentally handicapped, we can argue that their salvation is assured by the basic fact that they do not have the mental capacity to receive any type of conviction from the law of nature (cf. Rom 2:14–15) and because of the bounty of God's grace (cf. Ps 103:8).

29. Even though God has revealed himself in nature, according to Paul, this is not enough because all unregenerate people are naturally inclined to follow their corrupt desires and rebel against God (cf. Rom 1:20–21).

30. However, one question still remains: Is it *possible* that God can bring the gospel to an individual living in a remote place without any direct human communication? In terms of possibility, the answer to this question is in the affirmative since God can sovereignly use any method (e.g., dreams, angelic messengers, etc.) to bring the gospel to a particular individual. On the other hand, is it *likely* that God will use means other

## Penal-Substitutionary Atonement and the Christian Life

One of the common criticisms leveled against the traditional penal-substitutionary view of the atonement is that it runs the risk of undermining the biblical exhortations for Christians to live out the gospel mandate to be a sanctified and obedient people. In other words, if Christ's sacrificial death takes care of all the sins of Christians what purpose is there for them to live sacrificially for God? Although on the surface the argument appears to have some logical consistency, if examined beyond the surface the argument is flawed under scriptural scrutiny. Even though the penal-substitutionary death of Christ fully takes away the penalty of sin for those who belong to Christ, it is also the grounds for the moral and spiritual renewal of the believer. Through Christ's atoning work, believers are not only forgiven of their sins but also have their sinful passions crucified with him, as Paul states in Galatians 5:24. Furthermore based on the propitiatory sacrifice, they are united to Christ through the Spirit who transforms them and gives them new life (Rom 6:5; 1 Pet 1:23). Therefore, it is impossible for a person who has his or her sins forgiven through the sacrificial work of Christ to remain unchanged ethically and spiritually.

Contrary to being a doctrine that encourages antinomianism,[31] it is a doctrine, as J. I. Packer points out, that is intimately connected with Christian living and practice:

> The idea that since Christ's sacrifice covers all sins, including future sins, as indeed it does, we may now sin freely is out: it is a monstrous mistake (cf. Rom 6). Knowing that Christ was crucified as sin-bearer for us, we crucify sin in our personal moral system for him. Atonement, says Paul, is thus foundational to Christian holiness.[32]

Also, Thomas R. Schreiner puts it well when he remarks: "The love of God expressed in the reconciling and substitutionary work of Christ should

---

than direct human communication to bring the gospel to an individual living in a remote place? The answer to this is in the negative since Scripture makes it clear that the normative way of bringing the gospel message to others is through preaching or evangelism (cf. Rom 10:14–15). Having said that, we must firmly conclude that any individual who is saved on the last day is due solely to Christ's sacrificial work on the cross on his or her behalf (cf. 2 Cor 5:21).

31. The term *antinomianism* means against God's law (from the Greek words *anti* [against] and *nomos* [law]).

32. Packer, "Atonement in the Life of the Christian," 413–14.

motivate believers to live for Christ instead of themselves (2 Cor 5:15)."[33] Therefore, the penal-substitutionary death of Christ does not encourage in any way moral laxity in the lives of Christians. It is a doctrine that is connected to Christian ethics in a profoundly intimate way. Those who claim to be forgiven of their sins through Christ's substitutionary work yet show absolutely no evidence of the reality of the new birth in their lives have no right to any assurance that they are saved now and on their way to eschatological glory (cf. 1 Cor 6:9–10; Gal 5:19–21; Eph 5:5; Jas 2:14–26; 1 John 3:6, 9).

33. Schreiner, "Penal Substitution View," 96.

# CHAPTER 10

# The Holy Spirit and His Works

## 1. The Person of the Holy Spirit

IN HIS POPULAR WORK *Christian Theology*, Alister E. McGrath notes that the "Holy Spirit has long been the Cinderella of the Trinity. The other two sisters may have gone to the theological ball; the Holy Spirit got left behind every time."[1] This mindset has been buttressed in recent years by the fact that an anti-supernaturalistic tendency has progressively crept into professing Christianity in the last two hundred years in Europe and North America. Even in strictly evangelical circles, discussions of the Holy Spirit and his works are not given nearly the same amount of attention as the person and work of Christ in many systematic theology works. In some ways this is understandable. For one, the scriptural revelation is not as explicit regarding the identity and person of the Holy Spirit as compared to the Father and the Son.[2]

Secondly, the primary role of the Holy Spirit according to Scripture is to bring glory to Christ and make his name known among people (John 16:14) (although Scripture also states that the Holy Spirit's role in redemption is no less important as Christ's unique role in it). Finally, writing about the Holy Spirit is not a simple task. Out of the three persons of the triune Godhead the Holy Spirit is probably the least understood and the most

1. McGrath, *Christian Theology*, 279.
2. Erickson, *Christian Theology*, 863.

difficult to comprehend. Therefore, in some way, it is understandable why many Christian theologians throughout history have focused more of their time and effort discussing the Father and the Son than the Holy Spirit.

Although we acknowledge that writing about the Holy Spirit is not a simple task, a discussion of his personhood and works does deserve a separate treatment if a theological work is to be considered complete from a Christian standpoint.

## His Deity

Although the deity of the Holy Spirit is not as easily discernible in Scripture as the deity of the Son, there are several references in Scripture that indicate that the Holy Spirit is very much God as the Father and the Son are. For example, in Luke 1:35, the angel Gabriel tells Mary: "The Holy Spirit will come upon you, and the power of *the Most High* will overshadow you; therefore the child to be born will be called holy—the Son of God." Here, we see that Gabriel associates "the power of the Most High" with the Holy Spirit coming upon Mary to virginally conceive the Son of Man in her womb. When one reads the verse, one will notice the similarity between the Holy Spirit's work of conception in Mary's womb and the description given of God the Spirit hovering over the waters during the act of creation in the first chapter of Genesis (cf. 1:2).[3]

In Acts 5, when Ananias and Sapphira sinned by lying about how much they kept for themselves for the property they had sold, Peter tells Ananias that lying to the Holy Spirit (v. 3) is the same as lying to God himself (v. 4). In the same vein, he tells Sapphira not too long after her husband was struck down (vv. 5–7) that what they had done is to actually test the Spirit of God (v. 9). Right after that pronouncement she suffered the same fate as her husband for the deception (v. 10). The statements made by Peter to Ananias and Sapphira demonstrate that Peter understood the Holy Spirit as not a mere supernatural force (as some like to believe today), but as a person who can be lied to—more specifically, to God himself.

The apostle Paul also gives indications that the Holy Spirit is deity. In 1 Corinthians 3:16, he tells the Corinthian believers that they are "God's temple" and that God's Spirit dwells in them. He then warns them in the following verse: "If anyone destroys God's temple, God will destroy him" (v. 17). Later in the same letter, he tells them: "Do you not know that your

3. Hendriksen, *Luke*, 88.

body is a temple of the Holy Spirit, who is in you, whom you have received from God? You are not your own; you were bought at a price. Therefore honor God with your body" (6:19–20, NIV). We can see here that Paul identifies the Holy Spirit with God. His equating of "God's temple" with the "temple of the Holy Spirit," and his statement that having the Holy Spirit dwelling in them is the same as God living in them, reveals that Paul affirmed without question the Holy Spirit's divine nature. Lastly, the author of Hebrews states that Jesus offered himself up to God as an unblemished sacrifice "through the eternal Spirit" for the purification and conversion of believers (Heb 9:14). Since only God is eternal, and this verse asserts that the Holy Spirit is eternal, we must conclude that the author fully acknowledges the divinity of the Holy Spirit based on what he wrote.

Even though there are numerous Scripture references that demonstrate to the full deity of the Holy Spirit, we can also provide evidence of his deity by the way he works in the lives of human beings (especially in the work of redemption). In fact, the way the Holy Spirit works in the lives of people can only be done by God himself. In Romans 8:11, for example, Paul states: "If the Spirit of him who raised Jesus from the dead dwells in you, he who raised Christ Jesus from the dead will also give life to your mortal bodies *through his Spirit who dwells in you.*" Since only God can raise Christ Jesus from the dead and give life to mortal beings this demonstrates, according to the passage, that the Holy Spirit possesses all the attributes of deity. In another passage, Paul states that salvation is by God's grace alone by "the washing of regeneration and renewal of the Holy Spirit" (Titus 3:5). Here again the Holy Spirit does something in the lives of believers that only God can do.

Another example is the way the Holy Spirit inspired the writers of Scripture so that the word of God can be passed down to future generations of believers. In 2 Timothy 3:16, Paul writes: "All Scripture is breathed out by God and profitable for teaching, for reproof, for correction, and for training in righteousness." Something similar is stated in 2 Peter 1:21, when Peter writes: "For no prophecy was ever produced by the will of man, but men spoke from God as they were carried along by the Holy Spirit." Since only God can inspire human beings to write a book that has all the characteristics of having a divine origin (i.e., infallibility and inerrancy), the Holy Spirit's deity is clearly attested to when looking at how all the books of the biblical canon came into existence.

Finally, another way to establish the deity of the Holy Spirit is by examining how the third person of the Trinity is related to the other two. Although all three persons of the Trinity are distinct, as discussed in chapter 2, the Scriptures make it clear that the Holy Spirit is equal with the Father and the Son in regards to deity. For example, in Jesus' Great Commission to his disciples, he tells them to go "and make disciples of all nations, baptizing them in the name of the Father and of the Son and of the Holy Spirit." Another example is found in 1 Corinthians 12:4–6, when Paul talks about the gifts of the Spirit: "Now there are varieties of gifts, but the same Spirit; and there are varieties of service, but the same Lord; and there are varieties of activities, but it is the same God who empowers them all in everyone." In another Pauline passage the apostle gives this benediction to his readers: "The grace of the Lord Jesus Christ and the love of God and the fellowship of the Holy Spirit be with you all" (2 Cor 13:14). Finally, the apostle Peter, writing to the scattered elect, tells them that they "have been chosen according to the foreknowledge of God the Father, through the sanctifying work of the Spirit, for obedience to Jesus Christ and sprinkling by his blood" (1 Pet 1:2, NIV).

We can see here that Jesus, Paul, and Peter ascribe equal status to the Holy Spirit with the Father and the Son, especially in the work of salvation. Although each member of the triune Godhead has distinct roles to play in the work of salvation, all three persons of the Trinity *possess equal status as God*. Therefore, the whole work of redemption establishes the deity of the Holy Spirit when looking at his role in it in relation to the Father and the Son.

## The Holy Spirit as a Person

Some pseudo-Christian organizations like the Watchtower Society of the Jehovah's Witnesses assert that the Holy Spirit is not a person with emotions, a will, and an intellect but merely a "power" or "force" that comes from God.[4] In other words, according to this group, the Holy Spirit is merely "God's active force."[5] However, Scripture clearly portrays the Holy Spirit as a person with all the essential attributes of personhood. The Spirit is never addressed in Scripture as an "it" but is addressed as "thou" or "you" (cf. John 16:7). Also, the masculine pronoun is used whenever he is the

4. Hoekema, *Four Major Cults*, 239–41.
5. Quoted in Martin, *Kingdom of the Cults*, 102.

subject of discussion in Scripture (John 16:13–14). It would be grammatically incorrect to use personal pronouns to address a mere power or force (cf. Eph 1:13–14). Jesus and the biblical writers, with their trinitarian understanding of God, understood the Holy Spirit as a person.

Other evidences that demonstrate to the personhood of the Holy Spirit are the numerous passages in Scripture that talk about how people are to respond to the Holy Spirit. In Ephesians 4:30, Paul exhorts the Ephesians not to "grieve" the Holy Spirit of God. Also, in 1 Thessalonians 5:19, he warns the Thessalonians not to "quench" the Spirit. Paul also talks about how the Spirit is sent into the hearts of believers and enables them to cry out "Abba! Father!" (Gal 4:6). In addition to Paul's statements, Jesus warns his hearers in Matthew 12:31–32 and Mark 3:29 that there will be no forgiveness for those who commit the blasphemy against the Holy Spirit. Also, Jesus tells his disciples that he will ask the Father to send another "Helper" or "Comforter" (Gk. *paraklētos*) to be with them after he has gone to be with the Father (John 16:7), and that this Paraclete will teach them all things and remind them of everything that he had told them (John 16:13). Lastly, in Acts 7:51, Stephen chides his fellow Jews for always resisting the Holy Spirit. Only persons can be resisted in the manner Stephen is speaking of. The fact that the Holy Spirit can be grieved, quenched, blasphemed against, lied to, resisted, and is able to guide and teach Christ's disciples clearly shows that the Holy Spirit is not an impersonal force but a person.

## Why Is Affirming the Deity and Personhood of the Holy Spirit Important?

One obvious importance of affirming the deity of the Holy Spirit is that he is also to be seen as the rightful focus of our worship. The Holy Spirit's deity should evoke in us a desire to worship and follow him. In other words, because he is fully divine, he "is to be accorded the same honor and respect that we give to the Father and the Son. It is appropriate to worship him as we do them."[6] Also, because he is fully God we can trust in his leading and prompting. We can also take great comfort knowing that his work of salvation in our lives will one day reach complete fulfillment (cf. 2 Cor 1:22; 5:5; Eph 1:13; 4:30). Lastly, knowing that the Holy Spirit is not an impersonal force but a person, we can joyfully remind ourselves that we can have a personal relationship with him. In fact, he is the Spirit of God who comes

6. Erickson, *Christian Theology*, 879.

close to each and every believer in genuine fellowship. Thus, through the Holy Spirit, believers can enjoy a kind of close intimacy with the triune God never experienced before the ascension of Christ.

## 2. The Works of the Holy Spirit

### The Holy Spirit's Work in Creation

In the Old Testament there are several passages which discuss the role of the Holy Spirit in creation. In Genesis 1:2, the verse reads that the "earth was without form and void, and darkness was over the face of the deep. And *the Spirit of God* was hovering over the face of the waters." The verse in Genesis shows that God's Spirit was at work bringing order out of chaos and having the role as the Father's Co-agent (along with the Son) in creating everything out of no pre-existing materials.[7] Another notable passage that talks about the Spirit's role in creation is Psalm 33:6. The Psalmist declares, "By the word of the Lord the heavens were made, and by the breath of his mouth all their host." In addition, the Holy Spirit's work in creation is also testified to by the fact that he gives life to living creatures, whether human or non-human. We see this in Job 27:3 when Job declares, "as long as my breath is in me, and the spirit of God is in my nostrils." This, according to T. S. Caulley, reveals that as "an agent in creation, God's spirit is the life principle of both men and animals (Job 33:4; Gen. 6:17; 7:15)."[8] Other passages that make reference to the role of the Holy Spirit in the act of creation include Job 26:13; Psalm 104:30; Isaiah 32:15; and 40:12–14.

### The Revelatory Works of the Holy Spirit

In the Old Testament the Holy Spirit worked mightily among the prophets to reveal God's will and his truth to the people of Israel. For example, in Ezekiel 2:2 the prophet declares: "And as he spoke to me, the Spirit entered into me and set me on my feet, and I heard him speaking to me." Later on, he also declares: "And the Spirit of the LORD fell upon me, and he said to me, 'Say, Thus says the LORD: So you think, O house of Israel. For I know the things that come into your mind'" (11:5). Other Old Testament passages that speak of the revelatory role of the Holy Spirit include Numbers

7. Cf. Reymond, *New Systematic Theology*, 391.
8. Caulley, "Holy Spirit," 521.

24:2; 1 Samuel 10:6, 10; and Zechariah 7:12. This revelatory role of the Holy Spirit, as mentioned above, is confirmed by the apostle Peter when he writes: "For no prophecy was ever produced by the will of man, but men spoke from God as they were carried along by the Holy Spirit" (2 Pet 1:21; cf. 1 Pet 1:11). In addition, Acts 1:16 and 4:25 make it clear that the Holy Spirit spoke through the mouth of David. Finally, the Holy Spirit played a pivotal role in the composition and formation of the Scriptures for Israel and the church. For instance, as mentioned earlier, Paul tells Timothy that "All Scripture [the Old Testament] is breathed out by God [Gk. *theopneustos*] and profitable for teaching, for reproof, for correction, and for training in righteousness" (2 Tim 3:16). Also, in John 16:13, the Lord Jesus tells his disciples that when "the Spirit of truth comes," he will guide them into all truth and declare to them the things that are to come. We see here that one of the key roles of the Holy Spirit is to reveal the truths of God to those appointed to speak on his behalf.

## The Holy Spirit's Role as Sanctifier

The Holy Spirit not only creates and reveals but is an agent of sanctification for God's people. When sinners come to Christ in faith, the Holy Spirit immediately begins the work of sanctification in their lives. This begins at the moment when the Holy Spirit gives them new hearts and minds and brings about the cleansing of sin (typically called *regeneration*) (cf. John 3:3, 5–6). The Holy Spirit then starts to continually work in the lives of believers to enable them to overcome sin in their lives and to live in a way characterized by righteousness, which glorifies God and benefits others. That is why Paul tells the Christians at Rome that "all who are led by the Spirit of God are sons of God" (Rom 8:14). Only those who are led by the Holy Spirit, as the apostle points out, are the true children of God. The evidence of being led by the Holy Spirit is that one does not live according to the flesh but, instead, lives according to the Spirit and sets his or her mind on the things of the Spirit (vv. 5–11). In another place, Paul tells the believers at Corinth (despite their spiritual immaturity and struggles) that they "were washed, [they] were sanctified, [they] were justified in the name of the Lord Jesus Christ and *by the Spirit of our God*" (1 Cor 6:11). Even new believers who still have much room to grow in their faith are being progressively sanctified by the Holy Spirit. Paul also makes it clear that the Holy Spirit brings about the "fruit [singular] of the Spirit" in the lives of believers. The fruit of the Spirit includes "love, joy, peace, patience, kindness, goodness, faithfulness, gentleness, self-control" (Gal 5:22–23), and these are set in contrast to the "works of the flesh" that characterize the lives of those who are perishing (vv. 19–21). Therefore, one of the evidences that one is a true child of God is that he or she experiences the Holy Spirit's work of sanctification (with the accompanying fruits) throughout his or her life.

## The Holy Spirit as Comforter and Assurer

Not only does the Holy Spirit sanctify his people, he also comforts and gives them assurance of their salvation. In Acts 9:31, Luke tells us that the "church throughout all Judea and Galilee and Samaria had peace and was being built up. And walking in the fear of the Lord and *in the comfort of the Holy Spirit*, it multiplied." As we read in the passage, one of the ways God facilitates growth in the church and the spiritual lives of believers is by providing them the comfort that comes only through the Holy Spirit. In addition, when trouble or difficulty ensues in the lives of believers the Holy Spirit bestows his comforting presence by assuring them of the full inheritance kept for them until the time of complete renewal (cf. Gal 5:5; 1 Pet 1:4–5). As Craig L. Blomberg writes, "The Spirit's presence in a believer's life is a promise of more to come, a partial installment of future blessings, and a divine guarantee of preservation by God."[9] This assurance is a subjective perception experienced by the believer—it reveals to him or her that he or she is indeed God's child who has been elected by grace. As the apostle Paul states in Romans 8:16, the Holy Spirit himself "bears witness with our spirit that we are children of God." Also, not only does the Holy Spirit give believers assurance of God's salvific grace, his presence in their lives reveals that God is abiding in them and they in him (1 John 3:24; 4:13).

Therefore, the Holy Spirit plays a powerful role in comforting and assuring believers while they struggle to run the race of faith with perseverance in this spiritually hostile age.

---

9. Blomberg, "Holy Spirit," 347.

## Excurses: The Debate over the "Charismatic Gifts" for the Present Age

In evangelical circles in the last several decades there has been an impassioned debate among Christians on whether the charismatic "gifts of the Spirit" are still operative during the present period of redemptive history. On one side of the debate are those who belong to the Pentecostal and Charismatic traditions (although not necessarily restricted to those two traditions) who argue that the so-called charismatic gifts of the Spirit (e.g., tongues, prophesies, etc.) are still operative in the present age.[10] This position is often called the *continuationist* view. Others, typically from Lutheran, Reformed, and dispensationalist backgrounds argue that these gifts of the Spirit are no longer operative in the present age and ceased at the end of the apostolic period. This position is usually referred to as the *cessationist* view.[11]

To determine which position is the most consistent with the biblical witness, we first need to understand accurately what is being said by Paul in 1 Corinthians 13:8–13 (apparently, the scriptural focal point among evangelicals when this subject is brought up). The passage in the English Standard Version reads:

> Love never ends. As for prophecies, they will pass away; as for tongues, they will cease; as for knowledge, it will pass away. For we know in part and we prophesy in part, but when the perfect comes, the partial will pass away. When I was a child, I spoke like a child, I thought like a child, I reasoned like a child. When I became a man, I gave up childish ways. For now we see in a mirror dimly, but then face to face. Now I know in part; then I shall know fully, even as I have been fully known. So now faith, hope, and love abide, these three; but the greatest of these is love.

The key phrase of this passage is found in verse 10 when it states that "when the perfect comes, the partial will pass away." Scholars have often debated on what Paul exactly meant when he said "when the *perfect* comes." Continuationists like Wayne Grudem argue that the word "perfect" (Gk. *teleion*) in the verse means the moment when Christ returns at the end of the present

---

10. This is the position of Wayne Grudem (cf. *Systematic Theology*, 1031–46). Cf. also Williams, *Renewal Theology*, 2:212–20.

11. A classic treatment of the issue from a cessationist position is found in B. B. Warfield's work *Counterfeit Miracles*; cf. also Gaffin, *Perspectives on Pentecost*.

age.[12] Thus, the charismatic gifts will continue to be operative after the apostolic period until Christ's second coming. Others, however, argue that the word refers to the closing of the biblical canon. Therefore, tongues and prophecies ceased after the canon was completed because those gifts are no longer needed.[13]

Coming to a firm conclusion on this matter is not an exegetically simple task. Both sides have solid scriptural arguments to support their respective positions. However, we must say from the start that, exegetically, the interpretation that the word "perfect" means the parousia of Christ appears to be more persuasive. The argument that the word refers to the closing of the biblical canon seems quite strained when examined closely and within the context of the entire passage. W. Harold Mare, a cessationist himself, makes a noteworthy point when he states that it

> is difficult to prove the cessation of these gifts at the end of the first century A.D. by taking *teleion* to refer to a completion of the canon at that time, since that idea is completely extraneous to the context. While *teleion* can and does refer to something completed at some time in the future, the time of that future completion is not suggested in v.10 as being close.[14]

In addition, Simon J. Kistemaker makes this insightful note that one of the problems with the "completion-of-the-canon" reading of *teleion* in verse 10 is "that we cannot expect the Corinthians in A.D. 55 to link perfection to the closing of the canon in the last decade of the first century."[15]

Making the claim that *teleion* in verse 10 refers to the second coming of Christ, however, does not mean that the apostle Paul necessarily viewed the gifts of tongues and prophesies as continuing on after the apostolic

---

12. Grudem, *Systematic Theology*, 1032–35. Grudem gives three reasons why the "perfect" should be understood as the parousia of Christ: 1) In verse 12, Paul states that believers for now "see in a mirror dimly, but then face to face." Since it is Christ's physical face believers will see visibly at the end of the age, it must mean that the "partial" (or "imperfect")—knowing and prophesying—will pass away only at Christ's return; 2) Paul desires to emphasize the greatness of love—which will have enduring value even after the return of Christ (unlike the miraculous gifts of the Spirit); and 3) Paul ties the spiritual gifts to the activity of waiting for Christ's return (*Systematic Theology*, 1033–35).

13. Walvoord, *Holy Spirit*, 178–79.

14. Mare, "1 Corinthians," 269. Mare also maintains that the Greek words *telos* and *teleō* in a number of contexts are used in reference to the second coming of Christ (cf. 1 Cor 1:8; 15:24; Jas 5:11; Rev 20:5, 7; 21:6; 22:13) (cf. "1 Corinthians," 269).

15. Kistemaker, 1 *Corinthians*, 467.

period. Although we cannot entirely rule out that the modern "tongues phenomenon" is prompted by the Holy Spirit, we should not conclude confidently also that these experiences are *in fact* brought about by the Holy Spirit. During Paul's time, the gift of tongues was strictly governed and accompanied by interpretation, and speaking in unknown tongues was considered a lesser gift (1 Cor 14:6–11). In addition, the apostle exhorted the Corinthian believers to regulate their public worship in an orderly fashion (1 Cor 14:26–33). Finally, we should also be wary of demonic counterfeits that deceive people into thinking that these verbal utterances are from God when in fact they are not.

In regards to prophecies, we should not expect this gift to play a role in God's redemptive-historical purpose after the end of the apostolic period. Although God's ministers should preach *prophetic* sermons to admonish believers to take seriously their spiritual duties before God, it would be premature to assume that the gift of prophecy is still being given to believers in the church today. One of the problems with the view that the gift of prophesy is still continuing in the church today is that there are no reliable ways to distinguish whether a so-called prophecy is from God or brought about by demonic influence. Additionally, if the gift of prophecy still continues in the church today how can we confidently trust that the canon of Scripture we have today is fully authoritative and sufficient for all matters regarding faith and doctrine? What if a "prophet" in the present day claims to have extra revelations from God that can be added to the biblical canon? How are we able to respond, in a way that is faithful to Scripture, to his or her claims of receiving extra divine revelation if we believe that the gift of prophecy extends beyond the apostolic period?[16] These are some of the factors that continuationists must consider when they examine the veracity of the gift of prophecy for the present-day church.

Despite taking a position that is closer to the cessationist position, we should not discount the fact that God works in supernatural ways in the present age to carry out his purposes for individuals, the church, and the world. For instance, God could miraculously heal a terminally ill cancer patient by directly removing the cancerous cells from his or her body. This understanding has the support of Scripture since James tells his readers

16. Grudem argues that one of the ways out of this impasse is by understanding what is happening in churches today as something that Reformed believers have traditionally understood as "illumination" (*Systematic Theology*, 1042). This still does not provide a satisfactory answer to how we can biblically distinguish between false prophets and those who are genuinely influenced by the Holy Spirit.

that if there are any among them that are sick that he or she should call on the elders of the church to pray for the healing of the body (Jas 5:14–15).[17]

Leaning towards a more cessationist perspective on the gifts of the Spirit, however, is not synonymous with absolutely denying that God miraculously works in history during the post-apostolic age. God cannot be fixed into a straitjacket, and he has the absolute authority and freedom to do as he pleases to carry out his perfect will on earth. In this regard, the best way to label the position proposed here is not strict cessationism but an "open but cautious" approach that leaves the door open for God to work supernaturally to fulfill his purposes on earth today.[18]

17. This, of course, does not mean that God will automatically answer all prayers for healing, as attested to by Paul's own experience (2 Cor 12:7–9).

18. Robert L. Saucy provides us with some words of wisdom regarding this issue when he states: "[T]he teaching of miraculous gifts as normal may place so much emphasis there that some believers lose the biblical emphasis that spirituality is evidenced primarily by the fruit of the Spirit and loving service to others" ("Open But Cautious View," 146).

# CHAPTER 11

# God's Sovereign Election of His People

To MANY PEOPLE IN the church today the doctrine of election is either a theologically fascinating subject or a belief that should be shunned and never to be discussed again in the church. Millard J. Erickson, for instance, states that the doctrine of election is "certainly one of the most puzzling and least understood" and "seems to many to be obscure and even bizarre."[1] Despite the discomfort that is usually associated with this doctrine, we should not, however, set it aside because of the possible intellectual and philosophical difficulties that may arise out of it. In an age where equality and fairness are highly esteemed values this doctrine has been viewed with great consternation by many today (even within the church). However, if we take Scripture as God's authoritative word for us, we must reckon seriously with this doctrine because it is taught throughout the pages of Scripture.

Before we examine what Scripture says on this subject we must first define what election is from a theological standpoint. The most satisfactory definition we can provide when describing this doctrine is this: *election is the sovereign act of God whereby, out of his own perfect and free will, he chooses a fixed number of human beings to enjoy his gift of salvation apart from their foreseen merits or worth.* If we go by this definition of election, it will be of no surprise that many modern people will find this doctrine objectionable for various reasons. One of the tasks of this chapter, therefore, is to respond to some of the common objections brought forth against this doctrine. Before we undertake that task, however, we will first discuss the

---

1. Erickson, *Christian Theology*, 921.

biblical basis for this doctrine and the nature of God's sovereign election of individuals.

## The Biblical Basis for the Doctrine of Election

There is no question that Scripture supports the position that God chooses certain individuals to be recipients of his special grace and salvation. Several key passages from the New Testament testifies to this truth:

> Acts 13:48: "And when the Gentiles heard this, they began rejoicing and glorifying the word of the Lord, and as many as *were appointed to eternal life* believed."

- In this verse we see that the reason why some of the gentiles in Antioch believed was due to the fact that they were divinely appointed to eternal life.

> Romans 8:28–29: "And we know that for those who love God all things work together for good, for those who are called according to his purpose. For those whom he foreknew he also predestined to be conformed to the image of his Son, in order that he might be the firstborn among many brothers."

- This passage teaches us that those who love God are those who are called according to his purpose. These individuals were foreknown[2] by God and *predestined* to be conformed to the image of the Son. There is no indication in this passage that those called according to God's purpose were chosen because of any foreseen faith or merit. God's calling of them for salvation was based purely on his sovereign mercy.

> Romans 9:10–13: "And not only so, but also when Rebekah had conceived children by one man, our forefather Isaac, though they were not yet born and had done nothing either good or bad—in

---

2. The word "foreknown" in Romans 8:29 is *proginosko* in Greek. Some claim that the word merely refers to "knowing beforehand." The word, however, has a more intimate connotation than just a mere intellectual knowledge of future events. According to Thomas R. Schreiner, the "background of the term should be located in the OT, where for God 'to know' (ידע, *yādaʿ*) refers to his covenantal love in which he sets his affection on those whom he has chosen (cf. Gen. 18:19; Exod. 33:17; 1 Sam. 2:12; Ps. 18:43; Prov. 9:10; Jer. 1:5; Hos. 13:5; Amos 3:2)" (*Romans*, 452).

order that God's purpose *of election might continue*, not because of works *but because of him who calls*—she was told, 'The older will serve the younger.' As it is written, 'Jacob I loved, but Esau I hated.'"

- Here we see that Paul makes it clear that the choosing of Jacob over Esau does not have anything to do with any worthiness on Jacob's part but due entirely on account of God's gracious purpose of election. Although some have argued that Romans 9 is only talking about the *corporate* election of Israel for *service* (not eternal salvation),[3] this argument does not stand up under careful exegetical scrutiny. Paul makes it clear that he is talking about eternal salvation in the entire chapter because in verses 22–23 he lets his readers know the contrast between the vessels of *wrath prepared for destruction* and the vessels of *mercy which God has prepared beforehand for glory*.[4] Also, it does not make sense, as Thomas R. Schreiner points out, if Paul here is only talking about the salvation of a *corporate body* of people. If God elects a corporate body of people to enjoy his salvific mercy, he is certainly electing *individuals* within that corporate body for salvation and eventual glory. In other words, you cannot separate the corporate body from the individuals within it.[5]

  Ephesians: 1:3–6: "Blessed be the God and Father of our Lord Jesus Christ, who has blessed us in Christ with every spiritual blessing in the heavenly places, even as *he chose us in him before the foundation of the world,* that we should be holy and blameless before him. In love he *predestined us* for adoption as sons through Jesus Christ, according to the purpose of his will, to the praise of his glorious grace, with which he has blessed us in the Beloved."

- Here again we see that Paul seeks to point out to his readers that their election in Christ took place *before the foundation of the world.* He also adds that God *predestined* all believers to be adopted as sons through Christ. Again, this divine act of electing and adopting was not due to

---

3. Pinnock, "Divine Election as Corporate, Open, and Vocational," 276–314.

4. In fact, the main theme of Romans 9–11 is not about God's election of certain people for service but about the undeserved salvation of individuals by God's grace for his glory (cf. Rom 10:1–4; 11:4–10, 14, 17–24, 26–27).

5. Schreiner, "Does Romans 9 Teach Individual Election Unto Salvation?," 1:98–105.

any foreseen merits in the elect but according to the purpose of God's gracious will.

> 1 Thessalonians 1:4–5: "For we know, brothers loved by God, *that he has chosen you*, because our gospel came to you not only in word, but also in power and in the Holy Spirit and with full conviction. You know what kind of men we proved to be among you for your sake."

- Paul makes it clear that the reason why his addressees are loved by God is due to the fact that God *had chosen them* to be the objects of his love before the creation of humankind. This bestowal of love had nothing to do with the worthiness of the Thessalonian Christians but was rooted in God's grace alone. Regarding this passage, Robert L. Thomas writes: "'He has chosen' stands for *eklogēn*. This is God's sovereign choice of certain individuals, including the Thessalonian believers, prior to Adam's appearance on earth (cf. Eph 1:4)."[6]

> 2 Thessalonians 2:13: "But we ought always to give thanks to God for you, brothers beloved by the Lord, because God *chose you* as the firstfruits to be saved, through sanctification by the Spirit and belief in the truth."

- Paul again tells the Thessalonian believers that God chose them as the firstfruits for salvation. The sanctification by the Spirit and belief in the truth are based on the sovereign work of God among the elect. There is no indication in the verse that the Thessalonians in any way prepared themselves for this divine work of sanctification to take place in them or for them to believe in the truth (v. 14).

> 2 Peter 1:10: "Therefore, brothers, be all the more diligent *to confirm your calling and election,* for if you practice these qualities you will never fall."

- The apostle Peter in this verse exhorts his readers to be diligent in confirming their calling and election. He does not say that they should cultivate the virtues mentioned in verses 5–7 to *earn* God's calling and election, but that they should cultivate these virtues in their Christian

6. Thomas, "1 Thessalonians," 243.

lives to *confirm* (Gk. *bebaian*) their divine calling and election. Peter presupposes the election of those who are truly redeemed in Christ through the Spirit's work of regeneration (cf. 1 Pet 2:9).

> Revelation 13:7–8: "Also it [the beast] was allowed to make war on the saints and to conquer them. And authority was given it over every tribe and people and language and nation, and all who dwell on earth will worship it, everyone whose name has not been written *before the foundation of the world* in the book of life of the Lamb who was slain."

- John is describing a time when an intense period of persecution against God's people will occur right before Christ's return. John states that those who worship the beast that came out of the sea are those whose names have *not* been written in the Lamb's book of life *before the foundation of the world*. This indicates that the names of those who will enjoy eschatological salvation were already recorded before the earth was created, meaning that their election happened before God laid the first building blocks of the earth.

As these passages make clear, God's election of individuals for salvation is entirely based on his sovereign mercy *and* occurred before the creation of the world. The doctrine of election is not a philosophically deduced dogmatic construct to reinforce the teaching that salvation is entirely by God's grace. Rather, Scripture speaks quite clearly in numerous places that God elects certain people for salvation apart from their merits. However, one will still ask: why did God elect certain people for salvation and leave the rest to suffer his righteous wrath? To answer this question we now turn to discuss the nature of God's gracious act of election.

## The Nature of God's Election of His People

### God's Election of Individuals for Salvation Is Grounded in His Love and Grace

When the doctrine of election is brought up in a discussion we must always emphasize foremost that God's decree to elect certain individuals for salvation is grounded upon his pure grace. Divine election is not an arbitrary selection of some to salvation while leaving the rest to damnation. Rather, it is a divine act that occurred in eternity *grounded in God's sheer kindness, love, and mercy.* Oftentimes, the doctrine of election is understood as a capricious act done by God that does not involve his loving kindness and mercy to helpless sinners. However, Scripture speaks of God's election of individuals as something that happens as a result of his love. For instance, in Ephesians 1:4–6, Paul tells his readers that "In *love*" God "predestined us for adoption as sons through Jesus Christ, according to the purpose of his will, to the praise of his glorious grace, with which he has blessed us in the Beloved." The doctrine of divine election, therefore, is not an impersonal concept based on an abstract dogmatic construct but a doctrine that is very personal and rooted in God's divine love for his people.

### The Doctrine of Election Should be a Source of Comfort and Assurance

A corollary of knowing that election is not an arbitrary act by an impersonal deity but a divine act of love by the triune God is the recognition that election should be understood as a source of assurance for those who are in Christ. Divine election, oftentimes, is viewed as a source of dread because of its seemingly inscrutable character. Scripture, however, views God's election of individuals as a source of comfort and assurance. We see this clearly in passages like Romans 8:28–29 and Ephesians 1:4–6. It is because God's election of individuals is an act of utter grace that believers can take comfort knowing that their election is not by some capricious deity but from a personal God who loves them. This truth is what enabled Paul to persevere with joy even in the midst of the most difficult trials during his time as an apostle. As Bruce A. Ware states, "What is often to us a 'controversial' and 'potentially divisive' doctrine to be ignored, at best, and repulsed, at worst, was for Paul, most notably, one of the sources of his greatest joy and strength."[7] Instead of causing morbid fear, divine election should lead believers to greater assurance that God is *always* for them despite the circumstances of life (cf. Rom 8:31–39).

---

7. Ware, "Divine Election to Salvation," 1.

## God's Election of Individuals Is Unconditional

One of the greatest attractions of the Reformed or Calvinistic understanding of election is its *unconditional* character.[8] Contrary to the Arminian or Wesleyan understanding of election (where election is based on God's foreknowledge of a person's faith and/or obedience),[9] the Reformed/Calvinistic view of election states without compromise that God's election of individuals for salvation is totally apart from any foreseen faith or obedience.[10] This is what makes God's election of individuals a sheer act of grace, according to the Calvinistic perspective. If God's election is based on the foreseen faith of the individual then one has to conclude that divine election is not unconditional but based on something that the sinner has done to earn God's salvific favor. However, Scripture presents election as a divine act that is grounded in God's good and sovereign pleasure alone. Therefore, we argue that the unconditional understanding of election, as articulated

---

8. Within Reformed circles there is an ongoing debate regarding the order of the divine decree to save. One position, *supralapsarianism*, states that God's decree to elect individuals happened *before* the fall; while another position, *infralapsarianism*, states that God's decree to elect individuals happened *after* the fall. One of the strengths of the supralapsarian position is that it is logically consistent with the entire Calvinistic scheme. One of its weaknesses, however, is its liability to portray God as being unjust because the decree to create the elect and non-elect happened *before* the decree to permit the fall. Also, it may be argued that this position makes election nonsensical since the decree occurred before the creation of any human being. The strength of the infralapsarian position is that it escapes the charge that God is being unjust in his dealings with people—since the decree to save certain individuals happened *after* the fall of man. However, one of the major weaknesses of this position is that it does not explain why the act of election has to occur after the fall if God is all knowing and all sovereign from eternity. A third position, *sublapsarianism* (sometimes called Amyraldism—after Moses Amyraut [1596–1664]), argues in a similar fashion to infralapsarianism but adds that salvation is provided for all *and then* God chooses certain individuals to receive this salvation (cf. Erickson, *Christian Theology*, 927–31).

9. For example, Robert E. Coleman writes: "As to the election from time immemorial, Arminians understand this divine choice to refer to persons who believe in Christ. The elect, then, are those who respond to the Gospel call. Those persons were foreknown before the worlds were made, and 'whom he foreknew he also predestined to be conformed to the image of his Son' (Rom. 8:29). So it is believed that divine foreknowledge determines the divine decrees" (*Heart of the Gospel*, 146).

10. Berkhof, *Systematic Theology*, 115. The nineteenth-century Anglican Reformed theologian E. A. Litton puts it well when he states: "Election to eternal life is not conditional, in the sense of being *on account* of foreseen repentance and faith" (*Introduction to Dogmatic Theology*, 350).

by the classic Reformed/Calvinistic tradition, is consistent with the biblical truth that the salvation of believers is *by grace alone*.

### God's Election Is Unchangeable

Another aspect of divine election that we must highlight is that it is a divine act that is forever unchangeable. When God elected certain individuals for salvation before they came into existence that decree will remain steadfast and inviolable. For instance, Paul declares forthrightly that the "gifts and the calling of God are irrevocable" (Rom 11:29). Later, in 2 Timothy 2:19, Paul also states: "But God's firm foundation stands, bearing this seal: 'The Lord knows those who are his.'" These passages make it clear that God's election of certain individuals for salvation will always remain unchanged. An elect person cannot fall out of his or her election in Christ; nor can a non-elect person add himself or herself to the scroll of the elect by doing something noteworthy. In other words, the number of the elect company is fixed and will always remain so. If this were not the case, we must conclude that salvation is ultimately based on human decision rather than God's sovereign mercy.

## Common Objections Against the Doctrine of Election

### Objection 1: The Doctrine of Election Is Unjust

One of the most common objections against the Reformed or Calvinistic understanding of unconditional election is that it is unjust. If God is just, holy, and loving how could he elect only a certain number of individuals to receive the gift of salvation while leaving the rest to suffer eternal torment in hell? Should not a God of love and mercy *offer the gift of salvation equally to all*? On the surface this objection appears to be an effective argument against the doctrine of unconditional election. However, the objection only appears valid on the surface.

First, God owes no single individual salvation from his eternal wrath. Instead, every fallen human being deserves nothing less than eternal damnation for the sins he or she has committed against an absolutely holy God. If God were to always act according to his strict and perfect justice *no* human being will ever experience salvation from his wrath (cf. Rom

1:18—2:11). To save even a few individuals is an utterly astonishing act of grace on the part of God.

Second, God is not only a holy and just God but also a *sovereign* God. Since he is the Creator of the universe he has the right to do as he pleases, as long as it does not contradict his holy character. Since he is sovereign over all things, he can dispense with his gifts (including salvation) to whom he is pleased to give them. In fact, Paul, anticipating the hostile reactions to this understanding of election (cf. Rom 9:14, 19), responds by telling his readers in Rome that God has the right to do what he pleases with his creation. He states in Romans 9:19–21 in response to a hypothetical interlocutor: "You will say to me then, 'Why does he still find fault? For who can resist his will?' But who are you, O man, to answer back to God? Will what is molded say to its molder, 'Why have you made me like this?' Has the potter no right over the clay, to make out of the same lump one vessel for honorable use and another for dishonorable use?"

Third, since we are all fallen creatures our understanding of fairness is marred and imperfect. Just because the doctrine of unconditional election appears unfair on the surface does not mean it is so in reality. God's dealings with human beings will always be perfectly just and fair. God's conception of justice is infinitely far more superior to ours (our conception of it only being a faint mirror reflection of God's) and, therefore, we can never truly fathom how he thinks and why he does certain things. Hence, we, as fallen human beings, have no right to accuse God of being unfair because he has decided to elect certain individuals for salvation while passing over the rest.

*Objection 2: The Doctrine of Election Undermines Godly Living*

Another common objection against the doctrine of unconditional election is that it undermines the biblical exhortations to godly living for Christians. If Christians have been predestined by God to enjoy the blessings of salvation what motivation is there to live a godly or righteous life? This objection, again, appears to have some validity at first glance. However, if we seek the counsel of God's word on this subject we will see that Scripture never presents God's election of his people as a decree so that they can merely escape the agonies of hell. Rather, election is also to a life of service and godliness. For instance, in Ephesians 2:10, Paul states that believers are the "workmanship" of God "created in Christ Jesus *for good works, which God prepared beforehand,* that we should walk in them." In another letter, Paul tells Timothy that God "saved us and *called us to a holy calling,* not because of our works but because of his own purpose and grace, which he gave us in Christ Jesus before the ages began" (2 Tim 1:9).

According to Scripture, therefore, God did not elect believers so that they can merely avoid being consigned to hell and suffer its torments. Rather, God predestined believers so that they will also experience the transformation of their hearts and lives that accompany the whole package of salvation. In fact, a life characterized by virtue is an indicator that one has been elected by God (cf. 2 Pet 1:5–11). As Charles Hodge points out, "Such is the clear doctrine of the Bible, men are chosen to be holy. The fact that God has predestinated them to salvation is the reason why they are brought to repentance and a holy life."[11]

### Objection 3: The Doctrine of Election Provides No Motivation for Evangelism

Those who object to the Calvinistic understanding of election often point out that the doctrine provides no motivation for evangelism. They will typically argue that since God has already ordained who will receive the gift of eternal life that there really is no purpose in sharing the gospel to the lost. However, this objection is also faulty when examined carefully under the light of Scripture. For instance, even though Paul states clearly in several passages, as shown above, that God sovereignly elects certain individuals to salvation (cf. Rom 8:28–29; 9:10–13; Eph 1:3–7; 1 Thess 1:4–5; 2 Thess 2:13), he tells believers in Rome without ambiguity that the gospel must reach unbelievers in order for them to hear about Christ and believe in him for eternal life (Rom 10:14–17).

What this entails is that despite an individual's salvation being ultimately a result of God's sovereign choice, the church must send out missionaries in order for the gospel to be made known to the unbelieving world so that the spiritually dead may believe and live. Christ made this mandate for believers very clear in passages like Matthew 28:18–20 and Luke 24:46–48. In addition, since no human being knows whose names have been written in the Lamb's Book of Life we are required to evangelize to *every* human being regardless of whether they have been elected to salvation or not. Instead of tormenting our minds wondering whether a particular relative or friend is elect, Christians need to simply obey God by

11. Hodge, *Systematic Theology,* 2:342.

sharing the gospel to them and let God's sovereign work of salvation take care of the rest. As Gordon R. Lewis and Bruce A. Demarest insightfully note, since "no human knows that any given unrepentant person is not among the elect, we must present the Gospel to all (Acts 1:8; 17:30). We do not know that any given person is not among those whom the Holy Spirit will call redemptively."[12] Therefore, it is a duty of every Christian, whether Arminian or Calvinist, to make every effort to share the gospel to the lost and bear witness to Christ.

*Objection 4: The Doctrine of Election Is Contrary to the Scriptural Witness*

Some will still contend that the problem with the Calvinistic understanding of election is that it is not consistent with numerous passages in the New Testament that state that Christ's propitiatory death is for *all* human beings (cf. John 3:16; 12:32; Rom 3:22–26; 8:32; 2 Cor 5:14–15; 1 Tim 2:4–6; Titus 2:11–14; Heb 2:9; 1 John 2:2). Despite the forcefulness of this argument against the Calvinistic view, the argument loses its strength when we recognize that God's offer of salvation to all human beings does not necessarily contradict God's sovereign election of some individuals to eternal life. God's desire for the salvation of every unsaved individual is a genuine one (as witnessed in verses like Ezekiel 33:11; Acts 17:30; Romans 10:13; and 2 Peter 3:9). However, Scripture also speaks of God ordaining a fixed number of individuals to receive this gift of salvation. What we must conclude, therefore, is that God desires the salvation of all unredeemed human beings *and* he sovereignly chooses, in his infinite wisdom and grace, who will receive this gift of eternal life. Ultimately, what saves an individual from judgment is God's sovereign and electing grace and not the individual's "decision of faith." The fact that it is God's sovereign grace, and not the sinner's worthiness, that saves individuals from eternal judgment demonstrates to the truthfulness of unconditional election, even though God desires all sinners to come to repentance and salvation.[13]

12. Lewis and Demarest, *Integrative Theology*, 3:62.

13. Cf. Piper, "Are There Two Wills in God?," 107–31.

## Excurses: Does the Doctrine of Election Require the Doctrine of Reprobation?

Theologians within the Augustinian-Calvinist tradition have passionately debated since the Reformation on the scriptural validity of the converse of divine election: the reprobation of the non-elect (the view that God, by his sovereign decree, actively passes over those he has not decided to save and consigns them to eternal condemnation at the end). Many people throughout the history of the church have reacted with revulsion when first confronted with this doctrine. Even John Calvin, who is considered by many to be one of the forefathers of Reformed evangelicalism, once confessed that the doctrine of reprobation is "dreadful indeed."[14] On the other hand, Lutherans, who generally agree with the Reformed on the *monergistic* character of the gift of salvation, diverge with their Reformed counterparts when it comes to the issue of reprobation (Lutherans traditionally adhered to a *single predestinarian* view of election).[15] Also, many in the Arminian and Wesleyan traditions consider this doctrine a monstrosity that goes against God's goodness and justice, and maintain that it should have no place in a church's confession of faith or witness.[16] Despite the emotional discomfort and philosophical difficulties that result from this doctrine, the more important question is whether or not Scripture teaches reprobation when examined on its own terms.

A few notable passages in Scripture teach that God does in fact pass over non-elect sinners so that they will not receive the gift of salvation. For instance, in Matthew 11:25–26, Jesus declares to the Father, "I thank you, Father, Lord of heaven and earth, that you have hidden these things from the wise and understanding and revealed them to little children; yes, Father, for such was your gracious will." Another passage that speaks of God actively passing over certain people for salvation is Romans 11:7 when Paul writes about the current situation of his fellow Israelites: "What then?

---

14. Calvin, *Inst.* 3.23.7. Calvin's exact words in Latin are: "*Decretum quidem horribile, fateor.*" Calvin does not mean that he found the doctrine of reprobation "horrible" (as the word is often understood by those who read Calvin's *Institutes* for the first time), but that he found God's decree to elect some to salvation and leaving the rest to damnation as something to be reverently awestruck about.

15. Cf. Mueller, *Christian Dogmatics*, 606–10. Those who hold to "single predestination" deny that God's leaving certain individuals for eternal condemnation is a proactive decree.

16. Cf. Pinnock, "Divine Election as Corporate, Open, and Vocational," 298–313.

Israel failed to obtain what it was seeking. The elect obtained it, but the rest were hardened." Paul makes it clear to his readers that the unregenerate within Israel failed to obtain salvation because their hearts were *hardened by God*. In 1 Peter 2:8, Peter tells his audience that those who reject Christ do so because they "were destined" to do so. The word "destined" in that verse is *tithēmi* in Greek. According to Wayne Grudem, the Greek word is "a term which elsewhere is also used to speak of God's *appointing* or *pre-destining* a particular event or situation long before it happens (Acts 1:7; Rom. 4:17; 1 Thes. 5:9; Heb. 1:2; probably also Jn. 15:16; Acts 13:47), or of God's *establishing* someone in a certain situation not long beforehand but at a certain point in time (*cf.* Mt. 22:44; 20:28; Rom. 9:33; 1 Cor. 12:18, 28)."[17] Finally, in Jude 4, the author tells his readers that the false teachers who have slipped into the church are those "who long ago were *designated* for this condemnation, ungodly people, who pervert the grace of our God into sensuality and deny our only Master and Lord, Jesus Christ." The verse seems to suggest that God ordained the condemnation of these false teachers who promote false teachings and licentiousness.

The scriptural testimony is clear that God not only elects certain people to salvation but also actively passes over the rest so that salvation will never be realized in them. Although we may feel a certain apprehension about this doctrine at first glance, we do ourselves a disfavor by ignoring it for the sake of lessening any emotional uneasiness that may come out of it. If we take Scripture as God's divinely inspired and authoritative word we must accept the doctrine of reprobation as a revealed biblical teaching. However, we should never view this reprobating act as something that God takes delight in or something that he is pleased with (cf. Ezek 18:32).

Furthermore, Scripture does not teach the doctrine of reprobation with joy. Scripture does speak of God's electing grace as a reason for rejoicing, but it does not speak of his reprobating act in the same way (Rom 9:1–4; cf. Ezek 33:11). In fact, to speak of election and reprobation in symmetrical ways is not only unbiblical but pastorally unwise. That is why when a congregation member brings up the subject of predestination to the pastor, the pastor should always respond: "Don't focus on reprobation, but focus on election. The reason why the Bible talks about election is so that Christians will have full assurance of God's grace towards them in Jesus Christ. That is also why Augustine, Luther, Calvin, and others emphasized this truth to

17. Grudem, 1 *Peter*, 107.

their listeners. Therefore, don't dwell on the negative side of predestination but the positive!"[18]

Finally, we must never accuse God of being the author of sin when discussions of reprobation come to the fore. God did ordain *everything* that will happen in the world (cf. Isa 37:26; 46:10), but that does not mean he is the *author* of sin (cf. Jas 1:13). Instead, human beings, as a result of Adam and Eve's original transgression, are the ones corrupted by sin and who commit sins. Even though God passes over certain individuals so that they will never attain salvation, the responsibility of sin still lays squarely at the feet of rebellious human beings (Rom 3:9–20; 5:12–14, 17–19). Eternal condemnation, therefore, is the righteous judgment that results from the individual's transgression of God's law despite the fact that God had ordained before the foundation of the world that the individual in question will never receive the gift of eternal life.

18. John M. Frame makes this astute observation about the relationship between election and reprobation: "We should recognize, as do the Canons of Dordt (one of the Reformed confessions), that election and reprobation are not simple parallels to one another. When God elects people to salvation, he decrees that they will be saved apart from their works. But when God reprobates, he decrees that they will be punished because of their works. Works, then, play a role in the outworking of reprobation that they do not play in the outworking of election" (*Salvation Belongs to the Lord*, 181).

# CHAPTER 12

# The Call of the Gospel and Regeneration

## 1. The Call of the Gospel

ONE OF THE MOST important questions a Christian can ask himself or herself is "What is the gospel?" Since the time of the Reformation numerous attempts have been made to answer this question with some coherency. Many of the proposals put forth since the early days of the church diverged quite sharply from the testimony of Scripture to the point that they could no longer be thought of as being faithful to the true *kerygma* proclaimed by the apostles. In the contemporary period theologians still debate amongst themselves what the content of the biblical gospel is *and how the church can proclaim it faithfully.* Within the Reformed tradition there are still vociferous debates surrounding the relationship between the external call of the gospel to all people and the internal call that is given only to the elect.

In the first section of this chapter we will discuss what the gospel call is and what relationship it has to the effectual call prompted by God's sovereign work of grace. A discussion of the so-called "well-meant offer" will also be discussed at the end of this section.

## The Gospel Call

Scripture portrays God as a God who calls sinners to faith and repentance for forgiveness of sin and salvation. He calls them out of the realm of darkness and into his kingdom of light, as the apostle Peter testifies in 1 Peter 2:9. Paul, in Romans 8:30, states that those whom God predestined he "also called, and those whom he called he also justified, and those whom he justified he also glorified." This calling, in addition, is not only a calling out from spiritual darkness into eternal salvation but also into the "fellowship of his Son, Jesus Christ our Lord" (1 Cor 1:9). Although Scripture is clear that God sovereignly elects certain individuals to eternal life, it is also clear that God calls *all* sinners to repentance and faith for salvation (Matt 11:28; 22:1–14; Luke 14:16–24; Acts 17:30; Rev 22:17). The questions then must be asked: if God calls every human being to faith and repentance for salvation how are we to convey that message, *and* what are the contents of that message that must be believed in for forgiveness and eternal life to result? This is where we attempt to provide answers to these two important questions of the Christian faith.

### *The Contents of the Gospel Must be Clearly Proclaimed*

One of the principal duties of the church is to make the contents of the gospel known to the unbelieving world without alteration or deviation. Regrettably, serious distortions of the gospel message have proliferated in churches in recent times that the church's witness has considerably weakened. In mainline churches, the gospel is often synonymized with certain liberal socio-economic policies or ecological ethics, while in many evangelical churches the gospel has been turned into a therapeutic self-help plan or a blanket promise of prosperity and health. There is little or no mention of sin, God's righteous judgment, the atoning work of Christ, and the need for true repentance and faith. Scripture, on the other hand, clearly portrays the gospel as the *kerygma* of salvation from the guilt and dominion of sin.

This gospel message is founded upon the perfect obedience and costly sacrifice of Jesus Christ on behalf of sinners (1 Cor 15:3–4). The gospel convicts sinners of their sin (Rom 3:23) and calls them to repentance and faith for forgiveness and salvation from God's wrath (Luke 24:47; Acts 20:21; Rev 22:17). Without the mentioning of sin, God's coming judgment on the impenitent, the propitiatory work of Christ through his sacrificial death, and the necessity of repentance and faith for forgiveness and life, there is no gospel message being proclaimed no matter who proclaims it or where it is heard.

## The Gospel Call Demands That Sinners Turn to Christ in Repentance and Faith for Salvation

It is all too common for churches today to avoid discussing the necessity of faith and repentance for forgiveness and salvation from divine judgment. It is often viewed as being too exclusivistic or judgmental. What is more important, it is commonly argued, is that the average lay person sitting in the pew feels "accepted" or "loved" no matter what situation he or she is in life. This sentiment is not only expressed in mainline Protestant churches but also in many confessing evangelical ones as well. Scripture, however, presents the situation in a very different light. Scripture is emphatic that repentance and faith are the *necessary means* to enjoy the benefits of salvation earned by Christ (Luke 24:46–47; John 3:16; Acts 3:19; 5:31; 20:21; 2 Cor 7:9–10).[1] This summons to repentance and faith is not a mere suggestion but a direct command given by a sovereign God to all (with dire consequences if ignored).

In one sense, then, the reception of the forgiveness of sins and eternal life are *conditional* blessings dependent upon the exercise of faith and repentance by those who hear the gospel. As Anthony A. Hoekema states, "The gospel invitation is not one a person may feel free to accept or decline, as one might with an invitation to go bowling, but it is an order from the sovereign Lord of all creation to come to him for salvation—an order that can be ignored only at the cost of one's eternal perdition."[2]

Although some may contend that this summons to *all* to repentance and faith is inconsistent with God's sovereign election of certain individuals for salvation, the Scriptures do not view this as a theological conundrum and/or problem. Ministers and evangelists, regardless of their view of predestination, have a duty to tell *everyone* the need for repentance and faith for forgiveness of sin and salvation from God's coming wrath.

1. More on this will be discussed in the next chapter on conversion.
2. Hoekema, *Saved by Grace*, 69.

*The Gospel Call Also Proclaims the Good News
of God's Forgiveness and New Life*

The gospel call not only demands repentance and faith from its hearers, but also promises forgiveness of sins and new life in Christ to the penitent. If there is no inclusion of these promises in the gospel call then the gospel has not been truly proclaimed. This is exemplified in Christ's words to his Jewish audience when he tells them, "Truly, truly, I say to you, whoever hears my word and believes him who sent me has eternal life" (John 5:24). Paul also makes this clear in 2 Corinthians 7:10 when he tells his readers, "For godly grief produces a repentance that leads to salvation without regret, whereas worldly grief produces death." Peter's preaching of the gospel also demonstrates to this truth when he tells his listeners, "Repent therefore, and turn back, that your sins may be blotted out" (Acts 3:19).

In addition, it is important to include in the gospel call the promise that all those who come to Christ in genuine repentance and faith will be accepted into his kingdom, and that none of them will be lost (John 6:35, 37–40). If these elements are not included in the gospel call then the call becomes nothing more than a didactic message without a promise. It is important, therefore, that Christians make clear the promises of the gospel when evangelizing to unbelievers or else the core message of the gospel is lost and the call is rendered useless in effecting salvation for its hearers.[3]

## Effectual Calling

Within the Reformed theological tradition there has historically been a clear distinction made between the external call of the gospel *given to all people* and the internal call *given only to the elect*. According to the confessional Reformed tradition, it is only those who have been internally called by the Spirit that receive the new birth, forgiveness of sins, justification, adoption, and eternal life. This internal call, which is only given to the elect

3. Although God is the one who ultimately saves an individual by sovereignly electing and calling him or her to repentance and faith, a distorted gospel message—which is no gospel at all—cannot bring about salvation (cf. Gal 1:8–9). The Spirit of God draws sinners to genuine faith and salvation only if it is coupled with a proper reception of the biblical gospel. This does not mean that correct preaching of the gospel trumps God's sovereignty but that God uses earthly means (one of which is the correct preaching of the gospel) to bring about the repentance and salvation of his elect. Nowhere in Scripture is it suggested that the effectual call occurs apart from the proper proclamation of the gospel.

and *always* leads to genuine repentance and faith, has historically been termed *effectual calling*. Thus, only those who are effectually called by God are able to respond to the external call of the gospel and receive the benefits of Christ's atoning work. According to Reformed theology, this effectual call is necessary because everyone borne in Adam is dead in sin and unable to respond positively to the summons to repentance and faith apart from God's gracious initiative. It is only by the Spirit's operation in the sinner's heart that he or she is able to respond to the gospel in repentance and faith that leads to salvation.[4] Therefore, if we were to give a precise definition of effectual calling we would define it as *God's effective calling of the sinner, through the operation of his Spirit in concurrence with the proclamation of the gospel by human agents, in which he summons the sinner to repentance and faith that leads to the forgiveness of sins and new life in Christ.*

*Effectual Calling According to Scripture*

In the Scriptures there is ample evidence to support the idea that only those who are effectually called by God are able to exercise true repentance and faith that leads to forgiveness and salvation. For example, Paul states quite plainly that the "natural person does not accept the things of the Spirit of God, for they are folly to him, and he is not able to understand them because they are spiritually discerned" (1 Cor 2:14; cf. Rom 8:7). Paul tells the believers at Ephesus that they were once "dead in the trespasses and sins in which you once walked" (Eph 2:1–2), but that "God, being rich in mercy, because of the great love with which he loved us, even when we were dead in our trespasses, *made us alive* together with Christ" (Eph 2:4–5). Christ also makes this clear when he tells Nicodemus that unless one is "born of water and the Spirit" he or she cannot enter the kingdom of God (John 3:5). This truth is repeated by Christ in a different way when he tells the Jews, "No one can come to me unless the Father who sent me draws him" (John 6:44). In fact, at the end of the Parable of the Wedding Feast, Jesus states that "many are called, but few are chosen" (Matt 22:14). In 2 Peter 1:10, the apostle Peter exhorts his readers to "be all the more diligent to confirm your calling and election." Indicating that one of the ways a believer can confirm that he or she has been effectually called by God is by practicing the virtues listed in verses 5 to 7 in the same chapter. Lastly, one of the clearest examples of God's effectual calling of an individual to salvation is found

4. *Westminster Confession of Faith*, X/1–2.

in Acts 16:14. There, Luke tells us that after Lydia heard the gospel, "The Lord opened her heart to pay attention to what was said by Paul."

These examples demonstrate that Scripture clearly speaks of God effectually calling sinners to salvation, and that this calling is necessary because of the fact that sinners, in and of themselves, are unable to exercise true faith that leads to salvation. Therefore, the exercise of repentance and faith is not something done by the sinner's own strength but originate in God's empowering grace through the Spirit (John 3:8).

### Effectual Calling Is Passive

One important feature of the effectual call is its passive character. Due to the corruption of sin and its pervasive character, as mentioned earlier, unredeemed individuals are not able to summon themselves to true repentance and faith. This calling is done by God alone apart from our own volition or power. If this summons to repentance and faith is a result of our own "decision-making processes" then we must conclude that salvation is a result of our own efforts or will. Salvation, then, becomes something that is partially based upon our merits. John Murray, however, makes this astute point about the passive character of this effectual call:

> We do not call ourselves, we do not set ourselves apart by sovereign volition any more than we regenerate, justify, or adopt ourselves. Calling is an act of God and of God alone. This fact should make us keenly aware how dependent we are upon the sovereign grace of God in the application of redemption. If calling is the initial step in our becoming actual partakers of salvation, the fact that God is its author forcefully reminds us that the pure sovereignty of God's work of salvation is not suspended at the point of application any more than at the point of design and objective accomplishment.[5]

According to the Augustinian-Reformed tradition, therefore, this effectual call must be passive and have its origins solely in God or else salvation becomes something that is partially earned by our own actions (namely, our own elicitation to repent and believe). It is only by stressing the divine origins of this call that salvation can be genuinely understood as a pure gift given to those who will inherit eternal life.

---

5. Murray, *Redemption—Accomplished and Applied*, 89.

## The Results of the Effectual Call

Although the effectual call of the elect is solely a work of God apart from a person's own volition, this does not mean that the effectual call does not have practical consequences in the life of the believer. The effectual call not only leads the elect to repentance and faith for the forgiveness of sins (Col 2:13–15), eternal life in Christ (1 Tim 6:12), and entrance into God's glorious kingdom (1 Thess 2:12), but also leads them to a life of fellowship with Christ (1 Cor 1:9) and the way of obedience (1 Thess 4:7; cf. Eph 4:1–3; Phil 3:14; 2 Tim 1:9; Heb 3:1). This summons, then, pertains not only for the elect to believe the gospel but also *to repent of sin.* Although their repentance and obedience will never be perfect in this life, those effectually called will lead lives *characterized* by ongoing repentance and obedience. Again, Murray makes this insightful comment regarding the relationship between the effectual call and its practical ramifications in the life of the believer:

> The life into which the people of God are ushered is one that separates them from the fellowship of this present evil world and imparts to them a character consonant with that consecration. If we find ourselves at home in the ungodliness, lust, and filth of this present world, it is because we have not been called effectually by God's grace. The called are "the called of Jesus Christ" (Rom. 1:6), called to be his property and peculiar possession, and therefore they are "called to be saints" (Rom. 1:7). The called must exemplify in their conduct the calling by which they have been called and have no fellowship with the unfruitful works of darkness.[6]

This effectual call is not a powerless call but a call that enables believers to live lives that are pleasing to God. This divine calling empowers believers to overcome the evil powers of this present age and live in a way that is consistent with the ethics of God's kingdom. Therefore, those who are divinely called have the capacity to live for Christ, and their obedience to God serves to provide the necessary evidence that they have effectually been called to repentance and salvation.

---

6. Murray, *Redemption—Accomplished and Applied,* 91–92.

## Excursus: The Debate Over the "Well-Meant Offer" of the Gospel in the Reformed Tradition

In recent years within the evangelical Reformed tradition there has been an ongoing debate regarding the so-called "well-meant offer" of the gospel to the non-elect (or the universal offer of the gospel). Certain groups within the orthodox Reformed tradition contend that the well-meant offer view is inconsistent with God's sovereign election of individuals and, therefore, argue that God does not genuinely offer the promises of the gospel to the non-elect. This view is espoused by certain Reformed denominations like the Protestant Reformed Church in America.[7] Others in the Reformed tradition, like Murray[8] and Hoekema,[9] argue that the offer of the gospel to the non-elect is a genuine one. On the surface the view of the Protestant Reformed Church in America seems to be more logically consistent with the classic Calvinistic/Reformed view of divine election and effectual calling. Those on the opposing side will argue that there are numerous passages in the Scriptures that clearly state that God desires all people to repent and be saved. So how does one attempt to resolve this apparent conundrum?

What we must state from the outset is that the scriptural witness always takes precedence over any type of rationalistic argument when deciding upon which doctrinal perspective is correct. This is no different when it comes to the universal call of the gospel. Although Scripture can never contradict itself, it does not always offer logically neat answers to some difficult theological questions. Hoekema is correct to maintain that we must never offer a rationalistic solution when discussing the issue of the external call—either in the Arminian direction (that God does provide salvation to all who believe and repent through their own volition) or the hyper-Calvinistic one (that God does not genuinely offer the gospel to the non-elect).[10]

As mentioned in chapter 11 on election, Scripture is clear in numerous places that God desires the salvation of all people (cf. Ezek 18:23; 33:11; Matt 23:37; John 3:16; 6:40; Acts 17:30; Rom 10:13; 2 Pet 3:9; Rev 22:17). This desire of God for the salvation of all people must never be pitted against God's sovereign decree to elect certain individuals for salvation. Both are

---

7. One notable theologian in the Protestant Reformed Church who wrote against the well-meant offer view is Herman Hoeksema (see his *"Whosoever Will"*).

8. Murray, *Collected Writings of John Murray*, 4:113–32.

9. Hoekema, *Saved by Grace*, 72–79.

10. Hoekema, *Saved by Grace*, 79.

true. God genuinely offers salvation to the non-elect and *he will save them* if they will repent and trust in Christ. This is no mock offer but an authentic external summons. However, God, according to his secret decree, does not effectually call the non-elect to repentance and faith. They are left to their own devices and are judged on the last day for their sins. This is a mystery that Christians need to accept and not attempt to figure out using logically tight rationalistic deductions. It may not make sense on the surface to our finite intellects, but God is much more complex than our human minds can fathom, and we will never fully understand how God works on this side of eternity when it comes to the redemption of human beings.

## 2. Regeneration

In a well-known discourse in Scripture, Jesus tells a renowned Jewish religious leader named Nicodemus that "unless one is born again he cannot see the kingdom of God" (John 3:3). Jesus highlights the necessity of the new birth before a person can enter the kingdom of God. It is commonplace for lay evangelicals today to speak of the new birth as a "born again" experience. In more technical theological language this new birth is typically called *regeneration*.

In this section of the chapter, we will discuss three issues that are pertinent to the doctrine of regeneration: 1) the nature of regeneration; 2) the relationship between conversion and regeneration; and 3) the results of regeneration.

### The Nature of Regeneration

*Regeneration Is Totally a Work of God*

Scripture presents the work of regeneration as wholly originating in God. It is a miraculous event where dead sinners are spiritually quickened and made alive by the Spirit. Human beings have no role whatsoever in bringing this new birth about. This means that regeneration cannot be the product of a sinner's cooperation with the divine call, as taught by semi-Pelagianism and some brands of Arminianism. This is due to the fact that fallen human beings are spiritually dead (Rom 3:9–20) and are unable to respond to the external call of the gospel by their own will (1 Cor 2:14). Reformed theologians typically call this condition *total depravity*.

The notion that regeneration is entirely a work of God is demonstrated unambiguously in Scripture. For example, John declares that "to all who did receive him, who believed in his name, he gave the right to become children of God, who were born, *not of blood nor of the will of the flesh nor of the will of man, but of God*" (John 1:12–13; cf. 3:6–7). Also, the apostle Paul declares to the Ephesian believers that "even when we were dead in our trespasses," God "made us alive together with Christ" (Eph 2:5). Elsewhere, Paul tells the Colossian believers: "And you, who were dead in your trespasses and the uncircumcision of your flesh, God made alive together with him, having forgiven us all our trespasses" (Col 2:13). In another place, Peter tells his readers that God the Father, according "to his great mercy, he has *caused us to be born again* to a living hope through the resurrection of Jesus Christ from the dead" (1 Pet 1:3). This regeneration (or new birth), according to these passages, is something that comes from above and not by the sinner's own will.

Just like human beings do not choose when they are physically born into this world, those who are appointed for eternal life by God do not choose when they will be made alive spiritually: *God alone makes sinners to become spiritually alive.* Reformed theology has been consistently faithful to Scripture on this point by arguing for the purely passive character of regeneration. As the apostle Paul states in Titus 3:5, God "saved us, not because of works done by us in righteousness, *but according to his own mercy,* by the washing of regeneration [*palingenesia*][11] *and* renewal of the Holy Spirit." J. I. Packer captures the matter well when he writes:

> Infants do not induce, or cooperate in, their own procreation and birth; no more can those who are "dead in trespasses and sins" prompt the quickening operation of God's Spirit within them (see Eph. 2:1–10). Spiritual vivification is a free, and to man mysterious, exercise of divine power (John 3:8), not explicable in terms of the combination or cultivation of existing human resources (John 3:6), not caused or induced by any human efforts (John 1:12–13) or merits (Titus 3:3–7), and not, therefore, to be equated with, or

---

11. This word is found in only one other place in the New Testament: Matthew 19:28. In that passage, the word *palingenesia* is used to describe the restoration of all things when Christ returns and establishes his kingdom on earth. This clearly indicates that regeneration also involves the restoration of the whole human being as we will discuss below.

attributed to, any of the experiences, decisions, and acts to which it gives rise and by which it may be known to have taken place.[12]

Gordon R. Lewis and Bruce A. Demarest essentially make the same point when they write: "The newness of heart and life is *a gracious gift* from God's Spirit; it is never earned. Regeneration is freely given as the Spirit wills (James 1:18). New life is not of works but is entirely unmerited, for we have seen that there is no merit in the human responses of repentance and faith."[13]

If we are to maintain a consistently monergistic view of salvation that emphasizes God's sovereign grace in all aspects of redemption, we must conclude that regeneration is solely the work of God. Sinners dead in their trespasses cannot by their own volition bring about any type of movement towards God—not to mention making themselves alive spiritually. We must conclude, therefore, that regeneration is an exclusive work of God on behalf of sinners for their spiritual resurrection and renewal of their hearts and minds.

*Regeneration Is Instantaneous*

Another important aspect of regeneration that needs to be stressed is its instantaneous character. Regeneration is not a drawn out, gradual process that reaches a climax at the end of one's life but an instantaneous change that occurs at one single moment at the beginning of the Christian life. For example, one clear example from Scripture that demonstrates to this truth is mentioned in Acts 16:14 where it describes Lydia's conversion. The verse narrates that the Lord opened Lydia's heart at an instantaneous moment so that she can come to believe the gospel message. Even though we cannot know for certain when regeneration occurs in an individual's life (and in some instances, new converts are not consciously aware that this regenerative work has already occurred in them), we can say for certain that it is a work of God that happens at one moment. One is either spiritually dead *or* spiritually alive but not somewhere in between. As Millard J. Erickson notes:

> [I]t appears that the new birth is itself instantaneous. Nothing in
> the descriptions of the new birth suggests that it is a process rather

12. Packer, "Regeneration," 925.

13. Lewis and Demarest, *Integrative Theology*, 3:106.

than a single action. It is nowhere characterized as incomplete. Scripture speaks of believers as "born again" or "having been born again" rather than as "being born again" (John 1:12–13; 2 Cor. 5:17; Eph. 2:1, 5–6; James 1:18; 1 Peter 1:3, 23; 1 John 2:29; 5:1, 4—the relevant Greek verbs in these references are either in the aorist tense, which points to an occurrence without reference to duration, or in the perfect tense, which points to a state of completion). While it may not be possible to determine the precise time of the new birth, and there may be a whole series of antecedents, it appears that the new birth itself is completed in an instant.[14]

Regeneration, therefore, is an instantaneous event that is completed at one time and never to be repeated again.

In addition, regeneration is a necessary prerequisite for the progressive sanctification of the believer.[15] We must keep this proper distinction between regeneration (which is a one-time event) from progressive sanctification (which is a lifelong process) to avoid any confusion about the proper ordering of salvation. Regeneration is only the starting point of that gradual process of inner transformation that is necessary to prepare the believer for future glory and habitation in God's eschatological kingdom.

*Regeneration Affects the Whole Person*

Another important facet of regeneration that needs to be pointed out is that it is a supernatural event that affects the *whole person*. One of the deep mysteries of regeneration is how it involves every facet of the inner human being. Even though the physical body of the regenerate person is slowly wasting away due to sin, the new birth quickens the heart and changes the whole inner person instantaneously. The new birth transforms a person so profoundly that it affects the deepest parts of his or her inner being. This means that the way a regenerate person thinks, feels, worships, prioritizes, etc. are all affected by this new birth. Before the new birth, every human being is hostile to God and is unable to respond to him positively (Eph 2:1); after the new birth, the whole person is so changed that he or she is a *new creation* in Christ, with the old person progressively passing away (2 Cor 5:17; cf. Ezek 36:26–27).

14. Erickson, *Christian Theology*, 957.

15. When discussing the doctrine of sanctification in chapter 15 we will demonstrate that sanctification has both positional and progressive aspects to it.

This does not mean that the regenerate person is morally perfect, but that there is a change so profound that occurs inside him or her that he or she is no longer the same person as before. Nor does regeneration mean an impartation of a new substance into the converted person. It is true that people who are regenerated have their inner selves transformed by God's grace but that does not mean a new element is implanted into them. They are the same individuals but only that their hearts have been renewed by the Spirit to respond to God in obedience.

## The Relationship between Conversion and Regeneration

One of the more difficult questions that keep plaguing discussions about the new birth within the Reformed or Calvinistic tradition is how one should understand the temporal relationship between conversion and re-generation. All Reformed or Calvinistic Christians agree that regeneration is totally a work of God who imparts new life to those he has chosen for eternal life. They also unanimously agree that salvation, from beginning to end, is a work of God by his grace alone. The debate, however, centres around *when* this work of regeneration takes place: is it *before* or *after* the sinner's conversion to Christ? One solution that is typically set forth by Reformed theologians is to argue that God regenerates individuals *so that they will* repent and believe the gospel for salvation. In this view, therefore, regeneration *precedes* the exercise of repentance and faith (conversion) that result from hearing the gospel. In other words, individuals are made alive by the Spirit *first*, and then are they able to repent of their sins and trust in Christ.[16] Others, however, like Erickson, argue that conversion is prior to regeneration.[17] Both views have their merits, and it is admittedly difficult to decide which view is more consistent with the witness of Scripture.

Despite some of the merits of the view that regeneration is temporally prior to repentance and faith, we must argue that this perspective is not consistent with the biblical witness. Many passages in Scripture state that salvation is *a result* of a person's repenting and believing. If regeneration is included in the entire package of salvation, then we must conclude that re-generation takes place *after* conversion. For instance, in John 3:16, the verse reads that "God so loved the world, that he gave his only Son, that whoever *believes in him should not perish but have eternal life.*" In another example,

16. Cf. Bavinck, *Reformed Dogmatics*, 4:121–26.
17. Erickson, *Christian Theology*, 945.

in Acts 2:38, Peter tells his fellow Hebrews to "Repent and be baptized every one of you in the name of Jesus Christ for the forgiveness of your sins, *and you will receive the gift of the Holy Spirit*." Finally, Paul chides the Galatian believers because they have been misled by the Judaizers (Gal 1:6; 3:1) and then rhetorically asks them, "Let me ask you only this: Did you receive the Spirit by works of the law or by hearing with faith?" (Gal 3:2). This verse suggests that Paul believed that people receive the Spirit *after* they have entrusted themselves to Christ through faith. Therefore, based on the scriptural references above, we see that regeneration happens as a *result* of a believer repenting and trusting in Christ.

Others may argue that the problem with the view just espoused is that spiritually dead people cannot come to repentance and faith unless they are first made alive (or regenerated) by God's work of grace. However, if we distinguish between God's effectual calling and his work of regeneration then this problem is easily resolved. As discussed in the previous section on the call of the gospel, we argued that effectual calling is the internal call of God to his elect so that they are enabled to respond to the gospel message in repentance and faith. We agree with the Reformed theologians who temporally place regeneration prior to conversion that fallen human beings cannot come to faith by their own volition, but we also argue that the ability to repent and believe does not have to be brought about by God's act of regeneration. God's internal or effectual calling is powerful enough to lead an elect sinner to genuine repentance and faith, which then leads to regeneration and reception of the other benefits of salvation. It may not be the same as the complete transformation that is entailed in regeneration but it is effective enough to awaken the elect sinner's heart and bring him or her to saving faith in Christ.[18]

## The Results of Regeneration

*Regeneration Leads to a Decisive Break with Sin*

One of the great blessings of regeneration is that the believer makes a decisive break with the powers of sin. Scripture is clear that those who have been regenerated by God are no longer enslaved by their sinful natures. Although they may not be totally free from the sinful tendencies residing in them, the new birth enables them to make a decisive break with sin and,

18. Erickson, *Christian Theology*, 945.

therefore, no longer sin *as a way of life*. The apostle John makes this clear in his first letter when he tells his readers that "No one born of God makes a practice of sinning, for God's seed abides in him, and he cannot keep on sinning because he has been born of God" (1 John 3:9).[19] The verse does not teach that regenerate people no longer sin *at all* (cf. Jas 3:2; 1 John 1:8–2:1), but that they are no longer *characterized* by a life of sin. As Sinclair B. Ferguson writes: "The new birth radically and totally transforms our relationship to sin. Christ Jesus makes men whole, and has begun the process of making all things new! This is what it means to be 'born again' from above."[20] Those who continue to wallow in sin and remain impenitent demonstrate that they do not truly know Christ and his new life. This is an important biblical truth to emphasize in an age where churches are filled with people who have a distorted understanding of the gospel and have never experienced the new birth that comes from the Spirit.

### Regeneration Leads to a Transformed Life That Is Pleasing to God

Another important result of regeneration is that the believer now lives his or her life in a way that is pleasing to God. No longer is the believer enslaved to sin and self but is implanted with a new nature which desires to obey God and love others. The regenerate person, by God's gracious operation, will not only be able to crucify his or her sinful flesh with its ungodly passions (Gal 5:24) but will also bear the fruit of the Spirit (vv. 22–23) and practice the virtues that are commended by God (2 Pet 1:3–7). Jesus made it clear to his disciples that people will be known by their fruits (doctrine and lifestyle) (Matt 7:15–20), and that there will be many on the last day who will call him "Lord, Lord" but will be cast out of his presence forever because they failed to bear the fruits that spring forth from regeneration (Matt 7:21–23).

The new birth will, therefore, enable believers to love God (cf. 1 Cor 16:22), other believers (cf. 1 John 4:7–12), and even their enemies (cf. Matt

---

19. Even if John is not talking about sin being practiced as a settled way of life in this verse, as some scholars have argued (cf. Kubo, "I John 3:9: Absolute or Habitual?," 47–56; Wallace, *Greek Grammar Beyond the Basics*, 525), there are other passages in the New Testament that clearly state that regenerate people are no longer slaves to sin (cf. Rom 6:6–7; 1 Cor 6:11; 2 Cor 5:17; Gal 5:24; Eph 4:22; 1 Pet 2:9; 2 Pet 1:4). In contrast to Kubo and Wallace, John R. W. Stott argues for the "habitual sinning" view of 1 John 3:9 (cf. *Letters of John*, 129–31).

20. Ferguson, *Christian Life*, 54.

5:43–48). As Carl B. Hoch states, "The new birth is . . . a sovereign act of God by his Spirit in which the believer is cleansed from sin and given spiritual birth into God's household. It renews the believer's intellect, sensibility, and will to enable that person to enter the kingdom of God and to do good works."[21] The regenerate person now has the ability to do good works and bear fruit for God's kingdom which he or she did not have the ability to do before conversion.

### Regeneration Guarantees That the Believer Will be Sanctified Progressively and Persevere in the Faith

Not only does the gift of regeneration free the believer from the bondage of sin and enable him or her to live for God and others, it also guarantees that he or she will be sanctified progressively and persevere in faith. In other words, the new birth will assure that the believer will progressively grow in Christ and not apostatize from the gospel. This is illustrated in 1 Peter 1:3–5 when the apostle tells his readers, "According to his great mercy, *he has caused us to be born again to a living hope through the resurrection of Jesus Christ from the dead*, to an inheritance that is imperishable, undefiled, and unfading, kept in heaven for you, *who by God's power are being guarded through faith* for a salvation ready to be revealed in the last time." This is one of the most comforting passages in the New Testament pertaining to God's promise of an unbreakable and eternal salvation arising out of his sovereign work of regeneration. True believers can take great comfort knowing that the new birth they have experienced by God's grace results in an imperishable inheritance that cannot be taken away despite their vacillating faithfulness or the vicissitudes of this life.

21. Hoch, "New Birth," 559.

# CHAPTER 13

# Conversion: Repentance and Faith

## 1. Repentance

ALTHOUGH THE TERM *REPENTANCE* can be understood in a non-religious way (when it is understood as a person turning away from his or her unscrupulous way of life to become a more law-abiding member of society), the biblical understanding of repentance is typically understood as a sinner's positive response to the gospel summons whereby he or she consciously turns away from sin due to the convicting work of the Holy Spirit. This is one of the two aspects of Christian conversion.

There are many places in Scripture that call sinners to repentance for forgiveness and salvation. For instance, in Matthew 3:2, John the Baptist is recorded as telling his Judean contemporaries to "Repent, for the kingdom of heaven is at hand." Jesus, in Luke 13:1–5, warns his hearers that they will perish unless they repent. Later in the Gospel of Luke, Jesus tells his disciples that the call to repentance for the forgiveness of sins is part and parcel of what is to be preached among the nations (Luke 24:46–47). The apostle Paul states that God's kindness is meant to lead people to repentance (Rom 2:4), and "that godly grief produces a repentance that leads to salvation without regret" (2 Cor 7:10). At Pentecost, the apostle Peter tells his audience to "Repent and be baptized . . . in the name of Jesus Christ for the forgiveness of your sins" (Acts 2:38). Again, in 2 Peter 3:9, the same apostle tells a different audience that "The Lord is not slow to fulfill his promise as some count slowness, but is patient toward you, not wishing that any should perish, but that all should reach repentance."

Scripture, therefore, is very clear that repentance is a necessary component in the conversion of sinners for the reception of eternal life. Without the call to repentance the biblical message of salvation is truncated and a deficient gospel message is preached. If repentance is clearly demanded numerous times in Scripture for forgiveness and salvation, what exactly then does repentance mean from a biblical point of view?

## The Meaning of Repentance according to Scripture

In the Old Testament the most common word used to denote repentance is *šûb* (literally "to turn"). The verb occurs over 1,050 times in the Old Testament, although it is translated as "repent" only thirteen times.[1] The word is used in 2 Chronicles 7:14 to describe the repentance that is required of the Israelites if they desired forgiveness from God and healing of their land: "if my people who are called by my name humble themselves, and pray and seek my face and turn from [*šûb*] their wicked ways, then I will hear from heaven and will forgive their sin and heal their land." Another passage that uses the verb *šûb* to describe God's call for repentance is found in Isaiah 1:16–17: "Wash yourselves; make yourselves clean; remove the evil of your deeds from before my eyes; cease to do evil, learn to do good; seek justice, correct oppression; bring justice to the fatherless, plead the widow's cause." In addition, in Jeremiah 26:2–3, the prophet tells Jehoiakim, king of Judah:

> Thus says the Lord: Stand in the court of the LORD's house, and speak to all the cities of Judah that come to worship in the house of the LORD all the words that I command you to speak to them; do not hold back a word. It may be they will listen, and every one turn from [*šûb*] his evil way, that I may relent of the disaster that I intend to do to them because of their evil deeds.

These passages indicate that repentance in the Old Testament includes grieving for one's sins, turning away from those sins, and returning to God in obedience and trust. J. M. Lunde notes:

---

1. Dunnett, "Repentance," 671. A related Hebrew term is *nāḥam*. However, when this term occurs in the Bible the subject of the verb is God rather than human beings (cf. Gen 6:6; Exod 32:14; except in Job 42:5–6) (cf. Erickson, *Christian Theology*, 948).

> Repentance . . . involves the turning away from those actions and attitudes that are offensive to God and his nature (1 Sam. 7:3; Jer. 4:1; Ezek. 14:6). It naturally includes the confession of sin, appropriately accompanied by mourning and regret (Joel 2:12–13; Jer. 3:13). Given the covenantal context, this is often expressed as 'turning back' to God, (which explains the frequent translation of šû*b* as 'return': Deut. 30:2; 2 Chr. 30:6–9; Is. 31:6; Jer. 3:22; 31:18–19; Lam. 3:40; Hos. 6:1; 14:1–2, NIV).[2]

In the New Testament, the noun "repentance" and the verb "repent" are translated from the Greek words *metanoia* and *metanoeō*, respectively. Both Greek forms signify a changing of one's mind. In regards to the noun *metanoia*, it is used in Luke 3:8 when John the Baptist tells his hearers to "[b]ear fruits in keeping with repentance." Indicating that genuine repentance includes bearing fruits that are pleasing to God. In Romans 2:4, Paul uses the word *metanoia* to describe a person's heartfelt turning towards God due to God's kindness. Also, in 2 Peter 3:9, the apostle Peter uses the word to describe God's desire for sinners to turn away from their error so that they may not perish eternally. In regards to the verb *metanoeō*, it is used in John the Baptist's preaching in Matthew 3:2 when he tells his Jewish contemporaries to "Repent, for the kingdom of God is at hand." The same word is also used in Acts 3:19 when Peter tells his audience in Solomon's portico: "Repent therefore, and turn back, that your sins may be blotted out" (cf. Acts 2:38; 8:22; 17:30).

Another significant Greek term for repentance found in the New Testament is *metamelomai* (although it seldom occurs in Scripture). The term means "to experience remorse" or "to have a different feeling" about some matter.[3] One notable place the word is used is in Matthew 27:3 when it talks about Judas' remorse after betraying Jesus: "Then when Judas, his betrayer, saw that Jesus was condemned, he changed his mind [*metamelomai*] and brought back the thirty pieces of silver to the chief priests and the elders." Although the change of mind that Judas experienced did not lead to salvation, the meaning is still there that repentance is a change in the person's mind about a previous action.

We conclude, therefore, that both in the Old and New Testaments the meaning of repentance involves a person wholly turning away from sin with his or her mind, emotions, and will. It is not merely a change of one's

---

2. Lunde, "Repentance," 726.

3. Michel, "μεταμέλομαι," 626.

opinion about something (as the Greek term might be mistakenly thought to convey) but a radical turning away from the things that God finds offensive and a sincere turning towards God in humble obedience and trust. Repentance (*metanoia*), therefore, can be said to "denote that inward change of mind, affections, convictions, and commitment rooted in the fear of God and sorrow for offenses committed against him, which, when accompanied by faith in Jesus Christ, results in an outward turning from sin to God and his service in all of life."[4]

## The Nature of Repentance

Through our brief word study of the Hebrew and Greek meanings of repentance we have discovered that the biblical terms mean turning away from sin and, therefore, turning towards God. We still, however, need to discuss what this repentance entails and what the nature of true repentance is. This is where we now turn our attention.

### Repentance Is Necessary for Salvation

We have seen that the Scriptures are clear that repentance is necessary for the forgiveness of sins and deliverance from God's wrath (cf. Luke 24:46–47; Acts 3:19–20; 2 Cor 7:10; 2 Pet 3:9). Some have argued, however, that adding repentance as a prerequisite for forgiveness and salvation turns the gospel of grace into another type of works-righteousness message. The only requirement for salvation, they argue, is that a sinner "believes" in Jesus Christ and his work.[5] The inadequacy with this understanding is that Scripture never speaks of instances where a person can refuse to take up Christ's call to discipleship and remain indifferent to what pleases God, and still be considered a genuine follower of Christ. Biblical repentance involves not only that the person thinks the same way about sin as God does but that he or she is *willing* to take up his or her cross to follow Christ (Luke 14:27) and renounce everything for the sake of Christ's kingdom (v. 33). In other words, genuine repentance consists of dying to self, turning away from sin, and having the willingness to lead a life that is pleasing to God (cf. 2 Cor 12:21). True believers, then, are characterized by a life of discipleship,

---

4. Kromminga, "Repentance," 936.

5. This is the position of Zane C. Hodges (cf. his *The Gospel Under Siege*).

repentance, and obedience to God, although these will never be perfectly realized in this life.

Also, this dying to self includes forsaking the attempt to earn a place in God's kingdom by one's own moral performance. This involves renouncing all self-proclaimed good works for the attainment of salvation and, instead, trusting in Christ alone as the only suitable sacrifice for one's sin.[6] Thus, genuine repentance not only turns away from sin and turns toward Christ but also turns away from dead works that provide no escape from the coming judgment (Heb 6:1; 9:14).

## Repentance that Leads to Justification and Adoption Happens Only Once in a Believer's Life

The initial repentance that new believers experience for justification, adoption, and salvation only happens once in their lives. This repentance to eternal life does not need to be repeated again since at the moment of conversion God justifies the penitent person *for all time* and adopts him or her *forever*. Unlike the Roman Catholic or Arminian understanding of repentance, the Reformed view, being in most accord with the testimony of Scripture, argues that the initial repentance which brings new life need not be repeated again since justification and adoption are completed acts of God done at a single moment in a person's life. This is attested to in passages like Romans 8:1; Hebrews 10:14; and 1 Peter 1:3–5.

## Repentance Continues throughout the Believer's Life

Although the initial repentance that leads to justification and eternal life is something that does not need to be repeated in a believer's life, repentance from daily sins is a duty that believers are commanded to exercise for the rest of their Christian lives. The apostle John makes this clear when he tells his readers, "If we confess our sins, he is faithful and just to forgive us our sins and to cleanse us from all unrighteousness" (1 John 1:9). Also, knowing that believers still sin and continually need an intercessor on their behalf, he writes to them, "My little children, I am writing these things to you so that you may not sin. But if anyone does sin, we have an advocate with the Father, Jesus Christ the righteous" (1 John 2:1). That the apostle

---

6. Horton, *Pilgrim Theology*, 265.

is talking to saved people is made clear by the manner he addresses them throughout the letter. Jesus also makes this plainly evident when he tells his disciples to pray "forgive us our sins, for we ourselves forgive everyone who is indebted to us" (Luke 11:4).

The *initial* repentance that leads to salvation is the starting point for the future acts of repentance that the believer experiences for the rest of his or her life. One can even say that there is no substantive distinction between the initial repentance involved at the time of the sinner's conversion and the subsequent acts of repentance by the believer due to his or her need for forgiveness because of daily sins.[7] In other words, although all believers are completely washed of their sins by the blood of Christ, they still need to be cleansed on a daily basis due to the sins that they commit subsequent to their initial repentance. The biblical witness, therefore, is clear: believers need to continually repent of the sins they commit on a regular basis during their earthly pilgrimage.

### Genuine Repentance That Leads to Salvation Is Ultimately Grounded in God's Sovereign Work of Grace

Even though human beings are the ones who repent and turn from sin, the heartfelt contrition for offending God and the turning away from what is displeasing to him are ultimately grounded in God's sovereign work of grace. It is true that repentance is something that human beings do (cf. Acts 3:19; 2 Cor 12:21) and ministers of the gospel must call all sinners to repentance (cf. Luke 24:47), yet genuine repentance that leads to salvation is finally rooted in God's effectual and gracious calling of the sinner. This is demonstrated by the fact that Paul tells Timothy that he hopes that God may grant the opponents "repentance leading to a knowledge of the truth" because the servant of the Lord corrects his enemies with gentleness (2 Tim 2:25). Also, in Acts 11:18, the repentance of the gentiles is clearly described as something that occurs because of God's gracious work in their hearts: "Then to the Gentiles also God has granted repentance that leads to life." Therefore, we conclude that even though repentance is a genuinely human response to the gospel summons, it is *ultimately* grounded in God's work of grace in the sinner's heart.

---

7. Culver, *Systematic Theology*, 709.

## 2. Faith

The other critical component of a believer's conversion is the act of trust in Christ and his work for salvation. In common Christian parlance this component is called *faith*. That faith, along with repentance, is a necessary requirement for the forgiveness of sins and the receiving of salvation is clearly attested to in numerous passages in Scripture: Gen 15:6; John 1:12; 3:16; 6:53–58; 11:26; 20:31; Acts 16:31; Rom 1:16; 5:1; 9:30; 10:9; Gal 3:24; Eph 2:8–9; Heb 4:3; Jas 2:23; and 1 Pet 1:8–9. In fact, one can even say that while repentance is the negative side of conversion (where a sinner turns from his or her sins), faith is the positive side where the sinner entrusts himself or herself to Christ. In order to understand the nature of faith and what it entails we must examine, like the term repentance, what the word means in Scripture.

### The Meaning of Faith according to Scripture

In the Old Testament there are a number of Hebrew terms that are commonly associated with the English words "faith" and "faithfulness." According to Herbert L. Swartz, the Hebrew language has six terms that expresses what it means to believe, trust, and be loyal. These are: *bṭḥ* (which expresses a feeling of safety and security); *ḥsh* (which connotes a dependence on another for help); *qwh, yḥl,* and *ḥkh* (all of which mean persistence, hope, or waiting for); and the well-known *'mn* (which stresses firmness and stability).[8] After drawing out the meaning of faith based on these Hebrew terms, Swartz writes:

> The recognition and acknowledgment of the relationship into which God enters with people is a declaratory saying of "amen" to God and a special religious attitude of the people of God. The commands of God demand a proper response. Individuals are to acknowledge his demands, regard him as trustworthy, and be obedient to him. Faith is a spiritual attitude involving activity. The children of Israel stood condemned because they rebelled at God's command to take possession of the land he had given them. Fundamental to this rebellion is the claim: "You did not trust him or obey him" (Deut. 9:23). On the other hand, Abram stood approved when he acknowledged the promise of God, and trusted God's power to perform what he had promised: "Abram

8. Swartz, "Faith," 236.

believed the LORD, and he credited it to him as righteousness"
(Gen. 15:6). The Lord indicated to Abram his plan for history, and
Abram believed it to be something real and was filled with a firmness and security in the Lord. His subsequent exercise of patience
and obedient actions are clear indications of the meaning of faith.[9]

If we take up Swartz's analysis the meaning of faith in the Old Testament
consists of trust, covenant loyalty, and firmness of belief in the promises of
God. It is not a mere intellectual assent to a given set of facts but a personal
turning towards God in trust and covenant loyalty with the firm knowledge
that he will accomplish his purposes for his people.

When we turn to the New Testament the Greek terms commonly
used to express the meaning of faith belong in the *pist*-root word group: the
noun *pistis* ("faith"), the adjective *pistos* ("faithful"), and the verbs *pisteuō/
pisteuein* ("to believe" or "to trust in") and *peithein* ("to trust in" or "to
obey").[10] The verb forms of the *pist*-word group can take on two general
meanings: it can either mean believing something to be true based on what
someone says (what the apostle John tells his readers in 1 John 4:1 being
a good example) or it can mean personal trust that goes beyond a mental
affirmation that something is true to the hearer (this is when prepositions
like *en, eis,* or *epi* are used: examples include Matthew 27:42; Mark 1:15;
John 2:11, Acts 10:43; Romans 4:5; Galatians 2:16; Philippians 1:29; 1 Peter
1:8; and 1 John 5:13).[11] In the second meaning, there is an emphasis on
trusting *in* someone—in this case, Christ—for forgiveness of sin and eternal life. Faith, therefore, according to the New Testament writers is not only
about acknowledging that something is true (*notitia*) or trustworthy to
believe in (*assensus*), but, like the Old Testament, involves a heartfelt trust
in someone/something for liberation or deliverance (*fiducia*)—in this case,
Christ as Savior from God's eternal wrath—that also result in commitment
and loyalty to the object of that trust.[12]

---

9. Swartz, "Faith," 236–37.

10. Taylor, "Faith, Faithfulness," 488.

11. Erickson, *Christian Theology*, 952–53.

12. In Protestant theological circles saving faith is understood to have three elements:
*notitia* (the intellectual element—acceptance of a truth on the mental level), *assensus* (the
emotional element—being persuaded that something is true), and *fiducia* (the volitional
element—a personal trust in and commitment to the object of faith). Confessional Reformed theologians have always agreed that faith would be less than saving if the *fiducial*
element is lacking (cf. Berkhof, *Systematic Theology*, 505–6).

Going forward in our discussion based on our brief word study we will now turn to discuss what the nature of saving faith is and what it consists of.

## The Nature of Saving Faith

### Saving Faith Is a Gift from God

An important aspect of saving faith that needs to be emphasized is its gift-character. No orthodox Christian will doubt that faith is something that human beings must exercise for salvation; Scripture, however, also states that saving faith is something graciously given by God. One place in Scripture that demonstrates to this truth is found in John 6:44 (also v. 37) when Jesus tells his Jewish audience: "No one can come to me unless the Father who sent me draws him. And I will raise him up on the last day." Jesus makes it clear that the ability to believe in him for salvation is given by the Father. In another place, the apostle Paul tells the Philippian believers: "For it has been granted to you that for the sake of Christ you should not only believe in him but also suffer for his sake" (Phil 1:29).

On the other hand, the passage that is most often cited to argue that saving faith is a gift from God is Ephesians 2:8–9: "For by grace you have been saved through faith. And this is not your own doing; it is the gift of God, not a result of works, so that no one may boast." When commenting on this passage, Reformed scholars have typically argued that the "this" Paul talks about in verse 8 is faith in Christ, and therefore, the "gift of God" that he is talking about immediately following is the believer's "faith."[13] Thus, the gift that Paul mentions in this passage is saving faith. However, what makes this interpretation highly unlikely is the fact that the word "faith" in Greek (*pistis*) is feminine and the word "this" (*touto*) is neuter.[14] A better interpretation would understand *touto*, as Andrew T. Lincoln points out, as referring to the whole process of salvation from beginning to end (which includes the means of receiving that salvation, which is faith).[15] What Paul is saying, then, is that the entire package of salvation, along with faith, is a gift from God. Regardless of how one interprets Ephesians 2:8–9, the

13. Cf. Reymond, *New Systematic Theology*, 732.

14. Hoekema, *Saved by Grace*, 144–45.

15. Lincoln, *Ephesians*, 112. Even John Calvin argued that Paul is not restricting the Greek term to faith but to the whole gift of salvation. He writes: "His [Paul's] meaning is, not that faith is the gift of God, but that salvation is given to us by God, or, that we obtain it by the gift of God" (*Comm.* Eph. 2:9).

point is clear: saving faith, along with salvation, is a gift from God and not something that can be generated out of one's own volition. If saving faith is something that can be created out of one's own will then salvation cannot be considered a divine gift but something that is partially earned by one's "decision to believe."

### *Saving Faith Casts Off All Attempts to Earn God's Salvific Favor by Keeping the Law*

Along with its gift-character, another important aspect of faith that needs to be stressed is its intrinsic nature of being opposed to any endeavor to earn God's salvific favor by keeping the law. Genuine saving faith looks away from oneself but to Christ as the only appropriate sacrifice to deal with the guilt of sin. This is why it is important to stress in our preaching that the ungodly are justified through faith *alone* apart from any good works or observance of the law. This gospel truth is made clear in passages like Romans 3:28; 4:5; 10:4; Galatians 2:16; 3:11; and Philippians 3:9. In order for faith to be understood as a gift and eternal life as viewed as something that is freely given by God's sovereign grace, we must *always* set saving faith and personal law-keeping as antithetical principles in the reception of justification and salvation. Basing his argument on Paul's statement in Galatians 3:11–12, Calvin writes:

> The law, he says, is different from faith. Why? Because works are required for law righteousness. Therefore it follows that they are not required for faith righteousness. From this relation it is clear that those who are justified by faith are justified apart from the merit of works—in fact, without the merit of works. For faith receives that righteousness which the gospel bestows. Now the gospel differs from the law in that it does not link righteousness to works but lodges it solely in God's mercy.[16]

In summary, law and faith in God's economy of salvation do not mix. Faith must always be set in diametric opposition to law-keeping if God's gift of salvation is to remain untarnished by the error of any type of works-righteousness doctrine.

---

16. Calvin, *Inst.* 3.11.18.

## Saving Faith Has Christ as Its Object

Another important aspect of saving faith that needs to be highlighted is that it has Christ as its only object. This implies that even faith the size of a mountain is less than saving if it does not have Christ as its sole focus. Genuine saving faith, then, looks to Christ alone and rests on his sacrificial work for justification and eternal life. This is what makes saving faith efficacious and pleasing in the sight of God (even if this faith is small as a mustard seed [cf. Matt 17:20]). G. C. Berkouwer states it well when he writes that everything

> is really said in an unobtrusive phrase, *in Christ*. The possibility and reality of justification are concentrated in this one phrase. This appears most clearly in the manner in which faith is approached. It is not added as a second, independent ingredient which makes its own contribution to justification in Christ. On the contrary, faith does nothing but accept, or come to rest in the sovereignty of His benefit.[17]

Therefore, it is somewhat incorrect to say that sinners are justified *by* faith alone (as if faith itself is the *basis* for a sinner's justification before God). Rather, it is more proper to say that sinners are justified *through* faith alone *in* Christ alone (inferring that faith is merely the *instrumental means* to receive the salvific benefits of Christ's sacrificial work). The saving power of faith is not inherent in the act of faith itself but because it relies solely on Christ who gave himself up for the salvation of those who come to him in childlike trust. Genuine faith, in other words, looks outward and relies solely on the Incarnate One who does not turn away anyone who entrusts himself or herself to him for forgiveness of sins and eternal life.

## Saving Faith Is a Faith That Expresses Itself in Obedience to God and Love for Others

Since the Reformation period, there have always been voices of opposition to the traditional Protestant belief that sinners are justified through faith alone in Christ alone. They maintain that casting out good works in the procuring of the benefits of Christ's redemptive work will inevitably lead people down the road of moral indifference or a life of sinful debauchery. Although this response to the traditional Protestant view appears justifiable

17. Berkouwer, *Faith and Justification*, 43.

on the surface, it misunderstands the biblical view of faith and how faith operates in the life of the believer. Despite insisting that justification is always through faith alone in Christ alone, traditional Protestants have always argued that genuine faith expresses itself in obedience to God (Rom 1:5; Jas 2:14–26) and love for others (Gal 5:6; 1 John 3:14). If obedience towards God and love for others are consistently lacking in a professing believer's life, Protestant divines have typically argued that the person in question is more likely devoid of saving faith, and therefore, self-deceived. Francis Turretin, in response to the theologians of Rome who argued that the Reformation's *sola fide* doctrine led to moral license, wrote:

> The opinion of our opponents receives no better support from Jam. 2:26 where "faith without works" is said to be "dead" because this must not be understood of the causality of works to the life of faith *a priori*, as if works made faith living, but of a declaration that *a posteriori* because works demonstrate a living faith; as a body without spirit is said to be dead (i.e., it is known to be dead from the want of respiration and breathing; for here *pneuma* is used for *pnoē* or "respiration").[18]

Therefore, it is erroneous to conclude that the traditional Protestant understanding of faith as the only instrument in the reception of the gift of justification leads to ethical indifference or immoral living. Genuine faith expresses itself in keeping God's commandments. However, we must also contend that the keeping of God's commandments is only the *evidence* and *fruit* of genuine faith and salvation. It is not another instrument alongside faith in the reception of God's salvific gifts procured by Christ's redemptive work. Through this, the dual dangers of practical antinomianism *and* legalism are avoided.

## Special Issues Concerning Repentance and Faith in Contemporary Theological Discourse

### Must Sinners Receive Christ as Lord for Salvation?

One of the questions often asked within evangelical circles today is whether the gospel requires sinners not only to trust in Christ as Savior but also to submit to him as Lord of their lives. This debate regarding the terms of the gospel reached its height during the late 1980s and early 1990s among

---

18. Turretin, *Institutes of Elenctic Theology*, 2:581.

conservative evangelical scholars. On one side of the debate were those who sought to defend the freeness of the gospel and argued that trusting in Christ only as Savior was enough to obtain forgiveness and eternal life.[19] The inclusion of submission to Christ's lordship in the gospel message, they claimed, undermined the graciousness of salvation and led to a type of works-righteousness soteriology. On the other side of the debate were those who argued that submission to Christ's lordship is a necessary component of saving faith. A person cannot receive Christ as Savior if he or she refuses to submit to him as Lord.[20] This position is often pejoratively labeled "lordship salvation" by its opponents. The important question, therefore, to ask here is this: which side has more biblical support when all the scriptural evidence is taken into account?

One of the pitfalls that we must avoid when discussions of these types of issues come up is to never draw certain doctrinal and exegetical conclusions using an all-encompassing hermeneutical paradigm. This is one of the serious fallacies committed by those who oppose the position that submission to Christ's lordship is a necessary aspect of conversion. This fallacy occurs when they take up a single doctrinal principle (i.e., salvation by grace alone) and use it as the overarching hermeneutical lens to interpret all the relevant passages in Scripture dealing with this subject. This has resulted oftentimes in bizarre interpretive moves by those who fall into the "non-lordship salvation" camp.[21]

In response to this heterodox view, we must state again that biblical conversion not only involves a sinner entrusting himself or herself to Christ for salvation (faith) but also a *turning away from a life of sin* (repentance). As discussed earlier, Scripture nowhere states that a person can enjoy the blessings of salvation while wilfully, deliberately, and persistently remaining in rebellion against God. Those who come to Christ will receive eternal rest but they must also take up the yoke he places upon them (Matt 11:28–29) as *evidence* of this exercising of faith. Also, true believers are also Christ's disciples who obey him and continually follow him—even to

19. Hodges, *Absolutely Free!*; Ryrie, *So Great Salvation*; Lightner, *Sin, the Savior, and Salvation*, 200–214.

20. MacArthur, *Gospel According to Jesus*; Reisinger, *Lord and Christ*; Belcher, *Layman's Guide to the Lordship Controversy*.

21. For example, Zane C. Hodges's interpretation of James 2:14–26 as set forth in his work *The Epistle of James*. Hodges argues that the passage in James is not talking about salvation from God's eternal wrath but salvation from physical death (*Epistle of James*, 60–61).

the point of giving up their own lives if necessary (Matt 16:24–25; Luke 9:23). Taking up of Christ's yoke and becoming a disciple, therefore, are not options that people can pass over but essential and necessary aspects of the gospel message.

In addition, Christ's position as the Lord (*kyrios*) of the universe precludes the idea that people can come to him for salvation while rejecting him as Lord. Christ is not only the sacrificial priest who gave himself up for the salvation of sinners and the prophet who calls all people to rest in him, *but the king who is sovereign over all of creation* (as discussed in chapter 8). This sovereign lordship includes that those who come to him for salvation must also submit to him as the ruler of their lives. As Bruce A. Demarest helpfully points out:

> [S]eekers of salvation cannot partition Christ's work any more than his person. The Lord Jesus Christ exercised the redemptive ministry of prophet, priest, and king. . . . We cannot accept the prophet who speaks the saving Word and the priest who laid down his life on the cross while rejecting the king who rules over his subjects. A truncated ministry betrays a truncated Christ who would be no Savior at all. God, who is wiser than we, has wisely ordained that sinners embrace his Son as prophet (herald), priest (sacrifice), and king (sovereign over life).[22]

We must conclude, therefore, that any message of salvation that excludes the requirement for submission to Christ's lordship as the necessary consequence of genuine faith has widely missed the mark concerning Scripture's teaching on the contents and terms of the gospel. The biblical gospel teaches sinners not only to come to Christ to receive eternal rest but also to reorient their lives to conform to what is pleasing to him (Col 1:10; 1 Thess 4:1) and to follow him to the very end (Rev 2:26–27).

### Is Saving Faith Synonymous with Obedience?

A related issue that has provoked some discussion among evangelical scholars today is whether saving faith is synonymous with obedience to God. Some evangelical scholars in recent years, in order to avoid the dangers of "cheap grace" antinomianism, have argued that faith is virtually identical

---

22. Demarest, *Cross and Salvation*, 269–70.

to obedience.[23] For instance, Scott J. Hafemann, in his work *The God of Promise and the Life of Faith*, writes:

> Trusting God and obeying God are not two *different* ways to relate to him, as if the former expresses a passive, emotional, or merely intellectual acceptance of what God has done for us while the latter is an active attempt to do something for God. Rather, faith and obedience are organically related aspects of our one response to God's grace.[24]

Although the desire to avoid the dangers of antinomianism is laudable by those who espouse the view above, we must conclude that it is exegetically and theologically problematic to synonymize trusting in Christ with obedience to God's commandments. Instead, faith throws itself upon the mercies of God through Christ for salvation from all guilt after the sinner humbly acknowledges his or her sinfulness before God. This is why the apostle Paul writes in Romans 4:5 that to "the one who does not work but believes in him who justifies the ungodly, his faith is counted as righteousness." Further on in the same epistle, he states that if salvation "is by grace, it is no longer on the basis of works; otherwise grace would no longer be grace" (Rom 11:6).

Although it is true, as discussed above, that genuine faith results in obedience to God, it can never be viewed as being synonymous with obedience to God. Calvin even compared saving faith with "a kind of vessel" and explained this further by stating that "unless we come empty and with the mouth of our soul open to seek Christ's grace, we are not capable of receiving Christ."[25] In fact, shortly after in the *Institutes,* Calvin makes this point clearer when he declares: "But a great part of mankind imagine that righteousness is composed of faith and works. Let us also, to begin with, show that faith righteousness so differs from works righteousness that when one is established the other has to be overthrown."[26]

Therefore, we conclude that while saving faith will produce the good works that are pleasing to God, it is not something that is synonymous with obeying God's commandments.[27]

---

23. Cf. Fuller, *Gospel and Law*, 105–20; Ridderbos, *Paul*, 237–42.

24. Hafemann, *God of Promise and the Life of Faith*, 99–100.

25. Calvin, *Inst.* 3.11.7.

26. Calvin, *Inst.* 3.11.13.

27. In recent years, some scholars, like D. B. Garlington, have contended that Paul equates faith with obedience in Romans 1:5 (cf. 16:26) when he talks about bringing

## Is Assurance the Essence of Saving Faith?

One of the more contentious issues in Reformed circles since the Reformation is the relationship between assurance and faith. The debate centres on whether assurance is the essence of saving faith. Contemporary scholars on Calvin are divided regarding the Genevan Reformer's personal opinion on this matter. On one side of the debate are those who argue that Calvin taught that assurance is of the essence of faith. For example, R. T. Kendall maintains that Calvin described faith as a "firm" and "full assurance."[28] Also, M. Charles Bell, echoing Kendall, declares: "Without question, Calvin teaches that assurance of one's salvation is of the very essence of faith."[29] Some of Calvin's statements on this subject appear to give credence to this view. For instance, Calvin writes:

> Briefly, he alone is truly a believer who, convinced by a firm conviction that God is a kindly and well-disposed Father toward him, promises himself all things on the basis of his generosity; who, relying upon the promises of divine benevolence toward him, lays hold on an undoubted expectation of salvation.[30]

---

about the "obedience of faith" among all the nations (or Gentiles). Thus, the obedience that Paul talks about in the verse is virtually no different from entrusting oneself to God and Christ for salvation (cf. Garlington, "Obedience of Faith in the Letter to the Romans," 201–24). To support this position, Garlington argues that the Greek phrase *hupakoe pisteos* in Romans 1:5 can be interpreted as both "the obedience that consists of faith" and "the obedience that which is the product of faith" ("Obedience of Faith in the Letter to the Romans," 223–24). However, it is exegetically unlikely that Paul has both meanings in mind in that verse. Mark A. Seifrid notes that "confusion reigns throughout" one of Garlington's works (cf. Garlington, *Faith, Obedience, and Perseverance*, 10–31) due to his argument that *hupakoe pisteos* can have a twofold meaning in Romans 1:5 and 16:26 (Seifrid, *Christ, our Righteousness*, 135n18). Furthermore, Seifrid maintains: "The Greek terms for 'obedience' involved (*hypakoē, hypakouein, hypēkoos*), despite their semantic breadth, cannot be said to be synonymous with 'faith' in the biblical tradition. They bear the general sense of 'responding in subjection', thereby carrying connotations of 'hearing' or of response to a person. These associations do not in themselves entail the notion of 'faith' or 'believing' (e.g., Rom. 6:12, 16; Eph. 6:1, 5; Mark 1:27; 1 Pet. 3:6; Gen. 41:40)" (*Christ, Our Righteousness*, 135n18). Therefore, we argue that a better interpretation of *hupakoe pisteos* in Romans 1:5 is to see it as referring to the obedience that *flows* from faith. In other words, saving faith, for Paul, is never equated with obedience to God's commandments (Gal 3:12; Eph 2:8–9; Phil 3:9), even though it engenders positively ethical results in believers (Eph 2:10; Phil 2:12–13).

28. Kendall, *Calvin and English Calvinism to 1649*, 19.

29. Bell, *Calvin and Scottish Theology*, 22.

30. Calvin, *Inst.* 3.2.16.

Calvin even seems to suggest by this statement that those who lack assurance of salvation do not possess true faith at all.

On the other side of the debate are those, like Paul Helm, who argue that Calvin did not consider assurance as the essence of faith.[31] In addition, Joel R. Beeke maintains that there was no radical discontinuity between Calvin and later Reformed orthodoxy on this matter.[32] Finally, Richard A. Muller argues that Calvin taught a type of "practical syllogism"[33] in his doctrine of assurance.[34] When Calvin's statements on this matter are viewed in its entirety it appears that he qualified his statements regarding assurance being the essence of faith.[35]

Reformed theologians after Calvin, however, have generally agreed that even though assurance is an essential part of Christian experience, it should not be considered the essence of faith. For example, according to the divines at the Westminster Assembly: "This infallible assurance does not so belong to the essence of faith, but that a true believer may wait long, and conflict with many difficulties, before he be partaker of it."[36] Later Puritanism went further by sharply separating faith and assurance, and focusing more on the quality of a believer's faith for the building up of assurance (which sometimes led to excessive introspection and doubt).[37]

We must agree, therefore, with the Westminster divines and later Reformed orthodoxy that even though assurance is an important aspect of the believer's Christian experience, it is *not* the essence of faith. Even though it is true that faith, as the writer of Hebrews puts it, is the "assurance of things hoped for" (Heb 11:1), it is erroneous to conclude that genuine faith *must* have assurance as its essence. Genuine believers will go through periods of

---

31. Helm, *Calvin and the Calvinists*, 23–31.

32. Beeke, *Quest for Full Assurance*, 53.

33. The "practical syllogism" (*syllogismus practicus*) of later Reformed orthodoxy went as follows:
Major Premise: Every true believer obeys God's commandments.
Minor Premise: I obey God's commandments.
Conclusion: Therefore, I am a true believer and entitled to assurance of salvation.

34 Muller, *Calvin and the Reformed Tradition*, 247–58; cf. also Venema, *Accepted and Renewed in Christ*, 248–61.

35. For example, in one place in his *Institutes*, Calvin writes: "Surely, while we teach that faith ought to be certain and assured, we cannot imagine any certainty that is not tinged with doubt, or any assurance that is not assailed by some anxiety" (*Inst* 3.2.17).

36. *Westminster Confession of Faith*, XVIII/3.

37. Horton, *Christian Faith*, 586.

doubt in their pilgrimage of faith (due to a variety of factors), but that does not necessarily entail that saving faith is lacking. By taking the position that assurance is the essence of faith we are inadvertently conveying to believers that any trace of doubt is evidence that they are not genuinely saved (basically, assurance is gained by seeing if one has assurance!). Also, even though God's promise in the gospel is the *fundamental* pillar of assurance (1 John 5:13), Scripture is clear that personal assurance is cultivated when a believer obeys God (1 John 3:10) and bears good fruit (Gal 5:22–24; cf. Matt 7:15–20). In one sense, then, self-examination is a legitimate means of finding out whether one has true faith (2 Cor 13:5). That is why Peter tells his readers in 2 Peter 1:10 to "be all the more diligent to confirm your calling and election" by practicing the virtues that he lists in verses 5–7 in the same chapter, as discussed previously.

Having just argued that assurance is not the essence of faith, we must also point out that having assurance should be the normal experience of every true believer. Even though genuine believers will go through periods of doubt in their spiritual pilgrimage they should consistently have assurance of salvation. This is so because God's promises in Christ should be the principal foundation of assurance, not the believer's good works or quality of faith. If a professing believer is constantly plagued with doubt it *may* be an indication that he or she has never genuinely trusted Christ for salvation. In other words, constant doubting of one's salvation should not be the typical experience of a true believer.

# Chapter 14

# Justification

THE DOCTRINE OF JUSTIFICATION is viewed by many Christians to be one of the core doctrines of Christianity since the Protestant Reformation. Martin Luther, the father of the Protestant Reformation, recognizing the sheer importance of this doctrine wrote: "We must learn diligently the article of justification. . . . For all the other articles of the faith are comprehended in it: and if that remain sound, then all the rest are sound."[1] John Calvin, another great Magisterial Reformer, considered the doctrine of justification to be so fundamental to the Christian faith that he regarded it as "the main hinge on which religion turns," and therefore, believers must "devote the greater attention and care to it."[2] Over a century later, the renowned Puritan theologian John Owen viewed the doctrine of justification to be so crucial that he deemed it to be the "directive of Christian practice," and that "in no other evangelical truth is the whole of our obedience more concerned; for the foundation, reasons, and motives, of all our duty towards God, are contained therein."[3] Finally, in his fine treatment on the doctrine of justification from a classic Reformed perspective, the nineteenth-century Scottish theologian James Buchanan wrote that if

> the method of Justification by faith in a divine Redeemer, when it is considered intellectually, as a scheme of thought, be so profound in itself and so peculiar to the Gospel of Christ, that method, when

1. Luther, *Commentary on Galatians*, 171.
2. Calvin, *Inst.* 3.11.1.
3. Owen, *Doctrine of Justification by Faith*, 14.

it is considered practically, as the only remedy for the evils of our condition as sinners, and the only means of obtaining pardon and acceptance with God, must be regarded as of supreme importance.[4]

From these statements we see that the doctrine of justification (especially when viewed in its free and gracious character) has been a pivotal doctrine for many evangelical Christians since the Reformation.

In recent years, however, the traditional Reformation view that justification is received by grace alone (*sola gratia*) through faith alone (*sola fide*) has come under heavy criticism. These criticisms against the Reformation understanding, ironically, have not come from scholars of Roman Catholic persuasion but those who would generally be considered Protestant by profession. Although criticisms against the classic Reformation view of justification started to appear in the early to mid-twentieth century,[5] the work that was established to become the "Copernican turn" in Pauline studies on justification was E. P. Sanders's work *Paul and Palestinian Judaism*. In it, Sanders argued that the way orthodox Protestant scholars, especially those within the Lutheran and Reformed traditions, have typically understood Second Temple Judaism and the apostle Paul's relationship to it (particularly as it pertains to the law and righteousness) has been largely incorrect. For Sanders, Second Temple Judaism was not a works-based religion where people merit God's favor for salvation but a religion grounded in God's grace—with obedience to the law being the proper response to this grace *and* a means of maintaining one's covenant status (or "covenantal nomism").[6] Sanders also argued that Paul did not work from a "plight to solution" framework common in evangelical understandings of Paul's theology (where people are told they are sinners and need a savior), but from a "solution to plight" framework where God's grace is established first and figuring out how all human beings participate in that grace becomes a problem that needs to be solved.[7] Finally, Sanders argued that Paul basically takes up the structure of "covenantal nomism" found in Second Temple Judaism and applies it to his own soteriological framework (which developed into a new type of covenantal nomism).[8] Therefore, Paul's soteriology was not centered on the doctrine of justification *sola fide/sola gratia*, with

---

4. Buchanan, *Doctrine of Justification*, 408.

5. Cf. Schweitzer, *Mysticism of Paul the Apostle*; Davies, *Paul and Rabbinic Judaism*.

6. Sanders, *Paul and Palestinian Judaism*, 419–28.

7. Sanders, *Paul and Palestinian Judaism*, 442–47.

8. Sanders, *Paul and Palestinian Judaism*, 511–15.

its attendant pessimistic anthropology, but based on a "participationist" eschatology initiated by the Messiah and the new age of the Spirit.

As we will discuss in more detail below, Sanders's "revolutionary" thesis in Pauline studies has been taken up in considerable extent by notable New Testament scholars like James D. G. Dunn and N. T. Wright. This shift in Pauline studies on the law and justification in recent years has been labeled the "New Perspective on Paul" (NPP from now on).[9] Works by Dunn, Wright, and others have made this New Perspective view more accessible to the average layperson and seminarian. Furthermore, the debates surrounding the doctrine of justification are more amplified today than in previous eras due to a plethora of research on the critical study of the Bible and the ever-increasing desire for ecumenical dialogue between Protestants and Roman Catholics.

Before we discuss the nature of God's justifying act for sinners and recent developments in biblical scholarship on Paul's view of the law and justification, we will first briefly explore the terms used in Scripture for the concept of justification in the Old and New Testaments.

## Scriptural Terminology for Justification

In the Old Testament the Hebrew term that is used to describe the act of justification is the verb *tsadaq*. The *ṣdq* root in Hebrew basically denotes conformity to a norm. Basically, the person who is righteous in the Old Testament is the one who conforms to a given norm. It does not carry overtones of moral change or inner transformation, but is a term that signifies a type of relationship.[10] According to Mark A. Seifrid, the *ṣdq* terms, while often carrying a forensic sense, "generally signify the outcome of a 'contention' or 'lawsuit,' rather than the act of judging or its content." In addition, Seifrid continues, the "verbal forms denote the dispensing of justice in a positive sense: 'to give someone justice' is to vindicate them, to grant them salvation from injustice (e.g. Exod. 23:7; Deut. 25:1)."[11] In summary, the Old Testament term (*tsadaq*), which is translated into English as "righteousness" or "justification," does not describe the ethical quality of a person or his or her moral condition. Rather, the term is a description of a relationship between

9. Dunn was the first to coin the phrase "The New Perspective on Paul" to label this movement (cf. Dunn, "New Perspective on Paul," 95–122)

10. Ladd, *Theology of the New Testament*, 480.

11. Seifrid, "Righteousness, Justice and Justification," 740.

two parties, whether between two human beings or between a human be-ing and God, and is always set in a judicial context.

An example of this is found in Deuteronomy 25:1–2:

> If there is a dispute between men and they come into court and the judges decide between them, acquitting the innocent and con-demning the guilty, then if the guilty man deserves to be beaten, the judge shall cause him to lie down and be beaten in his presence with a number of stripes in proportion to his offense.

The judge does not make the guilty person morally upright but only *pro-nounces a judgment* based on what is heard in the case. In fact, God finds abhorrent anyone who pronounces the wicked as guiltless or declares the righteous as guilty: "He who justifies the wicked and he who condemns the righteous are both alike an abomination to the LORD" (Prov 17:15). This is clearly a forensic declaration since the verse states that God desires au-thorities to make right judgments in judicial cases. Therefore, the righteous person in the Old Testament is someone who is deemed guiltless (because he or she has done what God requires), which is then followed by a declara-tion of this fact: that he or she is indeed righteous.

The New Testament carries this forensic understanding of justification from the Old Testament. The English expression "to justify" is a translation of the Greek verb *dikaioō*. Related Greek terms are the noun *dikaiosunē* ("righteousness") and the adjective *dikaios* ("righteous"). That the *dik*-word group has forensic overtones without any suggestion of moral improve-ment is based on the fact that the terms, like their Hebrew counterparts, refer to a declaration of a condition. For example, in Luke 18:14, Jesus states that the tax collector, and not the Pharisee, went home *justified*: "I tell you, this man went down to his house justified, rather than the other." The tax collector had no exemplary qualities to boast about before God but was justified because he humbly acknowledged his sinful condition and begged God for mercy (v. 13). Another reason for arguing that justification in the New Testament is an exclusively forensic declaration is based on the fact that Paul sets faith and works in opposition to each other when it comes to the justification of sinners. For instance, in Romans 4:5 he states: "And to the one who does not work but believes in him who justifies the ungodly, his faith is counted as righteousness." One can clearly see that Paul has a forensic meaning in mind here because he states that God justifies the *un-godly* and not those who already made themselves practically righteous.

Also, in the verse, Paul states that righteousness is "credited" (*logizetai*)[12] to those who have faith in Christ. The forensic meaning is further reinforced when Paul states in Romans 8:33–34, "Who shall bring any charge against God's elect? It is God who justifies. Who is to condemn?" We see here that Paul sets justification and condemnation in opposition. Since condemnation is a judicial pronouncement, those who are justified are declared (not made) to be righteous.

Our analyses of the Hebrew and Greek terms and the examination of relevant biblical passages, therefore, reveal that justification is a juridical pronouncement made by a judge and not a term to describe the moral transformation of an individual (as Roman Catholicism teaches, as we will discuss below).

## The Nature of Justification

### Justification Is through Faith Alone

One of the corollaries of viewing justification as an exclusively forensic declaration is the belief that sinners are justified *through faith alone*. One of the battle cries of the Protestant Reformation is that individuals are not pronounced righteous by the good deeds they have performed but solely by the grace of God through faith *alone* in Christ. The Roman Catholic Church taught (and still does today) that believers partially merit eschatological salvation by their good works, and that justification is not only a judicial declaration but a progressive transformation of the moral condition of the believer (what Protestants normally call *sanctification*).[13] Scripture, on the other hand, against the Roman Catholic view, points in a different direction.

As discussed in chapter 13 on saving faith, we argued that Scripture sets faith and works in diametric opposition to each other when it comes to the believer's justification. One well-known biblical verse that supports this view is Galatians 2:16 when Paul writes: "yet we know that a person is not justified by works of the law but through faith in Jesus Christ, so we also have believed in Christ Jesus, in order to be justified by faith in

12. The Greek verb is from *logizomai* which means to "consider" or "reckon" (a declarative term).

13. Cf. Council of Trent, The Sixth Session; Ott, *Fundamentals of Catholic Dogma*, 250–69.

Christ and not by works of the law, because by works of the law no one will be justified." This point is made clearer in the epistle to the Romans when Paul tells his readers that the promise given to Abraham "depends on faith, in order that the promise may rest on grace and be guaranteed to all his offspring" (Rom 4:16). Paul also makes this sharp contrast between righteousness through faith and righteousness by works in Philippians 3:9 when he states: "and be found in him, *not having a righteousness of my own that comes from the law, but that which comes through faith in Christ*, the righteousness from God that depends on faith." Other noteworthy passages that teach that justification is received through faith alone include Genesis 15:6; Romans 3:28; 4:5; 5:1; 10:4; Galatians 3:10–12; and Titus 3:5.

Some, however, argue that the traditional Reformation view of justification through faith alone in Christ alone is inconsistent with the teachings of some passages in Scripture. The passage that is most often referred to is James 2:14–26. Those who argue against the Reformation view usually point to verse 24 to support their position: "You see that a person is justified by works and not by faith alone." On the surface this verse does seem to pose a great difficulty for the traditional Protestant view that sinners are justified through faith alone apart from their deeds. However, the difficulty is only apparent once we realize that James uses the word "justified" in a different sense than Paul. More specifically, James uses the word in a *demonstrative* sense, while Paul uses the word in a *soteriological* sense. In other words, Paul uses the word to talk about how believing sinners are declared righteous before a holy God apart from meritorious works (Rom 4:5); James, on the other hand, uses the word to talk about how believers give evidence of their faith before others by their good deeds (cf. Jas 2:18).[14] According to James, there is an intricate connection between faith and works (although he never equates the two). If genuine faith exists, then works of love will inevitably follow. In other words, saving faith necessarily produces good works, and these works provide the indispensable evidence that one is a true follower of Christ. James does not set himself against Paul

---

14. Cf. Calvin, *Comm.* James 2:21; Burdick, "James," 185. For an alternate explanation, see Moo, *James*, 108–10, 114–16. Douglas J. Moo argues that James uses the word "justify" (*dikaioō*) to refer to God's positive verdict of the believer at the last judgment *on account of* (not *on the basis of*) his or her good works. Although Moo's interpretation is plausible, it is unlikely that James had an eschatological focus in mind here. James is talking about how Abraham and Rahab vindicated their faith before others in temporal history by their concrete acts of obedience to God (cf. Gen 22:1–19 and Josh 2:1–21, respectively).

when it comes to the character and reception of justification but, in fact, endorses what Paul states in his letters (cf. Jas 2:23). Therefore, James does not reject the truth that sinners are justified through faith alone in Christ alone but only a distortion of it where faith becomes an empty slogan (Jas 2:19) with no practical effects in the life of the believer.

In conclusion, we must insist that upholding justification *sola fide* is vitally important to the Christian faith because it is also a defense of salvation *sola gratia*. When we mix faith and works in the reception of justification we in essence reject God's gracious work of salvation in our lives, and thus, attack the heart of the gospel.

## Justification Is Based on the Imputation of Christ's Righteousness

Another important component when viewing justification as a free and gracious gift of God received through faith alone is the understanding that Christ's perfect righteousness is the ground of this justification. Lutheran and Reformed theologians have typically argued that although the *means* of receiving God's positive declaration is through faith alone, the *basis* of this positive declaration is Christ's perfect obedience to God's law.[15] Reformed theologians go even further by saying that it is Christ's *active obedience* (his flawless obedience to God's law) which provides the basis for the divine justificatory verdict for those who believe. In addition, this active obedience is not something infused into believers so that they are internally changed by it (as Roman Catholicism teaches)[16] but is *imputed* to them so that they are *reckoned* righteous before God for all time.[17] Christ, therefore, not only takes away the sins of believers but also imputes his righteousness to them for their justification.

The classic scriptural text often referred to by evangelicals to argue for the imputation of Christ's righteousness is 2 Corinthians 5:21. There,

15. Cf. The Formula of Concord (Declaration III/4); *Westminster Confession of Faith*, XI/1.

16. Ott, *Fundamentals of Catholic Dogma*, 262. According to Roman Catholic teaching, the inner renewal that takes place in the life of the believer is justification. Believers first obtain this gift of justification by baptism, and then God gives them an *infused* righteousness so that they can cooperate with God by doing good works to merit final salvation. In addition, justification is not the same for every believer and can be increased by the believer's cooperation in grace (cf. *Catechism of the Catholic Church*, 535–37 [esp. nos. 1989, 1992, and 1993]).

17. Owen, *Doctrine of Justification by Faith*, 183–97, 251–69.

Paul states: "For our sake he made him [Christ] to be sin who knew no sin, so that in him we might become the righteousness of God." Paul states in the verse that Christ takes away the sins of believers *and* gives them his righteousness so that they might become "the righteousness of God." Some, however, object to this and argue that the verse is not talking about how Christ's righteousness is transferred to believers by imputation.[18] In response to this objection, we must say that since the verse states that the sins of believers are given to Christ by imputation (as D. A. Carson rightly points out),[19] it is only reasonable to assume that the transference of righteousness to believers is also imputative. Another well-known passage that speaks to the truthfulness of imputed righteousness is Philippians 3:9. There, Paul writes: "and be found *in him*, not having a righteousness of my own that comes from the law, but that which comes through faith in Christ, the *righteousness from God* that depends on faith." Paul makes it explicitly clear here that the righteousness that is required for salvation does not come by observing the law but through faith in Christ alone. Also, the truth of imputed righteousness is implicitly stated in Romans 5:12–21 when Paul discusses the Adam-Christ parallel in relation to unbelievers and believers, respectively. In that passage, Paul makes it clear that just like Adam's disobedience brought condemnation to all people (vv. 15, 18), Christ's obedience results in the righteousness for many (v. 19). As a result, there is now "no condemnation for those who are in Christ Jesus" (Rom 8:1). This truth is also revealed in Pauline passages like Romans 4:3–6 (cf. Gen 15:6, regarding the justification of Abraham) and 1 Corinthians 1:30.

We must also maintain that what is imputed to believers is *not* their faith but the righteousness of Christ. In recent years for example, some have argued that when Paul talks about God imputing righteousness to a believing sinner he is not talking about the righteousness earned by Christ but the believer's exercising of faith.[20] They typically look to Romans 4:9 to support their argument: "For we say that faith was counted to Abraham as righteousness." However, in response to this argument, we say that it is precisely because Christ is the object of faith that believers are reckoned righteous when they believe. Christ is the source of the believer's righteousness, which is necessary for a positive verdict in God's divine courtroom. If God reckons believers righteous because of their faith we must conclude that

18. Cf. Wright, *Justification*, 158–67.

19. Carson, "Vindication of Imputation," 69.

20. Gundry, "Nonimputation of Christ's Righteousness," 18.

faith, not Christ, is the ultimate basis for their justification before God. This in turn makes faith another work to earn God's salvific favor and, therefore, overturns the truth that salvation is by grace alone.

The imputation of Christ's righteousness for justification, therefore, is an important biblical teaching that needs to be stressed in our preaching and witnessing today. An absolutely holy God requires that his law be perfectly fulfilled for justification and salvation. A single transgression will condemn a person to eternal death with no hope of eternal life if left to his or her own devices. Only by Christ fulfilling the righteous requirements of the law and imputing his righteousness to believing sinners can they be found acceptable in God's divine courtroom and granted entrance into his kingdom on the last day.

### Justification Is a Permanent Declaration

Grounded in God's grace and Christ's righteousness, another important aspect of justification that needs to be mentioned is its permanency. In contrast to the Roman Catholic, Lutheran, and Wesleyan teachings on justification, the Reformed tradition has consistently maintained that justification is a *permanent* declaration given by God.[21] Although believers continue to sin and fall into periods of unfaithfulness, confessional Reformed theology has always maintained that justification, if genuinely conferred, can never be abrogated. This is what sets Reformed or Calvinistic evangelicalism apart from other traditions. In fact, the Reformed view of justification is the one that is most *consistent* with a monergistic understanding of salvation. That is why Lutheranism, as Michael Horton rightly points out, with its view that true believers can apostatize and lose their justification, is not consistently monergistic in its understanding of salvation.[22] This truth (of the permanency of justification) is highlighted most emphatically in Romans 8:1 when Paul writes: "There is therefore now no condemnation for those who are in Christ Jesus." Later on in the same chapter, Paul, in the famous "golden chain" passage, Romans 8:30, puts the believer's glorification in the past tense along with his or her justification: "And those whom he predestined he also called, and those whom he called he also justified, and

---

21. Cf. *Westminster Confession of Faith*, XI/5.
22. Horton, *Christian Faith*, 686.

those whom he justified he also glorified." So certain of the believer's future justification that Paul talks about it as if the believer already possesses it.[23]

Some will contend, however, that if justification is viewed as a gift that cannot be forfeited this will provide no motivation for believers to resist sin and keep God's commandments. This argument will soon prove to be spurious once we understand that believers are still obligated to keep God's law (1 Cor 9:21; Gal 6:2) and resist sin (Rom 6:12–14; Gal 5:13). Reformed Christians have typically argued that a person who claims to be a follower of Christ but is indifferent to God's commandments or allows sin to reign in his or her life gives evidence that he or she is not truly justified (cf. Rom 6:1–11; 1 Cor 6:9–10; Gal 5:19–21; Eph 5:5; Jas 1:26–27; 1 John 3:10; 3 John 11). As Wilhelmus à Brakel puts it, "He who desires justification and has no desire after holiness, gives evidence that his heart is not upright before the Lord. If he imagines himself to be justified, but is as yet without sanctification, he deceives himself."[24] Also, genuine believers who refuse to deal with sin in their lives will have their assurance of salvation taken away (Ps 51:11–12), bring upon themselves God's displeasure and chastisement (1 Cor 11:30–32; Eph 4:30; Heb 12:5–11), and risk losing eternal rewards in the heavenly kingdom (1 Cor 3:15; 2 John 8). Although true believers will never have their justification taken away for falling into sin, their disobedience can bring temporal suffering now and loss of heavenly rewards in the future.

## Justification Is a Present Reality and an Eschatological Hope

Evangelicals usually understand justification as something that occurs at the beginning of the Christian life. Justification is not often understood as something that happens in the future at the end of this present age. Scripture, however, presents justification as not only something that happens in a believer's present life but also something that the believer looks forward to in the future. Some passages that attest to the future aspect of justification include Matthew 12:36–37; Romans 2:13; 8:33–34; 1 Corinthians 1:8; Galatians 5:5; Colossians 1:22; 1 Thessalonians 3:13; 2 Timothy 4:8; and Jude 24. Even though Scripture talks about justification as a once-for-all declaration that happens in the present (Luke 18:14; Rom 3:28; 5:1; 8:1; 1 Cor 6:11; Gal 2:16; Titus 3:7), it also speaks about believers being present

23. Calvin, *Commentaries*, Rom 8:30.

24. Brakel, *Christian's Reasonable Service*, 2:408.

at the eschatological judgment to come (Rom 14:10; 2 Cor 5:10) to witness God's justifying verdict for them as a public vindication. In this sense, the New Testament concurs with Judaism when it talks about God's justifying act as having an eschatological dimension.[25]

Even though Scripture speaks of justification in two tenses (past and future), we should not construe from this that there is a disjunction between the two. It is incorrect, as some do, to identify one as a "present justification" through faith and the other as a "future justification" by works—as if Scripture is talking about an initial verdict through faith and an eschatological verdict through works of obedience.[26] A better way to understand this is seeing this one singular verdict of God as having two aspects: the "already" and the "not yet."[27] However, believers need not fear that their "not yet" justification will be in jeopardy if they fall into sin since the tie between the two aspects of justification cannot be severed (cf. Rom 5:9). If a person is justified in the present, he or she *will be* justified in the future—they have irreversibly crossed from the state of unrighteousness to righteousness. This is where the New Testament, especially Paul, significantly differs from Judaism when it views God's positive verdict of the believer as already having taken place.[28] As Thomas R. Schreiner states:

> The future has broken into the present, so that believers in Christ Jesus are now declared to be in the right before him. Believers grasp this verdict by faith, for it is hidden from the world and cannot be proved or demonstrated. The final heralding of the verdict will be on the last day. Therefore, believers are already righteous in Christ, but that verdict has not yet been promulgated throughout the world. They are righteous because they belong to the Christ, who has been declared to be righteous at his resurrection.[29]

Therefore, the eschatological aspect of justification should not bring fear to believers but give them more reason for hope since the past and future aspects of God's verdict of righteousness will always meet. Since God's irrevocable eschatological pronouncement has already been brought forward in history believers need not fear that they will be condemned on

25. Ladd, *Theology of the New Testament*, 483.

26. Dunn, "If Paul Could Believe," 119–41. Of course, Dunn rejects the idea that these works of obedience have any meritorious value at the last judgment.

27. Cf. Schreiner and Caneday, *Race Set Before Us*, 77–79.

28. Ridderbos, *Paul*, 164–65.

29. Schreiner, *King in His Beauty*, 555.

the final day when Christ returns to judge humankind and establish his kingdom on earth.[30]

## Justification Is the Ground of Adoption

When sinners come to Christ through faith and are justified from all guilt they are also adopted by God to be his children (John 1:12; 1 John 3:2). Adoption is the consequence of being justified and reconciled to God. One of the great privileges of being justified is not only that believers are free from guilt but are now treated as adopted sons and daughters in God's spiritual household. As John Murray states, "By adoption the redeemed become sons and daughters of the Lord God Almighty; they are introduced into and given the privileges of God's family."[31] As a result, believers no longer have to approach God as a distant Sovereign Judge but as someone who they can call "Abba, Father!" (Rom 8:14–17; Gal 4:4–7). This means that believers can come to God without fear or dread, and can converse with him like a human child does with an earthly father. That is why believers need not be hesitant when coming to God in prayer and supplication (Heb 4:16; 1 John 5:14).

Another privilege of adoption is that believers are co-heirs with Christ (Rom 8:17) and are now considered Christ's brothers and sisters (Rom 8:29; Heb 2:12).[32] As a consequence of being co-heirs with Christ, believers are assured of an eternal inheritance that awaits them in heaven (1 Pet 1:4). At

---

30. Ladd is helpful in this regard when he writes: "Since justification is an eschatological event, it belongs at the end of life when women and men will stand before the final judgment of God to answer for the entire course of their conduct. Its temporal location, therefore, is not really the point of belief; it is in fact no less than the final judgment that has in Christ thrust itself forward into the stream of history. As the final judgment, it retains its orientation toward the believer's entire life. One is justified not only from the sins committed before the time of belief; one is justified from *all* guilt" (*Theology of the New Testament*, 491).

31. Murray, *Redemption—Accomplished and Applied*, 132.

32. Christ, however, makes it clear that the way believers relate to the Father is not the same as the way he relates to the Father. This is made clear in John 20:17 when Christ declares: "Do not cling to me, for I have not yet ascended to the Father; but go to my brothers and say to them, 'I am ascending to my Father and your Father, to my God and your God.'" Christ's relationship to the Father is a unique one that can never be replicated. This relationship between the Father and Son has always existed in eternity and is far greater than the relationship that believers have with the Father. Believers are adopted children who relate to the Father in a way that does not arrive at the same level of intimacy as Christ relates (and always has related) to the Father.

the consummation, believers will even have the authority to judge angels due to their adopted position (1 Cor 6:3). Another blessing of adoption is that believers are led by the Holy Spirit (Rom 8:14) and sealed by him as a guarantor of their final redemption (Rom 8:23; 2 Cor 1:22; Eph 1:13–14; 4:30). God not only adopts the believer into his spiritual household but keeps him or her there forever (John 10:28–29). Finally, another result of being adopted by God is that believers now have new spiritual siblings that are tied by a common faith (Mark 10:30). Those who come to faith in Christ will enjoy being in a new family with all its attendant blessings.

One marvelous aspect of adoption is how people who were at one time enemies of God can now be received into his spiritual family based on Christ's work of reconciliation. Bruce Milne summarizes this thought well when he writes:

> When we recall what we were in our sins, the thought of adop-
> tion speaks most powerfully of the magnitude of God's mercy to
> us. That we should be pardoned of all our sin is wonder enough;
> but that the pardoned rebels should become God's very sons and
> daughters, installed within the intimacy of his own family circle, is
> surely wonder beyond wonder.[33]

Therefore, Christians should rejoice at the fact that God not only justifies them by the blood of Christ but that he also receives them as his own children with all the privileges involved in that adoption. Although God disciplines believers when necessary (cf. 1 Cor 11:30–32; Heb 12:5–6), they no longer need to fear God as an unapproachable judge but can come to him as a Father who loves and cares for them.

### Justification and Union with Christ

In Reformed theological circles, the doctrine of union with Christ takes up a pivotal place under the umbrella of soteriology. One issue that divides Reformed theologians to this day is whether justification is *based* on the believer's union with Christ or if justification takes place *prior* to the believer's union with Christ. Calvin appears to take the former position when he writes:

> Therefore, that joining together of Head and members, that
> indwelling of Christ in our hearts—in short, that mystical

---

33. Milne, *Know the Truth*, 259.

union—are accorded by us the highest degree of importance, so that Christ, having been made ours, makes us sharers with him in the gifts with which he has been endowed. We do not, therefore, contemplate him outside ourselves from afar in order that his righteousness may be imputed to us but because we put on Christ and are engrafted into his body—in short, because he deigns to make us one with him. For this reason, we glory that we have fellowship of righteousness with him.[34]

For Calvin, the reason why believers are imputed with Christ's righteousness, and consequently justified, is due to their mystical union with Christ. By being joined to Christ in this union, believers now receive all the salvific benefits of Christ's work of redemption, which includes justification.[35]

Louis Berkhof, on the other hand, argues for the latter view in which the believer's justification is prior to and not conditioned upon his or her union with Christ. He writes:

> It is sometimes said that the merits of Christ cannot be imputed to us as long as we are not in Christ, since it is only on the basis of our oneness with Him that such an imputation could be reasonable. But this view fails to distinguish between our legal unity with Christ and our spiritual oneness with Him, and is a falsification of the fundamental element in the doctrine of redemption, namely, of the doctrine of justification. Justification is always a declaration of God, *not on the basis of an existing condition*, but on that of a gracious imputation,—a declaration which is not in harmony with the existing condition of the sinner. The judicial ground for all the special grace we receive lies in the fact that the righteousness of Christ is freely imputed to us.[36]

In this view, therefore, justification is not rooted in the mystical union *but is the grounds for that union*.

The difficulty of deciding which view is correct is due to the fact that Scripture can be appealed to in support of both positions. The first view can be supported by passages like Romans 8:1; 1 Corinthians 1:30; 2 Corinthians 5:21; and Philippians 3:8–9 where Paul uses the "in Christ" language as the basis for the believer's justification. The second view can be supported by passages where Scripture does not mention the believer's union with

34. Calvin, *Inst.* 3.11.10.

35. In the contemporary period, this view is shared by Hoekema, *Saved by Grace*, 61–63.

36. Berkhof, *Systematic Theology*, 452 (emphasis added).

Christ as being the basis for his or her righteous standing before God but due to his or her faith *in Christ* (Rom 3:28; 4:3; 10:4; Gal 2:16; 3:11). Based on the biblical evidence alone we can see why it is difficult to decide which view has better scriptural support.

We must argue, however, that the view that justification is the grounds for the believer's union with Christ is more consistent with the whole biblical witness. God's verdict of righteousness is not based on the union between the believer and Christ but on Christ's righteousness being imputed to believers, as Berkhof rightly points out. Some may argue that this *prioritizing* of imputation will misleadingly give the impression that believers can receive the benefits of Christ "from afar" with no vital connection to Christ (with the false impression that justification has no ethical effects in the lives of believers). However, in response, we must argue that although justification is located in Christ's perfect righteousness it is not the *terminus* of God's salvific work for believers. God's work of redemption also includes that believers are vitally joined to Christ and live in him (and he in them) (John 15:4–5; Eph 3:17). The consequence of this is that they become new creatures with new appetites and desires, which flows out in God-pleasing behavior (Rom 6:11; 2 Cor 5:17; Eph 2:10). Through this union believers are also made spiritually alive now and assured of eternal life in the age to come (2 Tim 1:1; 1 John 5:11). Therefore, we must state that although the basis of a believer's justification is not his or her union with Christ, it is incorrect to assume that this understanding will extirpate the other facets of redemption found in Christ (like sanctification).

*Justification and Judgment According to Works*

One of the more difficult issues to arise in recent years when the subject of justification is discussed is the complicated relationship between justification through faith alone and judgment according to works. As discussed above, God's justifying verdict of believers has both a present and future dimension. That there will be a final judgment of believers is certainly attested to in Scripture (Matt 25:31–46; Luke 19:11–26; Rom 14:10–12; 1 Cor 3:11–15; 4:4–5; 2 Cor 5:10). Some Scripture passages seem to even suggest that final salvation is by works (Matt 25:34–40; John 5:29; Rom 2:13;[37] Phil

---

37. Taken at face value, Romans 2:13 ("For it is not the hearers of the law who are righteous before God, but the doers of the law who will be justified") seems to contradict Paul's other statements on justification (especially Romans 3:28 and Galatians 2:16).

2:12–13; 2 Thess 1:5; 1 Pet 1:17). When these passages are compared to numerous other passages that attest to the fact that people are justified and saved apart from works (Rom 4:4–5; 11:6; Gal 3:10–12; Eph 2:8–9; Phil 3:9; Titus 3:5–7), many of us will readily admit that the scriptural witness appears to contradict itself at this point.

The contradiction, however, is only apparent when we recognize that these two biblical truths do not truly conflict with each other. The good works of believers *will* play a role in vindicating them at the eschaton but *only as evidence* of their faith and salvation. These works will only demonstrate on the last day that they are genuine followers of Christ. Also, these works are not generated by the believers themselves but are brought about by the work of the Spirit. Furthermore, these works are never viewed as the *basis* of a believer's righteous standing before God or as the *instrumental means* to obtain a final justification on judgment day. Despite the language of Scripture that works will play an evidential role in the "not yet" justification of believers, salvation is still totally a work of God from beginning to end (Phil 1:6).

## Recent Developments in Biblical Scholarship on Paul's Understanding of the Relationship Between the Law and Justification

As discussed briefly in the introduction of this chapter, we mentioned how there was a significant shift in biblical scholarship over the last several decades regarding Paul's view of the law and justification. Sanders's so-called revolution in biblical studies essentially laid the foundation for contemporary reinterpretations of Paul's soteriology that significantly shifted away

---

Some have interpreted the verse to mean God's positive verdict of *a believer* based on the type of life he or she has lived (i.e., a life that is characterized by obedience to God). For instance, N. T. Wright writes: "[P]resent justification, as Romans makes clear, is the true anticipation of future justification. And in Romans, as elsewhere in Paul, it is present justification, not future, that is closely correlated with faith. Future justification, acquittal at the last great Assize, always takes place on the basis of the totality of the life lived (e.g. Romans 14.11f.; 2 Corinthians 5:10)" ("Law in Romans 2," 144). A more exegetically plausible interpretation would be to see Romans 2:13 as a statement of fact in light of God's perfect moral standard: a person who fulfills *all* the requirements of the law *will be justified.* However, since no human being, due to the fall, can obey God's law perfectly, this method of justification is forever out of reach. As a result, the only way fallen human beings can ever be justified before a holy God is by the perfect righteousness of Christ received through faith alone (cf. Harrison, "Romans," 30).

from the traditional Protestant understanding of Paul's view of justification. This shift is demonstrated in the writings of James D. G. Dunn,[38] N. T. Wright,[39] Don Garlington,[40] Terence L. Donaldson,[41] and others. Although all the scholars who have identified themselves with this new movement (NPP) do not agree on every point of biblical interpretation, they all agree that the traditional Reformation understanding of Paul is exegetically and historically unsatisfying.

At the outset we should note that the proponents of the NPP have done the evangelical world a service in some sense by making us re-examine our presuppositions and to look more carefully at the historical context of Paul's polemic against the Judaizers. They have also compelled us to re-evaluate the exegetical conclusions of evangelical scholars who are resolutely committed to their own confessional standards. Despite some of the helpful contributions that the NPP scholars have made in recent years, we must conclude that the NPP understanding of early Judaism and Paul is biblically and theologically unsatisfactory overall. We will argue this by: 1) contending that the Pauline phrase "works of the law" cannot be restricted to Jewish "boundary markers," and 2) maintaining that the relationship between the law and justification in Paul is much more dichotomous than the way NPP scholars assume it to be.

### The "Works of the Law": Boundary Markers or the Mosaic Law in Its Entirety?

One of the fundamental ways that NPP scholars diverge from the traditional Protestant understanding of Paul's soteriology and/or theological convictions is by interpreting the Pauline phrase "works of the law" (Gk. *ergon nomou*) in an entirely new way. Historically, Protestants have typically understood the "works of the law" as works done according to the Mosaic law *in its entirety* to earn God's justifying favor. These works not only include the ritualistic aspects of the Mosaic law but the *moral* aspects as well. For example, John Owen provides us with the classic Protestant interpretation of the "works of the law" when he writes:

38. Dunn, *New Perspective on Paul*.
39. Wright, *What Saint Paul Really Said*.
40. Garlington, *In Defense of the New Perspective on Paul*.
41. Donaldson, *Paul and the Gentiles*.

(1) That the law intended by the Apostle, when he denies that by the works of the law any can be justified, is the entire rule and guide of our obedience to God, even as to the whole frame and spiritual constitution of our souls, *with all the acts of obedience or duties that he requires of us.* And (2) that the works of this law which he so frequently and plainly excludes from our justification, and therein opposes to the grace of God, and the blood of Christ, *are all the duties of obedience, internal, supernatural, external, ritual, however we are or may be enabled to perform them,* that God requires of us.[42]

A perusal of works by other Protestant theologians since the Reformation will demonstrate that this interpretation of the "works of the law" has a long pedigree.[43]

In recent years, Owen's and the traditional Protestant understanding of the "works of the law" have come under considerable criticism by NPP scholars. The works that Paul condemns, they argue, has to do with those that exclude gentiles from entering the covenant, like circumcision and dietary laws (the "boundary markers").[44] The conflict between the works of the law and justification through faith, in essence, is not about soteriology but about *ecclesiology:* how do gentiles enter God's covenant family (and enjoy its blessings) without submitting to the law? Therefore, in Paul's polemic against his opponents in Galatians, he was not arguing against a type of Jewish merit theology but an exclusivistic theology espoused by the Judaizers that prevented gentiles from being part of God's new redemptive family.[45] Thus, the phrase "works of the law," according to NPP scholars, has a more narrow meaning than what Protestants have traditionally understood it to mean.[46]

42. Owen, *Doctrine of Justification by Faith,* 324 (emphases added).

43. Cf. Luther, *Galatians,* 65–66; Calvin, *Inst.* 3.11.13–20; Turretin, *Institutes of Elenctic Theology,* 2:640–42; Buchanan, *Doctrine of Justification,* 345–53; Fairbairn, *Revelation of Law in Scripture,* 386; Hodge, *Systematic Theology,* 3:137–38.

44. Dunn, *Theology of Paul the Apostle,* 354–66; Wright, *Justification,* 171–73.

45. Dunn, "New Perspective View," 193–94.

46. Some scholars argue that the phrase "works of the law" should not be understood as works in general or boundary markers but the attempt to earn God's salvific favor by legalistically *misusing* the law (see Daniel P. Fuller's essay "Paul and the 'Works of the Law,'" 31–33). However, the problem with this view is that the phrase *ergon nomou* is never used to mean a legalistic misuse of the law. This is supported by the fact that Deuteronomy 27:26 (cited in Galatians 3:10) does not have a legalistic misuse of the law in mind (cf. Bruce, *Epistle to the Galatians,* 158).

The argument that Paul used the phrase "works of the law" with a narrow meaning (as the ceremonial aspects of the Mosaic law that separate Jews and gentiles), however, is exegetically and lexically unconvincing. As some recent biblical scholars have maintained, the Greek term *ergon nomou* cannot be restricted just to the ceremonial aspects of the law. Rather, the terminology is used for the Mosaic law in its *entirety* with its requirements.[47] This understanding is reinforced by the fact that it is highly improbable that Paul, in Romans 3:20, was restricting the terms *ergon nomou* and *nomou* to ritualistic markers when he states that "by works of the law [*ergon nomou*] no human being will be justified in his sight, since through the law [*nomou*] comes knowledge of sin." In the verse, Paul primarily had the moral aspects of the law in mind when he talked about the sin-exposing function of the law. In addition, in Galatians 5:3, Paul states that a person who is circumcised "is obligated to keep the whole law [*holon ton nomon*]." One can see here that Paul connects the circumcision ritual with keeping of the entire Mosaic law. Based on Second Temple Jewish literature found at Qumran, Schreiner finds the holistic interpretation of the "works of the law" as being the most exegetically sustainable:

> It should be noted first of all that the phrase "works of law" does not occur in the Old Testament, and therefore we do not find such an expression in the LXX (Greek translation of the Old Testament). There are some parallels in Hebrew texts of Second Temple Jewish literature, and these support the thesis argued for here. For instance, in 4QFlor 1:7 there is the Hebrew equivalent "works of law," which is probably a reference to all the works commanded in the law since the context does not limit it precisely. There is a similar phrase "his works in the Torah" (1QS 5:21; 6:18) in the *Rule of the Community*. A careful reading of 1QS V-VII shows that general obedience to the law is described in this passage. . . . The laws that are demanded of members of the community focus on moral norms: lying, evil speech, blasphemy, anger, insulting others, revenge, evil words, falling asleep, walking naked, spitting, inappropriate jesting, grumbling (1QS 6:24—7:21). Nothing is said about boundary markers like circumcision, food laws, or Sabbath.[48]

47. Moo, "'Law,' 'Works of the Law,' and Legalism in Paul," 73–100. Even Dunn concedes that this is the general meaning of "works of the law" (Dunn, "New Perspective View," 194).

48. Schreiner, 40 *Questions About Christians and Biblical Law*, 44.

Based on the above analysis by Schreiner, the most appropriate way of interpreting the Pauline phrase "works of the law" is to understand it as the entire Mosaic law and its demands. The doing of the "works of the law" (including the moral codes) cannot confer justification to people because all fall short of perfection. Although Paul does not exclude Jewish exclusivism as one of the problems of attempting to be justified by the "works of the law" (cf. Eph 2:11–22), his main reason for pitting faith and "works of the law" against each other in regards to justification (Rom 3:21–26; Gal 2:16–17) is because, respectively, one is based entirely on grace and the other is based partially on human achievement. Paul's opponents in Galatia, on the other hand, were arguing that faith in Christ alone is insufficient for justification, and that observing the "works of the law" was also required if one sought to be justified before God.[49] These works, of course, included both the ritualistic (i.e., circumcision) and moral aspects of the Mosaic law. Therefore, the typical NPP interpretation that the "works of the law" only pertain to that which separates Jews and gentiles is inadequate if Paul's statements on the relationship between the law and justification are read in a larger context.

## The Relationship Between the Law and Justification in Paul

As mentioned above, NPP scholars maintain that the "works of the law" that Paul excludes from justification only pertain to the boundary marking aspects of the Mosaic law. Furthermore, they claim that the absolute antithesis between faith and works is foreign to the apostle Paul's soteriological pattern. Paul, therefore, does not condemn good works in general as a means to present or final justification but only those ritualistic works that separate Jews and gentiles. In fact, some NPP advocates even argue that Paul also framed his soteriology on a modified form of Jewish "covenantal nomism."[50] Traditional Protestants, on the other hand, have always argued that the antithesis between faith and "works of the law" in Paul's writings has to do with two diametrically opposed ways of relating to God: one by grace alone through faith alone and the other by human achievement through good works.[51] One can immediately see the stark contrast between

---

49. Scacewater, "Galatians 2:11–21 and the Interpretive Context of 'Works of the Law,'" 321.

50. Dunn, "New Perspective View," 198–200.

51. Cf. Owen, Doctrine of Justification by Faith, 311–26.

the NPP view and the traditional Protestant position on the law's relationship to justification in Paul's writings.

Protestant evangelicals do not deny that the law provides the means to justification and eternal life. However, they would add that the law cannot confer salvation because all human beings are sinners and fall short of that perfection that the law requires. If any person did in fact keep *all* the requirements of the law, they maintain, God would then be obligated to grant him or her justification and life (cf. Rom 2:13).[52] This is supported by the fact that in Galatians 3:10 Paul states (quoting Deuteronomy 27:26) that those who rely on the "works of the law" are under a curse because the law demanded complete compliance.[53] Jason C. Meyer makes this insightful point:

> [T]he sacrificial provisions [in the Mosaic covenant] prove that the law *did* require perfect obedience. The reasoning behind this inference is simple. The fact that every transgression of the law demanded atonement shows that perfect obedience is the expectation on which the law operates. Paul's quotation of Deut 27:26 reinforces this assertion because of the emphatic "all" (*pas*). One must abide by "all" the things written in the book of the law.[54]

As a result, fallen human beings must look outside themselves for righteousness and salvation (Phil 3:9). This righteousness that the law requires, as discussed earlier, is provided by Christ based on his perfect fulfillment of the law. By looking to Christ through faith, sinners receive this righteousness (via imputation) and are completely justified in God's sight (2 Cor 5:21). However, this justification is not a "legal fiction" since believers are truly righteous based on the righteousness that Christ has provided.[55]

52. In reference to Romans 2:13, F. F. Bruce writes: "The course of his [Paul's] argument goes on to indicate that, while one who was a 'doer' of the law would be justified, yet, since no-one does it perfectly, there is no justification that way" (*Romans*, 85–86).

53. We should note that Paul also has a redemptive-historical shift in mind when he talks about the inability of the law to provide righteousness and life. The traditional Protestant view that Paul sets law and gospel in absolute antithesis when it comes to justification, and the salvation-historical perspective that sees Paul viewing the law as coming to an end as a result of Christ's death and resurrection, should not be played off against each other. Both perspectives could have been in Paul's mind when he wrote his letters (cf. Moo, "Law of Christ," 324–43).

54. Meyer, *End of the Law*, 154.

55. Horton, *Pilgrim Theology*, 294–96.

Therefore, the traditional Protestant understanding that there is a sharp antithesis between law and gospel when it comes to the justification of the believer is more exegetically defensible than the NPP position.

# CHAPTER 15

# Sanctification and Perseverance of the Saints

## 1. Sanctification

SINCE THE PROTESTANT REFORMATION evangelical Christians have typically focused on the doctrine of justification as being pivotal for the church's mission and the life of the Christian. Oftentimes, therefore, they will overlook the equally important doctrine of sanctification in discussions about personal salvation. However, sanctification, just like justification, is viewed by the inspired writers of Scripture as an essential component of God's work of redemption. If sanctification is an essential component of God's salvific work for believers, Christians will want to know it means. If we were to provide a biblical definition of sanctification we may define it this way: *God's gracious work of setting apart believers for the purpose of freeing them from the dominion of sin, renewing their hearts and minds so that they will progressively conform to the image of the Son, and empowering them to live in obedience to him.*

In biblical terminology, the English word "sanctification" comes from the Greek word *hagiasmos*, which means "holiness"; while the verb form "sanctify" means "to make holy" (*hagiazō*).[1]

---

1. Mullen, "Sanctification," 708.

## Sanctification Is Both Positional and Progressive

Sanctification is typically understood by many Christians today as a work of God that only pertains to the renewal and transformation of the lives of believers. Scripture, however, sees sanctification as also having a positional aspect at the start of the Christian life. This is supported by passages like 1 Corinthians 1:2 when Paul states: "To the church of God that is in Corinth, to those *sanctified in Christ Jesus*, called to be saints together with all those who in every place call upon the name of our Lord Jesus Christ, both their Lord and ours." Despite the immaturity (1 Cor 3:1–3) and sinfulness (1 Cor 11:18–22, 27–30) of some of the believers at Corinth, Paul still identifies them as those "sanctified in Christ Jesus." That Paul is talking about positional sanctification is clear because some in the Corinthian congregation still needed to grow in obedience to Christ. Paul repeats this understanding in 1 Corinthians 6:11 when he tells them again that they have been "sanctified" (the Greek is in the aorist tense) in the name of Christ and by the Spirit in spite of the fact that some members of the Corinthian church lived very immoral lifestyles before their conversion (vv. 9–10). Also, in Acts 20:32, Paul talks about this positional sanctification of believers to the Ephesian elders when he declares: "And now I commend you to God and to the word of his grace, which is able to build you up and to give you the inheritance among all those who are sanctified." Finally, the author of Hebrews makes the same claim when he tells his readers: "And by that will *we have been sanctified* through the offering of the body of Jesus Christ once for all" (Heb 10:10; cf. 2:11; 9:13–14). It is clear that the author is talking about positional sanctification in this verse because he mentions Christ's once-and-for-all sacrifice as the basis for God's action of setting apart believers. As Donald Guthrie states regarding this verse, "Since Christ is perfectly sanctified through his perfect obedience to the will of God, it may be said that his sanctification is shared by all who believe."[2] The Scriptures without doubt state that believers are set apart by God's grace as a special possession at the time of conversion. This setting apart is the starting point of the believer's transformation of life and character: they have been delivered from the dominion of death and have been brought over to eternal life (Rom 6:11, 13, 22). God, therefore, sets apart believers for his holy purposes, and then the process of renewal begins to be actualized in their lives in concrete ways.

2. Guthrie, *Epistle to the Hebrews*, 206.

Although sanctification has a definite beginning at the moment of conversion, it is also a lifelong process that believers experience all the way to the end of their lives. This is made clear in passages like 2 Corinthians 3:18, where Paul states that the Corinthian believers "are being transformed . . . from one degree of glory to another." This transformation that the believers at Corinth are experiencing demonstrates to the authenticity of Paul's apostleship and message, against the accusations of his opponents. This is so because it is only by the power of the true gospel that sinners are transformed to become more like Christ progressively. Later in the same epistle, Paul exhorts the believers to "cleanse" themselves from "every defilement of body and spirit, bringing holiness to completion in the fear of God" (2 Cor 7:1; cf. Romans 12:2, where Paul tells the believers at Rome to "be transformed by the renewal of your mind"). In another letter, Paul tells the believers in Colossae that because of their new situation in Christ their "new self" is "being renewed in knowledge, after the image of its creator" (Col 3:10). That progressive sanctification is meant here is clear because the phrase "being renewed" (Gk. *anakainoumenon*) is in the present tense, indicating a continuing process of renewal.[3] Another passage that discusses the progressive character of sanctification is Hebrews 12:14. There the author writes: "Strive for peace with everyone, and for the holiness without which no one will see the Lord." The author tells his readers to "strive" after peace and holiness, meaning that this endeavor (albeit by God's grace) takes dedication, diligence, and effort. Finally, the apostle Peter tells his readers in 1 Peter 1:15 to "be holy in all your conduct." Meaning that holiness is a goal that believers are always to aim for in their daily lives.

Therefore, Scripture presents sanctification as both a positional gift *and* a gradual renewing process that takes place in the hearts of believers, which results in conduct pleasing to God.

## Sanctification Is Distinct from Justification

As mentioned in chapter 14, Roman Catholicism teaches that justification not only involves the judicial declaration of the believer but also the moral transformation of his or her life as a Christian. In other words, Roman Catholicism does not view justification and sanctification as two distinct salvific gifts of God but as one and the same. In contrast to Roman Catholic teaching, classic Protestantism maintains that there is a clear distinction

3. Vaughan, "Colossians," 213.

between these two salvific blessings, although both are inseparable in the life of the believer. Typically, Protestant soteriology understands justification as an instantaneous event that is forensic in character and completed at a moment, whereas sanctification is viewed as differing in degree in every believer and progressive in nature. The German Reformed theologian Heinrich Heppe expresses this distinction well:

> [J]ustification is an act of God resulting outwith man, by which God assigns to him an alien righteousness; whereas sanctification is an activity of God in man's inward part. The former rests directly upon the sacrificial death and merit of Christ, the latter on the contrary is an effect which the death and life of Christ produce indirectly in the person called. The former is a once-for-all act of God imparted in the same way; the latter is a gradual process variously completed according to the varying measure of the Spirit which the individual receives.[4]

Evangelical Protestants have always been careful to maintain this distinction in order to uphold the wholly gracious character of justification. If sanctification and justification are confused, they maintain, then the necessary outcome will be that believers partially merit a righteous standing before God by their practical holiness and renewal of life.[5] The consequence of this is that the biblical gospel of grace is undermined because we add our personal works to God's justifying act.

## God and Human Beings Cooperate in Sanctification

Although believers are totally passive in the instantaneous granting of justification, they are not so in regards to the life-long process of sanctification. This does not mean that sanctification is not of grace: many notable Reformed theologians over the centuries have argued that the process of sanctification, like the bestowal of justification, is rooted in God's grace alone.[6] For example, the Westminster Shorter Catechism states: "Sanctification is

---

4. Heppe, *Reformed Dogmatics,* 565–566. Even though Heinrich Heppe helpfully states here how justification and sanctification differ, his use of the word "imparted" may be misconstrued as teaching the Roman Catholic doctrine of infused righteousness (which he certainly does not).

5. Cf. Berkhof, *Systematic Theology,* 524, 536; Grudem, *Systematic Theology,* 729.

6. Cf. Hodge, *Systematic Theology,* 3:213–215; Bavinck, *Our Reasonable Faith,* 469; Berkhof, *Systematic Theology,* 532–533.

the work of God's free grace, whereby we are renewed in the whole man after the image of God, and are enabled more and more to die unto sin, and live unto righteousness" (Answer to Question 35). However, it is incorrect to deduce from this that believers play no role whatsoever in the process of sanctification. Believers are not wholly passive in regards to God's supernatural work of making them experientially holy. That is why fruit-bearing varies from one believer to another (cf. Mark 4:20; 2 Cor 3:18).

One notable passage that speaks of the cooperation between God and believers in the process of sanctification is Philippians 2:12–13: "Therefore, my beloved, as you have always obeyed, so now, not only as in my presence but much more in my absence, *work out your own salvation with fear and trembling, for it is God who works in you,* both to will and to work for his good pleasure." We see in the passage that Paul plainly states that believers are to "work out" their salvation because God is already working in them. No other passage in Scripture speaks compellingly about the cooperative nature of the believer's progressive sanctification. Another passage that speaks clearly about the believer's role in sanctification is 2 Corinthians 7:1. Here, Paul states: "Since we have these promises, beloved, *let us cleanse ourselves from every defilement of body and spirit,* bringing holiness to completion in the fear of God." Although God cleanses believers from the guilt of sin when he justifies them, the apostle states that the Corinthian believers *are to cleanse themselves* from "every defilement of body and spirit" in their daily pursuit of holiness. Finally, again, Hebrews 12:14 also speaks to the responsibility believers have in their pursuit of holiness: "Strive for peace with everyone, and for the holiness without which no one will see the Lord." The author of Hebrews makes it clear that his readers are to *strive* for peace and holiness, which is necessary if they wish to see the Lord at his return.

It is clear from the scriptural references above that believers are actively involved in their progress in sanctification. Although sanctification is rooted in God's supernatural grace, he also uses earthly means to achieve his salvific purposes for his people. Those means include the activation of the wills and affections of believers—which leads to behavior that is pleasing to God. As John Murray states:

> All working out of salvation on our part is the effect of God's working in us, not the willing to the exclusion of the doing and not the doing to the exclusion of the willing, but both the willing and the

doing. And this working of God is directed to the end of enabling us to will and to do that which is well pleasing to him.[7]

Therefore, it is not entirely incorrect to say that while justification is *monergistic* (God alone works), progressive sanctification is *synergistic* (God and believers work together).

## Sanctification and the Role of the Law

A divisive issue in evangelical circles in recent years is the role of the law in the believer's sanctification. Evangelical Christians who belong to the Reformed tradition have typically argued that the *moral* codes of the Mosaic law are still binding on believers today (which is normally identified as the "third use" of the law).[8] This view presupposes that the Mosaic law can be divided into three parts: ceremonial, civil, and moral.[9] However, as discussed in the previous chapter, there is no biblical justification for this tripartite division of the Mosaic law. The Mosaic law, as argued previously, was viewed as a single entity by the early Jews (and the biblical writers), and every aspect of the Mosaic law was understood in this unity.[10] In addition, the Mosaic covenant (along with its laws) was done away with and fulfilled in Christ, according to Paul (2 Cor 3:6–11; Gal 4:21–31). This is one of the key difficulties with the classic Reformed view of the law. We believe, therefore, that there is another perspective that avoids some of the problems associated with the classic Reformed view of the role of the law for today.

---

7. Murray, *Redemption—Accomplished and Applied*, 149.

8. Reymond, *New Systematic Theology*, 771–78.

9. Cf. *Westminster Confession of Faith* XIX/3–5. Those who espouse this position often look to Matthew 23:23 (Christ's distinction between the "weightier" and "lighter" matters of the law) to support their position. However, Jesus was not making a theoretical distinction between the ceremonial and moral laws but condemning the scribes and Pharisees for setting aside the more important aspects of the law (without ignoring the "lighter" ones) for their own convenience.

10. Joe M. Sprinkle insightfully notes: "Covenant theologians have traditionally divided laws into three categories: moral, civil, and ceremonial. . . . A problem with this approach is that the categories 'moral, civil, and ceremonial' are artificial. There is often a mixture of these categories: the ceremonial sabbath among 'moral' laws (Exod. 20:8), ceremonial food regulations among 'civil' laws (Exod. 21:28; 22:31), 'moral' motivations in civil laws (Exod. 22:21, 26–27) and in cultic laws (Exod. 20:26). There is considerable subjectivity in labeling laws as 'moral,' 'civil,' or 'ceremonial'" ("Law," 469).

The Scriptures are clear that new covenant believers are under God's moral authority. Although believers in the new covenant age are not bound to the obsolete Mosaic covenant, they are still exhorted to live in a way that pleases God (John 14:23; 1 John 3:22–24). In fact, when one reads the moral exhortations given in the New Testament, many of the commands are carried over from the Old Testament: Romans 2:21–22 (against stealing, adultery, and idolatry); Ephesians 4:28 (against stealing); 6:2 (honoring one's parents); Colossians 3:5 (against coveting); Titus 1:12 (against lying); Hebrews 13:4 (against sexual immorality and adultery); James 2:11 (against adultery and murder); 1 Peter 2:1 (against lying); 4:15 (against murder and stealing); and 1 John 3:12 (against murder). It is wrong to conclude, therefore, that believers are not under explicitly revealed laws for their sanctification because they can merely grow in obedience through the power of the Holy Spirit, as some dispensationalists argue.[11] However, it is just as problematic to argue that the New Testament commands are merely repetitions of the moral codes of the Mosaic law.

The more adequate approach to this problem is viewing the Mosaic law through its fulfillment in Christ. Now, under the new covenant, believers are obligated to fulfill the law of Christ (1 Cor 9:21)—which they do as the law is fulfilled in their lives through the power of the Spirit (Rom 8:4)[12]— while not being under the authority of the obsolete Mosaic covenant. The fulfilling of God's law through Christ not only includes right conduct but also the right attitude that accompanies it (Matt 5:21–30). Through their union with Christ and enablement by the Spirit, believers are now able to love God and others instinctively, and thus, genuinely fulfill the law. This does not mean that the importance of outward acts is lessened—believers are still commanded to refrain from conduct that is detrimental to others (cf. 1 Cor 8:9–13); however, believers are now motivated to obey God out of love. In this way, the biblical ethic of love is inextricably linked with the law of Christ (Rom 13:8–10). As George Eldon Ladd astutely points out:

11. Cf. Showers, *There Really Is a Difference!*, 195–205.

12. In Romans 8:3–4, Paul writes: "By sending his own Son in the likeness of sinful flesh and for sin, he condemned sin in the flesh, in order that the righteous requirement of the law might be fulfilled in us, who walk not according to the flesh but according to the Spirit." When Paul talks about the righteous requirement of the law being fulfilled in believers he is not talking about the imputed righteousness of Christ given to believers at conversion. Rather, he is talking about how believers practically fulfill the law in their lives through Christ's sacrificial work and the Spirit's empowerment (this is supported by Paul's statement at the end of verse 4: "who walk not according to the flesh but according to the Spirit") (cf. Bruce, *Romans*, 153).

In Christ, God has done what the law could not do, namely, condemned sin in the flesh, that the just requirement of the Law might be fulfilled in those who walk by the Spirit (Rom. 8:3–4). Here is paradox: by being freed from the Law, we uphold the Law (Rom. 3:31). It is obvious that the new life in Christ enables the Christian to keep the Law not as an external code but in terms of its higher demand, i.e., at the very point where the Law was powerless because it was an external written code. Thus Paul repeats that the essential Christian ethic of love, which is a gift of the Holy Spirit (1 Cor. 13; Gal. 5:22), is the fulfilling of the Law.[13]

The salvation-historical shift that has occurred in Christ, therefore, has put the Mosaic covenant to an end. Believers are no longer bound by the regulations of the Mosaic covenant and its external precepts. Despite this, new covenant believers are still commanded to love God and their neighbors as an expression of their fulfilling of the law of Christ and for their sanctification—which they do so by the Spirit. Even though believers today are not under the Mosaic covenant with its laws, the obligation to obey God's moral law given under Christ's authority is not abrogated in the least.[14]

## Sanctification Will Never be Perfect in This Life

In some Christian circles today the doctrine of "sinless perfection" (or "entire sanctification") is taught as a biblical teaching. Those who promote this teaching usually come from the Wesleyan-Holiness tradition.[15] Advocates of this position argue that believers can reach a moral state where they are completely free from sin and utterly blameless in conduct. Two passages that are most often invoked for support of this view are Matthew 5:48 and 1 John 3:6. In Matthew 5:48, Jesus declares: "You therefore must be perfect, as your heavenly Father is perfect," and in 1 John 3:6, John tells his readers: "No one who lives in him keeps on sinning" (NIV). Both verses appear to teach that a believer can reach a state of perfect holiness or complete sinlessness. However, on closer examination, both passages do not teach that

13. Ladd, *A Theology of the New Testament*, 553.

14. The view espoused here is similar to the view set forth by Douglas J. Moo in his essay "Law of Christ," 319–76.

15. Cf. Wood, "Wesleyan View," 95–118; Dieter, "Wesleyan Perspective," 11–46. Two well-known proponents of this view before the twentieth century include John William Fletcher (1729–85) and Charles Grandison Finney (1792–1875).

believers can attain sinless perfection in this life. In Matthew 5:48, Jesus is only giving us a standard by which God measures us when he judges the world according to his law—since God is *perfect*, only perfect righteousness is acceptable in his sight (which includes the right attitude when observing the law). Believers are, therefore, called to *strive* for this perfection (*teloioi*), even though they will never reach it in this life. In 1 John 3:6, John is not saying that believers do not sin (or can reach a stage where sin is totally eradicated in their lives) but that those who *persist in sin as a way of life* give evidence that they do not truly possess new life in Christ.[16] Therefore, as will be argued in more detail below, we maintain that the doctrine of sinless perfection is contrary to what is revealed in Scripture.

In response, we maintain that there are two key passages that speak against the sinless perfection doctrine: Matthew 6:12 and 1 John 1:8–10. In the first passage, which is contained in the Lord's Prayer, Jesus tells us to pray "forgive us our debts, as we also have forgiven our debtors." If Jesus thought that believers could reach sinless perfection in this life he would not have included this in the prayer. In the other passage, John writes: "If we say we have no sin, we deceive ourselves, and the truth is not in us. If we confess our sins, he is faithful and just to forgive us our sins and to cleanse us from all unrighteousness. If we say we have not sinned, we make him a liar, and his word is not in us." It is clear that John is speaking to believers since he addresses them as his "little children" shortly after (1 John 2:1). What John is saying, then, is that believers do need to regularly confess their sins and ask for forgiveness because they are not yet totally free from sin. In fact, John states that any person who claims to have not sinned as a believer is devoid of the truth (1 John 1:8) and is calling God a liar (v. 10). The good news for believers, however, is that they have Jesus Christ as their advocate before the Father when they do sin (1 John 2:1).

Other scriptural passages that contradict the sinless perfection doctrine include those that speak of the continual struggle that believers have with sin in the present age. One notable passage is Galatians 5:16–17: "But I say, walk by the Spirit, and you will not gratify the desires of the flesh. For the desires of the flesh are against the Spirit, and the desires of the Spirit are against the flesh, for these are opposed to each other, to keep you from doing the things you want to do." If sinless perfection is possible in this life, Paul would not use the language of struggle to depict the battle that constantly rages between the Spirit and the flesh inside the believer. In fact,

16. Kistemaker, *James and I–III John*, 299–300.

Paul exhorts his readers to "walk by the Spirit" so that their sinful desires will not be gratified (cf. Rom 13:14). In another passage, Paul warns the believers at Rome: "For if you live according to the flesh you will die, but if by the Spirit you put to death the deeds of the body, you will live" (Rom 8:13). Paul is not saying here that it is possible for a regenerate person to perish eternally if he or she acts according to the flesh, but that those who do live according to the flesh will suffer eternal death at the eschaton (because they lack the new life in the Spirit). Nevertheless, the power of the sinful flesh is ever so real in all believers that they must do their utmost to fight against it on a regular basis. Paul even admits of not attaining perfection in his own life when he writes in Philippians 3:13–14: "Brothers, I do not consider that I have made it my own. But one thing I do: forgetting what lies behind and straining forward to what lies ahead, I press on toward the goal for the prize of the upward call of God in Christ Jesus." Also, there are passages in other parts of Scripture that plainly speak to the fact that no human being is totally free from sin in this life (e.g., 1 Kgs 8:46; Ps 130:3; Prov 20:9; Eccl 7:20; and Jas 3:2).

Another problem with the sinless perfection view is that it results in a deficient *hamartiology* (or doctrine of sin). Those who espouse the sinless perfection view, especially in the Wesleyan tradition, argue that sins can be divided into two types: voluntary ("ethical") and involuntary ("legal"). The former type of sin carries more weight and compromises a believer's progress in sanctification, but the "involuntary" sins do not result in a believer becoming blameworthy.[17] However, there is no scriptural basis to say that those who commit "involuntary" sins, in contrast to those who commit "voluntary" sins, may still be considered blameless. James makes it clear that all believers "stumble in many ways. And if anyone does not stumble in what he says, he is a perfect man, able also to bridle his whole body" (James 3:2). In fact, Paul states clearly that he is "not aware of anything" against himself but that still does not make him "acquitted" of anything in his own judgment (1 Cor 4:4). Scripture is clear, then, that all sins, done wilfully or ignorantly, are an offense against God and those who commit them deserve his eternal wrath.

Based on the testimony of Scripture sanctification can never be perfect in this life. Sinless perfection will only be attained at the final consummation when believers receive their resurrected bodies. Therefore, believers,

---

17. Wood, "Wesleyan View," 112–13.

even though they are new creations in Christ, will still struggle with sin and constantly need to be exhorted to fight against the flesh in their daily lives.

## Sanctification and the "Old Person"

In Reformed circles in years past there was a debate concerning the condition of the "old person" (or the "old man") in the regenerate. Some Reformed theologians argued that the regenerate person is no longer the "old person" of his or her pre-conversion days. They maintain that at the time of regeneration, the old person is totally crucified and the believer is now only a "new person" in Christ. One notable Reformed theologian who held this view was John Murray. In his *Principles of Conduct*, he writes:

> When Paul says, 'our old man has been crucified' [Rom 6:6], we have to take into account the terms, the background, and the context of this statement. The term 'crucified' is that of being crucified with Christ, and therefore indicates that the old man has been put to death just as decisively as Christ died upon the accursed tree. To suppose that the old man has been crucified and still lives or has been raised again from this death is to contradict the obvious force of the import of crucifixion.[18]

The position advocated by Murray does have some merit but may be too excessive in its claims. Most evangelicals will agree that the believer is no longer the same person as he or she was before conversion. The supernatural change that has occurred in the believer's inner being delivers him or her from the dominion of sin, and he or she is now enabled to live in a way that pleases God. That is why true believers cannot fall into a state of utter carnality or remain in that state for an extended period of time.[19] In one sense, then, we can say that the believer is a "new person" who still has to struggle with the flesh until the end of his or her life. However, we should be cautious that we do not equate the spiritual resurrection that believers

18. Murray, *Principles of Conduct*, 212–13; cf. also Hoekema, *Saved by Grace*, 209–14.

19. Those who argue for the existence of the "carnal Christian" (a regenerate person who lives like an unregenerate person) often point to 1 Corinthians 3:1–3 to defend their position. However, Paul is not saying in the passage that there exists another category of believers called "carnal Christians." Rather, Paul is pointing out to these immature believers at Corinth ("infants in Christ") that they were behaving in a *fleshly manner* ("still of the flesh") (Gk. *sarkikos*) with their divisions and jealousies. True believers do fall into sin, as we have stated above, but their sinful flesh does not exert the same degree of influence or power as it did before their conversion.

experience at conversion with the obliteration of the "old person" (which happens at the future resurrection). The believer is in one sense still the "old person," even though this old self is being slowly overcome by the new person in Christ (2 Cor 4:16; Col 3:10). Even though the old person is no longer the dominant principle in the believer (Rom 6:17–18), it is still an ever-present threat. Therefore, Martin Luther's statement that believers are "simultaneously righteous and sinner" (*simul iustus et peccator*) is correct to a certain degree.[20]

We believe that the most adequate way to understand the relationship between sanctification and the "old person" is by viewing it through the lens of eschatology. It is unhelpful to make absolutist statements, like Murray does, that infer that the old person has completely died at conversion. The old person still remains in believers (Eph 4:22), but due to the fact that they have been taken up in the eschatological renewal of all creation (which still awaits complete fulfillment at the eschaton) they enjoy a foretaste of

---

20. Many Christians refer to Romans 7:7–24 in order to find support for the *simul iustus et peccator* doctrine. They argue that the passage describes Paul's inner struggle between the spirit and the flesh during his *post*-conversion life. This interpretation of the passage has a long history since Augustine and many modern exegetes still hold to it today. What makes this view attractive are four exegetical factors: 1) Paul switching from the past tense in verses 7–13 to the present tense in verses 14–24; 2) Paul's continual use of the "I" in verses 14–24 to describe the struggle that is going on within him; 3) Paul's mentioning of the believer's struggle against the flesh in other places (cf. 1 Cor 9:26–27; Gal 5:17; Eph 4:22–24); and 4) Paul stating that he "delights" in the law of God in his "inner being" (v. 22), which is difficult to ascribe to an unregenerate person. Despite some of the valid points of the post-conversion Augustinian interpretation, we find this view unpersuasive when examined carefully. One of the main difficulties of the Augustinian interpretation is that there is no mention of the Holy Spirit in verses 14–24. If Paul was describing his experience as a Christian why does he not mention the Holy Spirit as the agent that enables him to fight against the flesh? Another argument against this view is that Paul ends the chapter with a note of triumph—that through Christ one can find victory in one's battle against the flesh (v. 25). This connects well with what Paul says at the beginning of chapter 8 of Romans about the "law of the Spirit of life" setting believers free from the "law of sin and death" (Rom 8:2) as a result of Christ's sacrificial work (v. 3). It seems, therefore, best to read Romans 7 and Romans 8 sequentially—the plight of the unsaved (7:14–24) and the deliverance of the redeemed thereafter (8:1–17). We propose, therefore, that the most adequate way of understanding Romans 7:14–24 is viewing it as Paul's description of unregenerate humanity in the face of God's law. Although the law is good, for unregenerate people it only leads to defeat and death (7:13, 24). In short, the main purpose of Paul writing Romans 7:14–24 is to tell his readers that the law by itself cannot spiritually transform unregenerate people and that victory over sin can only come through Christ and the Spirit's work in them (Rom 8:1–4, 10–11) (cf. Seifrid, "Romans 7," 153–63).

the full redemption to come through the new birth. Therefore, it is best to view the matter of the believer's struggle between the old and new self as the reality of living in both the "already" and "not yet" of God's redemptive-historical timeline.

## 2. Perseverance of the Saints

The doctrine of the perseverance of the saints is a doctrine that brings great comfort to those who have genuinely entrusted themselves to Christ for salvation and give evidence of new life in the Spirit. It is also a doctrine that should encourage believers to greater obedience to God and care for their spiritual growth. In recent years this doctrine is sometimes called *the eternal security of the believer*,[21] but ever since the post-Reformation period the phrase *perseverance of the saints* is what has been used customarily to describe this doctrine. Therefore, this is the wording that will be used to describe this doctrine in this work. In regards to a definition, we believe the most satisfactory way to define this doctrine is *the truth that all regenerate persons will persevere in faith to the end by the keeping power of God, and that only those who persevere to the end will be saved.*

### The Biblical Support for the Doctrine of the Perseverance of the Saints

There are several notable passages in Scripture that indicate that true believers are kept by God's power and persevere to the end:

> John 5:24: "Truly, truly, I say to you, whoever hears my word and believes him who sent me has eternal life. He does not come into judgment, but has passed from death to life."

---

21. The term "eternal security" is not entirely incorrect if used with qualification. Oftentimes, this doctrine is misunderstood to mean that a person is saved (and will be saved at the end) no matter what he or she does after a so-called profession of faith. It is true that those who come to Christ will never experience condemnation (Rom 8:1) and that Christ will lose none of those who truly belong to him (John 6:39), but Scripture also makes it clear that not all those who profess to be Christians are truly saved (Matt 7:21–23; 1 Cor 5:9–13). Thus, the term *perseverance of the saints* more accurately describes the biblical teaching that none of Christ's own will ever be lost.

- Jesus here is emphatic that those who believe in him have crossed over from spiritual death to eternal life. This promise is not only for the age to come but the present. The irrevocability of the promise is necessitated by the fact that believers receive this gift of life immediately. Regarding this verse, George R. Beasley-Murray writes: "The promise becomes immediately effective; the hearer-believer *has* eternal life *now*. He has the judgment behind him, not before him, since judgment is for unbelief (3:18, 36), and he has crossed over from the realm of death into the sphere of the divine sovereignty, the characteristic of which is life for all who enter it (cf. Col 1:13)."[22]

> John 6:38–40: "For I have come down from heaven, not to do my own will but the will of him who sent me. And this is the will of him who sent me, that I should lose nothing of all that he has given me, but raise it up on the last day. For this is the will of my Father, that everyone who looks on the Son and believes in him should have eternal life, and I will raise him up on the last day."

- This is one of the strongest statements given by Jesus regarding the irrevocability of the believer's salvation. Jesus makes it clear that the will of the Father is that none of those who are given to the Son will ever be lost, but that they will receive eternal life in the present and be raised on the last day. On the other hand, if any believer perishes eternally this then would mean that Jesus failed in his mission to carry out his Father's will—something that is not possible for God to do.

> John 10:27–30: "My sheep hear my voice, and I know them, and they follow me. I give them eternal life, and they will never perish, and no one will snatch them out of my hand. My Father, who has given them to me, is greater than all, and no one is able to snatch them out of the Father's hand. I and the Father are one."

- Here is another resounding declaration by Jesus about the imperishable character of salvation. He makes it clear that his "sheep" (all believers) will never perish nor can anyone take them out of his hand. This security is also reinforced by the Father's hold on the believer. Both the Father and the Son work in unison to keep the believer from falling away and perishing.

22. Beasley-Murray, *John*, 76.

Romans 8:30: "And those whom he predestined he also called, and those whom he called he also justified, and those whom he justified he also glorified."

- This verse, as mentioned earlier, is sometimes referred to as the "golden chain" of salvation. Paul states here that there is an inextricable link between predestination and glorification insofar that he speaks of the latter as if it had already occurred for believers. Thus, those God predestined for salvation before creation *will* be glorified in the future. What one notices here is that all the aspects of salvation that Paul mentions (predestination, calling, justification, and glorification) are all those accomplished by God *alone*.

  Romans 8:38–39: "For I am sure that neither death nor life, nor angels nor rulers, nor things present nor things to come, nor powers, nor height nor depth, nor anything else in all creation, will be able to separate us from the love of God in Christ Jesus our Lord."

- This is one of the strongest affirmations by the apostle Paul that salvation is an irrevocable gift. He lists a number of factors in the created order that could possibly terminate God's love for his children but he emphatically states that none of those can do so. Even believers themselves, despite their sins, cannot cause God's love for them to be extinguished. The passage is straightforwardly clear that *nothing* in all of creation can cause a breach in the believer's saving relationship to Christ.

  Ephesians 1:13–14: "In him you also, when you heard the word of truth, the gospel of your salvation, and believed in him, were sealed with the promised Holy Spirit, who is the guarantee of our inheritance until we acquire possession of it, to the praise of his glory."

- Paul here states that the Holy Spirit who indwells all believers is the guarantee of the inheritance to come. In fact, believers are said to be "sealed" by the Holy Spirit as God's promise to them of their eschatological redemption (to indicate in the strongest possible way that believers truly belong to God without end).[23] One can even say that

23. In regards to Paul's use of the word "sealed" in this context, Francis Foulkes writes:

the sealing of the Holy Spirit is the "initial installment" of the final salvation to be revealed at the end of the age.

> Philippians 1:6: "And I am sure of this, that he who began a good work in you will bring it to completion at the day of Jesus Christ."

- This is another verse that speaks to the enduring character of God's work of salvation for believers. Some commentators have argued that Paul is referring to God using the financial generosity of the Philippians to carry out his good work until the return of Christ.[24] However, there is no exegetical or contextual reason to restrict the meaning of the verse in this way. Although Paul may have had the Philippians' monetary generosity in mind here, he is more likely referring to the whole work of salvation begun at their conversion. In regards to this verse, Homer A. Kent writes: "God not only initiates salvation, but continues it and guarantees its consummation. The apostle's thought relates not to the end of life but to the glorious coming of Jesus Christ that will vindicate both the Lord and his people. So Paul is asserting that God will bring his work to completion. Nothing in this life or after death will prevent the successful accomplishment of God's good work in every Christian."[25]

> 1 Peter 1:3–5: "Blessed be the God and Father of our Lord Jesus Christ! According to his great mercy, he has caused us to be born again to a living hope through the resurrection of Jesus Christ from the dead, to an inheritance that is imperishable, undefiled, and unfading, kept in heaven for you, who by God's power are

---

"In the ancient world the seal was the personal sign of the owner or the sender of something important, and thus, as in a letter, it distinguished what was true from what was spurious. It was also the guarantee that the thing sealed had been carried intact. In New Testament times certain religious cults followed the practice of having their devotees tattooed with the emblem of the cult, and the initiates were then said to have been sealed. This may have been in Paul's mind here, and in the very different context of Galatians 6:17, but not necessarily so. The Jews thought of circumcision as a seal (see Rom. 4:11). The Holy Spirit is the Christian's seal. The experience of the Holy Spirit in their lives is the final proof to them, and indeed a demonstration to others, of the genuineness of what they have believed, and provides the inward assurance that they belong to God as children (*cf.* Rom. 8:15–16; Gal. 4:6)" (*Ephesians*, 64).

24. Gundry, *Commentary on the New Testament*, 781–82.

25. Kent, "Philippians," 105.

being guarded through faith for a salvation ready to be revealed in the last time."

- The apostle Peter, like Paul, speaks of the believer's salvation as an inheritance. Peter describes this inheritance as a gift that is "imperishable," "undefiled," and "unfading." Peter uses these adjectives to make sure that his readers understand that unlike earthly goods salvation is something that is of enduring character. The security of this salvation is fortified by the fact that believers are "guarded through faith" by "God's power." Even though full redemption belongs only in the future, God guards the believers' salvation now *through faith* so that they may receive the full inheritance at the restoration of all things at the end. In regards to this passage, Simon J. Kistemaker states: "Earthly possessions are subject to constant variation and change, but our eternal inheritance is safely guarded by God in heaven. Not only is our salvation kept safe, but also, Peter declares, we, the possessors of this inheritance, are protected by God's power."[26]

> Jude 24–25: "Now to him who is able to keep you from stumbling and to present you blameless before the presence of his glory with great joy, to the only God, our Savior, through Jesus Christ our Lord, be glory, majesty, dominion, and authority, before all time and now and forever. Amen."

- Verse 24 makes it clear that God will keep (Gk. *phulassō*, "guard") believers "from stumbling" so that they will be presented "blameless" when Christ returns. Jude makes it clear that God's work of salvation includes believers being kept by his power so that they will not stumble to the point of completely turning away from Christ. God's keeping of the saints from falling away, therefore, is his work alone.

From the passages we have examined above, there is a consistent theme running throughout all of them: *God is the one who keeps believers in their salvation.* When it comes to the work of salvation from beginning to end, it is God alone who deserves all the credit. Although believers are exhorted to persevere in many places throughout Scripture, their perseverance is ultimately grounded in God's sovereign work of salvation on their

---

26. Kistemaker, *Peter and Jude*, 43.

behalf. [27] That is why it is not entirely wrong to view perseverance as more of a promise than a demand.[28] However, despite the numerous passages that support the doctrine of unconditional perseverance, many still find the doctrine objectionable on practical and biblical grounds. We now turn to engage with the practical and biblical objections typically laid against this doctrine.

## Objections Against the Doctrine of the Perseverance of the Saints

### The Doctrine Leads to Moral Carelessness or Indifference

One of the most common objections to the doctrine of the perseverance of the saints is that it leads to moral carelessness or indifference. If believers are assured that they will never fall out of grace, what is the point of exhorting them to obey God and refrain from a life of sin? This objection against the doctrine of perseverance is similar to the one set forth against the Reformation doctrine of justification *sola fide*. This objection, however, is founded on a misunderstanding of the nature of perseverance and the design of God's work of salvation. As noted above, the doctrine of the perseverance of the saints means that *saints* persevere to the end in faith and obedience. The doctrine does not assure professing believers that they are eternally secure apart from their perseverance.

The biblical and historic understanding of this doctrine keeps security and perseverance together, although both are different aspects of God's work of salvation. Rather than making believers indifferent to what God requires of them, the doctrine of perseverance spurs believers on to a life of active faith and obedience. As Murray aptly puts it:

> To say that a believer is secure whatever may be the extent of his addiction to sin in his subsequent life is to abstract faith in Christ from its very definition and it ministers to that abuse which turns the grace of God into lasciviousness. The doctrine of perseverance is the doctrine that believers *persevere*; it cannot be too strongly stressed that it is the *perseverance* of the saints. And that means that the saints, those united to Christ by the effectual call of the Father and indwelt by the Holy Spirit, will persevere unto the end.

27. Louis Berkhof puts it succinctly when he writes: "The denial of the doctrine of perseverance virtually makes the salvation of man dependent on the human will rather than on the grace of God" (*Systematic Theology*, 549).

28. Keathley, *Salvation and Sovereignty*, 189.

> If they persevere, they endure, they continue. It is not at all that they will be saved irrespective of their perseverance or their continuance, but that they will assuredly persevere. Consequently the security that is theirs is inseparable from their perseverance.[29]

In addition, Scripture is replete with warnings that those who continue in wickedness will not inherit the kingdom of God no matter what they profess to believe (1 Cor 6:9–10; Gal 5:19–21; Eph 5:5; Rev 21:8). Many who professed faith in Christ at one point will be cast away from Christ's presence at the final judgment because their failure to persevere revealed their unregenerate condition.

Finally, even though the doctrine of the perseverance of the saints can be misused (or even abused) by some people, this does not make the doctrine any less biblical or true. The truthfulness of a doctrine is not based on whether it can be protected from abuse or mishandling (cf. Rom 6:1), but if it is supported by the testimony of Scripture. However, as we have argued above, this doctrine, if rightly understood, does not promote any type of practical antinomianism. Scripture nowhere supports the idea that a person can claim Christ, continue in the way of rebellion against God, and still be on the way to eschatological glory.

### The Doctrine Is Contrary to What Is Taught in Scripture

Another common objection against the doctrine of the perseverance of the saints is that it is contrary to the teachings of Scripture. Opponents of the doctrine argue that there are numerous passages in the Gospels and epistles that view apostasy as a real possibility for genuine believers.[30] They argue that if true believers cannot fall away from the faith why do the Scriptures exhort believers to endure to the end to enter salvation (Matt 10:22; 24:13; Mark 13:13; Heb 3:14; 4:11; Jude 21), warn them of the dire consequences of apostasy (John 15:6; Rom 11:21–22; Heb 6:4–8; 10:26–31; 2 Pet 2:20–22), and give actual cases of such apostasy among professing believers (Mark 4:17 [cf. also Matt 13:20–21; Luke 8:13]; Gal 5:4; 2 Tim 4:10)? A quick glance at those passages seems to support the view that security and

---

29. Murray, *Redemption—Accomplished and Applied*, 154–55.

30. I. Howard Marshall presents a thoroughly biblical-exegetical case for the doctrine of conditional security in his work *Kept by the Power of God*. For a less technical work that espouses the same Arminian or Wesleyan perspective, see Robert Shank's *Life in the Son*.

perseverance are not guaranteed according to Scripture. However, we will argue that these three types of passages do not necessarily speak against the doctrine of the perseverance of the saints and the security of the true believer. We will discuss these three types of passages in order and provide a response for each of them immediately following.

1.  *Passages that exhort believers to endure to the end.* Wesleyan or Arminian Christians typically argue that if apostasy is impossible for true believers then the exhortations in Scripture to persevere lose their meaning and force. For instance, they argue, in the Gospels of Matthew and Mark, that Jesus tells his disciples of the necessity of endurance for final salvation (Matt 10:22; 24:13; Mark 13:13). In Mark's version it reads: "And you will be hated by all for my name's sake. But the one who endures to the end will be saved." Some scholars, especially those from a dispensationalist background, argue that the "end" that Jesus speaks of here is the end of the Great Tribulation. According to these scholars, believers will be *physically* saved at the end of the Great Tribulation if they endure.[31] However, there is nothing in the context, as Wesleyan or Arminian Christians rightly aver, to suggest that Jesus was restricting the terms "end" and "saved" in those ways. What Jesus meant in those verses was that believers need to persevere to the end (whether at the end of life or at his return) if they are to be eternally saved on the last day. This, therefore, poses a biblical-theological difficulty for Calvinist interpreters: if salvation is an irrevocable gift, why exhort believers to persevere to the end for eschatological salvation?

    We believe the best solution to this apparent dilemma is by understanding these exhortations as the *means* that God uses to keep his elect on the narrow path that leads to eschatological life.[32] These admonitions are genuine calls to perseverance (not "hypothetical" warnings) which *all* the regenerate do heed and, therefore, endure to the end as a result—unlike the unregenerate in the church who do not heed these exhortations and finally apostatize in the face of difficulties and trials (cf. Mark 4:17). Verses like Hebrews 4:11 and Jude 21 can also be understood this way.[33] In another key verse, Hebrews 3:14, the author of the letter is only reminding his readers that they have truly

31. Barbieri, "Matthew," 77.

32. Berkouwer, *Faith and Perseverance*, 83–124.

33. For an extremely helpful book on this subject from a Calvinistic point of view, see Schreiner and Caneday, *Race Set Before.*

come to "share in Christ" if they hold to their "original confidence firm to the end." Their perseverance is evidence that they are genuine partakers of Christ and his salvific benefits.

None of the passages mentioned above prove that it is possible for genuine believers to fall away and lose their salvation. They are only admonitions to believers to stay on the narrow path of eternal life. These exhortations, however, do not undermine the inseparable connection between the "already" and "not yet" aspects of salvation: they only reveal that believers need to endure to the end as evidence of their salvation, which will then result in them being received unto glory at the eschaton. This is based on the fact that even though believers are saved now, their full redemption is only complete when Christ returns (Heb 9:26–28).

2. *Passages that warn believers of the dire consequences of apostasy.* Another set of passages that appear to pose a problem for Reformed/Calvinistic interpreters are those that warn believers of the dire consequences of apostasy. Similar to the argument for the above set of passages, non-Reformed Christians maintain that the warnings against falling away will be bereaved of significance if true believers cannot turn away from Christ. One verse that is often referred to in support of the real danger and threat of apostasy is John 15:6. In the verse, Jesus declares: "If anyone does not abide in me he is thrown away like a branch and withers; and the branches are gathered, thrown into the fire, and burned." If genuine believers cannot be severed from Christ, why does Christ give this specific warning to his disciples? Again, this verse does not prove that true believers can lose their salvation; it only demonstrates that those who fail to produce fruit will be cut off because this reveals that their attachment to Christ was merely superficial (Judas being a prime example; cf. John 17:12).[34] In regards to this verse, Merrill C. Tenney writes: "An absolutely fruitless life is prima facie evidence that one is not a believer. Jesus left no place among his followers for fruitless disciples."[35]

Another passage that non-Reformed Christians commonly refer to in support of conditional perseverance is Hebrews 6:4–8. The passage in full reads:

34. J. Carl Laney notes that the description of judgment in the verse is strikingly similar to the judgment of the worthless vines in Ezekiel 15:6–7 (*John*, 275).

35. Tenney, "Gospel of John," 152.

> For it is impossible, in the case of those who have once been en-lightened, who have tasted the heavenly gift, and have shared in the Holy Spirit, and have tasted the goodness of the word of God and the powers of the age to come, and then have fallen away, to restore them again to repentance, since they are crucifying once again the Son of God to their own harm and holding him up to contempt. For land that has drunk the rain that often falls on it, and produces a crop useful to those for whose sake it is cultivated, receives a blessing from God. But if it bears thorns and thistles, it is worthless and near to being cursed, and its end is to be burned.

Many Christians will admit that this is one of the most troubling passages to read in Scripture. Countless exegetical battles have been fought over this one passage over the years by Bible scholars. Various interpretive proposals have been suggested regarding the meaning of the passage in relation to the doctrine of perseverance. The most commonly held position is that the writer is speaking in a straightforward manner: the author is describing a genuine saving experience and the real possibility of falling away and losing salvation. This interpretation of the passage is typically held by Roman Catholic, Lutheran, Wesleyan, and Arminian exegetes.[36] Another interpretation offered is that the author is speaking only hypothetically: the passage is describing a genuine Christian experience but the apostasy is only hypothetical—it only describes what *would happen* to true believers if they do apostatize (which is impossible; cf. verse 9). Millard J. Erickson holds this view.[37] Finally, an approach that is popular among Reformed/Calvinistic scholars is to view the people described in verses 4–6 as those who experience many spiritual blessings from the Holy Spirit but fall short of actually receiving salvation. Their apostasy is evidence that they were never genuinely saved.[38]

The problem with the first view is that there are numerous passages in Scripture that affirm the eternal security of the true believer (cf. John 6:38–40; 10:27–30; Rom 8:38–39; Phil 1:6; and others). The second view does not do justice to the seriousness of the warning given in the passage—the author is not talking about a hypothetical

36. Cf. Osborne, "Classical Arminian View," 111–15; Cockerill, "Wesleyan Arminian View," 272–80.

37. Erickson, *Christian Theology*, 1004–5. See also Hewitt, *Epistle to the Hebrews*, 110–11.

38. Cf. Grudem, "Perseverance of the Saints," 134–60; Morris, "Hebrews," 54–56.

situation but a real danger. The difficulty with the third view is that the way the author describes the apostates in verses 4–6 is not consistent with a superficial experience of grace that falls short of actual conversion. The people described in the passage were "once enlightened," "tasted the heavenly gift,"[39] "shared in the Holy Spirit," and "tasted the goodness of the word of God and the powers of the age to come." It is difficult to conclude that the experiences described in these verses refer to a "conversion experience" that is less than saving.

In contrast to the views suggested above, we argue that the most satisfying way to understand the passage is viewing the experiences described in verses 4–6 as those that indicate a genuine reception of salvation (along with a serious warning against apostasy). The author is not telling his readers that true believers can lose their salvation but, instead, is warning them that those who fail to persevere will not inherit God's salvific promises despite their past profession of faith. In other words, the author is not providing a dogmatic treatment about whether loss of salvation is a real possibility for his readers but giving them a pastoral admonition to persevere so that they will be received into Christ's kingdom at the end (v. 7). As mentioned previously, the elect heed these admonitions and persevere to the end (as indicated in verse 9), while the non-elect do not and apostatize when persecution comes (either by returning to Judaism, in the case of these Hebrew believers, or by falling into mere unbelief). Therefore, we should understand the warnings as another *means* God uses to keep the elect on the path of salvation so that they will be received into glory when Christ returns.[40]

Finally, another passage that is commonly brought up in defense of conditional perseverance is 2 Peter 2:20–22. The apostle Peter, describing the situation of the false teachers, writes:

> For if, after they have escaped the defilements of the world through the knowledge of our Lord and Savior Jesus Christ, they are again entangled in them and overcome, the last state has become worse

39. In Hebrews 2:9, the author states that Christ "tasted" death for everyone. The Greek word for "taste" in Hebrews 2:9 is the same word used in Hebrews 6:4 to describe the tasting of the heavenly gift. Just like Christ did not experience death in a superficial way (but experienced death in the fullest sense), the people described in Hebrews 6:4–6 did not have a superficial taste of the heavenly gift but experienced it in full measure (with all the attendant blessings).

40. Schreiner and Caneday, *Race Set Before Us*, 200–204.

for them than the first. For it would have been better for them never to have known the way of righteousness than after knowing it to turn back from the holy commandment delivered to them. What the true proverb says has happened to them: "The dog returns to its own vomit, and the sow, after washing herself, returns to wallow in the mire."

Unlike Hebrews 6:4–6, however, the experience of these false teachers fall short of actual conversion. Even though Peter tells his readers that these false teachers were those who "escaped the defilements of the world through the knowledge of our Lord and Savior Jesus Christ" (v. 20) and who had "known the way of righteousness," their turning back on the "holy commandment" that was delivered to them (v. 21) revealed that they were always "dogs" and "sows" (v. 22) who never really experienced the transforming grace of God. They were supposed converts to the faith who later repudiated the message of the cross and returned to their old pagan lifestyle (cf. also 1 John 2:19). Like the passage in Hebrews, it is wrong to infer that Peter was giving his readers a dogmatic treatise on perseverance and apostasy. Peter's purpose in writing this passage was not to tell his readers that they would lose their salvation if they fell into sin, but to tell them of the awful fate that awaits the false teachers who disavowed their supposed commitment to Christ in order to return to their previous way of life. Therefore, this passage is applied incorrectly if it used as a proof-text against the Reformed or Calvinistic understanding of perseverance.

3. *Passages that speak of actual cases of apostasy.* Lastly, non-Reformed Christians also refer to biblical passages that speak of actual cases of apostasy to argue that the Reformed/Calvinistic understanding of perseverance and security has no scriptural basis. They often refer to the "rocky ground" in Jesus' Parable of the Sower (Mark 4:17; cf. also Matt 13:20–21; Luke 8:13), those who "fell away" from grace in the church in Galatia (Gal 5:4), and the situation of Demas (2 Tim 4:10). They argue that if apostasy and loss of salvation cannot happen to true believers, why do the Scriptures provide such cases of apostasy? The problem with this argument is that none of the passages referenced above prove that the people in question were at one time genuinely saved. First, the "rocky ground" in the Parable of the Sower is set in contrast to the "good soil" (true believers) that produced fruit

in varying measure (Matt 13:23). Second, those who fell from grace in Galatia (Gal 5:4) were those who were attempting to be justified before God through faith in Christ *and* circumcision (or the "works of the law"). What Paul is saying in this verse is that if a person adds other requirements like observing the law for justification then he or she has in effect rejected God's grace in Christ. The verse is not talking about losing salvation but falling into Judaic legalism—which, thereby, invalidates Christ's work of salvation for the one who falls prey to its teaching. Lastly, Demas' case is not an appropriate example of a true believer who fell away and lost salvation. There is no indication in the text that Demas was at one time a true believer. In fact, Demas is a good example of an individual who once professed faith in Christ yet whose heart was still devoted to the world, and thus, demonstrated to others that his profession of faith was false and disingenuous (cf. Jas 4:4; 1 John 2:15).

## Conclusion

The doctrine of the perseverance of the saints is a glorious biblical teaching that needs to be preached in the pulpits of our churches today. A correct understanding of this doctrine will lead to greater obedience and assurance for believers in times of spiritual lethargy and doubt. Although believers will never be able to persevere to the end by their own will and strength, God, by his pure grace and mercy, provides all the necessary means to secure the believer's perseverance and salvation. Once dead to sin but now alive in Christ, believers now have the power through God's grace to finish the race that is set before them (cf. Heb 12:1).

# CHAPTER 16

# The Church

## 1. The Nature of the Church

### What Is the Church?

MANY CHRISTIANS THROUGHOUT HISTORY have asked: "What constitutes the church?" The answer to this question is fraught with difficulty since the church in the modern period is fractured with various denominations and confessional traditions. Not only is the visible church today divided between the East and West, but also between Roman Catholics and Protestants, Arminians and Calvinists, and liberals and evangelicals. In fact, some liberal Protestant churches today have veered so far off from the teachings of the apostles that one wonders if they should rightfully be included as part of the visible church of Christ. Therefore, one can readily understand the difficulty of answering this simple question in a straightforward manner.

If a basic definition of the church could be given, we could define it as *a fellowship of believers where the word of God is preached faithfully, the ordinances rightly administered, and church discipline is exercised when necessary.* It is necessary to point out that some churches come closer to this definition than others, but if these three elements are present in a local congregation then we can say that it is *a* church. Of course, the definition above pertains only to the visible church on earth. If we revised the definition to include only the "invisible church" we could define it as *the body of all saved individuals regardless of time and place.*

## The Church According to the Scriptural Witness

In the New Testament, the Greek term that is used to describe the gathering of God's people is *ekklēsia*—translated as "church" in our English Bibles.[1] The term is used this way 109 times out of the 114 occurrences in the New Testament. Most notable are in Paul's letters (in which he uses the term sixty-three times), whether addressing individual congregations (1 Cor 1:2; 1 Thess 1:1; Philem 2) or groups of congregations (Gal 1:2; 1 Thess 2:14). Jesus also used this word when he talks about building his church in the near future (Matt 16:18) and about disputes being settled in the church (Matt 18:17, although the usage here is debated). Other passages in the New Testament that use this term to refer to the church are Hebrews 12:23; James 5:14; 3 John 6, 9–10; and the numerous times when Jesus addresses the seven churches in the first three chapters of Revelation (and 22:16).

It is interesting to note that the Septuagint (LXX) translators translated the Hebrew word *qahal,* the Hebrew term for "assembly," into *ekklēsia.* The author of Hebrews, in fact, when quoting from Psalm 22:22 (of the LXX) in Hebrews 2:12 uses the term *ekklēsia* in regards to Christ's reference to the "congregation." In another New Testament text, Stephen refers to the Israelite assembly in the Old Testament as the *ekklēsia* (Acts 7:38). Thus, Stephen's designation of the Israelite assembly in the Old Testament as the *ekklēsia* suggests *some type* of continuity between Old Testament Israel and the New Testament church. Both are God's people despite a major shift having occurred in redemptive history with the coming of Christ. However, we should not conclude from this that the Scriptures teach that the visible church existed during Old Testament times. Scripture nowhere states that the Israel of the old covenant and the church of the new covenant are to be synonymized with each other (more on this will be discussed below).

It also must be said that the term *ekklēsia* applies to both the local and universal church. Although the former meaning is given more prominence in the New Testament (1 Cor 4:17; Gal 1:22; 1 Thess 1:1), the term is also used for those who constitute the church regardless of whether an actual assembling of believers takes place (Eph 1:22–23; Col 1:18). In this sense,

---

1. However, the term is also used in secular literature to denote an assembly of people (cf. Acts 19:32, 39, 41) (Tidball, "Church," 408).

local churches are *manifestations* of the one "universal church," even if they are churches *individually*.[2]

Therefore, according to Scripture, the church (*ekklēsia*) is an assembly of believers who are united to Christ through faith and gather together to worship God, hear God's word, and have fellowship with one another.

## The Attributes of the Church

According to the Niceno-Constantinopolitan Creed (381 AD), Christians believe that the church is "one, holy, catholic, and apostolic." This understanding of the attributes of the church has been affirmed by many Christian bodies and confessional traditions throughout history. Therefore, it is important that we discuss each of these attributes in order.

### The Oneness of the Church

The oneness of the church describes the essential unity that Christians have because of their belief in the triune God and confession of Christ as Lord. The apostle Paul emphasizes this oneness of the church when he states in 1 Corinthians 12:12–13:

> For just as the body is one and has many members, and all the members of the body, though many, are one body, so it is with Christ. For in one Spirit we were all baptized into one body—Jews or Greeks, slaves or free—and all were made to drink of one Spirit.

He also highlights this oneness in Ephesians 4:4–6 when he writes:

> There is one body and one Spirit—just as you were called to the one hope that belongs to your call—one Lord, one faith, one baptism, one God and Father of all, who is over all and through all and in all.

This unity of believers, it must be emphasized, is located in Christ. Due to his obedience and sacrifice, Christ unites all those who embrace him as their Lord and Savior through faith. Their personal union with Christ brings forth this unity and results in all believers being part of a single spiritual body (Rom 12:4–5). In fact, one of Christ's missions was to bring about this unity among all believers (John 10:16; 17:21). That is why disunity in

2. Saucy, *Church in God's Program*, 16–18.

the church is an aberration and expression of the fallen condition of humankind (1 Cor 1:10–17; 3:1–4). However, we must not confuse unity with *uniformity.*

Even though the church is one, this does not mean that every church must be identical to one another. Even in unity there will be a degree of diversity. That is why even if there are many denominations in evangelicalism today this does not necessarily negate the church's unity in Christ. As long as the church adheres to the apostolic tradition, the trinitarian theology of the early ecumenical creeds, and salvation by grace alone apart from human merit, then it may be considered part of this one body that Christ established.

### The Holiness of the Church

The church derives its holiness from God. In other words, it is holy because God is holy. Like individual Christians, the church's holiness is both positional and progressive: positional, because God has set apart the church as his treasured possession (Eph 5:25–27; 1 Pet 2:9); progressive, because the eschatological renewal of all things has yet to come (1 Pet 1:14–16). Therefore, despite the church being holy, there is no such thing as an absolutely pure church in the ethical sense during the interval between the first and second comings of Christ (cf. 1 Cor 5–6; 11:17–34). Even if the church is composed entirely of regenerate members, it would still not be absolutely sinless because even the regenerate stumble at times and fall into sin (Jas 3:2; 1 John 1:8—2:1).

In addition, the church's holiness is not something that is derived from an inherent righteousness of its members (whether infused or self-generated), but due to its vital connection to Christ and the Father's sovereign call by grace. However, this does not mean that the church is impeccably holy. The church is a body that is composed of individuals affected by the fall. Although at the eschaton the church will be made completely holy and free from sin, it still exists in the present age where sin reigns, and perfect holiness is something that the church progressively moves towards as the end of the age approaches.

## The Catholicity (or Universality) of the Church

The term "catholic" means universal. What this means is that the church cuts across all geographic, socio-economic, ethno-cultural, and temporal boundaries. Since the church has Christ as its head, no particular denomination or local church can claim that *it* is the universal church. Every local church that gives allegiance to Christ as Lord belongs to this universal church regardless of where and when it is located.

Scripture clearly attests to the catholicity of the church. One place in Scripture that speaks to this matter is Jesus' Great Commission to his disciples in Matthew 28:19–20: "Go therefore and make disciples of all nations, baptizing them in the name of the Father and of the Son and of the Holy Spirit, teaching them to observe all that I have commanded you. And behold, I am with you always, to the end of the age." Other passages that support the catholicity of the church come from Paul's writings. In Galatians 3:28, he writes: "There is neither Jew nor Greek, there is neither slave nor free, there is no male and female, for you are all one in Christ Jesus." Also, in Colossians 3:11, he states: "Here there is not Greek and Jew, circumcised and uncircumcised, barbarian, Scythian, slave, free; but Christ is all, and in all." That Paul speaks about the breaking down of cultural and socio-economic barriers in the church attests to the universality of the body of Christ. Finally, in Revelation 7:9–10, John reports of seeing a "great multitude that no one could number, from every nation, from all tribes and peoples and languages, standing before the throne and before the Lamb, clothed in white robes, with palm branches in their hands, and crying out with a loud voice, 'Salvation belongs to our God who sits on the throne, and to the Lamb!'"

As the above passages demonstrate, the universality of the church is an essential attribute of the church according to the scriptural testimony. It is an essential attribute because it signifies that all the churches are under the lordship of the one Lord Jesus Christ.[3]

## The Apostolicity of the Church

The apostolicity of the church means that the true and universal church will faithfully and consistently adhere to and proclaim the teachings of the apostles. This means that a church, regardless of confessional loyalties, can

3. Clowney, *Church*, 98.

only be considered apostolic if it witnesses to the world the gospel message proclaimed by the apostles and upholds the teachings of the apostles without deviation. In this sense, there is an unbroken continuity between the apostles and the true church today—the continuity being established through the teachings of the apostles passed down by God's providence. Also, the apostolicity of the church underscores the important truth that the reception of the teachings of the apostles is also the acceptance of the teachings of Christ. This is demonstrated in passages like Luke 10:16 (cf. also Matt 10:40; John 13:20) when Jesus tells the appointed seventy-two: "The one who hears you hears me, and the one who rejects you rejects me, and the one who rejects me rejects him who sent me." Those who reject the teachings of those commissioned by Christ, whether individually or corporately, also reject the Son of Man.

In fact, in Galatians 1:6–9, Paul pronounces an anathema upon those who deviate from the true gospel taught by the apostles:

> I am astonished that you are so quickly deserting him who called you in the grace of Christ and are turning to a different gospel— not that there is another one, but there are some who trouble you and want to distort the gospel of Christ. But even if we or an angel from heaven should preach to you a gospel contrary to the one we preached to you, let him be accursed. As we have said before, so now I say again: If anyone is preaching to you a gospel contrary to the one you received, let him be accursed.

According to Paul, those who teach and embrace another "gospel" are those under God's judgment, and thus, cannot be considered part of the true church.

It is important to emphasize the apostolicity of the church since there are many false religious organizations today that claim to be "Christian" but promote teachings contrary to Scripture and the biblical gospel. The church needs to constantly remind itself that only as it faithfully follows the teachings of the apostles can it be deemed the true church with Christ as its head.

## The Marks of the Church

As mentioned earlier, we stated that the church is a fellowship of believers where the word of God is preached faithfully, the ordinances rightly administered, and church discipline exercised when necessary. Some argue that church discipline is subsumed under the right administration of the ordinances and, therefore, that there are only two marks that constitute the church. Regardless of how these are set forth, evangelical scholars have generally agreed that the three marks mentioned above are the ones that constitute a church. We will discuss each of these in order now.

### The Faithful Preaching of the Word of God

It goes without saying that faithful preaching of the word of God is a necessary and essential mark of the church. This is a mark that the Reformers stressed heavily on when discussions of what constitutes a true church were brought up. For instance, John Calvin states that one of the two marks of the true church is "the Word of God purely preached and heard."[4] The importance of the preaching of the word of God is that the gospel—the message of Christ's obedience, death, and resurrection for our justification and new life—must be at the heart of the church's witnessing and teaching. The verbal proclamation of the true gospel is what makes preaching of the word one of the essential marks of the church. (One can even say that this is the principal mark of the church that superintends the other two.) As pointed out earlier, preaching a different gospel—which is no gospel at all, according to Paul—disqualifies a religious body or local congregation of being part of the universal church (Gal 1:8–10). This would include many liberal churches that reject the salvific efficacy of Christ's vicarious death or pseudo-Christian cults that espouse a works-based view of salvation.

This, however, does not mean that a church must interpret Scripture perfectly in order for it to be deemed part of Christ's church. Differences of interpretation among various churches on the mode of baptism or the nature and timing of the millennial kingdom will not determine whether one church is deemed as true and the other as false. Nevertheless, in order for a particular church to be considered as part of the universal church of Christ, it *must* espouse and preach the biblical gospel without compromise. The importance of upholding the gospel taught by Jesus and the apostles in our preaching and teaching is especially emphasized in passages like John 8:31; 2 Thessalonians 2:15; and 2 John 9–11. As Mark E. Dever correctly points out, "The right teaching of the true church, therefore, centers itself on a right understanding of the gospel."[5] Therefore, the correct preaching

---

4. Calvin, *Inst.* 4.1.9.
5. Dever, "Church," 615.

of the word of God, along with proclaiming the right gospel, is one of the basic and necessary marks of the church.

## The Right Administration of the Ordinances

Although baptism and the Lord's Supper will be discussed in more detail in the following chapter, it is appropriate to mention here that the right administration of the ordinances is another basic mark of the church. That baptism and the Lord's Supper are indispensable ordinances for the church's life is revealed in the Gospels. For instance, in Jesus' commission to his disciples, he commanded them to baptize converts in "the name of the Father and of the Son and of the Holy Spirit" (Matt 28:19). Also, before his crucifixion, Jesus instituted the Lord's Supper as a memorial ("Do this in remembrance of me") for his disciples to observe, as recorded in Luke 22:14–23 (cf. Matt 26:26–29; Mark 14:22–25). That the observance of the Lord's Supper was a regular part of the practice of the New Testament church is demonstrated in passages like 1 Corinthians 11:17–34.

The question then must be asked: what about organizations that profess to be Christian but do not baptize its members and observe the Lord's Supper?[6] Although some Christians will vehemently disagree with the position taken here, we must maintain with a tone of caution that these organizations have wilfully disobeyed the Lord and have removed themselves from the universal church. These are necessary ordinances that sets the church apart from the world. Even though observing these two ordinances does not justify a sinner in God's sight, deliberate refusal to observe these ordinances may legitimately call into question any profession of faith.[7] It is vitally important, therefore, that churches do not neglect these two ordinances in their regular life and practice.

Another question that some Christians may ask pertaining to this issue is: what constitutes a "proper" administration of the ordinances? In answering this question one must be careful not to provide rigid answers that will exclude traditions and/or churches that legitimately belong to the body of Christ. It is unwise, and even unbiblical, to exclude certain denominations or churches from the visible body of Christ because they do not observe the ordinances in a certain manner. As long as these two

---

6. A good example would be the Salvation Army or the Religious Society of Friends (Quakers).

7. Dever, "Church," 616.

ordinances are regularly practiced in one form or another we should not consider a particular church outside the boundaries of Christ's universal church. Even in those local churches that have fallen into serious doctrinal error (albeit, short of serious heresy), if they continue to observe these ordinances they are still providing visible evidence that they have not yet separated themselves from the universal body of Christ.

### The Exercise of Church Discipline When Necessary

Lastly, another basic mark of the church is the faithful exercise of church discipline, when necessary, towards those who promote heresies or live in unrepentant immorality. Regrettably, the practice of church discipline has declined in recent years and many churches today seldom implement church discipline even towards those who scandalize the people of God through heresies or grossly sinful living. However, Scripture is clear that church discipline is a necessary part of the church's life and practice. Jesus made this clear in Matthew 18:15–17 when he states:

> If your brother sins against you, go and tell him his fault, between you and him alone. If he listens to you, you have gained your brother. But if he does not listen, take one or two others along with you, that every charge may be established by the evidence of two or three witnesses. If he refuses to listen to them, tell it to the church. And if he refuses to listen even to the church, let him be to you as a Gentile and a tax collector.

It is clear from this passage that Jesus expected his church to administer discipline towards those who persist in wilful and unrepentant sin that causes the gospel to be reproached by outsiders.

In 1 Corinthians, Paul talks about the necessity of church discipline when he commands the Corinthians to expel the man out of the fellowship of believers who was engaged in an illicit sexual relationship with his stepmother (1 Cor 5:1–5). However, he also makes it clear that the discipline is not to be punitive but to be remedial so that the man's spirit "may be saved in the day of the Lord" (v. 5). At times, however, this discipline can be done in a spirit of gentleness as Paul makes clear in Galatians 6:1: "Brothers, if anyone is caught in any transgression, you who are spiritual should restore him in a spirit of gentleness." However it may be done, it is important to emphasize that church discipline is necessary not only to cleanse the church of spiritually harmful elements (1 Cor 5:6–8, 13) but to lead the offenders to repentance and salvation.

In addition, it is important to point out that church discipline is not something administered uniformly for every transgression. It is true, in extreme cases, that certain sins are so heinous that actual expulsion from the congregation is necessary. On the other hand, there are certain sins that may require pastoral attention from the leaders of the church yet do not necessitate actual exclusion from the fellowship of the saints. Every matter of church discipline must be judged on a case-by-case basis. Nevertheless, the administration of proper church discipline must be part of the church's life if it is to be considered a true church that follows the apostolic tradition (cf. Eph 5:6–7; 2 Thess 3:14–15; 1 Tim 1:20; 5:20; Titus 3:10).

## Special Issues Regarding the Nature of the Church

### The Relationship Between the Church and Israel

The subject of the relationship between the church and Israel is one of the most divisive issues in evangelicalism since the beginning of the twentieth century. Since the post-apostolic period, Christians generally viewed the church as having largely replaced Israel in God's redemptive-historical timeline (called *supersessionism*). In other words, the church became the "new Israel" and God was finished with physical Israel in terms of his overall plan in the history of redemption.[8] This was the prevailing view in the church until the rise of dispensational premillennialism[9] in evangelical

8. For an excellent survey of how some of the notable early church theologians viewed this matter, see Ronald E. Diprose's work *Israel and the Church*, 69–98.

9. Dispensationalism is a particular type of redemptive-historical system that arose in evangelicalism in the late-nineteenth and early-twentieth centuries (some notable dispensational scholars of this period include C. I. Scofield, James M. Gray, A. C. Dixon, and Lewis Sperry Chafer). Many evangelicals today still embrace this system as part of their overall theology and eschatology (some well-known writers who espouse dispensationalism in recent years include John F. MacArthur, Elliot E. Johnson, and Stanley D. Toussaint). There are even some notable seminaries in North America that espouse (or formerly did espouse) dispensationalism in their doctrinal statements. These include The Master's Seminary, Grace Theological Seminary, and Detroit Baptist Theological Seminary. Dispensationalism, especially in its older form, basically teaches that God has two distinct ways (along with two distinct promises) of redemptively dealing with Israel and the church: one by law and the other by grace, respectively. In recent years, there have been significant revisions to the system which resulted in something called *progressive dispensationalism*—which attempts to bring greater continuity between Israel and the

circles in North America in the early part of the twentieth century. Even in recent years, evangelicals are still divided on what role physical Israel still plays in God's redemptive-historical plan—most notably between dispensationalists and Reformed covenant theologians. The focus of the debate became accentuated in Christian circles after World War II (due to the horrors of the Holocaust). Many Christians since then have started to question the biblical, theological, and ethical viability of replacement theology in the church and academy. As George Lindbeck states, the "emotions that have motivated the rejection of supersessionism in our day may well have come mostly from horror at the Holocaust."[10] One of the tendencies that Christians must avoid, however, when this subject is discussed is providing simple and reductionistic answers to this very complex subject—either in the direction of supersessionism *or* a dual-covenant theory that accords a separate salvific covenant for Jews.[11] We believe that Scripture rejects both of these positions, and we will now endeavor to show why based on what the biblical writers had to say about this subject.

The Scriptures are clear that with the coming of Christ the Old Testament has been fulfilled and God's people today live under the new covenant administration (2 Cor 3:6 and Heb 8:6–13). With the arrival of Christ and the establishment of the new covenant, the blessings of the Abrahamic covenant are open to all people groups (Eph 2:11–22). In fact, all those who belong to Christ by faith in the present age, whether Jew or Gentile, are the true children of Abraham (Rom 3:29; Gal 3:7–9). In one sense, then, believers in Christ today constitute the "Israel of God" (Gal 6:16).[12] This is supported by the fact that Paul quotes Hosea 1:6–11 (a passage that has reference to Israel) in Romans 9:24–26 to show that the promise pertains not

---

church (cf. Saucy, *Case for Progressive Dispensationalism*). For a helpful introduction to traditional dispensationalist thought, see Charles C. Ryrie's work *Dispensationalism*.

10. Lindbeck, "What of the Future?," 362.

11. Although dispensationalists in the present time would vigorously deny that Jews are saved apart from Christ, some of the older dispensationalist theologians have drawn conclusions that appear to teach that Jews can be saved through their own law-based covenant. For instance, in the first edition of the *Scofield Reference Bible*, Scofield sets forth this dual-redemptive model of classic dispensationalism when he writes: "The point of testing [for the Jews] is no longer legal obedience as the condition of salvation, but acceptance or rejection of Christ" (*Scofield Reference Bible*, 1115n2).

12. It is also possible that Paul meant here the Jews during his day who trusted in Christ as their Savior and Messiah. As one scholar points out, "if 'the Israel of God' is a reference to the church, it would be the only instance where the apostle uses Israel with this meaning" (Saucy, "Israel and the Church," 246).

only to Jews but also to gentiles. Paul even states in Romans 2:28–29 that the "true Jew" is the one who has been circumcised in the heart by the Spirit and not by the external circumcision of the flesh. Therefore, according to the New Testament, Christ has fulfilled the promises of the Old Testament and believers now, whether gentile or Jew, are incorporated into this new spiritual body that Christ has established.

Some will argue that what has been set forth above is another form of supersessionism. However, it is incorrect to identify the fulfillment theology of Scripture with traditional replacement theology. Despite the Old Testament promises being fulfilled in Christ, it is clear that God is not done with Israel in his sovereign plan of salvation. This is what Paul was attempting to convey to his readers when he wrote Romans 11: The *complete* fulfillment of God's salvific purpose arrives when physical Israel is grafted back onto the olive tree (v. 24). According to Paul, once the "fullness of the Gentiles" has been reached (v. 25), "all Israel"[13] will then be saved (v. 26). This large-scale turning to Christ by the Jewish people will happen just prior to Christ's return: "The Deliverer will come from Zion, he will banish ungodliness from Jacob; and this will be my covenant with them when I take away their sins" (vv. 26–27). In this way, the promises of the Old Testament will not be missed out by the physical descendants of Abraham, Isaac, and Jacob.

Others, however, have concluded that Paul did not envision a large-scale conversion of Jews right before Christ's second coming. For instance, N. T. Wright argues that the phrase "all Israel" refers to all believers in Christ—whether Jew or gentile. Thus, "all Israel" refers to the church in its totality regardless of ethnicity.[14] This interpretation, however, is difficult to sustain considering that Paul consistently makes a distinction between physical Jews and gentiles throughout Romans 11 before he talks about the salvation of "all Israel" (vv. 7, 11, 13–15, 21, 25). It is, therefore, unlikely that Paul suddenly changed the meaning of "Israel" in verse 26.[15] Another interpretation that is offered, popular within some circles of Reformed evangelicalism, is to argue that "all Israel" refers to the *remnant* of Jews who turn to Christ throughout the new covenant age.[16] The difficulty with this

13. When Paul states that "all Israel" will be saved, he does not mean every single Jewish person living at that time but a very large number (cf. Bruce, *Romans*, 209).

14. Wright, *Climax of the Covenant*, 249–51.

15. Burns, "Future of Ethnic Israel in Romans 11," 212.

16. Cf. Berkhof, *Systematic Theology*, 698–700; Ridderbos, *Paul*, 358–59; Hoekema,

interpretation is that it reduces the climactic note Paul seeks to establish in order to highlight God's wondrous ways of saving his rebellious old covenant people (v. 15). Also, Paul sets a clear contrast between the remnant of Jews saved by grace throughout the church age and the salvation of "all Israel" at the end. This is supported by the fact that Paul awaits the "fullness" of salvation for the Israelites just prior to Christ's return (vv. 26–27)—a large-scale conversion unheard of in history, in contrast to the salvation of the remnant during the present period that is seen as only partial (v. 5).[17] Finally, Paul juxtaposes between the *full inclusion* of the gentiles (vv. 11, 25) and the *full inclusion* of the Jews (vv. 12, 26) throughout Romans 11:11–24. In other words, Paul is referring to gentiles and Jews *as a whole* and not remnants (as shown by his olive tree metaphor) in regards to God's sovereign work of redemption for his people throughout salvation history. Therefore, Paul anticipates a large-scale turning to Christ by the Jews right before the end of the age.

If what we have said above is true, some will then ask: if a large number of Jews will be brought to salvation through faith in Christ at the end of the age, will there be a special place accorded to them in the eschatological kingdom? Dispensationalists argue that Israel will have a special place in the coming millennial kingdom grounded in God's irrevocable promises given to the Israelites in the Old Testament (with the restoration of a literal temple and animal sacrifices).[18] Covenant theologians, on the other hand, typically argue that since the old covenant administration has ended and everyone is saved on the same terms and basis—faith in Christ's work alone—there will be no special status given to Israel, whether in a millennial kingdom or new earth.[19] Again, we must be careful that we do not provide simple and reductionistic answers to this complex question. It goes without saying that Israel will always be God's special possession, as dispensationalists correctly maintain. This is attested to in passages like Genesis 12:2 and Deuteronomy 7:6–9. However, salvation for the Jewish people, as covenant theologians correctly point out, must also be on the same terms and basis as given to the gentiles—faith in Christ alone. This does not mean that the distinction between gentile believers and Jewish believers is erased. Without drawing

---

*Bible and the Future*, 139–47; Hendriksen, *Romans*, 381–82; Reymond, *New Systematic Theology*, 1024–30.

17. Schreiner, *Romans*, 617–18.

18. Feinberg, *Millennialism: The Two Major Views*, 184–87.

19. Horton, *Christian Faith*, 730–31.

the same conclusions as dispensationalists, we believe that there will be a special place for Israel in the coming kingdom. We do not know what this will entail or what form it will take, but it is not incorrect to conclude that even though Israel's salvation is also dependent upon Christ's work alone this does not diminish her distinctiveness as God's special people in God's overall redemptive purpose for the world.[20]

## The Relationship Between the Church and the Kingdom

Another issue that provokes some debate among Christians in regards to ecclesiology is how we should understand the relationship between the church and the kingdom of God. Traditionally, Roman Catholic theology identifies the church *as* the kingdom of God. Therefore, the church, according to Roman Catholicism, is the kingdom made visible on earth. Protestants, on the other hand, correctly, have typically rejected this notion as being unbiblical, although they do acknowledge that there is a close connection between the two.[21] If there is a close connection between the two, we must then ask: what is the exact nature of the relationship between them? At the outset we should reject the view that maintains that there is no connection between the church and God's kingdom as advanced by some Anabaptist groups. The Scriptures are clear that there is a close relationship between the church and the kingdom of God (cf. Matt 16:18–19). Ladd has helpfully set forth five characteristics of the church-kingdom relationship in his *A Theology of the New Testament*. In it he maintains: 1) The church is never equated with the kingdom in the New Testament; 2) the church is created by the kingdom; 3) the mission of the church is to witness the kingdom; 4) the kingdom utilizes the church for its purposes; and 5) the church is the custodian of the kingdom.[22]

The common theme that is brought out in Ladd's analysis is that the church is always subservient to the kingdom of God. God's reign is manifested through the church and the hearts of the regenerate. As believers

20. For a helpful article on this topic, see Ladd, "Israel and the Church," 206–13. George Eldon Ladd may have found the right balance when he states at the end of the article: "Perhaps during the Millennium, we shall see for the first time in human history *a truly Christian nation*—Israel converted and brought to faith in Jesus as her Messiah" ("Israel and the Church," 213).

21. Grudem, *Systematic Theology*, 864.

22. Ladd, *Theology of the New Testament*, 111–17.

gather together and carry out God's will, God's kingdom is displayed on earth. However, the kingdom is manifested in imperfect ways by the church because it still exists under the present age of darkness and sin. Therefore, a biblical understanding of the relationship between the church and the kingdom avoids both an overrealized eschatology (where the church is identified with the kingdom, as taught by Roman Catholicism) and an underrealized eschatology (where there is a sharp separation between the church and the kingdom, as taught by some Anabaptist groups).

## When Was the Church Established?

According to the vast majority of Reformed theologians, the church began before the establishment of the new covenant by Christ.[23] Although there is diversity of opinion among Reformed scholars regarding the *exact* time of the commencement of the church, they all agree that the church was already in existence in the Old Testament.[24] Other scholars, especially those within dispensational circles, argue that the church did not exist until Pentecost (Acts 2). In order to determine which view is correct, we must look to Scripture again as the source for our conclusions.

As mentioned above, Scripture nowhere states that Israel and the church are to be seen as the same corporate redemptive entities. Although both communities belong to God, both were established with their own respective places and roles in redemptive history. It is interesting to note that the church is only mentioned twice by Jesus: in Matthew 16:18 and 18:17. The significance of the first passage is that he speaks of it in the *future* tense: "And I tell you, you are Peter, and on this rock, I will build my church, and the gates of hell shall not prevail against it." Furthermore, in the two biblical writings by Luke, Millard J. Erickson aptly notes that Luke never uses the term *ekklēsia* in his Gospel but employs it twenty-four times in Acts. Therefore, Erickson concludes that Luke never thought of the church as existing before the events recorded in Acts.[25] Based on the biblical evidence

23. This view is commonly held by Reformed evangelicals who hold to the Westminster Standards and the Three Forms of Unity.

24. For instance, Reymond states: "The church of God in Old Testament times, rooted initially and prophetically in the *protevangelium* (Gen. 3:15) and covenantally in the Genesis patriarchs (Rom. 11:28), blossomed mainly within the nation of Israel" (*New Systematic Theology*, 806).

25. Erickson, *Christian Theology*, 1058.

alone, therefore, we argue that the church began at the coming of the Spirit at Pentecost (Acts 2).

If the conclusion above is correct, this leads to the question of how we should view the status of the saints before the birth of Christ. Were pre-new covenant saints saved apart from joining the body of Christ? Some have attempted to solve this difficulty by arguing that the church began *spiritually* in the Old Testament but *institutionally* at Pentecost.[26] The problem with this view is that Scripture nowhere dichotomizes Christ's church in this manner by teaching that it existed only in part form (spiritually) in the Old Testament and exists in full form (spiritually and institutionally) after Pentecost. Another solution, which we find more satisfying, is given by Erickson. He argues that all the believers prior to the Pentecostal event were incorporated into the church. Old Testament saints, therefore, were saved on the same basis as post-Pentecost saints—by Christ's salvific and vicarious work—and, as a result, became part of the new covenant church *proleptically*.[27]

### The Visible-Invisible Distinction of the Church

One final issue concerning the nature of the church which should be briefly discussed here is whether the visible-invisible distinction of the church has support in Scripture. Some Christians, usually from high-church backgrounds, maintain that the visible-invisible distinction is not supported in Scripture and may, in fact, be counterproductive to the church's spiritual health and mission. According to these Christians, only the visible church exists or, at least, has priority. Others, with a more individualistic (or pietistic) understanding of Christianity, go to the other extreme and argue that when groups of individuals who have a personal relationship with Christ assemble together, that is all that is needed for a church to exist. Some even go so far as to deny that believers need to be part of an organized church or that a formal structure and professional clergy are necessary.[28] In this view, the invisible church has priority over the visible. In response to both of these views, we believe that it is necessary to uphold both the visible and invisible aspects of the church without prioritizing one over the other.

---

26. Lewis and Demarest, *Integrative Theology*, 3:344.

27. Erickson, *Christian Theology*, 1058.

28. For an explanation and critique of this view, see Erickson, *Christian Theology*, 1055.

According to classic Reformation ecclesiology, the visible church consists of all professing believers who gather together for worship, to hear the word of God, and to receive the other means of grace. On the other hand, the invisible church is a spiritual body that consists only of those who are in a saving relationship with Christ and have been baptized by the Spirit. In support for the legitimacy of the visible-invisible distinction, Scripture often speaks of the church as being an assembly that is comprised of both the regenerate and unregenerate. Many in this visible church have yet to truly trust in Christ and become sharers in the Holy Spirit. There will always be chaff among the wheat (Matt 3:12) and "bad fish" among the good (Matt 13:47–50). Jesus also warned that there are many who call upon him as "Lord" but will be revealed as never having a genuine saving relationship with him (Matt 7:21–23). Some who even belonged to the visible church will be revealed as imposters one day (1 John 2:19).[29] However, God's treasured possessions within the visible church are intimately known by him (2 Tim 2:19), and this will be made known openly at the eschatological renewal of all things. In this sense, the visible-invisible distinction can also be understood within an already-not yet framework: the remnant within the church is not fully known in the present but will be in the future.

## 2. The Purpose of the Church

In the evangelical world today, there are diverse opinions regarding the purpose and mission of the church. Those in more liberal churches often maintain that the church's main purpose is to serve the world by fighting against social injustice and defending the rights of the marginalized. Those in more conservative churches usually argue that the church's main purpose is to spread the gospel and spiritually nourish the members within its fold. A biblical understanding of this issue, however, holds that the church's

---

29. Calvin writes: "Often . . . the name 'church' designates the whole multitude of men spread over the earth who profess to worship one God and Christ. By baptism we are initiated into faith in him; by partaking in the Lord's Supper we attest our unity in true doctrine and love; in the Word of the Lord we have agreement, and for the preaching of the Word the ministry instituted by Christ is preserved. In this church are mingled many hypocrites who have nothing of Christ but the name and outward appearance. There are very many ambitious, greedy, envious persons, evil speakers, and some of quite unclean life. Such are tolerated for a time either because they cannot be convicted by a competent tribunal or because a vigorous discipline does not always flourish as it ought" (*Inst.* 4.1.7).

mission has both spiritual and material aspects in its service for the kingdom of God. These are to 1) witness the gospel; 2) serve as a place where believers worship God; 3) spiritually nourish believers; and 4) be a positive influence for the society at large. We will now discuss each of these in order below.

## The Church Is to Witness the Gospel

As discussed above, a church that does not preach and uphold the gospel cannot rightly be called a church. The heart of the ministry of the church is the gospel. Without the gospel being the center, the church will stray away from its true calling and its viability as a church belonging to Christ can be rightly questioned. Scripture is clear that any church that claims to be faithful to the teachings of Christ and the apostles must shape its life and purpose around the gospel. The Great Commission is unmistakably clear that followers of Christ must go out and "make disciples of all nations, baptizing them in the name of the Father and of the Son and of the Holy Spirit," and teaching these nations to observe all that Christ has commanded (Matt 28:19–20; cf. Mark 13:10). This is so that the entire world will one day know Christ, his redemptive work, and the ethical mandates of his gospel.

In another passage, Jesus highlights the central importance of the gospel in his ministry as narrated by Mark: "Jesus came into Galilee, proclaiming the gospel of God, and saying, 'The time is fulfilled, and the kingdom of God is at hand; repent and believe in the gospel'" (Mark 1:14–15). Jesus not only revealed to his hearers why he was sent to the world by the Father but that his earthly ministry was centered on the gospel. This is demonstrated in Matthew 9:35–38:

> And Jesus went throughout all the cities and villages, teaching in their synagogues and proclaiming the gospel of the kingdom and healing every disease and every affliction. When he saw the crowds, he had compassion for them, because they were harassed and helpless, like sheep without a shepherd. Then he said to his disciples, "The harvest is plentiful, but the laborers are few; therefore pray earnestly to the Lord of the harvest to send out laborers into his harvest."

For Jesus, the gospel was the lifeblood of his ministry, which he expected it to be for his church in future generations.

For the apostle Paul, as attested to in his writings, he viewed the gospel as the prime motivating foundation for his ministry. This is due to the fact that he understood Christ as *the* fulfillment of the Old Testament promises and the ultimate revelation of God's saving will for humanity. In Paul's mind, therefore, the gospel and the identity of Christ cannot be separated (Rom 15:19; 1 Cor 9:12; Gal 1:7; Phil 1:27; 1 Thess 3:2). If that was the case for Paul, what did he believe about the contents of the gospel? There are two passages where Paul delineates the contents of the gospel: Romans 1:1–4 and 1 Corinthians 15:3–5. In the first passage, he states:

> Paul, a servant of Christ Jesus, called to be an apostle, set apart for the gospel of God, which he promised beforehand through his prophets in the holy Scriptures, concerning his Son, who was descended from David according to the flesh and was declared to be the Son of God in power according to the Spirit of holiness by his resurrection from the dead, Jesus Christ our Lord.

We see here that Paul tells his readers that the gospel contains facts: that Jesus was promised beforehand by the prophets, was a descendant of David, was declared to be the Son of God in power through the Spirit, and was resurrected from the dead. In the second passage, Paul writes:

> For I delivered to you as of first importance what I also received: that Christ died for our sins in accordance with the Scriptures, that he was buried, that he was raised on the third day in accordance with the Scriptures, and that he appeared to Cephas, then to the twelve.

Here again, Paul lays out the necessary components that must be included in the gospel message: that Christ died for the sins of his people, was buried, and rose from the dead on the third day. Without these components, there is no gospel according to Paul. The reason why the gospel is so precious to Paul is because it brings salvation from God's wrath and liberation from the power of sin (Eph 1:13; 2 Tim 1:10).

Therefore, after briefly examining the ministerial teachings of Jesus and Paul, we argue that one of the key purposes of the church is to bear witness to the gospel. This witnessing, however, does not only happen outside the boundaries of the church but within. There are many people who regularly attend church service on Sundays without having a proper understanding of the gospel—let alone having embraced it through genuine faith. Leaders in the church need to make it a regular practice to make sure that the people sitting in the pews understand the true gospel through their ministries.

By witnessing the gospel, the church fulfills one of its core functions as the means by which God's glory and grace are made known to the world.

## The Church Is a Place where Believers Gather to Worship

Another key purpose of the church is that it is a gathering place for believers to worship and praise God. Worship is a necessary component of the church's life and God is pleased when believers gather together to offer him praise. In Ephesians 5:18–19, Paul exhorts the believers at Ephesus to be "filled with the Spirit" and to address "one another in psalms and hymns and spiritual songs, singing and making melody to the Lord with your heart." These exhortations are also repeated in Colossians 3:16 when Paul writes: "Let the word of Christ dwell in you richly, teaching and admonishing one another in all wisdom, singing psalms and hymns and spiritual songs, with thankfulness in your hearts to God." That worship is to be a regular part of the church's life is also demonstrated by the fact that the saints will gather together to serve and worship God forever in the new heaven and earth (Rev 22:3).

That one of the essential purposes of the church is to worship God is not debated among orthodox Christians. Debates surrounding worship usually center on how public worship should be conducted during services. Although it is important how believers should worship God within the church, it should also be stated that charity on this issue should be exhibited among Christians of differing opinions. As long as public worship is done in an orderly manner (1 Cor 14:40) and no one is scandalized by what is being witnessed, believers should be charitable amongst themselves regarding the form and structure of worship. This means that contemporary forms of singing and worship (like the use of contemporary worship songs or modern instruments) should not be shunned because of certain ecclesiological protocols found in some confessional traditions. As long as the worship songs are based on Scripture, edifying believers, and, most importantly, bringing glory to God, believers should maintain a stance of reasonable flexibility on this matter. What is advocated here, therefore, is a flexible form of the *regulative principle*.[30]

30. Regarding the meaning of the regulative principle, Dever writes: "The sufficiency of Scripture has many implications, including the conviction that Scripture should

## The Church Is to Nourish Believers Spiritually

In addition to being a gathering place to worship God, another purpose of the church is to spiritually nourish believers. One of the ways that the church does this is by edifying believers during their spiritual pilgrimage here on earth. Paul emphasizes the importance of edification within the church when he writes: "The one who speaks in a tongue builds up himself, but the one who prophesies builds up the church. Now I want you all to speak in tongues, but even more to prophesy. The one who prophesies is greater than the one who speaks in tongues, unless someone interprets, so that the church may be built up" (1 Cor 14:4–5). When discussing the issue of the Spirit gifts in Corinth, Paul highlights the superiority of prophesy because it can edify the whole church rather than just the individual believer. In Ephesians 4:11–12, he again stresses the importance of believers being edified in the church when he states that God gave "the apostles, the prophets, the evangelists, the shepherds and teachers, to equip the saints for the work of ministry, for building up the body of Christ." We should point out, however, that this edification is not only done by ministers or leaders of the church but by the whole body of Christ. Lay believers are to mutually edify one another. This mutual edification is achieved when they have regular fellowship, study the Bible together, and encourage one another.

Another way that the church nourishes believers is through teaching. One of the commands that Jesus gives his disciples in the Great Commission is to "teach" the nations to "observe all that I have commanded you" (Matt 28:20). The purpose of this teaching is not to ingrain believers with abstract theological knowledge but to equip them so that they can become more mature in the faith and bear good fruit (Col 1:28; 1 Tim 4:6–10). Through a steady flow of teaching based on a proper handling of Scripture believers can be prepared to give a sound defense of the faith to the outside world. They can also be prepared to teach others who are new to the Christian faith or who have yet to develop a deeper understanding of it. Therefore, teaching is one of the vital means to help believers to become more mature spiritually.

Finally, another component of the church's role as providing nourishment for believers is by being an exhortative voice. Because believers still

---

regulate the way God's people should approach God in worship. This principle has often been called the regulative principle. The regulative principle applies the Protestant belief in the authority of God's Word to the particular doctrine of the church. And it is most often referenced in discussions of public worship" ("Church," 635).

live under the fallen conditions of the present age, the church needs to constantly admonish them to fight against their own flesh and the sinful world around them (Gal 5:16–17; Eph 4:22–24). Believers are to be constantly reminded that they still have an obligation to obey God's moral law (1 Cor 9:20–21; Jas 1:22–25; 1 John 5:2–3), even though they are saved by grace apart from their works (Eph 2:8–9; Titus 3:5–7). The church also needs to admonish wayward believers that if they persist in their disobedience to God that he will chasten them until they repent (Heb 12:5–11). In certain situations, it is even necessary for the church to warn professing Christians within its visible sanctuary of the dangers of false conversion (Matt 7:21–23; 1 John 3:10) and the dire consequences of apostasy (John 15:2, 6; Heb 6:8). This aspect of the church's role as an exhortative voice needs to be stressed in an age where evangelical churches in large numbers are trying to be "seeker-friendly" and less prophetic in their ministries.

## The Church Is to Be a Positive Influence to the Society at Large

Although we have stated above that the gospel is the heart of the church's ministry, we must not exclude the church's positive role for the society at large in our discussion of the mission of Christ's church. Sometimes called "a ministry of mercy,"[31] the church, alongside its evangelistic ministry, is also called to physically minister to the poor and needy of the world. The church's role in this regard is a reflection of the way Jesus ministered while on earth. Jesus' concern for the physical well-being of people is clearly demonstrated in his miraculous feeding of the multitudes (Matt 14:13–21) and healing of the sick (Matt 14:34–36; John 5:2–9). Although these supernatural works were designed to show the people that he was the true Messiah and the embodiment of the kingdom of God, this does not diminish the fact that their physical well-being was of great concern to Jesus. This is also attested by the fact that in Luke 4:40, Luke tells us that Jesus healed *everyone* regardless of whether they accepted him as their Savior or not. Also, Jesus emphasized the importance of caring for others physically when he states in his Sermon on the Mount: "But when you give to the needy, do not let your left hand know what your right hand is doing, so that your giving may be in secret. And your Father who sees in secret will reward you" (Matt 6:3–4).

---

31. Grudem, *Systematic Theology*, 868.

What this means is that the church has a responsibility in becoming a positive influence for our societies. It is not only to concern itself with the spiritual health of its members (Gal 6:10) or to only bear witness to the gospel, but also to speak out against injustice, alleviate oppression, and help those who are downtrodden. In fact, the church is supposed to be a counter-cultural community that says *No* to those things that go against God's righteousness and justice. Even social sins must be struggled against in a world that is under the captivity of the evil one. This does not mean believers may use the force of arms in this struggle or attempt to gain victory through the establishment of a so-called Christian nation-state modeled on the civil law of the old covenant.[32] Rather, believers are to fight against these social sins by producing the fruits of the Spirit and practicing the good deeds that spring forth from faith (cf. Jas 1:27—2:1). However, we should always keep in mind that this should never overtake the primary mission of the church to the world: to spread the gospel and call everyone to saving faith and repentance. In fact, these works of charity that the church carries out should ultimately be about bearing witness to Christ's sacrificial love and God's saving grace. As Henry Clarence Thiessen states:

> The work of reformation, including philanthropy, must be definitely subordinated to the work of evangelization. The Christian should make all his charity and kindnesses bear testimony to Christ. Jesus may have fed five thousand as a humanitarian act, but he certainly did it primarily as a testimony to his own power and deity. When Jesus turned the water to wine he showed kindness to the wedding party, but he also "manifested His glory" (John 2:11). It appears that he healed the man born blind in order to win his soul (John 9:35–38). In other words, the Christian should make all his good works testify to Christ.[33]

Therefore, even though the principal mission of the church to the world is to bring the unsaved to Christ, one of the other basic purposes of

---

32. The belief that the civil laws of the Mosaic covenant should be implemented in modern societies, like in the old covenant nation of Israel, is called *theonomy*. This understanding of the Mosaic law and its political use in modern societies was first set forth by the Reformed apologist Rousas J. Rushdoony (1916–2001). Although most of those who identify with this movement come from the Reformed tradition, its advocates also come from other traditions as well. For an excellent critique of this movement, see the collection of essays in a work edited by William S. Barker and W. Robert Godfrey titled *Theonomy: A Reformed Critique.*

33. Thiessen, *Lectures in Systematic Theology*, 333.

the church is to carry out acts of mercy to the poor and marginalized in the world.

## 3. The Organization of the Church

That the Scriptures speak about the visible church being an organized body is evident by the manner in which the New Testament describes the church as being led by the apostles and elders. Some of the passages that attest to the existence of a leadership structure in the earliest churches include Acts 14:23; 1 Timothy 3:1–13; Titus 1:5–9; Hebrews 13:7; James 5:14; 1 Peter 5:1–3. Most Christians do not deny that the New Testament church had a leadership structure nor do they believe that the church in the present-day can function properly without an organized structure. What Christians over the centuries have disagreed over is *how* the church should be organized. In this section of the chapter, we will discuss the function of the churchly offices (the office of elders and the diaconate), and the various views pertaining to how the church should organize and govern itself (i.e., church government).

### The Offices of the Church

*The Office of Elders*

The existence of elders in the New Testament church is clearly attested to in various passages just mentioned above (1 Tim 3:1–13; Titus 1:5–9; 1 Pet 5:1–3). Elders are also usually called pastors or bishops according to the Scriptures. For instance, in Ephesians 4:11, the apostle Paul writes: "And He personally gave some to be apostles, some prophets, some evangelists, some pastors [Gk. *poimēn*] and teachers" (HCSB). The Greek term *poimēn* occurs here *only* to identify an office of the church, although the verb form of this term (which means "to shepherd) is found in Acts 20:28 and 1 Peter 5:2. Thus, elders are to shepherd the flock given under their care. Elders are also called "bishops" (*episkopos*) in 1 Timothy 3:1–2, which means the two terms are used interchangeably. This means that the elders/pastors/bishops are not only to shepherd the churches under their care but to teach believers rightly (1 Tim 3:2; Titus 1:9) and watch over them with godly concern (Heb 13:17; 1 Pet 5:2–3).

What are the qualifications to become an elder? Paul outlines plainly in two passages in his pastoral epistles (1 Tim 3:2–7 and Titus 1:5–9) the necessary qualifications that a man must possess in order to become an elder. In 1 Timothy 3:2–7, Paul writes:

> Therefore an overseer must be above reproach, the husband of one wife,[34] sober-minded, self-controlled, respectable, hospitable, able to teach, not a drunkard, not violent but gentle, not quarrelsome, not a lover of money. He must manage his own household well, with all dignity keeping his children submissive, for if someone does not know how to manage his own household, how will he care for God's church? He must not be a recent convert, or he may become puffed up with conceit and fall into the condemnation of the devil. Moreover, he must be well thought of by outsiders, so that he may not fall into disgrace, into a snare of the devil.

In Titus 1:5–9, he states:

> This is why I left you in Crete, so that you might put what remained into order, and appoint elders in every town as I directed you—if anyone is above reproach, the husband of one wife, and his children are believers and not open to the charge of debauchery or insubordination. For an overseer, as God's steward, must be above reproach. He must not be arrogant or quick-tempered or a drunkard or violent or greedy for gain, but hospitable, a lover of good, self-controlled, upright, holy, and disciplined. He must hold firm to the trustworthy word as taught, so that he may be able to give instruction in sound doctrine and also to rebuke those who contradict it.

When Paul states that these qualities must be present, he means that these characteristics must *consistently* be observed in the individual who seeks to be an elder. This is important to emphasize since any leadership position in the church must be filled by those who consistently exhibit godly attitudes and behaviors, and who do not bring reproach to the gospel by their lifestyles. They should not only be qualified to teach effectively but possess the spiritual qualities that are necessary to be godly examples for other believers (1 Tim 4:12; Titus 2:7).

---

34. The meaning "a husband of one wife" does not mean the individual has been married only once in his lifetime (as Roman Catholics teach), but that he is a husband of one wife *at the present* (i.e., someone who is not presently an adulterer or involved in a polygamous relationship).

Therefore, appointments into the eldership should never be handled haphazardly but must be done with utter care and thorough examination.

*The Diaconate*

The diaconate is also an important office in the New Testament church, and deacons played a pivotal role in the earliest churches. The English word *deacon* comes from the Greek word *diakonos*, which is the term normally used for "servant." According to Daniel L. Akin, the word "has both a general and technical sense in the New Testament. It may simply refer to any type of service or personal assistance performed for another. In the common usage of the day, the word meant to wait on tables or to assist or care for household needs. Eventually, the word came to mean 'to serve' in any capacity."[35] While the elders/pastors/bishops served for the *spiritual* well-being of the members of the church; deacons were to serve for the *physical* needs of the members of the church (usually in the form of proper distribution of goods). For instance, Acts 6:1–6 describes a situation where seven men of "good repute, full of the Spirit and of wisdom" were chosen to be responsible for the distribution of food because of a conflict over allocation of resources in the early Christian community. We can even say that the formal office of the diaconate was established at this time even though the term *deacon* is not used in the passage. Thus, the office of the diaconate did not function in the same way as the office of eldership but was concerned with "ministries of mercy" within the church, particularly as it pertained to helping poor members materially.

Like the nomination for eldership, the apostle Paul clearly lays out who are qualified to become deacons in the church in 1 Timothy 3:8–13. There, he writes:

> Deacons likewise must be dignified, not double-tongued, not addicted to much wine, not greedy for dishonest gain. They must hold the mystery of the faith with a clear conscience. And let them also be tested first; then let them serve as deacons if they prove themselves blameless. Their wives likewise must be dignified, not slanderers, but sober-minded, faithful in all things. Let deacons each be the husband of one wife, managing their children and their own households well. For those who serve well as deacons gain a good

35. Akin, "Deacon, Deaconess," 150.

standing for themselves and also great confidence in the faith that is in Christ Jesus.

Just like the individuals who seek to be elders in the church, individuals who seek to serve as deacons must be of upstanding character and be able to manage their own households well. Considering that they are responsible for the financial and administrative management of the church, the godly qualities Paul mentions must be present in order for them to serve in this capacity with integrity and impartiality.

Again, like the nominations for eldership, the church today must take the appointment of deacons with utmost seriousness, as the lifestyle and attitudes of the deacons reflect the church's identity as God's holy people.

## The Structure of the Church (Church Government)

As mentioned earlier, the idea that the church requires a structure with a formal leadership and governing body is not contested by most Christians. What is debated among Christians is what form this governance of the church should take and what structure is most faithful to what is revealed in Scripture. The three most common types of governing structures of the church throughout history are: *Episcopalianism*, *Presbyterianism*, and *Congregationalism*.

### Episcopalianism

Out of the three common forms of church government, *episcopalianism* is the most highly structured and hierarchical. The term *episcopalianism* comes from the Greek word *episkopos*, which means "overseer" or "bishop." This form of government is found in the Greek and Eastern Orthodox Churches, the Roman Catholic Church, the Church of the East, the Anglican or Episcopalian Church, and various Lutheran denominations. In this form of government, the archbishop oversees all the bishops. These bishops, in turn, have authority over local parishes within a diocese. Those in charge of a local parish are called *rectors* and possess the typical duties of a priest or minister. Although local parishes are ministered by the rectors, the bishop of a diocese is the one vested with greater authority. The bishop is responsible for the ordination of ministers and the administrative affairs of the church. The bishop views himself as the one who receives this governing power from Christ himself via the line of succession from the apostles.

Those who espouse this ecclesiastical structure argue that one of the advantages of this form of government is that it is highly organized. With such a highly organized structure, the danger of disunity and schism is significantly reduced and the governance of the church can be done in a more orderly manner. Others argue for the legitimacy of the episcopalian system by maintaining that the episcopalian form of government was the manner in which the church was structured universally during the post-apostolic period.[36] Still others maintain that the episcopalian structure arose during the early church period by the providence of God, and thus, should be considered the form of government providentially decreed by God for future generations.[37] Finally, supporters of this system claim that the legitimacy of the episcopalian form of government is based on the bishops having authority from Christ due to an unbroken line of succession from the apostles (the "apostolic succession").[38]

Non-episcopalians argue, however, that the New Testament provides no evidence that the earliest churches were organized in such a highly structured and/or hierarchical manner. The churches during the New Testament period appear to have been organized in a simple manner with believers gathering in people's homes. Even with the existence of the office of elders, there is no biblical evidence that the church during the apostolic period had an elaborate office of bishops overseeing a group of churches in various regions. In addition, as mentioned above, the biblical evidence seems to suggest that bishops and elders are not two separate titles or offices. Rather, both are used interchangeably as those who oversee and teach the flock.[39] Finally, the argument that bishops throughout the history of the church receive their authority from a direct line of succession from the apostles has no support in the New Testament.

## Presbyterianism

The presbyterian form of church governance is usually found in Reformed churches that adhere to the Westminster Standards or the Three Forms

36. Morris, "Church Government," 239.

37. Toon, "Episcopalianism," 24.

38. Cf. Gore, *Church and the Ministry*, 302–3.

39. Grudem, *Systematic Theology*, 924–25.

of Unity (although mainline Reformed churches also adhere to the presbyterian structure). In this form of government, unlike the episcopalian structure, authority is vested in a plurality of elders who are elected into a session. A local church is under the authority of a session, and in turn, the sessions are under a presbytery (where the elders of a given session may also be members of a presbytery). These presbyteries are then under the *general assembly*,[40] which is the highest governing authority in the presbyterian system. The presbyterian form is less hierarchical compared to the episcopalian one in that there is only a single level of clergy. There is no higher level of bishops that oversees a region of local churches. Also, in the presbyterian system, the local church has greater autonomy than in the episcopalian system, although this autonomy is also subject to regulation by doctrinal agreements and the mutual responsibilities that each local church has towards one another within the denomination.

Supporters of the presbyterian system argue that it provides a proper balance between the authoritarian dangers of a highly centralized episcopalian system and the lack of leadership accountability of the congregational system. For instance, Robert L. Reymond writes:

> Why is the matter of church government in general and of Presbyterian church government in particular important? Because Presbyterianism is not only the most biblically sound form of church government but also provides the most trustworthy, just, and peaceful way for the church to determine its direction, its principles, its practices and its priorities, and to resolve its differences. Lose balance in church government in one direction and one ends up with episcopal tyranny. Lose balance in the other direction and one has congregational anarchy, followed by the tyranny of the one or the few.[41]

Others also argue for the effectiveness of the presbyterian system based on the assertion that it provides doctrinal unity and greater cooperative ministry compared to the congregational system, which accords greater independence for local churches.[42]

In regards to some criticisms leveled at the presbyterian form of government, some have argued that there is no evidence in the New Testament that an elder has jurisdiction beyond his local church. According to the

---

40. In some Reformed denominations this is called a *general synod*.

41. Reymond, *New Systematic Theology*, 908.

42. Taylor, "Presbyterianism," 96–97.

critics of the presbyterian polity, elders only had authority over the churches that they were appointed to shepherd as revealed in the New Testament.[43] In addition, critics aver that the presbyterian form of government does not necessarily guarantee unity on doctrinal matters. Some local churches may even deviate from the denominational consensus given on a particular point of doctrine. In fact, there is some risk associated with this form of government considering that a general assembly (or a general synod) can rule in favor of a biblically unsound position and pressure more orthodox churches to adopt the position reached. Lastly, the presbyterian form of government, ultimately, like the episcopalian system, takes authority away from the laity and vests them in a small group of individuals (even though the elders may be considered servants of the church). If the laity believes that a decision taken by a presbytery is unfaithful to the teachings of Scripture they may have no recourse within the system to overturn it.

## Congregationalism

Lastly, the congregational form of church government is one that is embraced by many evangelical denominations in recent history (e.g., Baptists, Congregationalists, the Evangelical Free Church, etc.). Unlike the episcopalian and presbyterian forms of government, the congregational form situates authority in the local church and the members within it. There is no governing authority over the local church and every congregation is autonomous. Decisions on doctrinal matters are made by the local churches alone and every member of the church has a role in the decision-making process of the church (although local churches of the same doctrinal convictions may join together to form conventions). Congregational churches will usually have a single elder (or pastor) or a plurality of elders leading the local church. Regardless of whether a local church has only a single elder/pastor or a plurality of elders, the principal mark of the congregational form of government is that the local church is not under an external ecclesiastical authority.

Those who adhere to the congregational form of government argue that the main advantage of this arrangement is that local churches are free to make their own policies and draw up doctrinal statements without the oversight of a ruling body as long as they are consistent with the teachings of Christ and Scripture (cf. Matt 23:8). Also, supporters of this form

43. Grudem, *Systematic Theology*, 926.

of government argue that this is the polity practiced during the New Testament period. As Bruce Milne states:

> Adherents [of the congregational form of government] appeal to the significance of the local church in the NT. As we have seen, Scripture uses language concerning the nature of the church equally of the local and the 'total' church. Further, there is an absence of evidence in the NT of imposition upon the life of the local congregation by wider bodies or officials from beyond its ranks, with the obvious exception of the apostles or their personal delegates such as Titus and Timothy. Underlying this is the conviction that Christ's headship of the church implies his immediate presence among his people and his power to convey his will without the mediation of some other agent, whether personal or corporate.[44]

Therefore, one of the strengths of the congregational form of government is that its focus on ecclesiastical autonomy allows each local church to receive from Christ his authority and power directly without intervention from an external body.

The strength of the congregational form of government, however, may also be its weak point: without the oversight of an external ruling body there is no doctrinal or ethical accountability for individual churches. Leaders in these churches can form doctrines or policies that are contrary to Scripture without the possibility of being formally disciplined by an external authority. In addition, some might argue that the existence of apostolic authority (and the appointing of elders [cf. Acts 14:23]) during the New Testament period seems to be inconsistent with a congregational form of governance.

### Conclusion Regarding the Government of the Church

When all things are considered, however, we believe that the congregational form of government, with some reservations, best fits with the New Testament pattern for church governance. However, we must also state that the subject of how churches are to be governed is not a matter of orthodoxy or heresy. Genuine believers can be a member of a local church or denomination that adheres to any one of the three forms of church government discussed above as long as the gospel and other non-negotiable truths of Scripture are not being compromised with. Each view has their own strengths and weaknesses, and God has always used churches of various

44. Milne, *Know the Truth*, 326.

forms of governance to carry out his will and manifest his kingdom on earth.

# CHAPTER 17

## Baptism and the Lord's Supper

### 1. Baptism

THE VAST MAJORITY OF churches believe that baptism is an ordinance commanded by the Lord Jesus Christ (Matt 28:19). They also agree that the refusal to be baptized is an act of disobedience to the Lord. However, Christians throughout the centuries have disagreed on the meaning and efficacy of baptism for those in the church.

In this section of the chapter we will first discuss the major views on baptism held by various Christian traditions throughout history, and then discuss special issues that concern this initiatory ordinance.

### Major Views on Baptism in the Christian Tradition

#### *The Roman Catholic View: Baptism as a Necessary Means to Salvation*

The Roman Catholic view of baptism can be considered one of the two sacramentalistic views of baptism in the Western Church (the other being the Lutheran view). The Roman Catholic position states that baptism actually regenerates and confers salvation on its recipients. In fact, Roman Catholic theology teaches that the Roman Church itself is the channel where divine grace is imparted *through* baptism to all those within its ecclesiastical jurisdiction. In short, Roman Catholicism teaches an *ex opere operato* view of baptism where the *sacrament itself* (without the subjective experience of faith on the part of the recipient) conveys salvation to the baptized. As the Roman Catholic theologian Ludwig Ott writes, "The formula 'ex opere operato' asserts, negatively, that the sacramental grace is not conferred by reason of the subjective activity of the recipient, and positively, that the sacramental grace is caused by the validly operated sacramental sign."[1] This is one of the reasons why Roman Catholicism teaches that infants should be baptized (paedobaptism). According to Roman Catholic theology, infants who die without baptism will not enter heaven and will instead be sent to a place called the *limbus infantium* (where there are no sufferings of sense *or* enjoyments of redemption).[2] Baptism by itself, however, will wipe away original sin and provide salvation for the infant.

Therefore, by affixing saving grace in the baptismal sacrament itself, Roman Catholicism effectively undercuts the Pauline and Reformational principle of salvation by grace alone (more on this will be discussed below).

### The Lutheran View: Baptism as a Regenerative Rite

The Lutheran view is the other sacramentalist view of baptism within the broader Christian tradition. Like the Roman Catholic view, baptism possesses salvific efficacy for the recipients of this rite. However, the key difference between the two views is that the Lutheran view denies that baptism imparts grace *ex opere operato*. Lutherans argue that for baptism to have salvific efficacy, the recipient must also have faith in Christ. In other words, baptism works in tandem with the personal reception of the gospel. The Lutheran theologian John Theodore Mueller writes:

> Baptism, according to Scripture, is not a mere ceremony or church rite, but a true means of grace (*aqua divino mandato comprehensa et Verbo Dei obsignata*), by which God offers and conveys to men the merits which Christ secured for the world by His vicarious

---

1. Ott, *Fundamentals of Catholic Dogma*, 330.

2. Donnelly, "Limbo," 643. The problem with the Roman Catholic position regarding the fate of unbaptized infants is that it goes against what is stated in the Scriptures. For example, in 2 Samuel 12:22–23, David declares: "He said, 'While the child was still alive, I fasted and wept, for I said, "Who knows whether the LORD will be gracious to me, that the child may live?" But now he is dead. Why should I fast? Can I bring him back again? I shall go to him, but he will not return to me.'" Also, in Luke 18:16, Jesus, while gathering the children around him, states: "Let the children come to me, and do not hinder them, for to such belongs the kingdom of God." In addition, there is no scriptural support for the doctrine of the *limbus infantium* (cf. Heb 9:27).

satisfaction, Acts 2, 38. . . . Very aptly our dogmaticians have called Baptism "a means of justification" (*medium iustificationis sive remissionis peccatorum*), which belongs into the Gospel, not into the Law. That is to say, Baptism does not save as a work which *we* perform unto God (not as the fulfillment of an obligation), but rather as a work of God in which *He deals with* and blesses us.[3]

Essentially, Lutherans believe that baptism regenerates and creates new life for those who receive it as long as they also embrace the gospel through faith. In addition, baptism also strengthens the faith of those who believe.[4] Baptism, therefore, is the visible representation of the gospel, according to Lutheranism.

In regards to the situation of infants, Lutheran theology is more ambiguous than Roman Catholicism. Lutherans, like Roman Catholics, also espouse infant baptism. However, unlike Roman Catholics, Lutherans affirm that faith must be necessary in order for baptism to have salvific efficacy. If this is the case, how can baptism be efficacious for infants? Lutherans defend their particular paedobaptist position by arguing that faith can even exist in infants of believing parents (cf. Matt 18:6).[5] Since baptism has salvific efficacy if combined with faith, it is, therefore, wise for believing parents to baptize their children. In the case of unbaptized infants who die, the Lutheran tradition argues that the soul of the deceased child should be left in the hands of God who is boundless in mercy.[6] In addition, baptism lays the foundation of salvation for the children in the church by giving them new life in Christ and by showing them God's promises through the sacrament.[7]

Some, however, argue that the Lutheran position on baptism (especially as it pertains to infants) is inconsistent with the Lutheran view that justification is through faith in Christ alone.[8] If the justification of the sinner is through faith in Christ alone, how can Lutherans (with consistency) advocate that baptism possesses salvific efficacy and is a means of regeneration? Some Lutherans argue that despite baptism having the character of being regenerative and salvifically efficacious, it is not, unlike faith in

3. Mueller, *Christian Dogmatics*, 491.

4. Mueller, *Christian Dogmatics*, 493.

5. Mueller, *Christian Dogmatics*, 498.

6. Mueller, *Christian Dogmatics*, 498.

7. Kolb, "Lutheran View," 104.

8. Erickson, *Christian Theology*, 1101.

Christ, *absolutely* necessary for justification and salvation.[9] This, however, still does not resolve the dilemma faced by Lutherans in regards to the inconsistency between their particular view of baptism and their espousal of justification through faith alone.

### The Reformed View: Baptism as a Covenant Sign and Seal

In Reformed and Presbyterian circles, baptism, like Old Testament circumcision, is a sign and seal of the covenant. This view rejects the Roman Catholic teaching that baptism confers salvation *ex opere operato* or the Lutheran view that baptism is a means of regeneration (although Reformed Christians do maintain that baptism truly is a means of grace for believers when located in Christ alone). John Murray, a proponent of the Reformed view, writes:

> As a rite instituted by Christ, baptism is not to be identified with the grace signified and sealed. This is apparent from the terms of institution (Matt. 28:19), and from the nature of baptism as seal. The existence of the grace sealed is presupposed in the giving of the seal. The tenet of baptismal regeneration reverses the order inherent in the definition which Scripture provides. The efficacy resides entirely in the pledge of God's faithfulness. God not only brings men and women into union with Christ as the embodiment of covenant grace at the zenith of its realization, he not only gives exceeding great and precious promises that are yea and amen in Christ, but he seals this union and confirms these promises by an ordinance that portrays to our senses the certainty of his grace.[10]

Therefore, according to the Reformed tradition, baptism is a covenantal seal and sign that brings a person into the covenant of grace and seals his or her union with Christ through the ordinance. In this way, baptism truly is a means of grace for believers.

Reformed and Presbyterian Christians also believe, along with Roman Catholics and Lutherans, that infant baptism is a legitimate and scripturally-based practice. According to this view, New Testament baptism is parallel with the circumcision rite of the Old Testament. Just like infant males in Israel were circumcised under the old covenant, infants of believing parents are to be baptized in the present administration as a sign and seal of the

9. Mueller, *Christian Dogmatics*, 500.
10. Murray, *Collected Writings of John Murray*, 2:375.

covenant of grace. The justification for this belief is based on God's promise to Abraham in Genesis 17:7: "And I will establish my covenant between me and you and your offspring after you throughout their generations for an everlasting covenant, to be God to you and to your offspring after you." Reformed and Presbyterian believers argue that the above verse supports covenantal paedobaptism because the covenant of grace transcends the various administrations of redemptive history. In other words, the promises of Abraham are not restricted to Abraham's physical offspring but to *all* those—including their children—who believe in the promises of God through Christ.[11] Richard L. Pratt writes:

> When Reformed theology speaks of baptism as covenantal, the sacrament is viewed in the context of the unity of the covenant of grace. The meaning of baptism is not found in the teachings of the NT alone; it is also inferred from the manner in which baptism fulfills OT patterns of faith. This reliance on the covenantal unity of both the OT and NT is stated in general terms when the Westminster Confession identifies the ordinances administered. In the OT, the covenant of grace was "administered by promises, prophecies, sacrifices, circumcision, the paschal lamb, and other types and ordinances delivered to the people of the Jews" (7.5). Yet, "when Christ, the substance, was exhibited, the ordinances in which this covenant is dispensed are the preaching of the Word, and the administration of the sacraments of Baptism and the Lord's Supper" (7.6). Baptism administers the NT dispensation of the covenant of grace in ways that are analogous to the administration of the OT dispensation of that same covenant.[12]

Therefore, baptized infants of believing parents enter the covenant of grace and receive its promises just like the Israelite infants of the Old Testament.

Critics of the Reformed paedobaptist position argue that the view runs into several difficulties in light of the Reformed understanding of regeneration and salvation. Although Reformed theologians maintain that adult believers who are baptized assuredly receive the benefits of the sacrament,[13] they cannot say the same for infants who receive the ordinance. This is an undeniable difficulty found in the Reformed paedobaptist position. What if the baptized infant never personally appropriates the benefits of

11. Cf. Smith, *Systematic Theology*, 2:665; Frame, *Salvation Belongs to the Lord*, 280–81.

12. Pratt, "Reformed View," 65.

13. Hodge, *Systematic Theology*, 3:582.

Christ's death through faith later in life? What are we to make of his or her baptism as an infant? One way out of this difficulty is by saying that the infant is regenerated *in some way* at the moment of his or her baptism (or "presumptive regeneration") but may later demonstrate otherwise by his or her rejection of the faith (i.e., the grace given at baptism is only "effectual" when the infant grows up and personally receives Christ).[14] However, this understanding is inconsistent with the Reformed view that the Spirit effects regeneration for salvation, and that forgiveness only comes about through conscious faith in the Savior via the spoken word (John 3:14–15; Rom 10:8–17). Therefore, the difficulty with the Reformed paedobaptist position is that it inevitably leads to an incongruity between the sacramental efficacy of infant baptism and the Spirit's work of regeneration (and the need for conscious faith in Christ).

### The Believer's Baptism View: Baptism as an Outward Sign of Inward Grace

Another view of baptism held by many evangelicals throughout the history of the church is the position that baptism is only an outward sign of inward grace (often called "believer's baptism"). In this view, baptism has no salvific or sacramental efficacy. It is only an ordinance to symbolize that the believer has been forgiven of his or her sins and has received new life in Christ. However, this does not mean that baptism is unimportant, since those who espouse this position also argue that it is an ordinance clearly commanded by the Lord (Matt 28:19).[15] Furthermore, only those who make a credible profession of faith may receive this baptism. This does not entail that *only* adults may be baptized, since children who have the mental capacity to believe may also be baptized as long as they give a credible profession of faith. Finally, those who advocate believer's baptism usually argue that full immersion is the only proper mode since it most closely symbolizes the death and resurrection of Christ—which is the pattern the believer also follows spiritually through the new birth.[16]

---

14. The Dutch Reformed thinker Abraham Kuyper (1837–1920) advocated this view to address this incongruity in Reformed paedobaptist thinking (cf. Genderen and Velema, *Concise Reformed Dogmatics*, 798).

15. Dever, "Church," 618.

16. Saucy, *Church in God's Program*, 211.

Advocates of the believer's baptism position argue that there are various passages in Scripture that presuppose a credible profession of faith before baptism is conferred. In fact, the scriptural evidence suggests that the relationship between conversion and baptism is one of very close association. Some passages that support this understanding include:

- **Matthew 28:19:** "Go therefore and make disciples of all nations, baptizing them in the name of the Father and of the Son and of the Holy Spirit, teaching them to observe all that I have commanded you. And behold, I am with you always, to the end of the age."

- **Acts 2:38:** "And Peter said to them, 'Repent and be baptized every one of you in the name of Jesus Christ for the forgiveness of your sins, and you will receive the gift of the Holy Spirit.'"

- **Galatians 3:25–27:** "But now that faith has come, we are no longer under a guardian, for in Christ Jesus you are all sons of God, through faith. For as many of you as were baptized into Christ have put on Christ."

- **Colossians 2:11–12:** "In him also you were circumcised with a circumcision made without hands, by putting off the body of the flesh, by the circumcision of Christ, having been buried with him in baptism, in which you were also raised with him through faith in the powerful working of God, who raised him from the dead."

- **1 Peter 3:21–22:** "Baptism, which corresponds to this, now saves you, not as a removal of dirt from the body but as an appeal to God for a good conscience, through the resurrection of Jesus Christ, who has gone into heaven and is at the right hand of God, with angels, authorities, and powers having been subjected to him."

In addition, advocates of the position argue that nowhere does the New Testament provide evidence that baptism efficaciously imparts regeneration or salvation to the recipient, whether he or she is an adult or infant. Robert L. Saucy writes:

> [I]n every biblical example the inward, saving faith precedes baptism and, in some instances at least, it is clearly manifest that the gifts of salvation are bestowed as the fruit of that faith prior to baptism. The many instances where faith alone is mentioned

without baptism as the condition of salvation make it impossible to accept any doctrine of baptismal regeneration whereby baptism is necessary for salvation.[17]

Therefore, baptism, according to the believer's baptism position, has no salvific efficacy for those who submit to it.[18]

Critics of the believer's baptism position argue that the view takes infants out of the sphere of God's salvific grace by refusing them this rite of passage. By denying them this sacrament or rite, they argue, infants cannot participate in the life of the church and receive the spiritual nurturing that accompanies being part of Christ's ecclesial body.[19] This is one of the main arguments against believer's baptism by paedobaptists. Also, another criticism commonly laid against the believer's baptism position is that it undermines the sacramental nature of the rite by merely making it a symbol of grace rather than a means of grace.[20] Lastly, paedobaptists argue that infant baptism has a long history in the church, and therefore, should be viewed as having more legitimacy than the belief that only converts are to be baptized.[21]

In the following part of this section of the chapter, we will come to a decision regarding which of the four positions discussed above comes closest to the New Testament understanding of baptism by answering the three most commonly asked questions regarding baptism: 1) is baptism necessary for salvation?; 2) who should be baptized?; and 3) what is the biblical mode of baptism?

## The Three Most Commonly Asked Questions Regarding Baptism

### Is Baptism Necessary for Salvation?

One of the more divisive issues within Christianity is whether the ordinance of baptism actually confers salvation to those who submit to it. As

---

17. Saucy, *Church in God's Program*, 198.

18. However, some denominations, like the Churches of Christ and United Pentecostals, who believe in believers-only baptism, teach that baptism confers regeneration or salvation (see below).

19. Cf. Clowney, *Church*, 283–84; Reymond, *New Systematic Theology*, 954–55.

20. Berkhof, *Systematic Theology*, 641–42.

21. Dabney, *Systematic Theology*, 791–92.

mentioned above, the Roman Catholic Church teaches that baptism in and of itself possesses salvific efficacy. According to the Roman Catholic tradition, baptism is necessary in order to receive grace through the church, start the course of progressive sanctification (which is necessary for the maintenance of grace), and obtain glorification at the end. This position is consistent with the Roman Catholic view that salvation is *not* by grace alone through faith alone. However, there are groups besides the Roman Catholic Church that maintain that baptism is necessary for the forgiveness of sins and salvation. Groups like the Churches of Christ (Christian Churches) and United Pentecostals (Oneness Pentecostals) also maintain that baptism is necessary for forgiveness and salvation. The two most common scriptural passages appealed to for this position are Acts 2:38 and 1 Peter 3:21–22. We will examine these two passages below to determine if they both do teach that baptism is necessary for a person to be saved.

1. *Acts 2:38: "And Peter said to them, 'Repent and be baptized every one of you in the name of Jesus Christ for the forgiveness of your sins, and you will receive the gift of the Holy Spirit.'"* Advocates of the baptismal salvation position argue that Peter is unambiguous in this verse about the necessity of baptism for the forgiveness of sins. They maintain that Peter not only told his listeners to repent but to "be baptized" for the forgiveness of their sins. For instance, attempting to closely connect baptism with forgiveness of sin, John D. Castelein writes: "Baptism and repentance are both 'for the forgiveness of your sins' (Acts 2:38). In the 1600 occurrences of this preposition [*eis*] in the NT its meaning is always purposive or consecutive (it expresses the intended result of an activity) except, possibly, in four instances where its meaning may be more nuanced."[22] When taken at face value, the verse seems to support the position of Castelein and others who argue that baptism is necessary for forgiveness and salvation.

   Some have attempted to reconcile this passage with the biblical doctrine of justification through faith alone by arguing that a clear distinction must be made between the *instrumental cause* and the *efficient cause* of salvation: the instrumental cause being repentance-baptism and the efficient cause being God's grace through the work of Christ.[23] This argument still does not resolve the dilemma since baptism is still

22. Castelein, "Christian Churches/Churches of Christ View," 159n5.

23. Caneday, "Baptism in the Stone-Campbell Restoration Movement," 312. Caneday, of course, does not believe that baptism in and of itself confers salvation.

viewed as another instrumental means (alongside faith) that leads to forgiveness and eternal life. One may rightly ask how this is *practically* different from the Churches of Christ view where baptism is viewed as one of the components of conversion that are necessary for forgiveness and salvation. If there is a significant gap of time between the moment of the Spirit's work of effectual calling (that results in faith) and water baptism, was the believer's justified status "on hold" until he or she submitted to baptism? What was the salvific and legal status of the believer in the eyes of God between the time of faith and baptism? Although this is a valiant attempt to reconcile the Reformation's *sola fide* doctrine and Peter's statement on the significance of baptism in Acts 2:38, it does not satisfactorily address the apparent incongruity.

Without viewing baptism as another instrumental means (alongside repentance and faith) for forgiveness and salvation, the more satisfactory answer to how Acts 2:38 should be interpreted is given by Richard N. Longenecker. He believes that one must interpret the passage in the context of the Jewish religious mindset. For the Jews, the inward change (the new birth, for Christians) could not be divorced from its outward expression (baptism). Longenecker notes that wherever "the gospel was proclaimed in a Jewish milieu, the rite of baptism was taken for granted as being inevitably involved (cf. 2:41; 8:12, 36–38; 9:18; 10:47–48; 18:18; 19:5; also Heb 10:22; 1 Peter 3:18–21)."[24] This means that the relationship between repentance and baptism in Acts 2:38 is more likely the distinction between the conversion of the heart and its outward expression through baptism. Therefore, Peter is not stating that repentance *and* baptism are both involved at the same time in the believer's conversion to Christ for forgiveness of sins. Rather, he is stating that baptism is the expected visible outcome of those who have turned to Christ for forgiveness and have been baptized by the Spirit.[25] This interpretation also comports well with Peter's other statements in Acts where he stresses that forgiveness or salvation is through repentance and faith without mentioning the need for baptism (3:19; 5:31; 10:43; 13:38–39).

2. *1 Peter 3:21–22:* "*Baptism, which corresponds to this, now saves you, not as a removal of dirt from the body but as an appeal to God for a*

24. Longenecker, "Acts of the Apostles," 284.
25. Wallace, *Greek Grammar Beyond the Basics*, 370–71.

*good conscience, through the resurrection of Jesus Christ, who has gone into heaven and is at the right hand of God, with angels, authorities, and powers having been subjected to him."* This is another passage that is commonly appealed to by those who espouse that baptism is necessary for salvation. They argue that Peter again explicitly connects baptism with salvation in his epistle. However, this passage, when carefully examined, also does not support the view that baptism is necessary for salvation. The key to the passage is the statement "as an appeal to God for a good conscience." Peter does not say that the rite of baptism leads to, instrumentally or efficiently, the salvation of the individual. Instead, what he is pointing at is how baptism cleanses the believer's conscience before God. Baptism in this passage, according to Peter, therefore, is the outward expression of the inner renewal that has already taken place. In regards to this passage, Thomas J. Nettles writes:

> The text says that baptism does not remove the moral filth natural to life in this body. It affirms rather that we know that God has dropped his charges of condemnation against us because of Christ. Baptism represents the confident reliance on the judgment that Christ took for us, which judgment becomes our salvation. Baptism itself does not remove the damnable filth but expresses one's confidence that only the propitiatory death of Christ saves. We also express assurance that only the resurrection of Christ seals this transaction. His death satisfied all the demands of God's law so that, as Peter preached at Pentecost, death had no legitimate claim on its victim. The resurrection warrants the pledge, the affirmation after inquiry, of a good conscience unto God.[26]

Therefore, this passage cannot be justifiably used to teach that baptism in any way *leads to* forgiveness and salvation. Peter, like in Acts 2:38, is positing that the inward reality *must* be expressed in the outward form (baptism). Even though he intricately connects the ordinance of baptism with salvation, he does not state that the former is necessary, as an instrumental means or as the basis, for the latter.

Although we have examined two of the most common passages used by those who espouse baptismal regeneration/salvation with responses, we can also refute this position by providing an actual account of an individual who was saved apart from the rite: the thief on the cross (Luke 23:40–43).

26. Nettles, "Baptist View," 38.

At the end of the short account of the two thieves in Luke 23:40–43, Jesus tells one of the thieves: "Truly, I say to you, today you will be with me in Paradise" (v. 43). The declaration that Jesus makes to the thief is unambiguously clear: he is clearly telling the thief, as a result of his faith, that he will join him in Paradise after death. There is no mention of water baptism or any other ritual. The only thing that the thief did to enter Paradise that day was believe. The manner of the thief's salvation also agrees with other passages in the Scriptures that state that sinners are justified and saved through faith alone in Christ alone (John 3:16; Rom 3:28; Gal 2:16; Eph 2:8–9; Phil 3:9).[27] In addition, the view that baptism is necessary for forgiveness is practically no different from the position of the Judaizers who insisted that circumcision was also necessary for salvation (cf. Gal 3:1–14; 5:2–4). Therefore, when everything is taken into consideration, the Scriptures do not teach that baptism is necessary for salvation.[28]

### Who Should Be Baptized?

Another divisive issue among Christians in the past and present is the matter of the subjects of baptism. The topic of who is to be baptized can often lead to highly polemical debates, and history has shown that believers have even severed fellowships over this issue. As mentioned earlier in this chapter, those who advocate infant baptism argue that the practice has a long history in the Christian church, and that New Testament baptism not only substitutes but is a fulfillment of Old Testament circumcision. On the other hand, those who espouse believer's baptism (or credobaptism) argue that there is no clear evidence in Scripture that the New Testament church practiced infant baptism. Again, we must look primarily to Scripture, not tradition, to decide which view is correct.

---

27. Against the view of baptismal regeneration and/or salvation, James Montgomery Boice fittingly states: "We should know that such a conclusion is wrong because of the teaching of the rest of Scripture about the way in which a person is to be saved: by grace through faith in the death of Jesus Christ alone. If baptism is required for salvation, then the believing thief who was crucified with Christ is lost" (*Foundations of the Christian Faith*, 599).

28. Even though baptism is not required for salvation, it is still an ordinance that *all* believers must submit to if they desire to be obedient to Christ. Baptism publicly identifies a believer as belonging to Christ and his covenant community. In fact, a continual refusal to be baptized even when many opportunities to do so arise could call into question the genuineness of an individual's faith in Christ (cf. Luke 6:46).

Advocates of paedobaptism often argue that a case can be made for infant baptism when we look at the cases of "household baptisms" in the book of Acts (16:15, 31–34; 18:8) and 1 Corinthians 1:16. They argue that if these households included infants then they must have also been baptized along with the adults in the household. However, this is more of a conjecture than evidence for infant baptism. There is no evidence that there were infants in these households, and even if there were, there is no evidence that they were baptized along with the adults. Baptism presupposes that the recipient understands the gospel and receives it in faith. For instance, in Acts 16:34, Luke tells us that the Philippian jailer and his *entire* household rejoiced because he "had believed in God." In fact, the account also tells us that Paul and Silas spoke the word of the Lord to the jailor "and to all who were in his house" (Acts 16:32). The passage seems to indicate that the entire household of the Philippian jailor accepted the gospel message through faith (which would naturally exclude infants).[29] The same can be said of the household of Stephanas (1 Cor 16:15). In the case of Lydia (Acts 16:14–15), there is not enough information to determine if there were any infants in her household or if everyone received the gospel. Robert L. Reymond attempts to justify infant baptism on the grounds that there is no indication that everyone apart from Lydia and the Philippian jailor came to faith in these "household baptism" accounts. He then argues that despite their profession of faith (or lack thereof), all within their respective households received baptism.[30] However, this goes against several passages in the New Testament that closely connect baptism with conversion (cf. Acts 2:38; Gal 3:25–27; 1 Pet 3:21–22). Also, there is no indication in the New Testament that unbelievers, whether adult or infant, can receive baptism just because the head of their household is a believer.

Defenders of infant baptism also use a theological argument to support the view that infants should be baptized. Especially among Reformed Christians, there is the argument that since infants in the Old Testament were circumcised, New Testament infants should also be baptized. As already discussed above, the underlying assumption of this view is that the Scriptures must be read as a unity with the "covenant of grace" being the "golden thread" of this unity. Since the covenant of grace has the same terms and promises throughout redemptive history, infants in the new covenant church, as it is argued, should be baptized just as the male infants

29. Beasley-Murray, *Baptism in the New Testament*, 315.
30. Reymond, *New Systematic Theology*, 942.

in the nation of Israel were circumcised.[31] However, the main argument against this theory is that the Scriptures stress the clear discontinuity between the old and new covenants in redemptive history (2 Cor 3:7–11; Gal 3:15–29: 4:21–31; Heb 8:13). Although one can make a case that there is *some degree* of parallelism between Old Testament circumcision and New Testament baptism, this parallelism cannot be stretched too far. Old Testament circumcision was intended for the children of the nation of Israel and the rite inducted them into the theocracy. New Testament baptism, on the other hand, is for those who have received new life through the Spirit and forgiveness of sins (in which baptism marks them off as members of the new covenant community).[32] Additionally, while the old covenant included both the regenerate and unregenerate, the new covenant includes *only* those who have experienced the new birth and forgiveness of sins (cf. Jer 31:31–34).[33] In other words, unlike the old covenant, the circle of the new covenant is no bigger than the circle of the regenerate.

Finally, there is no solid scriptural support for the classic Reformed doctrine of the covenant of grace that theologically unites both Testaments. In this way, it may be exegetically and biblically questionable to argue that infant baptism should be practiced in the new covenant church because of an underlying "covenant of grace" that unifies the various administrations of redemptive history. As Stephen J. Wellum aptly notes:

> If we are not careful . . . the notion of *the* "covenant of grace" may be misleading, because Scripture does not speak of only one covenant with different administrations. Rather, Scripture speaks in terms of a *plurality* of covenants (e.g., Gal 4:24; Eph 2:12; Heb 8:7–13), which are all part of the progressive revelation of the one plan of God that ultimately is fulfilled in the new covenant. In reality, the "covenant of grace" is a comprehensive *theological* category, not a biblical one.[34]

Therefore, there is no scriptural justification to support the notion that New Testament baptism is parallel with circumcision in the Old Testament.

---

31. Reymond, *New Systematic Theology*, 944–45.

32. J. Rodman Williams maintains that the basic error of paedobaptism lies "in the failure to recognize the *difference* between the old and new covenants" (*Renewal Theology*, 3:232).

33. Cf. Schreiner, *Run to Win the Prize*, 90–92.

34. Wellum, "Baptism and the Relationship between the Covenants," 126.

After examining the biblical and theological arguments for paedobaptism, we maintain that the New Testament does not promote the practice of infant baptism. Rather, baptism, according to the New Testament, is only given to those who have committed themselves to Christ through faith and have received new life in the Spirit.

## What Is the Biblical Mode of Baptism?

One final issue pertaining to baptism that still provokes debates among Christians is the matter of the ordinance's mode. Roman Catholics, Anglicans/Episcopalians, Lutherans, Presbyterians, and Methodists argue that the mode of baptism can take on various forms: sprinkling, pouring, or immersion. Baptists and other credobaptist groups argue that full immersion is the only proper mode of baptism. Although the mode of baptism is not an issue that Christians should be divided over, the scriptural evidence strongly suggests that immersion was the way the first-century Christians conducted baptisms.

Those who believe that immersion is the only legitimate mode of baptism argue that one of the strongest supporting evidences for their position is the Greek word used when referring to water baptism in Scripture: *baptizein* (the verb form being *baptizō*). R. E. O. White states that the root word *baptizein* means "to plunge, immerse, sink; hence to wash; to be immersed, overwhelmed (in trouble)."[35] Thus, when examined lexically, the meaning of the Greek word supports the view that the proper mode of baptism is by immersion only. Some, however, argue that one cannot come to a firm conclusion regarding the mode of baptism by merely examining the Greek word apart from the immediate context. In fact, by looking at some biblical accounts in Scripture (e.g., Acts 9:18; 10:47–48 16:25–33), it does not appear practicable that baptism was performed only by full immersion.[36] Gregg R. Allison, however, points out that whenever the administration of baptism is referenced in the New Testament only the word *baptizō* is used.[37]

Another reference used by those who support immersion-only baptism is the language Paul uses in Romans 6:3–4 to identify a believer's baptism in water with Christ's death and resurrection: "Do you not know that all of us who have been baptized into Christ Jesus were baptized into his

35. White, "Baptize, Baptism," 50.

36. Berkhof, *Systematic Theology*, 630–31.

37. Allison, *Sojourners and Strangers*, 353.

death? We were buried therefore with him by baptism into death, in order that, just as Christ was raised from the dead by the glory of the Father, we too might walk in newness of life." The fact that Paul mentions that Christ was buried indicates, according to the immersion-only advocates, that believers spiritually and symbolically re-enact Christ's death most faithfully when they are fully immersed during baptism (cf. Col 2:12).[38]

As mentioned above, the mode of baptism is not an issue that Christians should be divided over. Charity should be shown towards other believers who disagree on this matter. However, at the same time, it is not an unimportant issue that we should nonchalantly set it aside and never have it discussed again. This is so because when believers submit to baptism they are tangibly showing to the outside world that they have spiritually identified themselves with Christ's death and resurrection.

Therefore, after examining the evidence above, we believe that baptism by full immersion most faithfully signifies our spiritual resurrection in Christ.

## 2. The Lord's Supper

In this section of the chapter we will discuss the other ordinance given and commanded by Christ for the life of the church: The Lord's Supper. The first part of this section will discuss the major views of the Lord's Supper found in the broader Christian tradition; the second part will discuss issues that are of significance to the church today regarding this ordinance.

### Major Views of the Lord's Supper in the Christian Tradition

#### The Roman Catholic View (Transubstantiation)

According to the Roman Catholic view of the Lord's Supper (called the Eucharist) the elements (the bread and wine) undergo a supernatural change where they transform into Christ's literal body and blood. Although the bread and wine retain their actual molecular properties, Christ's flesh and blood are actually present in their respective elements (transubstantiation). As the Roman Catholic scholar Brother Jeffrey Gros states, "Externally, the bread and wine retain their appearance even after consecration. Yet at the same time the whole Christ is sacramentally present in them—the whole

---

38. Grenz, *Theology for the Community of God*, 531.

Christ, body, and blood, soul and divinity."[39] Thomas A. Baima also provides a typical understanding of the Roman Catholic view of the sacramental elements when he states that the "accidents of bread and wine contain the reality of the body and blood, soul and divinity of Jesus Christ."[40] Therefore, when Jesus gave bread to his disciples and told them, "Take, eat; this is my body" (Matt 26:26), and when he gave them the cup of wine and told them, "Drink of it, all of you, for this is my blood" (vv. 27–28), Roman Catholics take these statements to be literal (cf. also John 6:53–56). In their view, when a person partakes of the Eucharist they are literally consuming the flesh and blood of Christ.

Another essential feature of the Roman Catholic view is the belief that the Eucharist "re-presents" Christ's vicarious sacrifice on the altar. Although Roman Catholics deny that their view undermines the salvific efficacy of Christ's vicarious death on the cross, their view essentially sees the Eucharist as an offering up again of Christ as an atoning sacrifice for the sins of the participants. For instance, Gros writes:

> In the sacrifice of the Lord's Supper, the same victim is indeed offered but in an entirely different *way*: sacramentally. By virtue of this sacramental re-presentation, the Eucharist—far from being "basically nothing but a denial of the one sacrifice" (as the Heidelberg Catechism claims)—renders present the unique and unrepeatable sacrifice of Jesus Christ. At the Last Supper, Christ left the church with "a visible sacrifice (as human nature demands)," which in a bloodless manner "re-presents," makes present, the bloody sacrifice that was once-for-all accomplished on the cross. In this way the "salutary power" of the cross "is applied for the forgiveness of sins" (Trent, session 22, chap. 1). In the "unbloody oblation" of the Eucharist, the "fruits" of the bloody oblation are "received" (Trent, session 22, chap. 2).[41]

In this way, the Eucharist performs the salvific function of cleansing the members of the church of their sins when they come to the table. However, the sins that can be washed away at the table only apply to "venial" sins and not "mortal" sins that have yet to be dealt with.

A final feature essential to the Roman Catholic position is the understanding that only validly ordained priests may consecrate the elements.

---

39. Gros, "Roman Catholic View," 17.

40. Baima, "Roman Catholic View," 129.

41. Gros, "Roman Catholic View," 19.

Thus, this means that either a presbyter or bishop must be present in order for Holy Communion to take place.[42] Without an ordained priest to administer the Eucharist, the bread and wine remain as they are without any metaphysical change. This sacerdotal character of the Roman Catholic position is what separates it from the various Protestant views of the Lord's Supper.

Protestants have typically objected to the Roman Catholic view for its highly literalistic understanding of Matthew 26:26–28. Protestant exegetes since the Reformation, rightly, find it difficult to accept that Jesus literally meant that people consume his flesh and blood at the table. The problem with the Roman Catholic interpretation of Matthew 26:26–28, according to Protestant interpreters, is twofold: 1) Jesus' listeners often missed the spiritual meaning behind some of his statements when they were understood too literally (John 2:20–21; 4:13–15; 9:38–41; 10:19–20); and 2) it is impossible that Jesus meant in the passage that his disciples should literally take his flesh and blood for consumption since he was still physically with them at the time.[43] In addition, if Christ's body and blood are literally present in the elements, how does this position agree with the view that Christ is physically raised to the Father's right hand and will remain there until his return? This is another difficulty with the Roman Catholic view of transubstantiation.[44]

A more fundamental problem with the Roman Catholic view, according to Protestants, however, is its understanding that the Eucharist re-presents Christ as the atonement for sins. Scripture makes it clear that anyone who trusts in Christ and his work alone has irrevocably passed from death to life (John 5:24; Rom 8:1; Eph 2:1–10; 1 John 3:14). The author of Hebrews makes it clear in two places that Christ's death is fully efficacious to deal with the sins of believers and that his sacrifice does not need to be repeated anymore. In Hebrews 9:24–28, he writes:

> For Christ has entered, not into holy places made with hands, which are copies of the true things, but into heaven itself, now to

42. Baima, "Roman Catholic View," 134.

43. As rightly pointed out by William Hendriksen in his *Matthew*, 909.

44. Roman Catholic scholars respond by saying that the conversion of the elements occurs through *adduction*. Which means Christ is brought into the Eucharist without leaving his place in heaven (Baima, "Roman Catholic View," 129). The inconsistency of this view is that both Christ's flesh and blood *truly are not* present in the elements if adduction is true *or* Christ's humanity is dichotomized during the transformation of the elements.

appear in the presence of God on our behalf. Nor was it to offer himself repeatedly, as the high priest enters the holy places every year with blood not his own, for then he would have had to suffer repeatedly since the foundation of the world. But as it is, he has appeared once for all at the end of the ages to put away sin by the sacrifice of himself. And just as it is appointed for man to die once, and after that comes judgment, so Christ, having been offered once to bear the sins of many, will appear a second time, not to deal with sin but to save those who are eagerly waiting for him.

Also, in Hebrews 10:11–14, he states:

And every priest stands daily at his service, offering repeatedly the same sacrifices, which can never take away sins. But when Christ had offered for all time a single sacrifice for sins, he sat down at the right hand of God, waiting from that time until his enemies should be made a footstool for his feet. For by a single offering he has perfected for all time those who are being sanctified.

By re-presenting Christ's death at the Mass and viewing the Eucharist as a repeated atonement for sins, the Roman Catholic Church is adopting a ritualistic system that is essentially no different from the ineffectual old covenant sacrificial system (Heb 10:1–4). Not only is the Roman Catholic position of the Eucharist biblically unsupportable, it also undermines assurance among true believers as they will never have the subjective surety that Christ's death was fully efficacious to deal with their sins (contra 1 John 5:13).

### The Lutheran View (Consubstantiation)

The Lutheran view of the Lord's Supper is another view that affirms that Christ's body and blood are truly present in the Eucharist. However, it differs from the Roman Catholic view by stating that the bread and wine do not actually change into Christ's flesh and blood, but that Christ's flesh and blood are present "in, with, and, under" the elements (consubstantiation). In this way, Lutherans also understand Christ's statement in Matthew 26:26–28 in a literal way. As David P. Scaer writes:

In the Lord's Supper, the Spirit as God's creating agent (Gen. 1:2) raises the created things of bread and wine to a higher and more sacred level in making them Christ's body and blood. Nevertheless, at the heart of the Lutheran arguments for Christ's presence in the Supper are the words of institution: "This is my body . . . this [cup] is my blood of the covenant" (Matt. 26:26, 28). Through these words Christ effects the sacrament. The word *is* is taken literally and not figuratively. Words spoken by the minister do not have their power from him, nor do they possess an autonomous power—a kind of magic—but their power resides in Christ's institution.[45]

The benefit of Christ's body and blood being present in the elements, according to Lutherans, is that it washes away the sins of the believers who partake of the Supper. By truly, not figuratively, feeding on Christ's body and blood (*mundacatio*),[46] the communicants receive the salvific benefits of Christ's propitiatory death. Drawing upon Christ's statement to his disciples in Luke 22:19–20 (cf. Matt 26:26–28; Mark 14:22–24), John Theodore Mueller writes:

> It is true, these words also *describe* the body and blood of Christ as His real and true body and blood. At the same time, however, they also show the *purpose* of the eating and drinking; for as the body was given into death and the blood was shed for the remission of our sins, so in the Holy Supper they are offered and imparted to the communicant for the remission of his sins.[47]

For Lutherans, therefore, the Lord's Supper is truly a means of grace for the participants. It is not merely a gracious reminder of Christ's death but a genuine sacrament that conveys the benefits of his sacrificial work. However, only genuine believers receive these blessings through the sacrament. Unbelievers or unworthy individuals who partake of the Supper will do so to their own condemnation.[48]

Evangelicals outside of the Lutheran tradition, however, have criticized the view because it, just like the Roman Catholic transubstantiation view, undermines the full humanity of Christ with its principle of *ubiquity* (that Christ's human nature can be everywhere). Lutherans respond

---

45. Scaer, "Lutheran View," 96–97.

46. In regards to the *mundacatio*, Mueller writes: "The Lutherans . . . regard the sacramental union between the bread and the body and between the wine and the blood as so real and intimate that in the sacramental act the communicant receives Christ's true body and blood in, with, and under the bread and wine (*mundacatio oralis*), the bread and wine indeed in a natural manner (*mundacatio naturalis*), but the body and blood in a supernatural, incomprehensible manner" (*Christian Dogmatics*, 527–28).

47. Mueller, *Christian Dogmatics*, 533.

48. Scaer, "Lutheran View," 92.

by arguing that the resurrected Christ is not bound by the ordinary rules of space and time. In other words, he can be in one place and another at the same time![49] However, the ubiquity of Christ's humanity is a teaching nowhere found in Scripture but merely a necessary contrivance to support the consubstantiation view.[50] Also, Lutherans have traditionally held that Christ's human nature was "interpenetrated" by his divine nature in order to justify the doctrine of ubiquity—which veers close to a Eutychianistic or Monophysite Christology.

## The Reformed View (Spiritual Presence)

The Reformed view makes a clear break from the Roman Catholic and Lutheran views by insisting that Christ's presence in the Lord's Supper is only a *spiritual* one. For instance, in the Westminster Confession of Faith, it states that "the body and blood of Christ" are "really, but spiritually, present to the faith of believers in that ordinance, as the elements themselves are to their outward senses" (XXIX/7). This spiritual presence, however, does not mean that Christ's flesh and blood are *truly* present *in* the elements;[51] although it does not mean that the presence is "unreal" either.[52] What it does mean, according to Morton H. Smith, is that even though "the bread and wine remain bread and wine," there is "a spiritual application of the Gospel to the hearts of believers as they partake. Thus, we take the bread in the mouth, and the body of Christ as given for us is received in the heart. The same is true of the cup."[53] Therefore, Christ is spiritually present in the Supper as believers partake of his flesh and blood through faith (spiritual manducation), in which case it truly becomes a means of grace for them. As Francis Turretin states:

49. Scaer, "Lutheran View," 92–93.

50. Grudem, *Systematic Theology*, 994. Reymond's words are stronger when he writes that both the Roman Catholic and Lutheran views on the real presence "destroy the true humanity of Christ" and "forsake Chalcedon's Christology" (*New Systematic Theology of the Christian Faith*, 960).

51. John Calvin at times spoke of the presence of Christ's body and blood in the elements just like the way his Lutheran contemporaries did. For instance, he writes: "But if it is true that a visible sign is given us to seal the gift of a thing invisible, when we have received the symbol of the body, let us no less surely trust that the body itself is also given to us" (*Inst.* 4.17.10).

52. Cf. Genderen and Velema, *Concise Reformed Dogmatics*, 810–11.

53. Smith, *Systematic Theology*, 2:695.

He is indeed corporeally in heaven with respect to the existence of his body, but he is nonetheless present to our minds through faith with his spiritual presence. Therefore Christ's body is truly present corporeally in heaven and truly spiritually present in our souls or to our faith, by which we receive him. And it is an improper inference, if spiritually then not truly; for nothing is done more truly than what is done by the Spirit.[54]

If the presence of Christ in the Supper is not real in the way Roman Catholics and Lutherans understand it, in what way then does the sacrament spiritually benefit the communicant according to Reformed Christians? Herman Bavinck provides this answer when he writes:

So among the Reformed . . . Christ is truly and essentially present with his divine and human nature in the Supper, only in no way other than he is present in the gospel. Christ is no more enclosed physically in bread and wine than he is in the Word proclaimed, but those who believingly accept the sign also, according to the divine ordinance, receive true communion with the whole Christ. Along with the sign, not in and under the sign, Christ bestows the thing signified, that is, himself with all his benefits.[55]

What the believer receives in partaking of the Supper, in other words, is the strengthening of his or her communion with Christ.[56] In addition, as they regularly feed on Christ, they re-appropriate the benefits of Christ's redemption and begin experiencing "spiritual nourishment, growth in grace, and renewal of thanksgiving and engagement to God."[57] However, this must be received *in faith* or else the elements confer no benefit to the communicant.[58] Therefore, the Lord's Supper is not only a reminder of Christ's vicarious death but also a means of grace where believers are enabled to draw closer to Christ, have their faith strengthened, and have their progress in sanctification fostered.

Critics of the Reformed view, on the other hand, accuse the view of being inconsistent with its attempt to uphold the localized physicality of Christ after his ascension, while arguing for the position that Christ is somehow spiritually present in the Supper. In other words, how can one

---

54. Turretin, *Institutes of Elenctic Theology*, 3:518.

55. Bavinck, *Reformed Dogmatics*, 4:577.

56. Bavinck, *Reformed Dogmatics*, 4:578.

57. Reymond, *New Systematic Theology*, 966.

58. Berkhof, *Systematic Theology*, 656.

consistently hold that the sign and the signified are identified with one another and yet maintain that Christ is physically present in heaven? In its attempt to make the Lord's Supper truly a means of grace, the critics argue that the Reformed view ends up falling into inconsistencies by confusing the sign and the signified in the sacrament while rejecting the Lutheran doctrine of Christ's ubiquity.[59]

## The Zwinglian View (Commemoration)

The fourth prevalent view of the Lord's Supper is the view articulated by the Swiss Reformer Huldrych Zwingli (1484–1531). This view is sometimes erroneously labeled the *memorialist* view (Zwingli taught that more than a mere remembering is done at the Supper).[60] However, even though Zwingli did not see the Supper as a mere memorial, his particular understanding of the ordinance kept the commemorative aspect as the fundamental one. Also, Zwingli did not deny a localized spiritual presence of Christ in the Supper, as some of those who adopted his position later did (like the Anabaptists).[61] Nevertheless, this spiritual presence is only meant for those who receive the Supper in faith.[62] Furthermore, the Supper's main purpose according to Zwingli, going back to his emphasis on the commemorative aspect of it, is to signify one's faith in Christ and reliance on his vicarious death through the eating of the bread and drinking of the wine.[63] Therefore, believers who participate in the Supper do receive the benefits of Christ's death by partaking of the elements. This means that they truly receive, through faith, the assurance of what Christ did for them by his sacrifice. However, like the Reformed view, those who lack faith in Christ cannot receive these benefits.[64] Finally, Mark E. Dever states that those who adopt this position argue that even though the Supper is not an "essential conduit

---

59. This is the criticism given by Roger E. Olson in response to Leanne Van Dyk's essay in his "Baptist Response [to the Reformed view]," 87–88. However, we should be mindful of the fact that Olson was criticizing Calvin's particular view of Christ's presence rather than the view of orthodox Reformed theologians of later generations.

60. As noted by Hodge in his discussion of Zwingli's view in the third volume of his *Systematic Theology* (*Systematic Theology*, 3:626–28, 631–37).

61. Erickson, *Christian Theology*, 1128.

62. Saucy, *Church in God's Program*, 223.

63. Saucy, *Church in God's Program*, 223.

64. Erickson, *Christian Theology*, 1128.

for God's grace," it still should be observed by Christians since it is an ordinance commanded by Christ, and therefore, the normal means of marking out those who belong to him (the church) from those who do not (the world).[65]

The common criticism leveled against this view is that it undermines the ordinance as being a true means of grace by deemphasizing the concept of the believer's communion with Christ in the Supper (cf. 1 Cor 10:16).[66] Therefore, by not being a true means of grace for believers the ordinance loses its sacramental character according to its critics.

## Significant Issues in Regards to the Lord's Supper

### How Is the Lord's Supper Spiritually Efficacious for Believers?

Although all of the views we have surveyed agree that the ordinance is commanded by Christ and should be regularly observed by Christ's followers (Matt 26:26–29; 1 Cor 11:23–26), they differ amongst themselves in regards to how the Lord's Supper is spiritually efficacious. Certainly we can say from the outset that the Roman Catholic view that the Supper is a re-presenting of Christ's sacrifice and a means to atone for the sins of believers is nowhere supported in Scripture. As mentioned in our discussion of the Roman Catholic view, passages like Hebrews 9:24–28 and 10:11–14 make it clear that Christ's death is a once-and-for-all atoning sacrifice that does not need to be repeated again in the church. The salvific efficacy of Christ's death lies at the crucifixion and not at the Eucharist (cf. Rom 3:25). However, it is equally unscriptural to say that the ordinance is a mere memorial that does not bring believers into a true participation or communion with Christ at the Supper (cf. 1 Cor 10:16). Therefore, the truth must lie somewhere in between those two extremes.

Before we discuss the efficacy of the Lord's Supper for believers, we must mention that the Lutheran view of a real bodily presence, and its accompanying doctrine of Christ's ubiquity, is not supported in Scripture. In fact, the Lutheran view leads to a type of Christology with problematic theological implications. As discussed above, the Lutheran view of consubstantiation falls into the same problem as with the Roman Catholic transubstantiation view when it maintains that Christ is both physically present

65. Dever, "Church," 648.

66. Saucy, *Church in God's Program*, 223.

in heaven *and* in the Eucharistic elements. By this move, the Lutheran view of the real presence, along with the Roman Catholic view, ends up undermining Christ's full humanity (and his incarnation) and dichotomizes his human nature (by allowing the possibility that Christ can be in more than one place at the same time). In short, this understanding inevitably leads to certain theological problems related to Christ's personhood. We must conclude, therefore, that if Christ is present in the Supper he is present only in a spiritual way.

This leads finally to the subject of what purpose the Lord's Supper serves in Christ's church. It must be mentioned from the outset that the spiritual benefits of the Supper are only conveyed to those who partake of it in a worthy manner. This means that only those who come to the table already trusting in Christ for salvation *and* not living in a way that brings reproach to the gospel may receive the blessings of the ordinance. Those who partake of the bread and wine in an unworthy manner will be subject to God's judgment (1 Cor 11:27–32).[67] This also means that the Supper does not impart grace to the participant in an *ex opere operato* way. In other words, the benefits of the ordinance are not given unconditionally irrespective of the faithlessness or spiritual apathy of the communicant.

In what way, then, does the ordinance bring blessing to believers who partake of the bread and wine in a worthy manner? The principal blessing of the ordinance is that Christ spiritually comes down to make his presence known to the church and spiritually nourishes believers by reminding them of his vicarious sacrifice for their sins. In this way, the Supper becomes a *means* of sanctification for believers as they are assured of Christ's sacrificial death as applying to them, and by freshly appropriating his work by partaking of the elements. As Robert L. Saucy writes:

> The two basic provisions of the new covenant were the forgiveness of sins and the gift of the Holy Spirit (cf. Jer 31:31–34; Eze 36:25–27). Although these were received initially in salvation and symbolized in baptism, the Christian's walk is not static but dynamic. He has been saved but he is also being saved. Involved in

---

67. Those who fell ill (and even died) as a result of abusing the Lord's Supper with their neglecting of the poorer members of the church were more likely believers who suffered God's disciplining judgment (v. 30). This is evident by the way Paul contrasts their physical punishment with the eternal punishment that awaits those who still belong to the world (v. 32) (cf. Schreiner, *New Testament Theology*, 733). Nevertheless, regardless of who is being addressed in the passage, the same principle still applies: unworthy participants of the Supper will experience God's judgment.

this continuous walk is the fresh need of forgiveness of sins and the power of the Spirit. In the Lord's Supper these are offered anew in order that the one partaking in faith might have fresh assurance of sin forgiven and a new appropriation of the life which is in Christ by the Spirit. . . . Partaking at the Lord's table in faith means nothing less than increasing in that life through a fresh appropriation of the Saviour.[68]

The efficacy of the Lord's Supper is found in Christ offering himself anew to believers during the meal. This ordinance, however, goes beyond being a mere remembrance of what Christ has done for those who belong to him. We argue instead that the Supper truly is a means of grace because it strengthens the faith of believers and enables them to make progress in their sanctification as they receive Christ's death afresh.

## How Often Should the Lord's Supper Be Observed?

One of the more debated questions discussed among Christians pertaining to the Lord's Supper is the frequency of its observance. Although the New Testament does not provide us with an explicit answer to this question, the scriptural evidence suggests that the ordinance was observed on a frequent basis by the earliest Christians (cf. 1 Cor 11:17–22, 26). This, however, does not necessarily mean that it was observed on a daily basis. Rather, it is more likely that the earliest churches observed the Supper on a weekly basis— and, therefore, we believe, this should be the normal pattern for churches today.[69]

Even though we believe that a weekly observance should be the norm for churches, we also maintain that charity should be expressed among believers of differing convictions on this matter. Some churches will observe the ordinance on a monthly basis but that does not necessarily make those churches theologically or spiritually suspect. What is more important is how the ordinance will spiritually benefit those who partake of it. If the ordinance becomes too procedural because of its frequency then it can lose its intended purpose. On the other hand, we should not allow the ordinance to be observed with long intervals of time, which will result in believers losing out on its benefits. Erickson finds the appropriate balance when he states that the ordinance should "be observed often enough to prevent long gaps

---

68. Saucy, *Church in God's Program*, 228.

69. Cf. Moule, *Worship in the New Testament*, 29.

between times of reflection on the truths it signifies, but not so frequently as to make it seem trivial or so commonplace that we go through the motions without really thinking about the meaning."[70]

## Who Should Administer the Lord's Supper?

As mentioned above, the Roman Catholic Church, due to its sacerdotal understanding of the church, believes that only validly ordained priests can consecrate the Eucharist. In other words, a priest must be present in order for the elements to be changed into Christ's body and blood and for the sacrament to have salvific efficacy. Scripture, however, does not clearly state who may administer the ordinance. Therefore, there is no biblical justification that only ordained ministers of the church may administer the Lord's Supper. On the other hand, in order to protect the Supper from potential abuse, we believe that in *ordinary* situations a pastor or church leader should officiate over the ordinance.[71]

## Who Should Be Allowed to Participate in the Lord's Supper?

The question of who may partake of the Lord's Supper is another issue that confronts Christians of various confessional traditions. Some Christian groups, like the Independent Baptists, practice what is sometimes called *closed communion*. According to this view, only members who have met certain requirements set forth in a particular local church may participate in the Lord's Supper. Usually, what this means is that the table is closed off to non-members (even if they are believers) or those who do not meet specific doctrinal or ecclesiastical requirements (e.g., baptism by immersion) of that church. On the other side of the spectrum are those who argue that the table should be open to all true believers in Christ. According to this view, even those who are not members of the local church administering the bread and wine or have yet to be baptized may partake of the Lord's Supper as long as they give evidence of having genuine faith. This is called the *open communion* view. Still others, however, argue for a mediating position called *close communion* where only *baptized* believers who are in good standing in their respective churches may partake of the Supper even if

70. Erickson, *Christian Theology*, 1134.
71. Grudem, *Systematic Theology*, 998.

they do not belong to the church administering the ordinance.[72] Those who advocate this position argue that the terms for participating in the Supper are the same as the conditions for membership in the church. This means that in order for a person to be qualified to take part in the Supper he or she must meet the membership requirements of the local church he or she is *already* a part of.[73]

Although all three views have their strengths and weaknesses, we believe that the *open communion* view has the least problems associated with it from a practical and theological point of view. If genuine believers are barred from participating in the Supper because they do not meet certain requirements of a local church (or denomination) then we are doing them a great disservice by depriving them of the spiritual benefits that come with participating in the Supper. Even in the more moderate version of *close communion*, if we demand that genuine believers be baptized before they are allowed to come to the table then we are in essence saying that they do not truly belong to Christ's spiritual body, and therefore, not entitled to the privileges and benefits of being in a saving relationship with Christ (1 Cor 10:16–17). This, however, does not mean that churches may allow anyone who professes to be a Christian to partake of the Supper despite their heretical opinions or profligate lifestyles (cf. 1 Cor 5:9–13). There are many people in churches today who call themselves Christians (and even get accepted as members of a local church) who have yet to experience the new birth by the Spirit and God's grace of forgiveness. To avoid situations where unregenerate individuals can have access to the Supper, churches must be extra vigilant in making sure that those who participate in Christ's holy meal are true believers in Christ. Therefore, only those who make a credible profession of faith and give evidence of the new birth may partake of the Lord's Supper.

### Should Infants of Believing Parents Be Allowed to Participate in the Lord's Supper?

In the Eastern Orthodox Church and certain segments within the Anglican and Reformed traditions, there is an idiosyncratic view of the Lord's Supper where baptized infants may participate in the ordinance (this is commonly called *paedocommunion*). This view has been rejected by the vast majority

72. Allison, *Sojourners and Strangers*, 404–6.
73. Allison, *Sojourners and Strangers*, 405.

of Christians throughout history because of its unscriptural nature, yet it is regularly practiced by some churches and groups today. One of the strongest biblical arguments against the paedocommunion position is found in 1 Corinthians 11:28–29. In the passage, Paul states: "Let a person examine himself, then, and so eat of the bread and drink of the cup. For anyone who eats and drinks without discerning the body eats and drinks judgment on himself." Considering that infants do not yet have the mental capacity to examine their own spiritual condition, it is wrong, if we consistently follow through with Paul's line of thinking, to allow infants to have access to the table. Secondly, we maintained elsewhere that only those who have faith in Christ may participate in the Supper and receive its benefits. Infants are not capable of exercising faith in Christ and, therefore, this naturally excludes them from taking part in the ordinance. Lastly, when taken to its logical end, the paedocommunion view turns the Supper into an *ex opere operato* means of grace.[74]

Therefore, due to these significant problems associated with the paedocommunion position, we must uncompromisingly reject the practice and conclude that it is not in accord with the teachings of Scripture.

74. Smith, *Systematic Theology*, 2:688.

# CHAPTER 18

# The Last Things, Part 1: Personal Eschatology

## 1. Death

### The Certainty of Death as a Consequence of the Fall

ONE OF THE CERTAINTIES of life is that all human beings are susceptible to death due to the fall. That all human beings have a finite span of time to live is clearly attested to in Scripture (1 Cor 15:22; Heb 9:27). Death is also something that modern people generally like to avoid discussing because it reminds them that we all will have to confront it someday. In fact, regardless of how hard a person tries to postpone his or her death in numerous ways all will inevitably succumb to it in one way or another. Although death is inevitable for all, Scripture also views human death as an abnormality in the created order—something that was not part of the original design of creation (Gen 2:17). This is due to Adam's rebellion against God in Eden (Gen 3:19; cf. Rom 6:23)—which plunged the human race into sin, corruption, and death (Rom 5:12, 17, 19). In fact, Paul calls death the "last enemy" to be destroyed through Christ's work of redemption (1 Cor 15:26). As Michael Horton states, "the death of human beings is not part of a natural cycle; it is the curse for disobedience (Ge 2:17; 3:19, 22; 5:5; Ro 5:12; 8:10; 1Co 15:21). As such, it is not a friend.

Rather, it is 'the last enemy' (1Co 15:26)."[1] Therefore, one of the consequences of living in a fallen world is that everyone is subject to death.

## The Believer's Relationship to Death

Even though physical death is a certainty for all due to the fall, it is not something that will have ultimate victory over those who have been spiritually resurrected in Christ. Although believers will experience the everyday hardships and difficulties of living in a fallen world, succumbing to death is not something for them to dread over as many unbelievers do. To put it differently, death loses its sting for those who are in Christ and who long for God's eschatological renewal of all creation (1 Cor 15:54–55). The reason why believers need not fear death is because they have been forever reconciled to the Father through Christ and have been given new life by the Spirit (Rom 8:1–11). In fact, one of the reasons why the Son entered the world in human flesh is so that death would be conquered (Heb 2:14–15). As Anthony A. Hoekema writes, "The conquest of death . . . is to be seen as an essential part of Christ's redemptive work. Christ not only redeems his people from sin; he also redeems them from the results of sin, and death is one of them."[2]

Also, the Spirit who gives new life to believers is also the same Spirit who will give eternal life to their mortal bodies at the eschaton (Rom 8:11). Believers, therefore, have a foretaste of this victory when they experience eternal life now through God's grace in Jesus Christ (John 5:24; 11:25–26), even though this final victory over death still awaits a future fulfillment (Rev 21:3–4; cf. Isa 25:8). As a result, even death, as the apostle Paul makes clear, cannot separate believers from the love of God in Christ Jesus (Rom 8:38–39).

## The Unbeliever's Relationship to Death

Unlike believers, death, for unbelievers, is the ultimate curse because it cuts them off from God and all hope of obtaining redemption.[3] The author of Hebrews makes it clear that after death awaits judgment (Heb 9:27), and

1. Horton, *Pilgrim Theology*, 422.
2. Hoekema, *Bible and the Future*, 84.
3. Grenz, *Theology for the Community of God*, 577.

those outside of Christ will immediately experience God's wrath at death (Luke 16:23–24)—even though a fuller experience of God's judgment belongs in the future (Rev 20:14; 21:8). Therefore, for unbelievers, death is not something that should be received with expectation and joy (as if death will transition them to a better existence), but an awful enemy to be feared. For this reason believers should feel great sorrow for those who die apart from Christ and God's saving mercy.

## 2. The Intermediate State

### What Is the Intermediate State?

In chapter 5, we discussed how human beings are both material and immaterial. We argued that the Scriptures teach that human beings are an organic unity of body and soul (Matt 10:28; 2 Cor 7:1; Jas 2:26). However, Scripture also teaches that the immaterial part of the human being carries on after it has left the body (Luke 16:22–31; Rev 6:9–11). Christian theologians have traditionally called the condition between a person's death and his or her future bodily resurrection as the *intermediate state*. It is a time when the human soul exists outside the body until the general resurrection when the body and soul of the person are reunited.

In the Old Testament and Judaism, there is no detailed teaching of what happens to the individual after he or she dies. Death was generally understood as something that ended the person's productive existence on earth and where he or she could no longer know anything (Eccl 9:5, 10).[4] Although there is scant information regarding the situation of the deceased in the Old Testament, the Old Testament does provide some glimpses of what happens to the soul after death. For instance, it is believed that all souls—whether righteous or wicked (Eccl 9:2–3)—went to a place in the lowest parts of the earth called *Sheol*. Unlike the world of the living, there is no loving, hating, envying, working, knowing, or having wisdom in Sheol (Eccl 9:6, 10).[5] From the way Sheol is described in the Old Testament, it appears to be a bleak place lacking light (Job 10:21–22), remembrance (Ps 6:5), or praise for God (Isa 38:18). The souls there exist in a shadowy form (Isa 14:9–10) and there is no hope of escaping from Sheol's grasp (Job

---

4. Ferguson, "Death, Mortality," 155.

5. Nelson, "Sheol," 735.

17:13–16).[6] However, the righteous dead will not remain in Sheol forever: one day they will be rescued by God from Sheol's clutches (Ps 16:10; Hos 13:14). At the end, there will be a resurrection and final judgment where individuals will be judged based on how they lived on earth (Eccl 12:14; Dan 12:2). Therefore, the Old Testament does speak of an intermediate state of the deceased before the general resurrection.

When we come to the New Testament more information is provided regarding the condition of the soul between death and resurrection, even though the information provided is also quite limited. However, there is still enough evidence given to indicate that the souls of individuals are not extinguished at death. For example, Jesus tells us that once a person dies he or she either enters into God's blessed presence (Luke 16:22; 23:43) or ends up in Hades (Luke 16:23). Also, when Stephen cried out to Christ "Lord Jesus, receive my spirit" (Acts 7:59) right before his death at the hands of the members of the Sanhedrin, he knew that his soul would be in the presence of God after he departed the world. Furthermore, the apostle Paul tells us in 2 Corinthians 5:3 that the intermediate state is similar to being "naked" (or "unclothed" [HCSB]) due to the temporary separation of body and soul. However, Paul also states that believers will be "at home with the Lord" after they die (2 Cor 5:8), and that death is actually "gain" for them because of this (Phil 1:21, 23). Therefore, these passages in the New Testament demonstrate that the souls of the deceased will be fully aware of their condition, either in God's presence in heaven or in Hades suffering his wrath. As John Murray states, "The Scripture represents the disembodied state as one of full consciousness. Man is spirit and, though man's spirit is separated from the natural and normal relationship, it nevertheless continues to exist and to be active in its own distinct identity as the spirit of the person."[7]

## What about Soul Sleep?

Some Christians, in order to stress the unity of the body and soul, argue that the deceased believer will not be aware of his or her condition during the intermediate state because he or she will exist in a state of unconscious non-existence. This teaching is typically called the doctrine of "soul sleep." This view is embraced by the Seventh-Day Adventist Church and

---

6. Nelson, "Sheol," 735.

7. Murray, Collected Writings of John Murray, 2:402.

the Watchtower Society (Jehovah's Witnesses).[8] Those who advocate this position argue that the biblical writers describe the death of believers as "falling asleep" rather than entering into another state of consciousness. They refer to several passages in Scripture to defend this viewpoint. For example, they argue that in John 11:11 Jesus tells his disciples that Lazarus had "fallen asleep" as a way of telling them that he had died (v. 13). Also, in Acts 7:60, Luke describes how Stephen "fell asleep" (i.e., died) as a result of being murdered for his faith in Christ, they maintain. Finally, they point out that in 1 Corinthians 15 (vv. 6, 18, 20, 51) and 1 Thessalonians 4 (vv. 13–15) Paul uses the word "sleep" to describe the death of Christians. If Jesus, Luke, and Paul described the death of Christians as "falling asleep," would not this description be more consistent with the view that people enter into a state of temporary unconscious non-existence after death as argued by the proponents of the "soul sleep" doctrine?

First, the problem with the "soul sleep" view is that Scripture emphatically states, as mentioned above, that human beings are composed of both body and spirit. Although a person must have body and soul joined together to be fully human, these two aspects of the human person are still kept distinct in Scripture (Matt 10:28). Since human beings are both material and immaterial, therefore, the immaterial part of the human being must continue to exist after death. Second, as mentioned previously, Scripture sets forth clearly that those united to Christ immediately enjoy blessed fellowship with God in heaven after they die (Luke 16:22; 23:43; Acts 7:59; 2 Cor 5:8; Phil 1:21, 23). Likewise, those outside of Christ immediately experience the torments of Hades after their deaths (Luke 16:23–24). Third, there is no exegetical warrant to suggest that the use of the word "sleep" by Jesus and Paul meant the cessation of consciousness at death. Rather, we should understand it as a metaphorical way of describing the temporary nature of death.[9]

8. Cf. Hoekema, *Four Major Cults*, 345–71. However, we must clarify that the Seventh-Day Adventist Church is a Christian denomination that upholds the orthodox view of the Godhead and Christ's deity. The Watchtower Society, on the other hand, is a pseudo-Christian cult group that espouses teachings that are contrary to the beliefs of the early apostolic church and orthodox Christianity (e.g., the denial of the Trinity).

9. Grudem, *Systematic Theology*, 820.

## Is There a Place Called Purgatory?

Traditional Roman Catholic teaching states that believers who do not have all their sins dealt with during this life must go to a place called *purgatory* to have their souls purified so that they can be suited for life in heaven. In purgatory, believers are punished for the sins they have committed on earth which were not atoned for before death. Thus, there is an expiatory purpose for purgatory. As the Roman Catholic scholar Zachary J. Hayes writes:

> [T]he notion of a purgatory is intimately related to the convic-
> tion that our eternal destiny is irrevocably decided at the moment
> of our death and that, ultimately, our eternal destiny can be only
> heaven or hell. But not everyone seems "bad enough" to be con-
> signed to an eternal hell. And most do not seem "good enough" to
> be candidates for heaven. Therefore, something has to happen "in
> between." But this cannot mean a coming back to this life and get-
> ting another chance since our destiny is decided at the moment of
> our death. Therefore, some sort of a cleansing process is postulated
> between death and the entrance into heaven.[10]

Roman Catholic theologians primarily look to 2 Maccabees 12:43–45 to support this doctrine. The passage in the Revised Standard Version reads:

> He [Judas Maccabeus] also took up a collection, man by man, to
> the amount of two thousand drachmas of silver, and sent it to Jeru-
> salem to provide for a sin offering. In doing this he acted very well
> and honorably, taking account of the resurrection. For if he were
> not expecting that those who had fallen would rise again, it would
> have been superfluous and foolish to pray for the dead. But if he
> was looking to the splendid reward that is laid up for those who
> fall asleep in godliness, it was a holy and pious thought. Therefore
> he made atonement for the dead, that they might be delivered
> from their sin.

Catholics appeal to the fact that the passage talks about making "atonement for the dead" so that the dead "might be delivered from their sin" (v. 45). However, the passage in question is not part of the inspired canon of Scripture and, therefore, should not be used as a prooftext to develop a doctrine that is already exegetically and theologically questionable.

Another passage that Catholics often appeal to is Matthew 12:32. There, Jesus states: "And whoever speaks a word against the Son of Man will

---

10. Hayes, "Purgatorial View," 99.

be forgiven, but whoever speaks against the Holy Spirit will not be forgiven, either in this age or in the age to come." Catholics typically argue that Jesus is telling his listeners in the verse that there are some sins that can be forgiven in the "age to come" (i.e., in purgatory).[11] However, Jesus is not talking about the possibility of another chance for forgiveness of sins after death, but about the dire situation of those who blaspheme against the Holy Spirit. This type of blasphemy, according to Jesus, is tantamount to rejecting the gospel and, therefore, there is no possibility of forgiveness for anyone who commits this type of sin—either in this age or in the age to come.

Lastly, Catholics also look to 1 Corinthians 3:11–15 to support their doctrine of purgatory.[12] The passage reads:

> For no one can lay a foundation other than that which is laid, which is Jesus Christ. Now if anyone builds on the foundation with gold, silver, precious stones, wood, hay, straw—each one's work will become manifest, for the Day will disclose it, because it will be revealed by fire, and the fire will test what sort of work each one has done. If the work that anyone has built on the foundation survives, he will receive a reward. If anyone's work is burned up, he will suffer loss, though he himself will be saved, but only as through fire.

Catholic exegetes claim that when Paul speaks of the believer who builds with inadequate materials being saved "but only as through fire" (v. 15), they understand this to mean that the believer experiences for a period of time the fires of purgatory before they are allowed entrance into heaven. However, this interpretation is highly unlikely due to the fact that the judgment Paul speaks of is an event that will happen when Christ returns (i.e., "the Day" [v. 13]). Also, Paul never says in this passage that the believer who produces shoddy work will have to go through a period of purgation. Rather, what Paul is saying is that *despite* the inadequate work that some of Christ's servants produce, they will still be saved (though barely) even though everything they have built up will be destroyed.[13]

Although the exegetical difficulties with the doctrine of purgatory are quite obvious, a more fundamental problem with the doctrine of purgatory is theological: it undermines the finality of Christ's work on the cross (contra 1 Peter 3:18). If believers have to enter purgatory to be purified

---

11. Hayes, "Purgatorial View," 105.

12. Sungenis, *Not by Faith Alone*, 514–15.

13. Morris, *1 Corinthians*, 66.

of remaining sin before they are admitted into heaven we must conclude, then, that salvation is not by grace alone and that Christ's sacrifice is not sufficient to deal with all sin. In fact, the doctrine of purgatory goes directly against the gospel of grace taught by the apostles. The Scriptures are clear, however, that once a person has put his or her trust in Christ he or she has been forgiven of all sin and has irrevocably passed from death to life (John 5:24; 6:37, 40; 10:27–29; Rom 8:1; 11:29; Col 2:13–14; Heb 10:14). Therefore, we must conclude that there is no scriptural basis for the doctrine of purgatory.

## 3. The Glorification of Believers

### What Will the Saints' Glorified Bodies Be Like?

The Scriptures are clear that unconscious non-existence is not the final condition of humankind. All human beings, whether believer or unbeliever, will be raised from the dead and their bodies and souls reunited one day (John 5:29; Acts 24:15). However, for believers, the resurrection will be a glorious event because they will receive new bodies that are completely free from the corruptions of sin. In fact, the glorification of the saints can be seen as the ultimate goal of God's work of human redemption (Rom 8:30). Although the Scriptures do not tell us in detail what these glorified bodies will look like or what they are capable of doing, the apostle Paul gives us a glimpse of what they will be like in 1 Corinthians 15:35–49. Based on what Paul wrote in the passage, three things will characterize the new bodies that believers will receive at the eschaton.

First, according to the passage, the new bodies that believers will receive will not be subject to disease, decay, and death ("imperishable," v. 42). It will be a body that will be raised in glory and power (v. 43). This means that everything that corrupted the physical and mental faculties of the present earthly body due to sin will be completely removed. Inherited disorders, diseases contracted in this life, and permanent injuries suffered on earth (like loss of a limb) will no longer be part of the believer's new body in the glorified state.

Second, the new body will be a "spiritual body" (v. 44). This does not mean that the new body will be immaterial or shadowy. Rather, what Paul means here is that the believer's glorified body will be thoroughly filled and governed by the Holy Spirit.[14] Believers will no longer be ruled by a sinful flesh but will be ruled by the Spirit instead. Their wills and faculties in the glorified state will perfectly conform to what honors and pleases God. In addition, glorified believers will be able to do greater physical activities (yes, work will still be part of the new creation) and enjoy God's creation in ways that are much more satisfying than when they were in their corrupt earthly bodies.

Last, there will still be some continuity between the old and new bodies of believers. Paul makes this evident when he uses the analogy of the bare kernel and wheat in verses 37–38. Paul even states elsewhere that Jesus "will transform our lowly body to be like his glorious body" (Phil 3:21; cf. Rom 8:11). We do not know exactly what processes God will use to resurrect the decayed corpse of a deceased believer, but Paul does state that the old earthly body will somehow play a role in the resurrection of the new spiritual body.[15] Also, another argument for the continuity between the old and new bodies of believers is that in the future kingdom believers who have known one another in this present life will recognize one another there (cf. Luke 9:30, 33). Even though the bodies of believers will be raised to glory, the believer's unique physical characteristics that he or she possessed in the present age will not be erased in the age to come.

## The Blessedness of Glorification

As discussed above, there are significant blessings associated with the believer's glorification at Christ's return. The hope of a new body that is free from sin and infirmity should encourage Christians to put their hope in the life to come rather than investing too much of their time and energy in the present world. The present world, even with all its splendor, will one day pass away (1 Cor 7:31), and nothing we have achieved in terms of worldly success will count in the kingdom (Matt 6:19–20). Even regrets for not being able to fulfill some personal goal in life should not matter in the grand scheme of things for those who hope in Christ. That is why believers who suffer from chronic illnesses should not be disheartened by their current situation. When Christ returns their broken bodies will be raised anew and they will be free from the sufferings that are associated with living with a sin-corrupted body. In fact, believers will become more fully human than

14. Kistemaker, 1 Corinthians, 575.
15. Bavinck, Reformed Dogmatics, 4:697–98.

they ever could imagine in the coming age. In the new heaven and earth everything will be set right and all things that are broken in this present created order will be completely removed (Rom 8:19–22). There will be no more crying or weeping (Rev 21:4) as believers will rejoice knowing that they will spend eternity with God in a glorified state with glorified bodies (Rev 21:1—22:1–5).

## The Resurrected Bodies of Unbelievers

As already discussed, the Scriptures clearly teach that unbelievers will also be raised from the dead. No one human being can escape the general resurrection because judgment must come to all (Dan 12:2; Acts 24:14–15; Heb 9:27; Rev 20:12–13). Unlike believers, however, the bodies of those outside of Christ will not be characterized by power and glory. Rather, the resurrected bodies of unbelievers will still retain the characteristics that are inherent in a body corrupted by sin. Although Scripture does not provide much information regarding the nature of the resurrected bodies of unbelievers, we can assume that it will not be of the same quality as the resurrected bodies of believers. Also, despite being qualitatively different from the bodies of glorified believers, the resurrected bodies of unbelievers will not be subject to physical decay and extinction. Unbelievers, like believers who are raised to glory, will also live forever in their new bodies. Their resurrection from the dead is necessitated by the fact that God requires righteous judgment for the unforgiven sins they have committed in this life (Rom 2:8–9; 2 Pet 3:7; Rev 21:8). Therefore, the resurrection of unbelievers will not be a blessed event but a dreadful time of God's righteous judgment for rejecting his gift of salvation.

# CHAPTER 19

# The Last Things, Part 2: General Eschatology

THE CHRISTIAN FAITH HAS always believed that a day will come when this present age will end and God renews all of creation by removing the effects of sin and abolishing death forever. This is set in direct contrast to the secular view of history where the world keeps continuing on until we annihilate ourselves or a catastrophic disaster puts an end to the human race. Without the belief in Christ's return to the earth, a final judgment, and the eschatological renewal of all things, the Christian religion would essentially be no different from the secular philosophies that stress only the importance of the present life (cf. 1 Cor 15:32). We can say, therefore, along with Gordon R. Lewis and Bruce A. Demarest, that the whole of theology according to Christian thought is "eschatological in orientation."[1]

In the final chapter of this book, we will discuss three topics that are traditionally the focus of discussion in Christian theological discourse regarding the end of history: Christ's second coming, the millennium, and the eternal states.

## 1. Christ's Second Coming

### The Nature of Christ's Return

The Scriptures are clear that Christ *will* return one day (cf. Matt 24:44; John 14:3; Acts 1:11; 1 Thess 4:16; Heb 9:28; Jas 5:8; 2 Pet 3:10; 1 John 3:2; Rev 1:7; 22:20). The expectation of Christ's second coming is something that

1. Lewis and Demarest, *Integrative Theology*, 3:369.

all orthodox Christians have held to since the earliest days of the church. In fact, the *parousia*[2] of Christ is one of the fundamental teachings of the church universal throughout its history. This is clearly attested to in one of the earliest ecumenical creeds of the faith: The Nicene Creed. In the creed, one of the lines read: "he [Christ] shall come again, with glory, to judge both the quick and the dead; whose kingdom shall have no end." All the other early ecumenical creeds (The Chalcedonian Creed, The Athanasian Creed, and The Apostles' Creed) concur that Christ's physical return is an event that will certainly happen one day in the future. Although Christians throughout history have disagreed on the exact details surrounding Christ's second coming, all of them agree that he will come back one day in glory and judgment.

In this section of the chapter, we will discuss the nature of Christ's return based on what is revealed in Scripture.

### Christ's Return Will Be Personal, Bodily, and Visible

The Scriptures clearly teach that Christ will return personally, physically, and visibly. For instance, in Acts 1:11, right after Christ ascends to heaven, two angels proclaim to the disciples: "This Jesus, who was taken up from you into heaven, will come in the same way as you saw him go into heaven." Undoubtedly, the disciples saw Jesus go up to heaven in a bodily and visible manner (Acts 1:9). Therefore, in the same way, Jesus will return visibly, and all will see him in full glory and power. Another verse that demonstrates to the visible and bodily return of Christ is Revelation 1:7. In the verse, John tells the seven churches: "Behold, he is coming with the clouds, and every eye will see him, even those who pierced him, and all tribes of the earth will wail on account of him." John unambiguously states that *every eye will see him*. The only way that human beings will visibly see Christ returning to earth is if his return is bodily. Other passages that confirm that Christ's return will be personal, physical, and visible include 1 Thessalonians 4:16 ("For the Lord himself will descend from heaven with a cry of command") and Hebrews 9:28 ("so Christ, having been offered once to bear the sins of many, will appear a second time, not to deal with sin but to save those who are eagerly waiting for him").

---

2. The word *parousia* is a Greek term that means "presence" or "arrival." In the Christian theological context it refers to the return of Christ.

In recent years, however, some biblical scholars have maintained that the Scripture's teaching on Christ's second coming is only referring to a metaphorical or spiritual coming. For example, the liberal theologian William Newton Clarke writes: "No visible return of Christ to the earth is to be expected, but rather the long and steady advance of his spiritual kingdom."[3] This view is not only espoused by liberal theologians who deny the divine origin of Scripture but also by those who purportedly have more conservative theological convictions (for example, those who hold to "realized eschatology"[4] or full preterism[5]). However, we must maintain that this spiritualized view of Christ's second coming is biblically unsupportable and contrary to the doctrinal beliefs of the early Christians. Aside from the biblical evidence discussed above, it is spiritually detrimental to argue that Christ's return is only metaphorical or spiritual and that the world will keep continuing on with no end in sight. The earliest Christians, on the other hand, expected Christ's physical return and the visible establishment of his kingdom to happen very soon.[6] In fact, that very expectation is one of the factors that energized the faith of the earliest Christians and gave them hope in the midst of tribulations (Acts 1:6; 2 Cor 4:16–18; 1 Thess 4:13–18; 2 Pet 3:11–13). Therefore, contrary to the views of some biblical scholars in modern times, the biblical understanding of Christ's return involves a personal, bodily, and visible coming.

3. Clarke, *Outline of Christian Theology*, 444; cf. also Tillich, *Systematic Theology*, 3:356–57; Robinson, *In the End, God . . .*, 80. Albert Schweitzer, on the other hand, argued that Jesus did believe that there would be an imminent establishment of God's kingdom during his lifetime. However, when he realized that this expectation would not be materially realized he gave up his life on the cross. This view has been typically called "consistent eschatology" by Christian theologians (cf. Schweitzer, *Quest of the Historical Jesus*, 368–69).

4. Dodd, *Apostolic Preaching and Its Developments*, 85.

5. The full preterist view, in contrast to the partial (or orthodox) preterist view, states that all the eschatological prophecies like the physical return of Christ, the resurrection of the dead, and the final judgment were all fulfilled in the first century and that we are now living in the new creation described in Revelation 21–22. Despite having a small but vociferous following within the visible Christian body, full preterism is a heretical doctrine that goes against the clear statements of several passages in Scripture (cf. John 5:28–29; 1 Cor 15:35–58; Titus 2:13; Rev 20:4–5, 11–15) and is, therefore, outside the scope of orthodox Christianity. For a detailed advocacy of this position, see Max R. King's lengthy work *The Cross and the Parousia of Christ*.

6. Allison, *Historical Theology*, 684.

*Christ's Return Cannot Be Predicted*

In recent times, there have been many individuals and groups proclaiming to know the exact date of Christ's second coming. For instance, the Jehovah's Witnesses claim that Christ's "second coming" occurred on October 1, 1914 in an "invisible" way (in fact, this is not really a "return" in the normal sense of the term, but Christ reigning from heaven starting on that date according to their eschatology).[7] Others, with more evangelical convictions, have written books purporting to know when the "secret rapture" or the parousia of Christ will occur.[8] However, all predictions of the timing of Christ's return have so far been wrong. This is not surprising considering that Jesus told his disciples that no human being knows the time of his return. For instance, in Matthew 25:13, after teaching his disciples about spiritual readiness through the Parable of the Ten Virgins, he tells them: "Watch therefore, for you know neither the day nor the hour." In another passage, in Luke 12:40, after providing them with an illustration of the importance of readiness, he declares to them: "You also must be ready, for the Son of Man is coming at an hour you do not expect." Finally, in Mark 13:32–33, the passage that clearly sets forth the truth that *only* the Father knows the time of the parousia, Jesus states: "But concerning that day or that hour, no one knows, not even the angels in heaven, nor the Son, but only the Father. Be on guard, keep awake. For you do not know when the time will come."

Based on these unambiguous statements by Jesus, it is obvious that anyone who claims to know the exact time of Christ's second coming is clearly going against what is revealed in Scripture. In fact, anyone who states that they know the time of the parousia is acting in disobedience to the obvious teachings of Christ and Scripture. Therefore, we must be careful that we do not set dates in reference to Christ's return since this knowledge only belongs to the Father. Scripture only calls Christians to remain vigilant in their faithfulness to Christ without knowing when the end will come.

---

7. Cf. Hoekema, *Four Major Cults*, 297–99.

8. For example, see Edgar C. Whisenant's book 88 *Reasons Why the Rapture Is in* 1988.

*Christ Will Return to Deliver His Saints and Destroy Those Who Oppose Him*

Another important point to underscore regarding the second coming is that Christ is not only coming to deliver his saints but also to destroy those who oppose him right before he establishes his kingdom on earth. Yes, there will be a holy war fought on the earth between the armies of Christ and the armies of the antichrist at the time of his return, as John mentions in Revelation 19:11–21. This will reveal to the world that the Christ who was crucified on a Roman cross is the same Christ who will rule the world unopposed (Luke 1:33; Heb 1:8). Also, his return will be characterized by great power and glory (Mark 13:26; also Matt 24:30; Luke 21:27) as he prepares to deliver his people and vanquish the earth.

Christ's victorious return, therefore, will demonstrate to the whole world that nothing can ultimately oppose the will of God and his reign over all of creation.

## Signs of Christ's Soon Return

We have mentioned above that the exact time of Christ's return cannot be known or predicted by any human being. However, Scripture does give us information regarding what events will take place in the world (i.e., the signs) just prior to Christ's second coming. In this section, we will discuss four major signs that are mentioned in Scripture that indicate that Christ's return is imminent.

### The Spread of the Gospel to All Parts of the World

One event that must be fulfilled before Christ returns is the promulgation of the gospel to all parts of the world. This is clearly taught by Jesus when he tells his disciples: "And this gospel of the kingdom will be proclaimed throughout the whole world as a testimony to all nations, and then the end will come" (Matt 24:14; cf. also Mark 13:10). Once the gospel is known throughout the world we know that Christ's return is going to happen very soon. With the rise of telecommunications technology and rapid modes of transportation in recent decades the fulfillment of this sign is now becoming an ever-present reality.

## The Great Tribulation of the World

Since the commencement of the church, there have always been perse-cutions, appearances of false christs, wars, earthquakes, and famines in various parts of the world (Matt 24:5–8). The whole world has always been groaning for redemption from the corruptions of sin (Rom 8:22), and be-lievers have always suffered under the hands of tyrants for their commit-ment to the gospel (cf. Phil 1:29; 2 Thess 1:4; 2 Tim 3:12). However, Jesus states that there will be a time of intense tribulation in the future that is unmatched in the history of the world. For instance, Jesus tells his disciples in Matthew 24:21: "For then there will be great tribulation, such as has not been from the beginning of the world until now, no, and never will be." In fact, so terrible is this period in world history that Jesus tells them that if "those days had not been cut short, no human being would be saved" (Matt 24:22). These distresses will begin when they see the "abomination of deso-lation" standing in the holy place (the temple in Jerusalem), as spoken of in Daniel 9:27 and 11:31. Immediately after the tribulation, there will be great cosmic signs: the sun will be darkened, the moon will not give its light, the stars will fall from heaven, and the powers of heaven will be shaken (Matt 24:29). After these cosmic disturbances, Christ will return and gather his elect from all four corners of the earth (Matt 24:30–31).

Some take Jesus' statements in the Olivet Discourse regarding the ter-rible things that will transpire in the future (Matt 24, Mark 13, and Luke 21) as referring to the great tribulation at the end of the present age.[9] Usually, interpreters embracing a dispensational eschatology hold this view. Others have argued that the tribulation that Jesus spoke of is an event that will occur in *his* near future at the time around the destruction of Jerusalem in AD 70.[10] However, we believe that both of these views are inadequate in and of themselves. Against the dispensationalist view, it is clear that in Matthew 24:15 Jesus is referring to the historical temple in Jerusalem owing to the context of the passage (for instance, his remark about the flight not taking place on the Sabbath, Matt 24:20).[11] However, it is equally strained to maintain that Jesus was restricting everything in the Olivet Discourse to

9. Barbieri, "Matthew," 76–79.

10. Gentry, "Great Tribulation Is Past," 33–66.

11. Also, in verse 34, Jesus tells his disciples: "Truly, I say to you, this generation will not pass away until all these things take place." The statement "this generation" suggests that Jesus is talking about the generation living when he spoke those words (cf. Carson, "Matthew," 507).

the events that would transpire during the time of Jerusalem's destruction in AD 70. The strict orthodox preterist interpretation of the entire passage does not do justice to Jesus' statement that his return will happen *immediately after* the tribulation (Matt 24:29–31).[12]

The most exegetically plausible position is that Jesus is telescoping the events that will happen in Judea in his very near future to the events that will happen right before the end of the present age. The persecution of believers (Matt 24:9) and the destruction of Jerusalem (Matt 24:1–2) in AD 70 are foreshadowings of the worldwide distress and tribulation that will occur right before his second coming. What the Jewish people during the time of the temple's destruction experienced was *a* great tribulation. However, right before Christ's return *the* great tribulation will occur all over the world with greater destruction and calamity. As J. Rodman Williams states, "What happened to an unbelieving Jerusalem in the first generation will happen manifoldly to an unbelieving world in the last generation."[13]

Therefore, one of the signs preceding Christ's return is a brief but intense period of persecution and hardship that will lead to immense devastation and sorrow on a global scale.[14]

### The Great Apostasy and the Appearance of the Man of Lawlessness

Another significant sign to look for right before Christ's second coming is the great apostasy and the appearance of the "man of lawlessness" (or the Antichrist). In 2 Thessalonians 2:1–12, Paul teaches that just prior to the return of Christ the man of lawlessness must appear on the world stage. The appearance of this global antichristian figure, however, will be preceded by a great apostasy (or falling away) never witnessed since the inception of the

12. Gentry understands Matthew 24:30, regarding Christ's coming in the clouds ("they will see the Son of Man coming on the clouds of heaven with power and great glory"), as referring to his ascension ("Great Tribulation Is Past," 60–61). However, this is the most unnatural way of reading the verse. The context suggests that Jesus is referring to his return. This interpretation is supported by the fact that his disciples asked him earlier: "Tell us, when will these things be, and what will be *the sign of your coming and of the end of the age?*" (Matt 24:3).

13. Williams, *Renewal Theology*, 3:364.

14. Dispensationalist scholars argue that the great tribulation (using the Jewish calendar) will be exactly seven years based on their interpretation of Daniel's seventy-weeks (Dan 9:24–27) (cf. Pentecost, "Daniel," 1361–65). However, it is wise not to come to firm conclusions regarding the exact time span of the great tribulation. All we know for certain is that this terrible period of world history will be of comparatively short duration.

church ("the rebellion" in verse 3). This will not be any ordinary denunciation of the Christian faith but a worldwide spiritual rebellion where all the forces of evil will work together to oppose anything that have to do with God or Christ. The occurrence of the definite article before the word "rebellion" suggests that Paul had a unique event in mind. Therefore, one sign to look for is a great apostasy throughout the world where the disobedient give open allegiance to Satan and begin actively opposing God and Christ.

After the great apostasy, Paul states that the man of lawlessness (or the Antichrist) will appear on the world scene.[15] That there is some type of connection between the apostasy and the appearance of this antichristian figure is demonstrated by the fact that Paul connects the two events with an "and" (Gk. *kai*) in verse 3.[16] In fact, it is likely that this individual will come out of this great apostasy.[17] Although many antichrists have appeared throughout the church's history (1 John 2:18, 22), there will come a climactic Antichrist who will be the culmination of all the previous antichrists who have emerged.

In 2 Thessalonians 2:1–12, Paul does provide some information of what this diabolical figure will be like and the circumstances of his appearing. First, this individual will oppose all rivals and exalt himself "against every so-called god or object of worship," and will even proclaim that he is God himself (v. 4). Second, even though there will be a time when it is necessary to reveal him so that he will carry out his worldwide reign of terror, he is currently restrained[18] according to God's sovereign will (vv. 6–7).

15. Some have argued that the number 666 in Revelation 13:18 is the number of Emperor Nero, the first-century emperor known for his brutality and the terrible ways he persecuted Christians. Therefore, the antichrist (i.e., the Beast) that John is describing in Revelation 13 is not an end-time figure but the historical emperor. Those who argue for this identification state that when Nero's name ("Neron Caesar") is calculated according to the Hebrew alphabet (*gematria*) its value turns out to be 666. However, we should be cautious of employing this method too readily to determine who John was trying to point at for his readers. Also, even if John was talking about Nero in the passage this does not necessarily preclude the appearance of a future antichrist figure just prior to Christ's return. It is possible that John used Nero as *a type* of the future antichrist figure whose reign will be much more diabolical than all the tyrannical Roman emperors combined (cf. Hamilton, *Revelation*, 275; Schnabel, 40 *Questions About the End Times*, 178–79).

16. Hoekema, *Bible and the Future*, 154.

17. Hoekema, *Bible and the Future*, 154.

18. There have been various interpretations throughout the history of the church regarding who or what the "restrainer" is in verses 6–7. Some have argued that it is the Roman Empire during Paul's time. Others have suggested it is the church and its spiritual influence over the world. Still others have concluded that it is the Holy Spirit. However,

Third, his appearance is by the activity of Satan and will be accompanied by false signs and wonders (v. 9). Last, his appearance will lead many astray because they refused to love the truth and had pleasure in unrighteousness (vv. 10, 12). Regardless of his power and might, Paul declares that shortly after his appearance Christ will return and destroy this diabolical man and end his satanic reign (v. 8).

Therefore, another significant sign to look for is the appearance of the man of lawlessness (or the Antichrist).

### The Salvation of Corporate Israel

In chapter 16 on the church, we discussed briefly how just prior to Christ's second coming there will be a large-scale conversion of Jews to the Christian faith as they receive Christ as their Messiah and Savior. That this is one of the signs of Christ's soon return is demonstrated by the fact that Paul states in Romans 11:26b that "The Deliverer will come from Zion, he will banish ungodliness from Jacob" (quoted from Isa 59:20). The fact that Paul states that the Deliverer (Christ) will "come from Zion" (from the heavenly realm) to banish all ungodliness from the elect Jews demonstrates that this great event will happen just before Christ's return.

Therefore, another sign that believers should look for is a large-scale turning to Christ by the Jewish people.

## How Do the Signs that Precede Christ's Return Harmonize with the Biblical Statements that the Parousia is an Unexpected Event?

One of the more difficult exegetical problems to wrestle with when it comes to Christian eschatology is the apparent incongruity between Scripture's teaching that certain signs must precede Christ's second coming and the biblical passages that declare that the Parousia is an unexpected event (Jas 5:8; 2 Pet 3:10). If Christ's return is unexpected, how is it possible to consistently claim that there will be certain signs manifested in the world that indicate that his return is very soon?

One attempt to harmonize this apparent inconsistency is by arguing that Christ will come in two stages: the first one for believers who will be

---

it is best to leave the identity of the restrainer a mystery. All we can surmise from Paul's statement is that one day this restrainer will be removed, which will then allow the antichrist to have free reign over the world.

taken up before the great tribulation (the "secret rapture"); the second one when Christ comes down to defeat his enemies and establish his millennial kingdom on earth. By separating the parousia of Christ into two stages (the first for the rapture of the church and the second for Christ's visible return), one seemingly is now able to uphold the biblical exhortations to constant watchfulness without contradicting the passages that state that certain signs must come to pass before Christ's second coming.[19] The problem with this view is that there is no scriptural warrant, as we will discuss in more detail below, for the idea that there are two separate comings of Christ—one secret and another visible. All attempts to argue for a secret rapture before the great tribulation are by conjecture and not based on solid biblical evidence.

Another approach to resolve this dilemma is by arguing that all the signs mentioned above have been fulfilled in the first century. Therefore, we no longer need to look for these signs and Christ will return at any moment without warning.[20] However, the problem with this view is that it does not agree with Paul's teaching that the destruction of the antichrist (2 Thess 2:8) will occur at Christ's return and the salvation of corporate Israel (Rom 11:26–27) will happen just prior to it.

Finally, an approach offered by some scholars to resolve this apparent inconsistency is by viewing the tribulation as having begun at the ascension of Christ but growing in intensity and reaching a final climax just prior to Christ's return. In one sense then the "last days" began with Christ's ascension, but in another sense the "last days" are still ahead just before the second coming of Christ (thus, we can argue that there is an "already/not yet" tension built into Scripture in terms of its eschatological chronology). This last stage of the tribulation will be short-lived but it will be the most intense and calamitous. It will be accompanied by great physical and spiritual disturbances on the earth, the appearance of the final antichrist, and the salvation of the great majority of the Jews. However, even when these signs appear, Christ's return will still be an unexpected event because no one knows the exact time the final stage of the tribulation will end.[21] As Thomas R. Schreiner puts it, "On the one hand . . . the timing of Jesus' return is unknown; on the other hand, other sayings suggest that certain signs precede

19. Thiessen, *Lectures in Systematic Theology*, 376–77.

20. Cf. France, *Matthew*, 333–52.

21. The fact that the parousia will be an unexpected event does not mean that Christ will suddenly return "out of the blue," but rather that no human being knows exactly when Christ will come back despite the signs of his soon return (as rightly argued by Douglas J. Moo in his "The Case for the Posttribulation Rapture Position," 207–11).

his coming that forecast his near appearance. Just as the leaves of the fig tree sprout when the fruit is about to appear, so too certain signs will precede Jesus' coming (Matt. 24:32–33 par.)."[22] We believe that this last position most adequately reconciles the apparent incongruity that exists between the passages that state that certain signs must precede Christ's return and the passages that state that his return is an unexpected event.

## 2. The Millennium

In Christian eschatological thought there are three conventional views on how Revelation 20:1–10 and the millennium should be interpreted. These three views are *amillennialism, postmillennialism,* and *premillennialism.* Even though most Christians throughout the centuries agree that the three millennial positions all fall within the scope of orthodox Christianity, there are still animated debates today over which view of the millennium is most consistent with the teachings of Scripture.

In this section of the chapter, we will discuss the three historic millennial positions as expressed in classic Christian eschatology. After providing a summary of each of the three millennial views, we will, then, discuss which view best accords with the evidence of Scripture.

### The Three Historic Millennial Views

#### Amillennialism

*Amillennialism* is the view that there is no literal millennial reign of Christ on earth. Out of the three millennial views this is the least complicated and easiest to comprehend. According to amillennialism, the present age will end with Christ's return, which will then be followed by a general resurrection and judgment of both believers and unbelievers. Immediately after the judgment, the eternal state will follow where believers will enter into the new heaven and earth, while unbelievers will be cast into the lake of fire. Furthermore, amillennialism holds that through Christ's victory at the cross Satan was dealt a decisive blow and his ability to deceive the nations greatly curtailed in the present age (cf. Matt 12:28–29; Luke 10:18; Rev 12:7–17). This restriction began at the binding of Satan mentioned in

---

22. Schreiner, *New Testament Theology,* 812.

Revelation 20:1–3.[23] Despite the restrictions placed on Satan during the present age, amillennialists also view the present time not as a period of churchly triumph but as a period of suffering and persecution. (If there is victory for God's people during the present age it is only in a *spiritual* manner.[24]) Therefore, total victory, according to amillennialism, will happen only when Christ returns to destroy all things that oppose God (1 Cor 15:23–28) and when he establishes his eternal kingdom (Rev 21–22).

In regards to how amillennialists interpret Revelation 20:1–10, they generally read the passage as a "recapitulation" of Revelation 19:11–21.[25] In other words, John is talking about the same event but describing it in two different ways. Also, the mention of a "thousand years" in Revelation 20 is not to be understood literally but symbolically (as the time between Christ's ascension and his return) since the entire book of Revelation contains much symbolism, according to the amillennialist hermeneutic.[26] Finally, and more significantly, amillennialists interpret the "first resurrection" mentioned in Revelation 20:5–6 as a *spiritual* rather than a physical resurrection. Therefore, what John is describing in that passage is not the bodily resurrection of the saints at Christ's second coming but rather the believer's new birth at conversion[27] or his or her soul's entrance into heaven at death.[28] During the meantime, those believers who have died will rule *in heaven* before Christ returns to earth and ends the present age.

One of the notable characteristics of the amillennial position is its simplicity in regards to understanding biblical eschatology. The main strength of the view, therefore, is its straightforward interpretation of how eschatological events will unfold: with one general resurrection, one final judgment of all, and the arrival of the eternal state. Also, it has been the majority view in the broader church since the time of Augustine, which makes its long history an attractive option for many.

23. Hoekema, *Bible and the Future*, 228–29; cf. also Strimple, "Amillennialism," 121–24.

24. Frame, *Salvation Belongs to the Lord*, 302.

25. Bavinck, *Reformed Dogmatics*, 4:682–84.

26. Morris, *Revelation*, 227.

27. Cottrell, *Faith Once For All*, 501.

28. Kistemaker, *Revelation*, 540; Hoekema, *Bible and the Future*, 233; Strimple, "Amillennialism," 127.

## Postmillennialism

Another view of the millennium held by a significant number of Christians throughout the history of the church (especially in the last few hundred years) is *postmillennialism*. According to postmillennialism, the thousand year reign of Christ started when the gospel started to spread out from Judea to the nations. As the nations of the world gradually turn to Christ and people are transformed by the Holy Spirit, this reign of Christ becomes increasingly realized on earth in the present. Hence, the reason why this view is called *post*millennialism (i.e., Christ's second coming happens *after* the millennial reign of Christ). As Loraine Boettner puts it:

> Postmillennialism is that view of the last things which holds that the kingdom of God is now being extended in the world through the preaching of the gospel and the saving work of the Holy Spirit in the hearts of individuals, that the world eventually is to be Christianized and that the return of Christ is to occur at the close of a long period of righteousness and peace commonly called the millennium.[29]

Postmillennialists will often point to Jesus' Great Commission to defend their particular view. For instance, they argue that in Matthew 28:19–20, Jesus tells his disciples to go and "make disciples of all nations" and to teach "them to observe all that I have commanded you." This commissioning is not merely for evangelistic purposes but to bring everything in the world under Christ's sovereign dominion. As the postmillennialist Kenneth L. Gentry states, "The Great Commission is world-encompassing. The ascended Christ mandates an expanded church. Would he assert his sovereign lordship so vigorously and command his disciples so majestically were it not his intention that they fulfill his obligation?"[30]

Postmillennialists agree with amillennialists that the term "the thousand years" in Revelation 20 is a symbolic reference to the present age. They also agree with the amillennialists that the binding of Satan happened during Jesus' earthly ministry, and that the "first resurrection" in Revelation 20:5–6 refers to a spiritual or non-bodily resurrection.[31] However, the

---

29. Boettner, "Postmillennialism," 117.

30. Gentry, "Postmillennialism," 46.

31. Gentry believes that the "first resurrection" refers to the regeneration of the soul and that believers *who are still alive* are reigning with Christ in the present ("Postmillennialism," 53–55). However, this interpretation is strained considering the context and what is being described in Revelation 20. If Revelation 20:4 is describing the reign of

similarities between both stop there. Postmillennialists are more optimistic in their outlook regarding the church's gradual influence over the world and the triumph of God's ethical principles over and against non-Christian claims.[32] Also, another significant difference between the two views is that postmillennialism asserts that Christ will return once the world has been thoroughly, but not totally, "Christianized." Amillennialism, on the other hand, maintains that the present age will always be characterized by both righteousness and wickedness, with both being in a constant struggle against one another until the end. Therefore, the postmillennial view, in contrast to the amillennial perspective, holds that God's progressive but certain subjugation of the world will happen through the church and the spread of the gospel.

The appeal of the postmillennial position is its optimistic outlook. If Christ has won a decisive victory over Satan at the cross, why should Christians be pessimistic about the influence of God's kingdom in all spheres of life? Also, another attractive aspect of the postmillennial position is that it takes God's sovereign rulership over creation seriously. Since God is the ultimate ruler of the universe it is difficult to construe how he can fail to reach his objective for the whole world even through earthly means.

## Premillennialism

Finally, the other major millennial view prevalent among contemporary evangelical Christians is *premillennialism*. According to this position, the millennial kingdom comes *after* the second coming of Christ (hence, the *pre* before *millennial*). Those who hold to this view argue that the millennial kingdom is a literal thousand-year reign of Christ that will happen after this age ends. Once Christ has defeated his enemies and established his throne at his return, he will visibly rule the world and institute absolute justice, righteousness, and peace among the nations (Ps 72:8–14; Zech 14:16–17). The earth will no longer be characterized by the curse of Genesis 3:17–19 and wild animals will live in harmony amongst themselves (Isa 11:6–9). Also, human lifespan will increase tremendously and people will be in much better physical condition than presently (Isa 65:20). Although

---

*living* believers in the present, how does this correspond with what John says about the beheaded martyrs just prior to that? The passage indicates that the reign happens *after* believers are resurrected from the dead and are seated on thrones.

32. Cf. Boettner, "Postmillennialism," 125–33.

there will be unbelievers living in the millennial kingdom with non-glorified bodies (cf. Rev 20:9), suffering and hardship in general will be greatly reduced due to the much-improved conditions.

Premillennialists maintain that the best evidence for a future thousand year kingdom is Revelation 20. Unlike the amillennial and postmillennial interpretations of Revelation 20, premillennialists argue that the most appropriate and natural way to read Revelation 20 is by understanding it as a literal description of what will happen after Christ's return. They understand the binding and confinement of Satan in the bottomless pit as a literal occurrence in the future, and usually take the phrase "the thousand years" to mean actual thousand calendar years.[33] More significantly, premillennialists argue that the best case for a future interim kingdom is John's mentioning of two types of *bodily* resurrections separated by a thousand years in Revelation 20:4–5.[34] They argue that the first resurrection is a bodily resurrection of all saints at Christ's second coming, while the second resurrection is a bodily resurrection of all unbelievers for judgment after the end of Christ's millennial reign. For instance, the premillennialist Walter C. Kaiser states regarding the passage: "We conclude . . . that the 'thousand years' spoken of here come *after* the second coming of Christ. And both resurrections are physical, serving as boundaries to the thousand years."[35] Therefore, the key to the premillennialist interpretation of Revelation 20 is not the statement "the thousand years" but John's mentioning of the two *physical* resurrections separated by a thousand year period.

Since the end of the nineteenth century, a subset of the premillennial position arose within evangelical circles called *dispensational premillennialism*. Dispensational premillennialism agrees with non-dispensational premillennialism in understanding the millennium of Revelation 20 as a literal thousand-year kingdom on earth after this present age. However, dispensational premillennialism diverges from the non-dispensational premillennial view by maintaining that the Old Testament promises to Israel will be literally fulfilled in the millennial kingdom (with a rebuilt temple, the restoration of the Jewish kingdom in Palestine, etc.) (cf. Ezek 37:21–28; Zech 10:6–12). Also, dispensational premillennialism differs with non-dispensational premillennialism by insisting that the church

---

33. However, some premillennialists interpret the phrase as a symbol for a long period of time.

34. Ladd, "Historic Premillennialism," 35–38.

35. Kaiser, *Promise-Plan of God*, 387.

will be raptured right before the great tribulation (the pretribulational rapture).[36] Dispensational premillennialists maintain that a pretribulational rapture is necessary to signify that God's redemptive program for the church has ended so that he can resume his kingdom program for Israel (Rom 11:11–32).[37] Regardless of the differences between dispensational premillennialism and non-dispensational premillennialism, both maintain that Christ will literally reign on earth for a lengthy period of time before the arrival of the eternal state.

One of the strengths of the premillennial position is its antiquity. This was the prevailing view among the early church fathers before the fourth century. Mention of a future millennial kingdom can be found in the writings of Papias, Justin Martyr, Irenaeus, Tertullian, Hippolytus, Methodius,

---

36. However, this is not to say that all dispensationalists hold to a pretribulational rapture. For example, Robert H. Gundry holds to a dispensational posttribulational position. See his *The Church and the Tribulation*.

37. Thiessen, *Lectures in Systematic Theology*, 374. Dispensationalists often refer to Revelation 3:10 to argue that Christ will deliver the church from the great tribulation through a secret rapture. The verse reads: "Because you have kept my word about patient endurance, I will keep you from the hour of trial that is coming on the whole world, to try those who dwell on the earth." Robert L. Thomas, for example, argues that the statement "I will keep you from the hour of trial" means that Christ will remove believers from the earth before the great tribulation because they have remained faithful to him. Thomas makes much of the fact that the Greek word *ek* ("out of") is used with the verb *tērēsō* ("I will keep") rather than *en* ("in") or *dia* ("through") when Christ promises believers protection from the coming tribulation (cf. John 17:15). Therefore, for Thomas, believers in the church age are spared from experiencing the horrors of the great tribulation not because Christ protects them *through it* but because he *takes them out of the earth* before it begins (cf. *Revelation 1–7*, 284–88). However, it is also possible to read the verse as saying that Christ protects believers while they are *in* the great tribulation. The fact that the word *ek* is used does not conclusively demonstrate that Christ meant that he will take believers "out of" the trials that will come upon the earth during that time (as Moo points out in his "The Case for the Posttribulation Rapture Position," 198). Also, it is difficult to exegetically demonstrate from other parts of Scripture that Christ's return will happen in two stages, as discussed earlier. In fact, Scripture closely links the taking up of the elect with the parousia of Christ at the end of the age (Matt 24:31; 1 Thess 4:16–17; 1 Cor 15:51–52). Furthermore, the pretribulational rapture view presupposes that there are two separate purposes in God's overall redemptive-historical plan—one for Israel and another for the church (as discussed in chapter 16). However, considering that Scripture presents God's salvific plan as being consistent throughout the various epochs of redemptive history, this view fails to do justice to the legitimate continuities that exist between Israel and the church. Finally, the Scriptures do not promise that believers will always be protected *from* whatever trials that may come their way (cf. John 16:33; Rom 5:3; 8:17; 1 Thess 3:3; 1 Pet 2:20–21; 4:12–19; Rev 2:10), which also includes the great tribulation to come.

and Lactantius.[38] Another strength of the premillennial position is its straightforward interpretation of Revelation 20:1–10: After the end of this present age, there will be a literal binding of Satan at the start of the millennium (v. 1–3), a literal resurrection of believers and their millennial reign (vv. 4–6), a literal release of Satan from the pit after the millennium (v. 7), a literal worldwide rebellion led by Satan (vv. 8–9), and a literal destruction of the satanic forces that encamp against God's people along with the final judgment of Satan (vv. 9–10). In other words, it does not need to resort to creative interpretive moves to make the passage apply to a period other than the one after Christ's return. Therefore, the average Christian can understand the premillennial interpretation of Revelation 20 without much difficulty. Finally, a premillennial interpretation of Revelation 20 best accords with some passages in the Old Testament that mention of a future period where the entire earth will be characterized by peace, prosperity, and abundance (cf. Ps 72:8–14; Isa 11:6–9; 65:20; Zech 14:5–17), while falling short of the sinlessness that characterizes the new earth (Rev 21:1–22:5).

## Which Millennial View Best Corresponds with the Witness of Scripture?

Before we attempt to determine which millennial view best agrees with what is revealed in Scripture, we must say from the outset that the subject of the millennium is not one that should divide Christians. Christians who hold to different millennial positions may fellowship together, hold conferences together, and work together to spread the gospel and promote societal good. The discussion about the millennium, therefore, should not be a matter of establishing who is to be judged orthodox or heterodox. Nonetheless, the subject is important enough to warrant a discussion in this work, and we should not set this subject aside casually because we believe everything will "pan out" in the end. The importance of this subject matter, therefore, deals with how we should view God's word on these issues and how we should go about interpreting biblical prophecy responsibly.

The first view surveyed was amillennialism. We mentioned that the strength of the amillennial position is its simplicity in interpreting biblical prophecy. However, the amillennial argument that the "first resurrection" spoken of in Revelation 20:4–6 is a reference to a spiritual (or non-bodily) resurrection is quite strained and difficult to support exegetically.

38. Clouse, "Millennium, Views of the," 716.

In regards to the second view surveyed, postmillennialism, we noted that its optimistic approach to God's work of worldwide redemption through the church is one of its appealing features. However, with the occurrence of the two World Wars in the twentieth century, genocidal campaigns still occurring in parts of the world today, the rapid moral decline of our modern societies, and the increase in hostility towards the Christian faith in the last hundred years or so it is very difficult to maintain that the postmillennial position is a biblically viable option. In fact, Jesus declared in Matthew 24:12 that right before his second coming there will be an increase in lawlessness and love will wane in many people. This hardly fits with a postmillennial hope.

The final view we surveyed was premillennialism. We mentioned that the strength of this position is that it reads Revelation 20 in a straightforward manner. Also, the premillennial interpretation escapes the difficulty of having to interpret the two resurrections in Revelation 20:4–5 as two different types of resurrections. Finally, the premillennial interpretation best fits with the Old Testament hope of a coming period of great peace and blessedness, while not corresponding exactly with the sinless condition of the new earth. However, one criticism that can be leveled against the premillennial position is that only once in Scripture is a millennial reign of Christ explicitly mentioned.

Despite the fact that all three views have their strengths and weaknesses, we believe that the non-dispensational premillennial view fits the language and pattern of Scripture most faithfully.

First, as mentioned above, the premillennial position does not face any exegetical difficulties compared to the amillennial and postmillennial views when it comes to interpreting the two resurrections in Revelation 20:4–5. The premillennial position rightly interprets both resurrections as bodily resurrections separated by a thousand years. This is demonstrated by the fact that the Greek verb *ezēsan* (from *zaō* ["live"]) is used for both the coming to life of the saints ("they came to life," v. 4) at the beginning of the millennium and the raising of the unbelievers to judgment after the end of the millennium ("the rest of the dead," v. 5).[39] This verb is also found

39. Craig A. Blaising also aptly points out a significant problem if both resurrections are interpreted as two different types of resurrections. Blaising writes: "Premillennialists have always argued that 'came to life' must mean the same thing in 20:5 as it does in 20:4. Typical amillennial and postmillennial interpretations usually try to acknowledge this point but face a problem with the universal extent of the phrase 'rest of the dead' and the implication that they too will come to life when the thousand years are ended.

in John 11:25; Acts 1:3; and 9:41, and the context of those verses reveal that a bodily resurrection is in view.[40] In addition, *zaō* is used in Revelation 1:18 and 2:8 in reference to the resurrection of Christ and, interestingly enough, for the resurrection of the sea beast in 13:14.[41] Furthermore, the statement "the first resurrection" in Revelation 20:5–6 is a translation of the Greek phrase *anastasis prōtē*. The word *anastasis* is found over forty times in the New Testament and is used almost exclusively to mean a physical resurrection.[42]

Second, the premillennial position avoids the chronological difficulties faced by the amillennial and postmillennial positions regarding the different times when the beast and the false prophet are condemned to the lake of fire (Rev 19:20) and when Satan joins them there later (Rev 20:10). That there is a chronological gap between the two events—by a thousand years—is demonstrated by John's statement in Revelation 20:10 that Satan is "thrown into the lake of fire and sulfur *where the beast and the false prophet are*" (HCSB).[43]

Lastly, the premillennial understanding that the binding of Satan will happen *after* Christ's return (Rev 20:1–3) makes the most sense in light of other passages in Scripture that depict Satan as being quite active during the present age. For example, Paul writes that "the god of this world [Satan] has blinded the minds of the unbelievers, to keep them from seeing the light of the gospel of the glory of Christ, who is the image of God" (2 Cor 4:4). Also, Peter warns his readers: "Your adversary the devil prowls around like a roaring lion, seeking someone to devour" (1 Pet 5:8). Furthermore, John tells his readers that the "whole world lies in the power of the evil one" (1 John 5:19). Even though Satan's power was greatly curtailed during Jesus'

---

Obviously, if 'came to life' means to have or begin to have *spiritual life*, then 'the rest of the dead' (whether physically or spiritually) will all receive *spiritual life* at the end of the Millennium, whatever the Millennium is taken to mean. Since 'the rest' appears to be comprehensive (few debate this comprehensiveness), then universalism would be the result!" ("Premillennialism," 225).

40. Thomas, *Revelation 8–22*, 417.

41. Ladd, "Historic Premillennialism," 37.

42. Johnson, "Revelation," 584.

43. Some amillennialists, to avoid this chronological difficulty with their position, argue that Revelation 19 and 20 refer to the same battle (cf. Beale, *Book of Revelation*, 976). However, the recapitulation between chapters 19 and 20 is difficult to sustain considering that the descriptions of both battles (19:17–21; 20:7–10) are very different. Also, John introduces the beginning of chapter 20 with the conjunction *kai* ("then" in the ESV, HCSB, and NASB), which indicates that he was about to describe a new sequence of events.

earthly ministry (Matt 12:28–29; Luke 10:18), this is not the same as his binding at the start of the millennium where he will be unable to influence the world to any degree or extent.

Therefore, after taking everything into account, we believe that the non-dispensational premillennial position best accords with the witness of Scripture.[44]

## 3. The Eternal States

Christians who believe that Scripture is God's infallible and authoritative word have always believed that there will come a day when all human beings will be judged by God to determine where they will spend eternity. They have also believed that there are only two eternal destinies for every human being: either in the renewed creation to enjoy God's blessed presence forever *or* in hell to experience his eternal wrath. Theologians have traditionally called these the eternal states.

In the final section of this chapter, we will discuss the subject of the eternal states which concerns the respective final destinies of unbelievers and believers. The first part of the discussion will deal with issues that concern the doctrine of eternal punishment (hell); the second part of the discussion will involve issues pertaining to the believer's everlasting rest in the new heaven and earth.

### The Eternal Destiny of Unbelievers: Hell

Whenever the topic of hell comes up in any theological conversation Christians must tread along carefully and soberly. That there will be countless numbers of people who will spend eternity separated from God and who

---

44. Some have argued that the difficulty with the non-dispensational (posttribulational) premillennial view is that it cannot explain how unbelievers with non-glorified bodies can exist in the millennial kingdom (Rev 20:8–9). In other words, if all unbelievers will be physically destroyed at the final battle (Rev 19:18–21) and all believers will be glorified when Christ returns (1 Cor 15:51–53), how is it possible for the millennial kingdom to be populated by unbelievers who have non-glorified bodies? However, nothing in Revelation 19:18–21 suggests that *all* unbelievers will be destroyed at Christ's second coming. The passage says that *only* those who joined the beast's army to wage war against Christ will be destroyed. Those unbelievers who did not join the great battle will be allowed to enter the millennial kingdom as long as they submit to Christ's reign (cf. Ladd, *Commentary on the Revelation of John*, 262–63).

will experience his everlasting wrath in hell is not a subject to be taken lightly. In fact, one of the reasons why Christians should take up Christ's Great Commission to the world with utmost fervency is so that unbelievers can hear the gospel, repent, and avoid ending up in this terrible place called hell. At the same time, however, it is imperative that believers tell unbelievers that hell is a real place because God must judge those whose sins have not been covered by the sacrifice of Jesus Christ. Therefore, one of the key components of evangelism is warning unbelievers about God's righteous judgment and the eternal punishment that awaits those who refuse to repent of their sins and trust in Christ for eternal life.

*The Nature of Hell*

The Scriptures are clear that hell is an unimaginable place of horror and anguish. In the New Testament, the term for hell is *Gehenna*. It may be a reference to the Valley of Hinnom, just south of Jerusalem, where garbage and dead bodies were thrown in and burnt (Jer 31:40; Isa 66:24). During the Old Testament period, the place became notorious because children were offered up to the pagan god Moloch by fire there (2 Kgs 16:3; 21:6; 23:10). Later on, the valley became a symbol of the eternal judgment to come on all the impenitent.[45] Some of the imagery used by Jesus to describe this awful place include: "the fiery furnace" (Matt 13:42, 50), "the unquenchable fire" (Mark 9:43), "the outer darkness" (Matt 22:13; 25:30), a place of "weeping and gnashing of teeth" (Matt 24:51), and an abode "prepared for the devil and his angels" (Matt 25:41). The reason why these dreadful imageries were used by Jesus to describe hell is because it is a place where all that is dark and diabolical are contained in one place. It is a place where no relief will be found for those who have chosen to remain in sin and darkness (Rev 22:15). It is also interesting to point out that Jesus spoke more about hell than any of the individual writers of the New Testament. In fact, one of the purposes of Christ's evangelistic work was to call sinners to repentance so that they will avoid being cast into hell at the last judgment (cf. Matt 10:28; Mark 9:43; Luke 16:19–31). The way Jesus and the biblical writers spoke about hell indicates that it is a place of conscious torment, despair, and loneliness.

Another aspect of hell that needs to be pointed out is that it is a place where God punishes the *whole* person. Hell is not a place where only the

45. Lightner, "Hell," 506.

387

spiritual aspect of the human being suffers but where the body also experiences affliction (cf. Matt 5:29–30; 10:28; Mark 9:43–47). One of the reasons why unbelievers are resurrected at the last judgment is so that their punishment in hell will be complete (John 5:28–29; Rev 20:11–15). God's righteous judgment requires that the entire person experiences his wrath. However, it is wise that we do not come to firm conclusions regarding the nature of the sufferings that the impenitent will have to endure. Some Christians have argued that the descriptions of hell should be taken literally and that the lost will be tormented in literal flames for eternity.[46] Although the descriptions of hell given by Jesus are graphic and terrifying, it is best to take these imageries as only metaphors of the horrible punishment that awaits the ungodly (how can fire and darkness coexist in the same place?). As Charles Hodge comments:

> There seems to be no more reason for supposing that the fire spoken of in Scripture is to be literal fire, than that the worm that never dies is literally a worm. The devil and his angels who are to suffer the vengeance of eternal fire, and whose doom the finally impenitent are to share, have no material bodies to be acted upon by elemental fire.[47]

This, however, does not mean that the non-literal view diminishes the terrible nature of the afflictions endured in hell by the ungodly, but only that Christians should be careful that they do not come up with fanciful descriptions of hell that go beyond what the Scriptures say.[48]

### Degrees of Punishment in Hell

Scripture teaches that not all the impenitent will suffer the same degree of punishment in hell. This is clearly taught by Jesus in Luke 12:47–48 when he tells his disciples: "And that servant who knew his master's will but did

---

46. Walvoord, "Literal View," 28.

47. Hodge, *Systematic Theology*, 3:868.

48. Furthermore, hell is not a place where the unrepentant are only in emotional agony because they will miss out on the blessings of heaven but also a place where they are actively punished. The torments of hell not only include being excluded from God's presence and his heavenly blessings but also the receiving of the positive afflictions for the sins not atoned for (2 Thess 1:8–9; Heb 10:26–31; Jude 7; Rev 21:8). Therefore, it is wrong to conclude that hell is merely a place of eternal regret. The imageries provided by Scripture describing hell go beyond a place of mere remorse and disappointment.

not get ready or act according to his will, will receive a severe beating. But the one who did not know, and did what deserved a beating, will receive a light beating." Jesus indicates here that in hell some will receive more punishment ("will receive a severe beating") than others depending upon how much exposure to God's saving truth they have received. Also, in Matthew 11:24, in his denunciation of the impenitent cities, he declares: "But I tell you that it will be more tolerable on the day of judgment for the land of Sodom than for you." Jesus is saying that those cities that did not receive his light will be punished less severely than those cities that knew about him but rejected him. Furthermore, Jesus states that the scribes will "receive the greater condemnation" (Mark 12:38–40; Luke 20:46–47) for their religious hypocrisy. Hypocrisy, according to Jesus, is a sin that deserves weightier punishment because it can cause others to stumble and bring disrepute to the truth.

The different degrees of punishment in hell is also necessitated by the fact that God is a perfectly just judge. God will judge unbelievers according to how they have lived and this will determine the degree of punishment they will receive in hell. Thus, an unbeliever who has not lived a remarkably wicked life will not receive the same degree of punishment compared to someone who has murdered millions of people in a genocidal campaign. As Millard J. Erickson puts it, the "different degrees of punishment reflect the fact that hell is God's leaving a sinful human with the particular character that the person fashioned for himself or herself in this life."[49] Therefore, based on the witness of Scripture and the nature of God's justice, the punishments suffered in hell will not be of the same degree for everyone consigned there.

## The Duration of Hell

Throughout the church's history, the vast majority of Christians have believed that hell is a place of punishment that will last for *eternity*.[50] This has been the majority opinion since the days of the early church to the post-Reformation period. In the modern period, however, the eternal nature of hell (and even hell itself) has been questioned by many who profess to be Christians. Some, especially those within more liberal theological circles, have argued that hell will be emptied, and that one day all human

49. Erickson, *Christian Theology*, 1248.
50. Cf. Allison, *Historical Theology*, 703–13.

beings will receive God's redemptive grace (*apokatastasis*).[51] However, this has been a very minor position within the broader Christian tradition, and a view for which it is very difficult to find support in Scripture (cf. Matt 25:31–46; John 3:16–18; 5:29; Rom 2:6–11; 2 Thess 1:9; Heb 10:26–27; 2 Pet 3:7; Rev 20:14–15; 21:8; 22:15).

In more recent years, some evangelical theologians have argued that hell will not be of eternal duration. Rather, they argue, unbelievers will simply cease to exist after the final judgment as a consequence of not having received eternal life. This view is typically called *conditional immortality.*[52] Those who advocate the conditional immortality view often maintain that hell cannot be of eternal duration because the final state of the unbeliever is often described in Scripture as his or her destruction (Matt 10:28; 1 Cor 3:17; Phil 1:28; 3:19; 2 Thess 1:9; Jas 4:12; 2 Pet 2:6, 12). They assert that the language of destruction used by the biblical writers is not compatible with the idea that unbelievers will suffer in hell consciously and eternally.[53] Also, those who reject the traditional view argue that the idea of human beings suffering in hell for eternity for the sins they have committed for a limited period of time on earth is not consistent with the goodness and justice of God.[54]

In response, we must argue that the objections against the traditional view are not biblically and theologically compelling. Biblically, the argument that the final judgment of unbelievers will simply consist of them being extinguished based on the terminological evidence is fraught with difficulties. For example, the passages listed above that describe the final fate of unbelievers as their "destruction" does not mean that they will simply cease to exist. The passages that talk about the final destruction of the wicked must be set alongside with those that talk about the unending nature of the sufferings of the wicked in hell (cf. Isa 66:24; Dan 12:2; Mark 9:43–48;

---

51. Cf. Schleiermacher, *Christian Faith*, paras. 117–20. In the contemporary period, universal salvation (or *apokatastasis*) has been espoused by the likes of John A. T. Robinson, Thomas Talbott, and John Hick.

52. Cf. Hughes, *True Image*, 398–407; Fudge, "Case for Conditionalism," 17–82; Pinnock, "Conditional View," 135–66. The Seventh-Day Adventist Church holds to a similar view called *annihilationism*, where unbelievers will eventually be destroyed after a set period of time in the lake of fire. Regardless of some of the differences in detail between the conditional immortality and annihilationist views, both views agree that unbelievers will not consciously suffer in hell for eternity.

53. Fudge, "Case for Conditionalism," 80–81.

54. Pinnock, "Conditional View," 140, 153–54, 163.

Matt 25:31–46; 2 Thess 1:9; Jude 7, 13; Rev 14:9–11; 20:10). In addition, although the Greek adjective *aiōnios* (translated into English as "eternal" or "forever") may not always indicate a condition without end, when the term is used on its own it usually carries the meaning as conventionally understood (e.g., the "eternal sin" in Mark 3:29). This is supported by the fact that Jesus states in Matthew 25:46 that unbelievers "will go away into eternal punishment, but the righteous into eternal life." If the final state of believers will be living eternally in the new heaven and earth, it only makes sense based on what is said by Jesus in that verse that the corresponding final state of unbelievers will be eternal existence in hell.[55]

Furthermore, the annihilationist/conditional view cannot be harmonized with the biblical passages that state that the impenitent will suffer different degrees of punishment in hell. If all the unbelievers will cease to exist after the final judgment, how can this be congruent with the biblical teaching that some will receive greater punishment in hell than others?

In addition, the theological argument that an eternal hell is contrary to the goodness and justice of God has no solid footing. Those who use this argument do not understand the severity of humanity's sin against God. An infinitely holy God requires an infinite payment for even the slightest sin in order for his perfect justice to be satisfied.[56]

Therefore, when all these arguments are considered together, there is no scriptural support for the idea that the final punishment of unbelievers will be their complete extinction.

## The Eternal Destiny of Believers: The New Heaven and Earth

Scripture describes heaven as a place of inexpressible and unending joy for those who have yielded their lives to Christ. Contrary to comical (and often boring!) depictions of heaven in modern times, Scripture presents the everlasting place of the redeemed as a place of untold beauty, peace, and delight. Heaven is not a place where people just sit on clouds playing musical instruments all day, but a place where humankind's ultimate purpose will be fully realized—to glorify God and enjoy him forever (cf. Isa 43:7; John 10:10). One of the original mandates of creation is that all human beings live in perfect fellowship with God and one another for eternity. Scripture

55. Phillips, "Hell," 340.
56. Walvoord, "Literal View," 27.

states that this will be perfectly fulfilled in the new heaven and earth (Eph 1:10; 2 Pet 3:13; Rev 21:3, 7, 23–26; 22:3–5).

In this section of the chapter, we will discuss what the new heaven and earth will be like and what the glorified saints will do there.

### The Nature of the New Heaven and Earth

The Scriptures make it clear that heaven is a real and definite place (John 14:2–3; Rev 21:2–3). It is not only a state of mind (as some modern Christians like to believe), but an actual place of habitation where people will live and engage in activities. In the present time, though, heaven is a place up above where God resides (Matt 18:10; Acts 7:55–56; Heb 9:24; 1 Pet 3:22) and is also considered his throne (Isa 66:1). In the future when the whole created order is renewed, God will dwell with the redeemed (Rev 21:3) and his glory will illumine the New Jerusalem (Rev 21:23). The dazzling description John provides of the New Jerusalem (Rev 21:9–21) reveals that it will be a city which no earthly city today can compare in terms of beauty and splendor. However, we should not press these descriptions too far and assert that the New Jerusalem will be literally composed of precious stones and metals.[57] The descriptions are symbols of the magnificence and holiness of the city (even though John is talking about a *physical* city coming down from heaven). The new heaven and earth, therefore, will far surpass the glory and beauty of the current heaven and earth. In fact, if one word could be used to summarize everything about the restored creation it is *glory*.

In addition, all evil and detestable things will be excluded from the New Jerusalem. Not only will sin and death be eradicated, but nothing unclean will be allowed to enter its precincts (Rev 21:27; 22:15). Only those who have been washed by the blood of the Lamb may enter and dwell in that place (Rev 22:14), which means that there will be no trace of disorder, corruption, or death on the new earth. All that causes mourning and weeping will be removed for good (Rev 21:4), and there will only be splendid beauty, harmony, and order in this renewed creation.[58] The disappearance of the sea (a symbol of chaos by the ancients) demonstrates to this fact (Rev

---

57. Johnson, "Revelation," 595.

58. Against the classic Lutheran position, we agree with the Reformed view that God will *renew* the present creation, not make an entirely new one (Heb 12:26–28) (cf. Genderen and Velema, *Concise Reformed Dogmatics*, 882–83).

21:1). Everything will be done according to God's will and nothing will depart from his lawful ordinance.

Lastly, the new heaven and earth will also be a place where the redeemed will dwell in glorified bodies. In their earthly bodies, it is not possible for the redeemed to inhabit the coming new creation (1 Cor 15:50). In the future when the redeemed receive their glorified bodies, they will be at home completely because their new bodies will be suited for the conditions of the new creation. The fact that the redeemed will live in the renewed creation in glorified *bodies* demonstrates that God has never devalued the physical aspect of his creation. In fact, God has always considered the material creation "very good" (Gen 1:31), and he will continue to do so for the rest of eternity.

### *The Activities of the Redeemed in the New Heaven and Earth*

The new heaven and earth will not be a boring or inactive place. This must be stated from the outset since many people today have this misinformed idea that heaven is a drab place where people will do nothing but sit around and contemplate about eternity in white robes. Scripture, however, describes heaven as a place where God's people will be engaged in various activities. Yes, the redeemed will rest in the new creation (Heb 4:9–11), but they will also engage in work by judging (Matt 19:28; Luke 22:28–30; 1 Cor 6:2–3) and ruling over cities (Luke 19:16–19). The work ordinance given to Adam in Genesis 2:15 will not be abolished in the new creation. Human beings were created for work, and one of the ways that a human being expresses his or her God-given identity is through his or her vocation. Aside from judging and ruling, however, we do not know what other types of work the redeemed will do or be engaged in. All we know is that unlike the situation after the fall under the old aeon, work will be delightful and fulfilling in the renewed creation.

The redeemed will also worship and offer up praises to God. There will be constant worship and singing in the new heaven and earth. A preview of the worship to come in the new creation is depicted in Revelation 19:1–6 when the multitude offer up praises to God before the close of the present age. Even though worshiping God can be tedious at times in our present fallen state, in the new creation worship will always be fervent, genuine, and enjoyable. As Lewis and Demarest state, "The joy of unbroken, fulfilling fellowship with our Creator and Redeemer will motivate authentic worship, adoration, and praise (Rev. 21:22)."[59]

There will also be greater enjoyment of God's creation in the new heaven and earth. During that time the saints will enjoy the splendor of God's created order with greater appreciation. Everything around them will be filled with inexpressible beauty and delight. Even though some Christians may think it implausible, it is not unreasonable to believe that there will be eating and drinking in the new creation (cf. Rev 22:2). The glorified saints will eat with Christ, just like Christ ate with his disciples after his resurrection (Luke 24:42–43).

Finally, the redeemed will not only enjoy perfect fellowship with God but perfect fellowship with one another. In the present age, all relationships, even among believers, are marred by sin. In the new creation to come, all relationships will be redeemed and there will be no more jealousy, deception, resentment, or anything else contrary to God's purpose for human relationships (cf. Col 3:7–10). Since God will perfectly fulfill the longings of the human heart, God's people will no longer be assailed by feelings of bitterness or envy.[60] Relationships in the new heaven and earth will indeed return to the way human relationships were intended to be—and much more—before sin entered the world.

---

59. Lewis and Demarest, *Integrative Theology*, 3:481.

60. Although in the new heaven and earth there will be different degrees of privilege and rewards (cf. Luke 19:16–19; 1 Cor 3:11–15), this will not result in jealousy or bitterness since even the saint with the least amount of rewards will be perfectly satisfied with being in the presence of God for eternity (Rev 21:3–4; 22:3–5).

# CHAPTER 20

# The Pilgrimage of Faith: Living as Christians

## Introduction

AT THE BEGINNING OF this work, we posited that Christian theology must foremost be practical in its purpose and outcome. Meaning that a theology that is biblically-grounded must ultimately be one that will invigorate believers to do God's will and serve his divine kingdom. Theology, therefore, must not be something that only stays in the minds of believers with no concrete effects in their lives; but instead, something that gets them to work diligently to be light and salt in the world. Many evangelical systematic theology works in recent decades, however, do not typically have a separate chapter dealing with the doctrine of the Christian life (or the theology of how to live as Christians in the world).[1] Normally these discussions are intermittently treated in sections dealing with conversion, sanctification, or perseverance.

Since theology is ultimately supposed to be practical, we have decided in the second edition of this work to include a separate chapter dealing with the Christian life. Although we briefly discussed the *why* and the *how* of the Christian life in the previous chapters dealing with the doctrines of conversion and sanctification, we have elected here to discuss the *character* of the Christian life.

1. However, some noteworthy exceptions include Morgan, *Christian Theology*, 551–574; and Williams, *Renewal Theology*, 2:411–445. From a Roman Catholic perspective, see Bauerschmidt and Buckley, 312–346.

What must be stated at the outset for our readers is that this chapter is not a formal treatment of the practical significance of the Ten Commandments in contemporary Christian living or about providing detailed treatments about specific ethical topics that preoccupy many modern evangelicals (e.g., abortion on demand, the use of force for the promotion of peace, divorce and remarriage, etc.),[2] but about providing a biblico-theological sketch of what the Christian life is supposed to be like. In other words, this chapter will deal with what it means to be a follower of Christ and what that entails based on the testimony of Scripture.

Before we provide a more detailed treatment of this topic under various sub-headings, we will reference some relevant Scripture passages to aid us in our thinking about what it means to be a Christian.

## Relevant Scripture Passages in Regards to the Christian Life

Scripture provides many statements in the Old and New Testaments that instruct believers on how to live their lives in obedience to God and his word. The Scriptures not only reveal the saving will of the triune God in the course of redemptive history but also offers numerous exhortations to believers on how to be a holy people in a spiritually dark world. Although the passages listed below are not exhaustive by any means, we have chosen some (in canonical order) that we believe are significant in the context of Christian living and ethics:

- Genesis 15:6: "And he [Abraham] believed the LORD, and he counted it to him as righteousness.

- Psalm 1:1–2: "Blessed is the man who walks not in the counsel of the wicked, nor stands in the way of sinners, nor sits in the seat of scoffers; but his delight is in the law of the LORD, and on his law he meditates day and night."

- Psalm 34:12–14: "What man is there who desires life and loves many days, that he may see good? Keep your tongue from evil and your lips from speaking deceit. Turn away from evil and do good; seek peace and pursue it."

---

2. Some helpful works on Christian ethics that deal with specific issues in great detail include Frame, *The Doctrine of the Christian Life*; Grudem, *Christian Ethics*; and Douma, *The Ten Commandments*.

- Proverbs 28:6: "Better is a poor man who walks in his integrity than a rich man who is crooked in his ways."

- Ecclesiastes 12:13–14: "The end of the matter; all has been heard. Fear God and keep his commandments, for this is the whole duty of man. For God will bring every deed into judgment, with every secret thing, whether good or evil."

- Isaiah 1:16–17: "Wash yourselves; make yourselves clean; remove the evil of your deeds from before my eyes; cease to do evil, learn to do good; seek justice, correct oppression; bring justice to the fatherless, plead the widow's cause."

- Hosea 6:6: "For I desire steadfast love and not sacrifice, the knowledge of God rather than burnt offerings."

- Micah 6:8: "He has told you, O man, what is good; and what does the LORD require of you but to do justice, and to love kindness, and to walk humbly with your God?"

- Matthew 7:12: "'So whatever you wish that others would do to you, do also to them, for this is the Law and the Prophets.'"

- John 8:12: "Again Jesus spoke to them, saying, 'I am the light of the world. Whoever follows me will not walk in darkness, but will have the light of life.'"

- Romans 12:2: "Do not be conformed to this world, but be transformed by the renewal of your mind, that by testing you may discern what is the will of God, what is good and acceptable and perfect."

- Galatians 5:16: "But I say, walk by the Spirit, and you will not gratify the desires of the flesh."

- Galatians 6:1–2: "Brothers, if anyone is caught in any transgression, you who are spiritual should restore him in a spirit of gentleness. Keep watch on yourself, lest you too be tempted. Bear one another's burdens, and so fulfill the law of Christ."

- Ephesians 2:10: "For we are his workmanship, created in Christ Jesus for good works, which God prepared beforehand, that we should walk in them."

- Ephesians 4:1–3: "I therefore, a prisoner for the Lord, urge you to walk in a manner worthy of the calling to which you have been called, with all humility and gentleness, with patience, bearing with one another in love, eager to maintain the unity of the Spirit in the bond of peace."

- Ephesians 4:32: "Be kind to one another, tenderhearted, forgiving one another, as God in Christ forgave you."

- Philippians 2:3–4: "Do nothing from selfish ambition or conceit, but in humility count others more significant than yourselves. Let each of you look not only to his own interests, but also to the interests of others."

- Colossians 3:8–10: "But now you must put them all away: anger, wrath, malice, slander, and obscene talk from your mouth. Do not lie to one another, seeing that you have put off the old self with its practices and have put on the new self, which is being renewed in knowledge after the image of its creator."

- Colossians 3:12–14: "Put on then, as God's chosen ones, holy and beloved, compassionate hearts, kindness, humility, meekness, and patience, bearing with one another and, if one has a complaint against another, forgiving each other; as the Lord has forgiven you, so you also must forgive. And above all these put on love, which binds everything together in perfect harmony."

- 1 Thessalonians 5:15: "See that no one repays anyone evil for evil, but always seek to do good to one another and to everyone."

- Hebrews 13:5: "Keep your life free from love of money, and be content with what you have, for he has said, 'I will never leave you nor forsake you.'"

- James 1:27: "Religion that is pure and undefiled before God, the Father, is this: to visit orphans and widows in their affliction, and to keep oneself unstained from the world."

- James 2:8: "If you really fulfill the royal law according to the Scripture, 'You shall love your neighbor as yourself,' you are doing well."

- James 2:26: "For as the body apart from the spirit is dead, so also faith apart from works is dead."

- 1 Peter 2:12: "Keep your conduct among the Gentiles honorable, so that when they speak against you as evildoers, they may see your good deeds and glorify God on the day of visitation."

- 1 Peter 4:1–2: "Since therefore Christ suffered in the flesh, arm your-selves with the same way of thinking, for whoever has suffered in the flesh has ceased from sin, so as to live for the rest of the time in the flesh no longer for human passions but for the will of God."

- 1 John 2:15–17: "Do not love the world or the things in the world. If anyone loves the world, the love of the Father is not in him. For all that is in the world—the desires of the flesh and the desires of the eyes and pride of life—is not from the Father but is from the world. And the world is passing away along with its desires, but whoever does the will of God abides forever."

- 1 John 5:4–5: "For everyone who has been born of God overcomes the world. And this is the victory that has overcome the world—our faith. Who is it that overcomes the world except the one who believes that Jesus is the Son of God?"

As stated above, this list is not exhaustive, and many more passages in Scripture can be called upon to show that God unwaveringly expects his people to live a certain way so that it brings honor to his name and effects blessings to others. One will also notice that what consistently shows up in these passages is the importance of *holiness, mercy, justice,* and *love* as characteristics of God's people.

In the next section of this chapter, we will discuss in more detail what it means to live the Christian life during the present age based on themes that are usually brought up in Christian theological discourse regarding this subject.

## Major Themes on Living the Christian Life

### A Holistic Practical Righteousness

No Christian today who faithfully embraces the teachings of Scripture would deny that Christian living and Christian ethics are closely inter-twined. In fact, living the Christian life and the moral law revealed in Scripture are so intricately connected that it is unfathomable to think that one can exist without the other. Not only did the Old Testament closely align God-honoring spirituality with an Israelite's careful devotion to the old covenant law (cf. Psalm 119); but also under the new covenant, Chris-tians are to demonstrate their genuine piety by living righteously under the law of Christ (Gal 6:2) and the moral commandments revealed by God (1 John 5:3). The challenging aspect, however, is how we understand what constitutes *righteousness* in the context of living the Christian life.

Christians are pilgrims in this world and are called to persevere in doing what is right, and uphold all that honors and pleases God: fighting for justice, showing mercy, practicing virtue, and loving others as themselves. They show their love for God by behaving, talking, and thinking in ways that are pleasing to him. Regrettably, however, many Christians throughout the centuries have developed "ethical" beliefs and practices that are not in complete harmony with Scripture. These may not take the form of outright opposition to the clear teachings of Scripture regarding the value of human life, property rights, the sanctity of marriage, idolatry, false witnessing, etc. (as is usually the case), but having more or less an incomplete understanding of biblical ethics as it relates to Christian living.

Some of the problems faced by Christians throughout the centuries when it came to biblical ethics was, using a common English idiom, the failure to "see the forest for the trees." Just like the Pharisees of Jesus' day, some Christians seem to not recognize that obeying God's moral law is a *holistic* endeavor. As discussed in chapter 6 on the doctrine of sin, God not only requires his people to refrain from acts that are blatantly sinful (murder, adultery, theft, idolatry, etc.), but also to act and speak in ways that are loving and considerate of others (cf. Gal 6:9–10). One can be a vocal opponent of certain scandalous sins that are clearly prohibited in God's word, but entirely miss the mark on following the ethics of God's kingdom because one consistently fails to be loving, kind, considerate, just, and merciful (cf. Matt 23:23–24). In fact, a warning must be issued at times in churches that merely appearing righteous to the outside world will not "cut it" in God's kingdom (cf. Matt 23:27–28). As F. Leroy Forlines points out in regards to this issue: "Some have given too much attention to form and not enough attention to substance."[3]

Another point we must highlight before we close this part of the discussion is the importance of a holistic righteousness as an antidote to a pernicious type of antinomianism (i.e., a rejection of God's law). People often mistakenly assume that the primary problem with the Pharisees of Jesus' time was that they attempted to merit a place in God's kingdom by rigorously following the Mosaic law and its rituals. Although that was one of the significant theological problems of the Pharisees (cf. Luke 18:9–12),

---

3. Forlines, *The Quest for Truth*, 247.

that was not the principal one. The principal problem with the Pharisees was that they drastically fell short of practicing the holistic righteousness revealed in the Scriptures that God endorses and approves of (i.e., not only refraining from the sensual sins common among the pagans, but also pro-actively practicing love, mercy, generosity, and justice). Jesus condemned them for "straining out a gnat and swallowing a camel" (Matt 23:24)[4] and for cleaning "the outside of the cup and the plate," while being filled with greed and self-indulgence (Matt 23:25). By only focusing on the externals of the law they actually lessened the requirements of the law for themselves (in a way, making it easier for themselves to obey). As a consequence, they were following the traditions of people rather than the moral will of God (Mark 7:8). In addition, in the Sermon on the Mount, Jesus warned his listeners that in order for one to enter the kingdom of heaven one's righ-teousness must exceed that of the scribes and Pharisees (Matt 5:20). What this entails is that one's righteousness must not be merely formal and ex-ternal, but must be rooted in the heart (Matt 5:22, 28) and driven by love (Matt 22:37–40). This does not mean, however, that a person must practice holistic righteousness (a righteousness that goes beyond mere ethical for-malism) in order to earn a place in God's kingdom, but that the consistent practicing of holistic righteousness (albeit imperfectly) is *evidence* that one is a partaker of eternal life and a member of God's kingdom (cf. Jas 2:14–26; 2 Pet 1:5–11; 1 John 3:10). In other words, a life characterized by holistic righteousness in varying degrees (Matt 13:23; Eph 4:24) is a sign that one truly belongs to Christ and the spiritual family of God (cf. 1 John 2:29).

## Between Legalistic Asceticism and Worldly Hedonism

Having discussed the nature of holistic righteousness and why it is impor-tant for Christian living today, we must also discuss how we can live this righteous life in a balanced way. A few centuries after the church's initial founding, some early Christians attempted to curb the sinful desires of the flesh and resist worldly temptations by escaping into the wilderness. Some early Christians (mistakenly) thought by withdrawing from the world and living like hermits that they could avoid the worldly temptations that

---

4. William Hendriksen astutely summarizes the meaning of this humorous illustra-tion given by Jesus: "The meaning is: they were paying no attention to the really impor-tant requirements of God's law but spending all their thought and energy on that which was totally unimportant" (*Matthew*, 833).

commonly plague humankind. This would allow them to devote more of their time and energy on the things of God without the distractions of the fallen world (even if those "distractions" were not prohibited in Scripture, like marriage). Church historians and theologians have typically called this movement *monasticism* (assumed to be started by St. Antony [251–356], who lived the remainder of his life in a desert of Egypt).[5]

Legalistic ascetic withdrawal, however, is not something that was restricted to the early church period. In modern times, certain Anabaptistic, neo-fundamentalist, and sectarian groups practice their own form of "worldly withdrawal" by not engaging with the outside world (or at least having a strong "us versus them" worldview mentality). For example, some very traditional Mennonite-Anabaptist groups (like the Amish) withdraw from modern society almost entirely (even avoiding the use of modern technology as a way to cultivate and preserve their faith), and live in a very communal way largely insulated from the rest of the world. In fact, discipline (or even excommunication) may be enacted towards those who violate their distinctive community regulations.

Although the examples given above are some extreme ones of legalistic ascetic withdrawal, mainstream evangelical Christians can also fall into this pattern in their private lives when they come up with their own personal rules about what is acceptable and unacceptable behavior. Some Christians, with weaker consciences, may avoid drinking alcohol, going dancing, dressing a certain way, listening to secular music, or watching secular movies. Some may even believe that only befriending Christian people and joining so-called Christian organizations are the only acceptable forms of social interaction. We may not condemn them for adopting these scruples (Rom 14:1, 5), but we can instruct them (lovingly and graciously) of the freedom they have in Christ because of his death and resurrection (cf. Gal 5:1). (In fact, Paul tells Timothy that one of the "teachings of demons" is the prohibition of marriage and abstinence of certain foods [1 Tim 4:1, 3], because the teaching is against the truth that "everything created by God is good" [1 Tim 4:4].) This freedom, of course, is never an excuse to indulge in sinful appetites, but rather to do what is pleasing in the eyes of God (Heb 13:16) and beneficial for others (Gal 5:13).

Having highlighted some of the problematic aspects of legalistic ascetic withdrawal, we must not swing wildly to the other side of the pendulum and believe that behaving and living like those who belong to this world

5. Allision, *Historical Theology,* 328, 528.

is not a problem to be concerned about. In fact, worldliness (or having an inordinate love for the present world) is utterly condemned in Scripture. For example, James warns his readers in his letter: "Do you not know that friendship with the world is enmity with God? Therefore whoever wishes to be a friend of the world makes himself an enemy of God" (Jas 4:4). Also, the apostle John wrote in his first epistle: "Do not love the world or the things in the world. If anyone loves the world, the love of the Father is not in him. For all that is in the world—the desires of the flesh and the desires of the eyes and pride of life—is not from the Father but is from the world" (1 John 2:15–16). Finally, the Lord Jesus tells his listeners in Matthew 6:19–20: "Do not lay up for yourselves treasures on earth, where moth and rust destroy and where thieves break in and steal, but lay up for yourselves treasures in heaven, where neither moth nor rust destroys and where thieves do not break in and steal." These statements reveal that believers in Christ do not belong to this world (even though they live in it presently); therefore, they must align their lives and values in accordance with this truth. As John Calvin once wrote:

> For the man who considers that he is a stranger in the world uses the things of this world as if they were another's—that is, as things that are lent us for a single day. The sum is this, that the mind of a Christian ought not to be taken up with earthly things, or to repose in them; for we ought to live as if we were every moment about to depart from this life.[6]

Although we understand that the true believer's ultimate home is not the present fading world, we should not, however, avoid all things of the present age. We still live in this world, and need to continually utilize the things of this world to continue the mission of being light and salt for the kingdom. Even though Jesus told his listeners to not store up treasures on earth, he did tell them to pray for their "daily bread" (spiritual *and* physical) (Matt 6:11), and that material necessities will be given to them if they seek first the kingdom of God and his righteousness (Matt 6:33). As the Lord who healed the sick, opened the eyes of the blind, and fed the hungry multitudes, he understood the importance of the physical well-being of people despite the temporary nature of the present life. The apostle Paul who told the Corinthian believers that "the present form of this world is passing away" (1 Cor 7:31), also told Timothy later on in his ministry that God is the One who "richly provides us with everything to enjoy" (1 Tim

6. Calvin, *Comm.* 1 Corinthians 7:29.

6:17). Although Paul recognized the transitory character of the present age, he did not encourage any type of ascetic withdrawal from life (1 Tim 4:3–5) or legalistic self-denial in regards to one's body (cf. Col 2:23).

In conclusion, what does this mean for Christians today in their spiritual pilgrimage in the present age? What it means is that they are not to become part of this fallen world system despite living in it presently. They are to live as "sojourners" and "exiles" (1 Pet 2:11) in a world that does not share their values, priorities, desires, and aspirations. As a consequence, they are to be spiritually different even though they dwell in this world with unbelievers and interact with them on a daily basis in various ways, personally and professionally. As the New Testament scholar George Eldon Ladd once wrote: "Christians live in this age, but their life pattern, their standard of conduct, their aims and goals are not those of this age, which are essentially human-centered and prideful."[7] However, this does not mean that Christians may quit their jobs, drop out of school, abandon their family responsibilities, and renege on their civic duties to society for the sake of pursuing a kingdom-oriented life. They are to continue their earthly vocations and responsibilities, while being a positive influence to those around them (cf. Gal 6:10; Col 4:5–6). In this way, they can take up the charge to be "light" and "salt" in this dying world (Matt 5:13–16), while interacting with this world in a socially and spiritually responsible way.

## Love: The Essence of the Christian Life

Jesus explained to a lawyer of the Sadducees that the first and greatest commandment (Matt 22:38) is to "love the Lord your God with all your heart and with all your soul and with all your mind" (Matt 22:37), and that the second is like it: "You shall love your neighbor as yourself" (Matt 22:39). In fact, he points out that the Law and the Prophets depend on these two commandments (Matt 22:40). In his first epistle to the Corinthians, the apostle Paul tells the Corinthian believers that among the triadic virtues of the Christian religion—faith, hope, and love—that love is the greatest of them all (1 Cor 13:13). James, the half-brother of the Lord Jesus, tells his readers that obeying the commandment to love one's neighbor (which he calls "the royal law") is the embodiment of "doing right" (Jas 2:8, NIV). Also, the apostle Peter tells his audience: "The end of all things is at hand; therefore be self-controlled and sober-minded for the sake of your prayers.

7. Ladd, *A Theology of the New Testament*, 569.

Above all, *keep loving one another earnestly,* since love covers a multitude of sins" (1 Pet 4:7–8). Here, Peter reveals one of the important functions of showing love to other believers: the covering of multitude of sins. Finally, the apostle John, in his first letter, tells his readers that one of the sure signs that someone possesses new life in the Spirit is that he or she loves other believers (1 John 4:7). The reason being? Because "God is love" (1 John 4:8). Based on the passages referenced above, one can make the case that love (for God and other people) is the *essence* of the Christian life. As J. Rodman Williams states:

> "Follow the way of love" is the ultimate imperative for Christian living. It is the way that we have entered upon through our Lord Jesus Christ, the way that we are commanded to follow amid all the vicissitudes and challenges of this life, and the way that has no end in the far reaches of eternity. To follow love is to follow God both now and always.[8]

One may still ask: What is this love that Scripture speaks of that we must regularly practice in our Christian walk? The Greek language during the days of Jesus and the apostles had various terms (six of them: *eros, ludus, pragma, storge, philia,* and *agape*) that were equivalent to the modern English word "love." However, the two significant ones found in the New Testament are *philia* and *agape*. The first one *philia* has to do with a deep emotional connection one has with a close friend. It is a type of love that is substantive and brings about a strong bond between two people. It does not carry the same meaning as understood by many in our Western culture today (where "friendship" can be viewed with an air of superficiality—for example, "friends" on social media pages). The other one *agape* (which is the most important to our discussion) is a type of love that is given to someone apart from any worthiness found in him or her (i.e., a self-giving love). Or as Harold W. Hoehner puts it, it is a love that "seeks the highest good in the one loved, even though that one may be underserving, and hence its prominence in the Bible can be understood."[9]

If a passage in Scripture can be used to summarize what this type of love looks like, we can use Paul's statement in Philippians 2:4: "Let each of you look not only to his own interests, but also to the interests of others." Although Paul does not use the word "love" in the verse, what he attempts to convey about the nature of this type of love is there: loving others

---

8. Williams, *Renewal Theology,* 2:444–445.

9. Hoehner, "Love," 657.

involves looking out for their interests, whether they deserve it or not. In his well-known passage on love, 1 Corinthians 13:1–13, Paul lists several characteristics of this type of love: it is patient and kind (v. 4); it is not envious or boastful (v. 4); it is not arrogant (v. 4) or rude (v. 5); it does not insist on its own way (v. 5); it is not irritable or resentful (v. 5); it does not rejoice at wrongdoing, but rejoices with the truth (v. 6); and it bears all things, believes all things, hopes all things, and endures all things (v. 7). Taking all these things into account, the love that the apostle Paul endorses is a type that seeks after the well-being and good of the other, even if this entails sacrificing one's own desires, ambitions, and convenience. In practical terms, believers express this *agape* love when they do good to others in society, seek after the well-being of their neighbors, and are concerned about the spiritual condition of their unbelieving colleagues, friends, and family members (as demonstrated in sharing the gospel to them).

If we understand this to be case, how are Christians to put this love into practice regularly as they interact with various people they encounter in life? First, this type of love does not mean that Christians must *like* everybody they meet in life. Some people in the world have questionable characters and unsavory personality traits. Our natural instinct is to shun these people and avoid them at all costs. Some people are just unlikeable in general; some just do not "click" with our personal preferences. However, Jesus commands (not suggests!) his followers to love all their neighbors (believer or non-believer, likeable or unlikeable) because they bear God's image in themselves (cf. Jas 3:9), and are to be treated accordingly (cf. Luke 10:29–37). In fact, he even commands his audience to love their enemies and pray for them (Matt 5:44; cf. Luke 6:27)!

Second, loving other people (even those we find objectionable) is a way of properly responding to the love that God has shown us in Jesus Christ. Even though we were once enemies of God and alienated from him (Eph 2:11–12), God decided to initiate his redemptive action through Jesus Christ (John 3:16) to bring reconciliation between him and us (Eph 2:16) so that we will no longer be "strangers" and "aliens" in a foreign land (Eph 2:19). As a consequence, we need to love our neighbors as we love ourselves because God first loved us by sending his Son to die on the cross for our sins. As the apostle John states: "We love because he first loved us" (1 John 4:19). Glenn E. Schaefer summarizes this truth well: "The command to love others is based on how God has loved us. Since believers have been the recipients of love, they must love."[10] In fact, the apostle John states that loving God and loving others (especially other believers) cannot be divorced from each other. Those who profess to love God but hate others contradict their profession (1 John 4:20).

Last, we reflect the Son's image in our own lives in concrete ways by showing love to others (2 Cor 3:18; Col 3:10). Human beings cannot accurately perceive what is inside another person's heart. They can only observe the new life of the regenerate person by his or her concrete actions of love. That is why James tells his readers that genuine faith can only be recognized by people in observable acts of love and kindness (Jas 2:18, 21, 25), and why the apostle John tells his audience that loving other believers is a *sign* that one has new life in Christ (1 John 3:14). This is so because God is the source of love and, in turn, he enables his children to love others (1 John 4:7). This does not mean that love must be perfect, since all believers at the present stumble in many ways (Jas 3:2) and still fall into sin time to time (1 John 2:1); but loving others must characterize the lives of believers because this shows that they are wholeheartedly following Christ and belong to him.

As we end this section, we must make a final note to remind ourselves that loving others must never be viewed as another path to earn God's salvific favor and merit a place in his kingdom (like a "new law" for making one's way into heaven). We love God and others, *because we have been completely forgiven and justified in Christ apart from any moral worthiness in ourselves* (a forgiveness and justification grounded in God's lovingkindness to us through the Son). As Sinclair B. Ferguson rightly states, believers "endeavor to fulfill the law, not in order to be justified but because they have already been justified, not in the flesh but in the Spirit, not out of merit-seeking but out of the response of faith which works by love."[11] Therefore, following the way of love is not a means to earn a place in heaven, but something that should *characterize* the lives of all Christians as a proper response to the salvific gifts given to them through the completed work of Jesus Christ.

## Virtue: The Quality of the Christian Life

If love can be viewed as the essence of the Christian life, one can argue that virtue can be seen as the *quality* of the Christian life. Although the

10. Schaefer, "Love," 494–495.

11. Ferguson, "The Reformed View," 69.

meaning and importance of *virtue* is not discussed much today in regards to ethics, it is something that is highlighted as being very important in several places in the Bible. In the Old Testament, the Hebrew word *chayil* denoted "power" or "might" (or even "force," "wealth," or "efficiency") (cf. Esth 8:11; Ps 110:3). However, *chayil* could also refer to "moral strength," as exemplified by the Moabitess Ruth (Ruth 3:11) for her "noble character" (HCSB) and the virtuous wife of Proverbs 31 (the NASB translates *chayil* as "excellent" in verse 10). In the New Testament, the Greek word *aretē* (usually translated as "virtue" or "excellence" in English) is used in only four verses: Philippians 4:8; 1 Peter 2:9; 2 Peter 1:3; and 2 Peter 1:5 (twice). The meaning of the Greek word is something akin to what we know as *moral excellence* or *ethical uprightness*.

When talking about the importance of virtue in the Christian life, one passage that stands out, however, is 2 Peter 1:5–11. In the English Standard Version, the passage in its entirety reads:

> For this very reason, make every effort to supplement your faith with virtue, and virtue with knowledge, and knowledge with self control, and self control with steadfastness, and steadfastness with godliness, and godliness with brotherly affection, and brotherly affection with love. For if these qualities are yours and are increasing, they keep you from being ineffective or unfruitful in the knowledge of our Lord Jesus Christ. For whoever lacks these qualities is so nearsighted that he is blind, having forgotten that he was cleansed from his former sins. Therefore, brothers, be all the more diligent to confirm your calling and election, for if you practice these qualities you will never fall. For in this way there will be richly provided for you an entrance into the eternal kingdom of our Lord and Savior Jesus Christ.

Here, the apostle Peter lists several things that constitute Christian virtue in verses 5–7. In the passage, he exhorts his readers to supplement their faith and virtue with these qualities: knowledge, self-control, steadfastness, godliness, brotherly affection, and love. We will now go over these qualities in sequential order as presented in the passage.

- *Knowledge.* When Scripture speaks of knowledge (Gk. *gnōsis*) it is not only talking about intellectual knowledge an individual receives through study or observation, but the knowledge one receives from God that leads to righteous or virtuous living (i.e., "sagacity" or "practical wisdom").[12] It is a type of knowledge that someone possesses to distinguish between the good and the bad. Peter uses this word to differentiate his ethical teaching from the heretical teachings of the false teachers who claimed to have superior knowledge of spiritual things. In fact, the knowledge that Peter talks about here is *understanding the will of God.*[13] The fact that Peter stresses the importance of knowledge in the pursuit of godliness reveals that believers of all ages and backgrounds need to cultivate in them, with the assistance of God's grace, godly wisdom and correct theological knowledge to live the Christian life properly.

- *Self-control.* The next item on the list is self-control (Gk. *enkrateia*). This word is not commonly found in the New Testament, but it is still an important virtue to be pursued by those who consider themselves to be followers of Christ. Also, it was considered by the ancient Greek philosophers to be a very important trait for a human being to possess. Simon J. Kistemaker notes that in the Hellenistic world of the apostles' time, this word pertained to the strict training athletes go through for their respective sport (cf. Paul's example in 1 Cor 9:25 regarding the parallels between training in sports and Christian discipleship).[14] For Peter, self-control is a very important virtue for Christians to seek after because the false teachers he was opposing possessed little to no self-control. It is a character trait that distinguishes a believer from someone who does not know God. Therefore, believers are called to constantly exercise self-control and discipline their bodies, in contrast to the unregenerate who easily give into their passions and desires. As Green states: "It meant controlling the passions instead of being controlled by them."[15] The apostle Paul even lists self-control as one of the things that belong to the fruit of the Spirit (Gal 5:23). The reason being that the self-control the believer exercises ultimately comes from the Holy Spirit.

- *Steadfastness.* After self-control, Peter lists steadfastness as another virtue to be pursued. Some versions, like the NIV and NET, translate the Greek word *hypomonē* as "perseverance." Regardless, the meaning

---

12. Green, *2 Peter and Jude,* 77.

13. Cf. Blum, "2 Peter," 269.

14. Kistemaker, *Peter, and Jude,* 251.

15. Green, *2 Peter and Jude,* 77.

is the same: to endure to the end despite the difficulties and challenges that come from one's commitment to Christ. As Peter H. Davids states, steadfastness (or perseverance) is "the virtue needed to stand firm in one's commitment to Jesus over the long haul in the face of persecution (thus its prominence in James and Revelation) or other hardships. In 2 Peter the need is to stand firm in their commitment in the face of the enticements of the teachers whom our author opposes."[16] In other words, Peter calls all his readers to remain steadfast in the faith, and to never deviate from the truth revealed by God in Christ (both ethically and doctrinally). This is another virtue that is of crucial importance to successfully live out one's Christian life in the world.

- *Godliness.* The next virtue Peter exhorts his readers to incorporate into their lives is godliness. The Greek word *eusebeia* can be understood as "piety or devotion to the person of God."[17] Green makes this interesting observation about why Peter included *eusebeia* on this list. He goes on to state that Peter is "at pains to emphasize that true knowledge of God…manifests itself in reverence towards him and respect towards men," unlike the false teachers who "were far from proper in their behaviour both to God and their fellow men."[18] What this means is that Christians are to properly relate to God by doing the things that please him, and behave in ways that are beneficial to their fellow human beings. They are not to dishonor God with shameful and immoral behaviors, and bring harm to their neighbors by acting and speaking in ways that damage them (physically, emotionally, and spiritually).

- *Brotherly affection.* The second-to-last item on the list is brotherly affection (Gk. *philadelphia*). This has to do with love that is shown to other believers in Christ. In the Greco-Roman world, the word *philadelphia* had to do with affection and generosity among physical kin (i.e., family members or close relatives), and this did not extend beyond the familial circle.[19] Peter uses this Greek word in the passage to admonish his readers to show love and godly affection towards *all* believers. Since all believers in Christ belong to a new family unit that

16. Davids, *The Letters of 2 Peter and Jude*, 181.
17. Blum, "2 Peter," 270.
18. Green, *2 Peter and Jude*, 79.
19. Davids, *The Letters of 2 Peter and Jude*, 182.

is superior to the physical bonds that unite earthly family members (cf. Matt 19:29; Eph 2:19), Peter tells his readers that they must love one another as brothers and sisters of the same spiritual household. In fact, as mentioned earlier, the apostle John states that loving other believers is evidence of being born from above (1 John 4:7).

- *Love.* Although we discussed at some length the importance of love in the previous section of the chapter, we need to discuss it again here because it is the capstone of Peter's "virtue list." While Peter talks about practicing "brotherly affection" among the believers in God's household, he entreats his readers to extend their love to outsiders. In fact, Peter wants his readers to be as comprehensive as possible in showing love to people. That is why he does not stop at brotherly affection on his list. Kistemaker makes this important point regarding this:

> Peter does not want us to restrict our love to the members of the church. He knows the teaching of Jesus, "Love your enemies" (Matt. 5:44). Love is a debt we owe our fellow man (Rom. 13:8) without exception. In other words, whereas we can limit the application of brotherly kindness to the Christian community, we are unable to restrict the practice of love.[20]

What is sometimes regrettable to observe today is how some sectarian-minded Christians think that they do not need to lovingly engage with people who are outside of the community of faith. This is not only wrong on a societal level, but it is also against the clear teachings of Scripture that exhort believers to love their neighbors (Matt 22:39) and to do good to *all* people (Gal 6:10). Christians are to be salt and light in this world, and the only way they can do this is by loving others regardless of their spiritual condition or religious commitments.

Having discussed the importance of virtue in the Christian life based on 2 Peter 1:5–7, one may still ask: why is this important? The importance of virtue in the Christian life is due to the fact that believers reflect the image of God in their lives by being virtuous towards others. Since God in Christ is the prime example of virtue, believers are to follow his ways in their relations and dealings with others (cf. Eph 5:1–2). In order for believers to become effective heralds of God's kingdom, they must behave in

20. Kistemaker, *Peter and Jude*, 253.

ways that do not bring disrepute to the gospel and cause God's name to be dishonored.

Another reason why Christians need to practice these virtues is because by doing so, they will not become "ineffective" or "unfruitful" in their "knowledge of [their] Lord Jesus Christ" (2 Pet 1:8). Possessing these virtues will not only prevent them from being insipid and powerless when resisting the onslaughts of the devil and the temptations of the world, but will also enable them to be effective ministers of the gospel and a positive influence to others in the world. Believers cannot do God's kingdom work effectively when they compromise on doing what is right and honorable.

Finally, one more reason why virtue is important for the Christian is due to the fact that it reveals who he or she really is in the eyes of others and to himself or herself. Shortly after exhorting his readers to put into practice certain virtues as members of God's household, Peter warns them that failure to put these virtues into practice will cause spiritual amnesia. He writes: "For whoever lacks these qualities is so nearsighted that he is blind, having forgotten that he was cleansed from his former sins" (2 Pet 1:9). Failure (or refusal) to put these virtues into practice *may* result in the undermining of assurance in a Christian's life. Those who lack virtue are spiritually blind and cannot see far ahead because they are unable to see the spiritual things of God. They have forgotten what their baptisms represent (which is what Peter was likely alluding to in the verse) and are no longer aware of what Christ's death and resurrection signifies.[21] This is why Peter also admonishes his readers to "be all the more diligent to confirm your calling and election, for if you practice these qualities you will never fall" (2 Pet 2:10). By cultivating these virtues in their lives, believers will have greater assurance of their salvific calling and election in Christ. This does not mean that putting these virtues into practice must be flawless, but that they must exist in the Christian's life in some significantly observable way. This is so because these virtues that exist in the Christian's life ultimately come from the Holy Spirit. As William Nigel Kerr states: "Christian character is the work of the Holy Spirit in the believer's life as the Word of God is applied and the means of grace employed."[22]

---

21. Kistemaker states: "By itself, baptism is no guarantee that a person is saved. Baptism is an external ceremony that must have its counterpart in an internal commitment to Christ. But if true faith is lacking in the heart of a person who has been baptized, all the other virtues that Peter mentions also are absent" (*Peter and Jude*, 255).

22. Kerr, "Virtue, Virtues," 1146.

## The Indicative and Imperative of the Christian Life

When talking about the Christian life in a pastoral context, it is important that the minister of the gospel does not present a skewed understanding of it where only the *indicative* (what God has done for us in Christ) is talked about *or* where the *imperative* (what believers must do in response to God's grace) is only presented. The Scriptures hold both in intricate unity and balance, and to emphasize one to the neglect of the other is to do a disservice to the gospel truths presented in God's word.

In contemporary evangelicalism, some well-intentioned believers argue that the gospel is *only* about God's forgiveness towards the sinner through the work of Jesus Christ. They argue that in order for the gospel to be truly good news for hopeless sinners we must never include the imperatives in our gospel preaching. Others, from a more pietistic or holiness background, maintain that the gospel is primarily about "doing" or "working"—in order to maintain a close relationship with God or to receive his salvific mercy. These individuals maintain that if the imperatives are not at the forefront of the gospel message, then Christianity will become nothing more than a quietistic religion with no significant ethical impact on believers. However, both tendencies err because the Scriptures present the gospel message as possessing both the indicative and the imperative in proper balance.

One clear example of both the indicative and imperative of the gospel message being held in proper balance is in the preaching of Jesus during his earthly ministry. For instance, in Luke 19:10, Jesus states that "the Son of Man came to seek and to save the lost;" yet, shortly after in Luke 19:11–27 (the Parable of the Ten Minas), he revealed to his listeners the utter importance of getting to work for God's kingdom (vv. 15, 17, 23, 26). In addition, Jesus at times spoke about the work he must do in order for sinners to be redeemed from sin and enjoy eternal life (cf. John 3:14–15; 6:38–40, 51; 10:10–11, 15), and yet he declares at another time that people must take up their crosses, deny themselves, and follow him to be his true disciples (Mark 8:34; cf. Matt 16:24). In fact, he even tells one particular audience that there is no point in calling him "Lord, Lord" if they will not put into practice his teachings (Luke 6:46–49; cf. Matt 7:21–27). Therefore, we see that Jesus held the indicative and the imperative together in proper balance in his gospel ministry.

In the New Testament epistles, the apostle Paul was a master at weaving together the indicative and the imperative in the Christian life in an appropriately balanced way. One prime example of this is found in Philippians 2:12–13: "Therefore, my beloved, as you have always obeyed, so now, not only as in my presence but much more in my absence, work out your own salvation with fear and trembling [the imperative], for it is God who works in you [the indicative], both to will and to work for his good pleasure." Another good example is found in Romans 12:1: "I appeal to you therefore, brothers, by the mercies of God [the indicative], to present your bodies as a living sacrifice [the imperative], holy and acceptable to God, which is your spiritual worship." Also, in 1 Corinthians 5:7, he states: "Cleanse out the old leaven that you may be a new lump [the imperative], as you really are unleavened. For Christ, our Passover lamb, has been sacrificed [the indicative]." Furthermore, in Ephesians 4:32, he writes: "Be kind to one another, tenderhearted, forgiving one another [the imperative], as God in Christ forgave you [the indicative]." Finally, another example we can give is found in Colossians 3:1–2: "If then you have been raised with Christ [the indicative], seek the things that are above [the imperative], where Christ is, seated at the right hand of God. Set your minds on things that are above, not on things that are on earth [the imperative]." We see from these passages that Paul held both aspects of the gospel message in proper balance and unity.

What must be highlighted here, however, is that the indicative *always precedes* the imperative. What sets Christianity apart from other religions is that Christians get to work and obey God's commands (the imperative) *because they have been called by God, justified from all guilt, and permanently adopted into the divine family* (the indicative). The other religions say, "Do the right things, and you will receive salvation;" but Christianity states, "You will do the right things, because you have received salvation."[23] A Christian's desire to be loving, virtuous, honorable, and upright is due to being forgiven and justified through the perfect work of Jesus Christ. One cannot emphasize this enough in preaching and evangelism. There is always the temptation among Christians to "put the cart before the horse" when it comes to salvation. The spectre of Pelagianism is an ever-present threat to the minds of many Christians. One way to free oneself from this Pelagianistic mindset is by looking to the cross of Christ and reflecting on all the salvific benefits bestowed upon us by God apart from our worthiness.

Having stressed the importance of putting the indicative before the imperative in our understanding of the Christian life, we must also point out that the Christian life is not a quietistic one that "lays back" and lets the

23. Cf. Keller, *The Reason for God*, 179–180.

flow of redemption move along in the course of history. The Christian life is a very active one where believers work assiduously to bring the gospel message to all unreached peoples and become shining examples to those around them. As the renowned British evangelical minister D. Martyn Lloyd-Jones wrote: "The opposite to a false trust in works is not indolence, lack of discipline and doing nothing, it is to be diligent and more diligent, to be zealous, and to add to your faith."[24] Being completely forgiven and justified in Christ does not remove responsibilities from Christians. In fact, having received the irrevocable salvific benefits of the new covenant, believers are now commanded to work diligently for God and be a blessing to other people (the ability to do these being a result of our union with Christ [John 15:5]). As Karl Barth once remarked: "So living by forgiveness is never by any means passivity, but Christian living in full activity."[25] Therefore, Christians who remain completely passive and are indifferent to God's commandments show that they are living in absolute contradiction to who they are in Christ.

## Simul Iustus et Peccator?

The great Protestant Reformer Martin Luther once declared that all Christians are *simul iustus et peccator* (the Latin phrase meaning "simultaneously righteous and sinner"). Luther knew full well that the justified individual still struggles with remaining sin within himself or herself. This was not only something he experienced in his own life, but also a phenomenon he understood to be a reality for all Christians based on the testimony of Scripture. As discussed in chapter 15 on the doctrine of sanctification, we argued that Scripture speaks of regenerate people as those still struggling with remaining sin and the fallen nature within themselves. We referenced passages like Matthew 6:12; 1 Corinthians 9:26–27; Ephesians 4:22; Philippians 3:13–14; James 3:2; and 1 John 1:8–9 to demonstrate that the regenerate in the present age have yet to obtain sinless perfection.[26]

One passage, however, that stands out the most when it comes to the *simul iustus et peccator* doctrine is Galatians 5:16–17. Paul states there: "But I say, walk by the Spirit, and you will not gratify the desires of the

24. Lloyd-Jones, *Spiritual Depression*, 211.

25. Barth, *Dogmatics in Outline*, 152.

26. We did not include Romans 7:7–24 because we do not believe this passage describes the situation of the regenerate (as discussed on page 282, footnote 20).

flesh. For the desires of the flesh are against the Spirit, and the desires of the Spirit are against the flesh, for these are opposed to each other, to keep you from doing the things you want to do." One can see from this passage that Paul is stating that the sinful flesh of the believer still harasses him or her during the present time. The condition of all regenerate people is that their fleshly natures still strive against the Spirit in a life-and-death struggle to the end. Although believers have had their hearts renewed by the Spirit so that they are no longer captives of sin (cf. Rom 6:6, 11; 2 Pet 1:4; 1 John 3:9), they still need to exert themselves (by God's grace) to fight against their own sinful tendencies remaining in them (cf. Rom 6:19; Col 3:5, 9). However, one must not think of this struggle against the fallen nature as an effortless task. The Spirit helps believers in fighting against the sinful inclinations in them that desire to produce the works of the flesh (like immorality, idolatry, drunkenness, jealousy, strife, etc.); but this does not mean that the sanctifying process will be an easy "marathon race" to the finish line.[27] As mentioned earlier in chapter 15, this process takes great striving and effort on the part of believers (Heb 12:14), and no Christian should think that the overcoming of his or her sinful tendencies within is easy as taking "a walk in the park."

Even though we just stated that the struggle against the fallen nature is a strenuous undertaking that requires great effort and striving, we must not fall into adopting a distorted understanding of the *simul iustus et peccator* doctrine where ethical transformation is seen as optional (as sometimes observed in contemporary evangelical teaching). Some evangelicals today believe that "simultaneously righteous and sinful" means that a person can be genuinely justified in God's eyes and yet remain utterly dissolute in his or her behavior and walk (which is akin to the "carnal Christian" theory). This is not what Luther had in mind when he used the phrase. What Luther meant was that even though true believers fall into sin time to time, those sins will not be held against them in the divine courtroom because of the righteousness imputed to them through faith. He writes:

> For the faithful assureth himself, by faith, that his sin is forgiven
> him, forasmuch as Christ hath given Himself for it. Therefore, al-
> though he have sin in him, and daily sinneth, yet he continueth
> godly; but contrariwise, the unbeliever continueth wicked. And
> this is the true wisdom and consolation of the godly, that although

27. As the Westminster Confession of Faith states, believers "ought to be diligent in stirring up the grace of God that is in them" (XVI/3).

they have and commit sins, yet they know that for Christ's sake they are not imputed unto them.[28]

Yet, we see here that Luther asserts that the forgiven man or woman, in contrast to the unbeliever, does not fall into utter moral destitution. He or she "continueth godly," despite the moral imperfections that remain in him or her. John Stott summarizes the daily experiences of every true child of God well: "We continue to be aware of sinful desires that pull us down; but we are now also aware of a counteracting force that is drawing us upward to holiness."[29] Therefore, the *simul iustus et peccator* doctrine does not mean "completely justified, yet utterly carnal;" but simultaneously living within the two realities of the present age and the inaugurated divine kingdom (or as some theologians like to say, living between the "already" and "not yet").

As a cautionary note before we end this discussion, when attempting to understand this doctrine we must maintain a sober view when it comes to relating it to our lives. Most believers are aware (in varying degrees) of the influence the old nature has on them in the present time. In fact, the apostle Paul was keenly aware of his own imperfections when he states in Philippians 3:12, "Not that I have already obtained this or am already perfect, but I press on to make it my own, because Christ Jesus has made me his own." That is why Paul exhorted his readers to put virtue and godliness into practice on a daily basis (cf. Rom 6:13; 8:12–13; 1 Cor 6:18; Eph 4:1, 17; Phil 2:14–16; Col 3:5–10; 1 Thess 4:1–6; etc.). Paul clearly understood how strong the sinful impulses are in every believer in the present time. As a matter of fact, one of the dangers of the "entire sanctification" (or "sinless perfection") doctrine found among certain Holiness-Wesleyan groups is that it does not fully appreciate how formidable the sinful flesh in believers can be. This can result in believers underestimating their own proclivity to sin and self-centeredness (cf. Matt 26:41).

Another reason why we must have a sober view of this subject is because it powerfully affects the Christian's assurance. If one takes every moral or spiritual failure as a sign that someone is not among the redeemed, then no genuine Christian can ever have assurance of salvation. Although obedience to God plays an important role in Christian assurance, it is subservient to the primary source of assurance: the promises of the gospel based on the work of Christ on our behalf. Even though believers are no longer under the dominion of sin (unlike the unregenerate [Rom 1:18–32; Eph

28. Luther, *Commentary on Galatians*, 338.
29. Stott, *Basic Christianity*, 122.

4:17–19]), they still give in to sin time to time (1 John 1:8–10). This is why we must also have a *biblically* realistic view of the presence of sin in the lives of the regenerate; lest we unintentionally undermine the assurance of those who are sincerely seeking to follow Christ and obey his word. As Sinclair B. Ferguson writes in his excellent book *The Whole Christ*:

> While guilt is gone and the reign of sin has ended, sin continues to indwell us and to beset us. It still has the potential to deceive us and to allure us. Once we understand this, we will not confuse the ongoing presence of sin with the absence of new life in us. Without that stability in our understanding, our assurance will be liable to ebb and flow.[30]

Therefore, when attempting to comprehend the truthfulness of the *simul iustus et peccator* doctrine, we must always vigilantly keep a level mind knowing that every Christian lives between the two ages of God's redemptive-historical timeline.

## The Christian Life and the Community of Saints

That the Christian is a visible member of the body of Christ (the church) is like saying that a quarterback under contract is a member of an American football team, or that an active military general is a member of the army. When a sinner converts, and becomes justified in Christ and is adopted by the Father, he or she now belongs to the community of the saints called the church (1 Cor 12:12–13, 27; Eph 4:4–7, 16). This is not something the new believer can choose to join after his or her conversion based on his or her desire; but something that becomes a permanent part of the new believer's life and identity. As George Eldon Ladd states: "When we believe in Christ, we are made members of Christ's body; we are joined to Christ himself and therefore to all others who in union with Christ constitute his body. In the biblical sense of the word, it is true that *extra ecclesiam nulla salus* ('outside the church there is no salvation')."[31]

The church is like a sanctuary in the midst of a spiritually dark world for those who have put on Christ through faith and have been given new life by the Spirit. It is like a "secure haven community" under a benevolent King that is separated from the surrounding hostile and precarious environment

---

30. Ferguson, *The Whole Christ*, 218–219.
31. Ladd, *A Theology of the New Testament*, 588.

(Eph 2:19–22). Additionally, the church *is* (not like!) a new family for all those who are mystically joined to Christ through the Father's election and calling (cf. Gal 6:10; Eph 2:19). This entails that the new household not only provides spiritual benefits and blessings for its members but also keeps them accountable when they err and go astray in their responsibilities. As discussed in chapter 16 on the doctrine of the church, one of the functions of the church is to keep believers accountable to their spiritual duties to God. In other words, the community of saints is to remind every member that they are obligated to keep God's moral commandments, to resist the temptations of the flesh and the world, and to be a positive influence to all those they encounter in life.

One of the ways that believers can keep each other accountable is by reminding everyone that the body of Christ is one (Rom 12:5). When one member of the body of Christ suffers, then the whole body suffers; when another member of the body is honored, all rejoice because of it (1 Cor 12:26). There is an intricate link that binds all believers together in this body—which is their union with Christ. As John Stott writes:

> One of the most striking pictures that Paul uses to express the unity of believers in Christ is that of the human body. The church, he says, is the body of Christ. Every Christian is a member or organ of the body, while Christ himself is the head, controlling the body's activities. Not every organ has the same function, but each is necessary for the maximum health and usefulness of the body.[32]

That is why when a believer starts going astray from the faith, we need to grieve and do all that we can to admonish him or her of the dangers of continuing on that perilous path (cf. Heb 3:13). When a believer attains some type of spiritual triumph, we need to rejoice with him or her knowing that God has done everything to bring that person to the healthy state he or she is in now (cf. Rom 8:28). Therefore, all believers share this life together in Christ, and this means that all believers are obligated to not only encourage one another but to hold each other accountable when one of them acts or speaks in ways that bring reproach to the gospel and dishonor to Christ's name.

Having said all this, an inquisitive believer may still ask: how is this related to the Christian life? We must point out first to any believer who asks such a question that ecclesiology and Christian living, under normal conditions, cannot be separated. Except under exceptional circumstances (like a

32. Stott, *Basic Christianity*, 125.

believer who is stranded alone on a small island or an elderly believer who is confined to bed due to a serious illness), the *regular* pattern of a believer's life is that he or she actively participates in the life of his or her local church. For the New Testament writers, it was unheard of for someone who confessed Christ as Lord and Savior to refuse to be part of a local assembly of saints (cf. Acts 2:42; Heb 10:24–25). Although all believers are completely forgiven and justified in Christ by grace alone through faith alone, it was considered highly abnormal by the inspired writers for someone to declare himself or herself as being a follower of Christ and yet deliberately and habitually refuse fellowship with other followers of Christ. Of course, this does not mean that if a believer stops attending church on a regular basis that he or she will forfeit his or her righteous standing in Christ (cf. John 6:37, 39–40; Rom 8:30); but a habitual refusal to participate in the life of the church, if the individual has the opportunity to do so, may be a sign that there is a serious spiritual problem (in which case, self-examination of one's spiritual condition may be required [cf. 2 Cor 13:5]).

In addition, it is important for Christians to belong to a local assembly of believers because, as stated above, it keeps them accountable to their spiritual duties to God and other people. As mentioned in the previous section, all believers must still contend with the allures of this world and their fleshly natures on a daily basis in the present age. When believers attempt to "go it alone" when it comes to progressing in the Christian life, they put themselves at great risk of losing the battle against the temptations of the world and the fallen nature residing in them. That is why Paul tells the Colossian believers to "let the peace of Christ rule in your hearts, to which indeed you were called in one body. And be thankful. Let the word of Christ dwell in you richly, *teaching and admonishing one another in all wisdom,* singing psalms and hymns and spiritual songs, with thankfulness in your hearts to God" (Col 3:15–16). And why the author of Hebrews tells his readers: "And let us consider *how to stir up one another to love and good works,* not neglecting to meet together, as is the habit of some, *but encouraging one another,* and all the more as you see the Day drawing near" (Heb 10:24–25). The importance of collective accountability and exhortation among God's people cannot be stressed enough. When believers graciously but firmly exhort a fellow church member of the spiritual perils of defying God's word (doctrinally or ethically), they are in fact acting in love. Although the admonition may not be comfortable or pleasant at the time, its aim is to produce a spiritually beneficial result for the individual in the long-term. If an erring believer refuses to heed the gentle warnings of other believers, God may have to take direct action against him or her, through divine discipline, to set things right again (cf. 1 Cor 11:30–32; Heb 12:5–11). Leaders in the church, because of their unique roles in God's spiritual family, have the added responsibility to aid believers in becoming more mature in Christ and helping them persevere in their spiritual duties. That is why Paul states that Christ gave "the apostles, the prophets, the evangelists, the shepherds and teachers" in order to "equip the saints for the work of ministry, for building up the body of Christ" (Eph 4:11–12). In addition, the reason why the author of Hebrews tells his readers to obey their "leaders and submit to them" is because they are there to keep "watch over your souls, as those who will have to give an account" (Heb 13:17). That is why judgment towards leaders in the church will be stricter, compared to those who are not in leadership positions, because people's eternal destinies are involved (Jas 3:1).

Before we end this discussion on the relationship between the Christian life and the church, we must maintain that the church is not the "be-all and end-all" of the Christian life. The church was given to believers by the triune God as a gift for their spiritual benefit and well-being. Furthermore, the church is only a means to an end: the end being the believer's complete communion with the triune God at the renewal of all things. This is not to say that the church is not important or necessary, but that we must hold a view of the church from a broader redemptive-historical perspective. Just like the old covenant nation of Israel was only a temporary arrangement to reveal to the surrounding pagan nations what the kingdom of God was like in shadow form, and to bring the Messiah-Savior into the world at the proper time (Gal 3:23–25; 4:21–31); the church (at least in its visible socio-institutional form) is also a temporary arrangement in the new covenant age for the spiritual well-being (through the means of grace) and discipline (through admonitions) of believers in their pilgrimage to the eschatological city. Although the mission and purpose of the church have eternal outcomes, the visible church itself, like the nation of Israel under the old covenant, will come to an end once it has served God's redemptive objective for his people. Once the new heaven and new earth arrive at the eschaton, the bride of Christ (the church with all her members) will have direct communion with Christ and behold his glory in fullness (Rev 21:22–23; 22:1–5).

## The Telos of the Christian Life: God's Glory

The Christian life has an ultimate purpose. There is a *telos* to the pilgrimage of faith that believers are on in the here and now. The Greek word *telos* can be rendered as "end," "fulfillment," or "realization."[33] We believe, however, that the word "realization" captures the best meaning within the context of how we understand the ultimate goal of the Christian life. When it comes to the Christian life, believers do not strive to become virtuous and loving just for the sake of being virtuous and loving. There is a greater purpose for a Christian's loving and virtuous actions toward others. That greater purpose being *bringing glory to God*. At the end of chapter 5 (on the doctrine of humanity), we quoted from the Westminster Shorter Catechism that the chief end of human beings "is to glorify God, and to enjoy him forever" (Q. and A. 1). The ultimate purpose for the creation of human beings was so that they would bring glory to God and enjoy fellowship with him forever in paradise. They were made in God's image in order to reflect his glory and carry out his divine mandate throughout creation. They were to do this by responsibly having dominion over creation and living in perfect harmony with one another.

In the post-fall situation, things are different. People do not live in an idyllic environment like the one Adam and Eve lived in before they transgressed God's command. Sin has tarnished the good creation, and human beings (in one way or another) experience the terrible fruits of the original transgression (cf. Rom 8:18–23). However, this does not absolve human beings of their responsibility to reflect God's image in their lives and bring glory to his name. Even in the post-fall situation, people are still obligated to do God's will and follow his word. They are to glorify God by living in a way that honors and pleases him (John 15:8). Believers do this by wholeheartedly worshiping God with their lives on a regular basis (John 4:24; Rom 12:1) and being worthy representatives of his kingdom (1 Thess 2:4). Furthermore, believers can glorify God even in simple tasks and activities. The apostle Paul, for example, states that believers should eat and drink to God's glory (1 Cor 10:31). A lot of Christians may wonder how the ordinary activities of eating and drinking can glorify God. However, Paul states clearly that this is possible if one has the right heart and mindset. In other words, there is no area in life that is not covered when it comes to a believer bringing glory to God in his or her daily walk. In the

---

33. Mounce, *The Analytical Lexicon to the Greek New Testament*, 447

context of living in a fallen world, believers glorify God by being salt and light through their actions and words before the audience of unbelievers. Believers indirectly show unbelievers the power of God's redemptive work by being loving, honest, kind, and generous to them. In this way, unbelievers can get a glimpse of God's goodness and grace as Christians assiduously live by the values of the kingdom (cf. 1 Pet 2:12).

Before we close this chapter, we must make this important point: even our salvation in Christ is ultimately about God. It is true that the Father sent the Son into the world to sacrifice himself for his people so that they will not suffer his righteous wrath in the future (cf. John 3:16; Rom 5:8); however, that is not the entire story. In Ephesians 1:3–6, the apostle Paul reveals to us why God willed the salvation of his people through Jesus Christ when he could have just left them to their own destruction:

> Blessed be the God and Father of our Lord Jesus Christ, who has blessed us in Christ with every spiritual blessing in the heavenly places, even as he chose us in him before the foundation of the world, that we should be holy and blameless before him. In love he predestined us for adoption to himself as sons through Jesus Christ, according to the purpose of his will, *to the praise of his glorious grace, with which he has blessed us in the Beloved.*

We see here what the ultimate purpose is for God the Father choosing people for salvation through his Son: *so that we can praise him for his glorious grace.* His glory is the ultimate reason why God chose to save people from their sins and bestow upon them eternal life. His primary purpose was not because he wanted to make his people happy for eternity or experience perpetual bliss in heaven, but because he wanted to bring glory to himself. This is important to highlight in a time when it is commonplace for churches to place human spiritual needs as the focal point of the gospel message rather than God and his glorious grace. Or, to put it another way more bluntly: the gospel of Jesus Christ is about God and not us. In this way, we can offer up praises to God knowing that he deserves all the glory and honor for saving his people from their sins and gifting them with eternal life that they never deserved.

# Bibliography

Akin, Daniel L. "Deacon, Deaconess." In *Evangelical Dictionary of Biblical Theology,* edited by Walter A. Elwell, 149–150. Grand Rapids: Baker, 1996.

———. "The Person of Christ." In *A Theology for the Church,* revised edition, edited by Daniel L. Akin, 391–437. Nashville: Broadman and Holman, 2014.

Alexander, T. D. *From Paradise to the Promised Land: An Introduction to the Pentateuch.* Grand Rapids: Baker, 2002.

Allison, Gregg R. *Historical Theology: An Introduction to Christian Doctrine.* Grand Rapids: Zondervan, 2011.

———. *Sojourners and Strangers: The Doctrine of the Church.* Wheaton, IL: Crossway, 2012.

Anselm. "An Address (Proslogian)." In *A Scholastic Miscellany: Anselm to Ockham,* edited by Eugene R. Fairweather, 69–93. Philadelphia: Westminster, 1956.

Augustine. *On Free Choice of the Will.* Translated by Anna Benjamin and L. H. Hackstaff. New York: Bobbs-Merrill, 1964.

———. *On the Trinity,* edited by Gareth B. Matthews. Cambridge, UK: Cambridge University Press, 2002.

Aulén, Gustaf. *Christus Victor: An Historical Study of the Three Main Types of the Idea of Atonement.* Eugene, OR: Wipf and Stock, 2003.

Baima, Thomas A. "Roman Catholic View: Christ's True, Real, and Substantial Presence." In *Understanding Four Views on the Lord's Supper,* edited by John H. Armstrong, 119–136. Grand Rapids: Zondervan, 2007.

Baker, David L. *Two Testaments, One Bible: The Theological Relationship Between the Old and New Testaments.* 3rd ed. Downers Grove, IL: InterVarsity Press, 2010.

Barackman, Floyd H. *Practical Christian Theology: Examining the Great Doctrines of the Faith.* 3rd ed. Grand Rapids: Kregel, 1998.

Barbieri, Louis A. "Matthew." In *The Bible Knowledge Commentary: New Testament,* edited by John F. Walvoord and Roy B. Zuck, 13–94. Colorado Springs, CO: Cook, 2000.

Barker, William S., and W. Robert Godfrey. *Theonomy: A Reformed Critique.* Grand Rapids: Zondervan, 1990.

Barth, Karl. *Church Dogmatics.* Translated by various authors. New York: T & T Clark International, 2004.

———. *Dogmatics in Outline.* Translated by G. T. Thomson. New York: Harper and Row, 1959.

Barth, Karl, and Emil Brunner. *Natural Theology.* Translated by Peter Fraenkel. Eugene, OR: Wipf and Stock, 2002.

Bartlett, Anthony W. *Cross Purposes: The Violent Grammar of Christian Atonement.* Harrisburg, PA: Trinity Press International, 2001.

Bauckham, Richard. *Jesus and the God of Israel:* God Crucified *and Other Studies on the New Testament's Christology of Divine Identity.* Grand Rapids: Eerdmans, 2008.

Bauerschmidt, Frederick C., and James J. Buckley. *Catholic Theology: An Introduction.* Chichester, UK: Wiley-Blackwell, 2017.

Bavinck, Herman. *Our Reasonable Faith: A Survey of Christian Doctrine.* Translated by Henry Zylstra. Grand Rapids: Eerdmans, 1956.

———. *Reformed Dogmatics.* 4 volumes, edited by John Bolt, translated by John Vriend. Grand Rapids: Baker, 2003–2008.

Beale, G. K. *The Book of Revelation.* New International Greek Testament Commentary. Grand Rapids: Eerdmans, 1999.

Beasley-Murray, George R. *Baptism in the New Testament.* Grand Rapids: Eerdmans, 1994.

———. *John.* Word Biblical Commentary. 2nd ed. Nashville: Thomas Nelson, 1999.

Beeke, Joel R, *The Quest for Full Assurance: The Legacy of Calvin and His Successors.* Edinburgh: Banner of Truth, 1999.

Belcher, Richard P. *The Layman's Guide to the Lordship Controversy.* Southbridge, MA: Crowne, 1990.

Bell, M. Charles. *Calvin and Scottish Theology.* Edinburgh: The Handsel Press, 1985.

Berkhof, Louis. *Systematic Theology,* new edition. Grand Rapids: Eerdmans, 1996.

Berkouwer, G. C. *Faith and Justification.* Translated by Lewis B. Smedes. Grand Rapids: Eerdmans, 1954.

———. *Faith and Perseverance.* Translated by Robert D. Knudsen. Grand Rapids: Eerdmans, 1958.

———. *Man: The Image of God.* Translated by Dirk W. Jellema. Grand Rapids: Eerdmans, 1962.

Blaising, Craig A. "Premillennialism." In *Three Views on the Millennium and Beyond,* edited by Darrell L. Bock, 155–227. Grand Rapids: Zondervan, 1999.

Blomberg, Craig L. "Holy Spirit." In *Evangelical Dictionary of Biblical Theology,* edited by Walter A. Elwell, 344–348. Grand Rapids: Baker, 1996.

Blomberg, Craig L., and Jennifer Foutz Markley. *A Handbook of New Testament Exegesis.* Grand Rapids: Baker, 2010.

Blum, Edwin A. "1 Peter." In *The Expositor's Bible Commentary,* vol. 12, edited by Frank E. Gaebelein, 207–254. Grand Rapids: Zondervan, 1981.

———. "2 Peter." In *The Expositor's Bible Commentary,* vol. 12, edited by Frank E. Gaebelein, 255–289. Grand Rapids: Zondervan, 1981.

Boettner, Loraine. "Postmillennialism." In *The Meaning of the Millennium: Four Views,* edited by Robert G. Clouse, 117–141. Downers Grove, IL: InterVarsity Press, 1977.

Boice, James Montgomery. *Foundations of the Christian Faith: A Comprehensive and Readable Theology.* Downers Grove, IL: InterVarsity Press, 1986.

Boyd, Greg A. *Oneness Pentecostals and the Trinity: A World-Wide Movement Assessed by a Former Oneness Pentecostal.* Grand Rapids: Baker, 1992.

Brakel, Wilhelmus à. *The Christian's Reasonable Service.* 4 volumes, edited by Joel R. Beeke, translated by Bartel Elshout. Grand Rapids: Reformation Heritage Books, 1992–1995.

Bray, Gerald. *The Doctrine of God.* Downers Grove, IL: InterVarsity Press, 1993.

Bridges, Jerry. *Respectable Sins: Confronting the Sins We Tolerate.* Colorado Springs, CO: Navpress, 2007.

Bruce, F. F. *The Epistle to the Galatians*. Grand Rapids: Eerdmans, 1982.

———. *Romans*. The Tyndale New Testament Commentaries. Grand Rapids: Eerdmans, 1985.

Brunner, Emil. *The Christian Doctrine of Creation and Redemption*. Translated by Olive Wyon. Philadelphia: Westminster, 1952.

Buchanan, James. *The Doctrine of Justification: An Outline of Its History in the Church and of Its Exposition from Scripture*. Grand Rapids: Baker, 1970.

Bulgakov, Sergius. *The Comforter*. Translated by Boris Jakim. Grand Rapids: Eerdmans, 2004.

Burdick, Donald W. "James." In *The Expositor's Bible Commentary*, vol. 12, edited by Frank E. Gaebelein, 159–205. Grand Rapids: Zondervan, 1981.

Burns, J. Lanier. "The Future of Ethnic Israel in Romans 11." In *Dispensationalism, Israel and the Church: A Search for Definition*, edited by Craig A. Blaising and Darrell L. Bock, 188–229. Grand Rapids: Zondervan, 1992.

Calvin, John. *Institutes of the Christian Religion*. Translated by Ford Lewis Battles. Philadelphia: Westminster, 1960.

Caneday, Ardel B. "Baptism in the Stone-Campbell Restoration Movement." In *Believer's Baptism: Sign of the New Covenant in Christ*, edited by Thomas R. Schreiner and Shawn D. Wright, 285–328. Nashville: Broadman and Holman, 2006.

Carson, D. A. "Matthew." In *The Expositor's Bible Commentary*, vol. 8, edited by Frank E. Gaebelein, 1–599. Grand Rapids: Zondervan, 1984.

———. "Reflections on Assurance." In *The Grace of God, the Bondage of the Will*, vol. 2, edited by Thomas R. Schreiner and Bruce A. Ware, 383–412. Grand Rapids: Baker, 1995.

———. "The Role of Exegesis in Systematic Theology." In *Doing Theology in Today's World: Essays in Honor of Kenneth S. Kantzer*, edited by John D. Woodbridge and Thomas Edward McComiskey, 39–76. Grand Rapids: Zondervan, 1991.

———. "The Vindication of Imputation: On Fields of Discourse and Semantic Fields." In *Justification: What's at Stake in the Current Debates*, edited by Mark Husbands and Daniel J. Treier, 46–78. Downers Grove, IL: InterVarsity Press, 2004.

Castelein, John D. "Christian Churches/Churches of Christ View: Believers' Baptism as the Biblical Occasion of Salvation." In *Understanding Four Views on Baptism*, edited by John H. Armstrong, 129–144. Grand Rapids: Zondervan, 2007.

*Catechism of the Catholic Church*. New York: Doubleday, 1995.

Caulley, T. S. "Holy Spirit." In *Evangelical Dictionary of Theology*, edited by Walter A. Elwell, 521–527. Grand Rapids: Baker, 1984.

Chang, Andrew D. "Second Peter 2:1 and the Extent of the Atonement." *Bibliotheca Sacra*, 142 (January, 1985) 52–63.

Childs, Brevard S. *Biblical Theology of the Old and New Testaments: Theological Reflection on the Christian Bible*. Minneapolis: Fortress Press, 1993.

Clark, David K. *To Know and Love God: Method and Theology*. Wheaton, IL: Crossway, 2003.

Clark, Gordon H. *The Atonement*. 2nd ed. Hobbs, NM: The Trinity Foundation, 1996.

———. *God and Evil*. Unicoi, TN: The Trinity Foundation, 2004.

Clarke, William Newton. *An Outline of Christian Theology*. New York: Scribner, 1901.

Clouse, Robert G. "Millennium, Views of the." In *Evangelical Dictionary of Theology*, edited by Walter A. Elwell, 714–718. Grand Rapids: Baker, 1984.

Clowney, Edmund P. *The Church*. Downers Grove, IL: InterVarsity Press, 1995.

Cobb, John B., and David R. Griffin. *Process Theology: An Introductory Exposition.* Philadelphia: Westminster, 1976.

Cockerill, Gareth L. "A Wesleyan Arminian View." In *Four Views on the Warning Passages in Hebrews,* edited by Herbert W. Bateman IV, 257–292. Grand Rapids: Kregel, 2007.

Coleman, Robert E. *The Heart of the Gospel: The Theology Behind the Master Plan of Evangelism.* Grand Rapids: Baker, 2011.

Cottrell, Jack. *The Faith Once For All: Bible Doctrine for Today.* Joplin: MO: College Press, 2002.

Crisp, Oliver D. *God Incarnate: Explorations in Christology.* London: T & T Clark International, 2009.

Culver, Robert Duncan. *Systematic Theology: Biblical and Historical.* Ross-shire, UK: Mentor, 2005.

Dabney, Robert L. *Systematic Theology.* Edinburgh: Banner of Truth, 1996.

Darwin, Charles. *The Origin of Species.* New York: Signet Classic, 2003 (first published 1859).

Davids, Peter H. *The Letters of Second Peter and Jude.* The Pillar New Testament Commentary. Grand Rapids: Eerdmans, 2006.

Davies, W. D. *Paul and Rabbinic Judaism: Some Rabbinic Elements in Pauline Theology.* London: SPCK, 1948.

Deiter, Melvin E. "The Wesleyan Perspective." In *Five Views on Sanctification,* edited by Melvin E. Dieter, 11–46. Grand Rapids: Zondervan, 1987.

Delitzsch, Franz. *A System of Biblical Psychology.* Grand Rapids: Baker, 1966.

Demarest, Bruce A. *The Cross and Salvation: The Doctrine of Salvation.* Wheaton, IL: Crossway, 1997.

Dever, Mark E. "The Church." In *A Theology for the Church,* revised edition, edited by Daniel L. Akin, 603–668. Nashville: Broadman and Holman, 2014.

Diprose, Ronald E. *Israel and the Church: The Origin and Effects of Replacement Theology.* Waynesboro, GA: Authentic Media, 2004.

Dodd, C. H. *The Apostolic Preaching and Its Developments.* New York: Harper, 1936.

Donaldson, Terence L. *Paul and the Gentiles: Remapping the Apostle's Convictional World.* Minneapolis: Fortress Press, 1997.

Donnelly, John Patrick. "Limbo." In *Evangelical Dictionary of Theology,* edited by Walter A. Elwell, 642–643. Grand Rapids: Baker, 1984.

Douma, J. *The Ten Commandments: Manual for the Christian Life.* Translated by Nelson D. Kloosterman. Phillipsburg, NJ: Presbyterian and Reformed, 1996.

Dumbrell, William J. *Covenant and Creation: A Theology of Old Testament Covenants.* Nashville: Thomas Nelson, 1984.

Dunn, James D. G. "If Paul Could Believe Both in Justification by Faith and Judgment According to Works, Why Should that Be a Problem for Us?" In *Four Views on the Role of Works at the Final Judgment,* edited by Alan P. Stanley, 119–141. Grand Rapids: Zondervan, 2013.

———. "New Perspective View." In *Justification: Five Views,* edited by James K. Beilby and Paul Rhodes Eddy, 176–201. Downers Grove, IL: InterVarsity Press, 2011.

———. *The New Perspective on Paul,* revised edition. Grand Rapids: Eerdmans, 2008.

———. "The New Perspective on Paul." *Bulletin of the John Ryland's Library* 65 (1983) 95–122.

———. *The Theology of Paul the Apostle.* Grand Rapids: Eerdmans, 1998.

Dunnett, Walter M. "Repentance." In *Evangelical Dictionary of Biblical Theology*, edited by Walter A. Elwell, 671–672. Grand Rapids: Baker. 1996.

Dyk, Leanne Van. "How Does Jesus Make a Difference?" In *Essentials of Christian Theology*, edited by William C. Placher, 205–220. Louisville: Westminster/John Knox, 2003

Enns, Paul. *The Moody Handbook of Theology*, revised and expanded. Chicago: Moody, 2014.

Erickson, Millard J. *Christian Theology*. 2nd ed. Grand Rapids: Baker, 1998.

Fairbairn, Patrick. *The Revelation of Law in Scripture*. Grand Rapids: Zondervan, 1957 (originally published 1869).

Feinberg, Charles L. *Millennialism: The Two Major Views*. Winona Lake, IN: BMH, 1985.

Feinberg, John S. *No One Like Him: The Doctrine of God*. Wheaton: IL: Crossway, 2001.

Ferguson, Paul. "Death, Mortality." In *Evangelical Dictionary of Biblical Theology*, edited by Walter A. Elwell, 154–156. Grand Rapids: Baker, 1996.

Ferguson, Sinclair B. *The Christian Life: A Doctrinal Introduction*. Edinburgh: Banner of Truth, 1989.

———. *The Holy Spirit*. Downers Grove, IL: InterVarsity Press, 1996.

———. "The Reformed View." In *Christian Spirituality: Five Views of Sanctification*, edited by Donald L. Alexander, 47–76. Downers Grove, IL: InterVarsity, 1988.

———. *The Whole Christ: Legalism, Antinomianism, and Gospel Assurance—Why the Marrow Controversy Still Matters*. Wheaton, IL: Crossway, 2016.

Fiddes, Paul S. *Past Event and Present Salvation: The Christian Idea of Atonement*. Louisville: Westminster/John Knox, 1989.

Foh, Susan T. "What Is the Woman's Desire?" *Westminster Theological Journal* 37 (1974/1975) 376–383.

Forlines, F. Leroy. *The Quest for Truth: Theology for Postmodern Times*. Nashville, Randall House, 2001.

Foulkes, Francis. *Ephesians*. The Tyndale New Testament Commentaries. 2nd ed. Grand Rapids: Eerdmans, 1989.

Frame, John M. *The Doctrine of God*. Phillipsburg, NJ: Presbyterian and Reformed, 2002.

———. *The Doctrine of the Christian Life*. Phillipsburg, NJ: Presbyterian and Reformed, 2008.

———. *Salvation Belongs to the Lord: An Introduction to Systematic Theology*. Phillipsburg, NJ: Presbyterian and Reformed, 2006.

France, R. T. *Matthew*. The Tyndale New Testament Commentaries. Grand Rapids: Eerdmans, 1985.

Fudge, William Edward. "The Case for Conditionalism." In *Two Views of Hell: A Biblical and Theological Dialogue*, 19–82. Downers Grove, IL: InterVarsity Press, 2000.

Fuller, Daniel P. *Gospel and Law: Contrast or Continuum?* Grand Rapids: Eerdmans 1980.

———. "Paul and the 'Works of the Law.'" *Westminster Theological Journal* 38 (1975–1976) 28–42.

———. *The Unity of the Bible: Unfolding God's Plan for Humanity*. Grand Rapids: Zondervan, 1992.

Gaffin, Richard B. *Perspectives on Pentecost*. Grand Rapids: Baker, 1979.

Garlington, Don. *Faith, Obedience, and Perseverance: Aspects of Paul's Letter to the Romans*. Tübingen: Mohr-Siebeck, 1994.

———. *In Defense of the New Perspective on Paul: Essays and Reviews*. Eugene, OR: Wipf and Stock, 2005.

———. "The Obedience of Faith in the Letter to the Romans: Part I: The Meaning of *hupakoe pisteos* (Rom 1:5; 16:26)." *Westminster Theological Journal* 52 (1990) 201–224.

Garret, James Leo. *Systematic Theology: Biblical, Historical, and Evangelical,* vol. 1, 2nd ed. N. Richland Hills, TX: BIBAL Press, 2000.

Genderen, J. van, and W. H. Velema. *Concise Reformed Dogmatics.* Translated by Gerrit Bilkes and Ed M. van der Maas. Phillipsburg, NJ: Presbyterian and Reformed, 2008

Gentry, Kenneth L. "The Great Tribulation is Past: Exposition." In *The Great Tribulation: Past or Present?,* 33–66. Grand Rapids: Kregel, 1999.

———. "Postmillennialism." In *Three Views on the Millennium and Beyond,* edited by Darrell L. Bock, 11–57. Grand Rapids: Zondervan, 1999.

Gentry, Peter J., and Stephen J. Wellum. *Kingdom through Covenant: A Biblical-Theological Understanding of the Covenants.* Wheaton, IL: Crossway, 2012.

Gill, John. *A Body of Doctrinal Divinity,* new edition. Paris, AR: The Baptist Standard Bearer, 2004.

Girdlestone, Robert B. *Synonyms of the Old Testament.* 2nd ed. Grand Rapids: Eerdmans, 1973.

González, Justo L. *The Story of Christianity: The Early Church to the Dawn of the Reformation,* vol. 1. New York: HarperCollins, 1984.

Gore, Charles. *The Church and the Ministry,* revised edition. London: Longmans, Greens, 1919.

Green, Michael. *2 Peter and Jude.* Tyndale New Testament Commentaries Grand Rapids: Eerdmans, 1987.

Grenz, Stanley J. *Theology for the Community of God.* Grand Rapids: Eerdmans, 2000.

Grogan, Geoffrey W. "Isaiah." In *The Expositor's Bible Commentary,* vol. 6, edited by Frank E. Gaebelein, 1–354. Grand Rapids: Zondervan, 1986.

Gros, Brother Jeffrey. "The Roman Catholic View." In *The Lord's Supper: Five Views,* edited by Gordon T. Smith, 13–31. Downers Grove, IL: InterVarsity Press, 2008.

Grudem, Wayne. *1 Peter.* The Tyndale New Testament Commentaries. Grand Rapids: Eerdmans, 1988.

———. *Christian Ethics: An Introduction to Biblical Moral Reasoning.* Wheaton, IL: Crossway, 2018.

———. "Perseverance of the Saints: A Case Study from Hebrews 6:4–6 and the Other Warning Passages in Hebrews." In *The Grace of God, the Bondage of the Will,* vol. 1, edited by Thomas R. Schreiner and Bruce A. Ware, 133–182. Grand Rapids: Baker, 1995.

———. *Systematic Theology: An Introduction to Biblical Doctrine.* Grand Rapids: Zondervan, 1994.

Gulley, Norman R. *Systematic Theology.* 4 volumes. Berrien Springs, MI: Andrews University Press, 2003–2016.

Gundry, Robert H. *The Church and the Tribulation: A Biblical Examination of Posttribulationism.* Grand Rapids: Zondervan, 1973.

———. *Commentary on the New Testament.* Peabody, MA: Hendrickson, 2010.

———. "The Nonimputation of Christ's Righteousness." In *Justification: What's at Stake in the Current Debates,* edited by Mark Husbands and Daniel J. Treier, 17–45. Downers Grove, IL: InterVarsity Press, 2004.

Guthrie, Donald. *The Epistle to the Hebrews.* The Tyndale New Testament Commentaries. Grand Rapids: Eerdmans, 1983.

Hafemann, Scott J. "The Covenant Relationship." In *Central Themes in Biblical Theology: Mapping Unity in Diversity,* edited by Scott J. Hafemann and Paul R. House, 20–65. Grand Rapids: Baker, 2007.

———. *The God of Promise and the Life of Faith: Understanding the Heart of the Bible.* Wheaton, IL: Crossway, 2001.

Hamilton, James M. *Revelation: Spirit Speaks to the Churches.* Wheaton, IL: Crossway, 2012.

Harpur, Tom. *The Pagan Christ: Recovering the Lost Light.* Toronto: Thomas Allen, 2004.

Harrison, Everett F. "Romans." In *The Expositor's Bible Commentary,* vol. 10, edited by Frank E. Gaebelein, 1–171. Grand Rapids: Zondervan, 1976.

Hayes, Zachary J. "The Purgatorial View." In *Four Views on Hell,* edited by William Crockett, 91–118. Grand Rapids: Zondervan, 1996.

Helm, Paul. *Calvin and the Calvinists.* Edinburgh: Banner of Truth, 1982.

———. *The Providence of God.* Downers Grove, IL: InterVarsity Press, 1993.

Hendriksen, William. *Luke.* New Testament Commentary. Grand Rapids: Baker, 1978.

———. *Matthew.* New Testament Commentary. Grand Rapids: Baker, 1973.

———. *Romans.* New Testament Commentary. Grand Rapids: Baker, 1981.

Heppe, Heinrich. *Reformed Dogmatics,* edited by Ernst Bizer, translated by G. T. Thomson. Eugene, OR: Wipf and Stock, 2007.

Hewitt, Thomas. *The Epistle to the Hebrews.* The Tyndale New Testament Commentaries. Grand Rapids: Eerdmans, 1960.

Hick. John. *Evil and the God of Love.* London: Macmillan, 1966.

Hiebert, Robert J. V. "Create, Creation." In *Evangelical Dictionary of Biblical Theology,* edited by Walter A. Elwell, 132–136. Grand Rapids: Baker, 1996.

Hoch, Carl B. "New Birth." In *Evangelical Dictionary of Biblical Theology,* edited by Walter A. Elwell, 558–559. Grand Rapids: Baker, 1996.

Hodge, Charles. *Systematic Theology.* 3 volumes. Grand Rapids: Eerdmans, 1970.

Hodges, Zane C. *Absolutely Free!: A Biblical Reply to Lordship Salvation.* Dallas: Redención Viva, 1989.

———. *The Epistle of James: Proven Character Through Testing,* edited by Arthur L. Farstad and Robert N. Wilkin. Irving, TX: Grace Evangelical Society, 1994.

———. *The Gospel Under Siege.* Dallas: Redención Viva, 1981.

Hodgson, Peter C. *Winds of the Spirit: A Constructive Christian Theology.* Louisville: Westminster/John Knox, 1994.

Hoehner, Harold W. "Love." In *Evangelical Dictionary of Theology,* edited by Walter A. Elwell, 656–659. Grand Rapids: Baker, 1984.

Hoekema, Anthony A. *The Bible and the Future.* Grand Rapids: Eerdmans, 1979.

———. *Created in God's Image.* Grand Rapids: Eerdmans, 1986.

———. *The Four Major Cults.* Grand Rapids: Eerdmans, 1963.

———. *Saved by Grace.* Grand Rapids: Eerdmans, 1989.

Hoeksema, Herman. *"Whosever Will."* Grand Rapids: Eerdmans, 1945.

Horton, Michael S. *The Christian Faith: A Systematic Theology for Pilgrims On the Way.* Grand Rapids: Zondervan, 2011.

———. *Covenant and Salvation: Union with Christ.* Louisville: Westminster/John Knox Press, 2007.

———. *God of Promise: Introducing Covenant Theology.* Grand Rapids: Baker, 2006.

———. *Pilgrim Theology: Core Doctrines for Christian Disciples.* Grand Rapids: Zondervan, 2011.

Hughes, Philip E. *The True Image: The Origin and Destiny of Man in Christ.* Grand Rapids: Eerdmans, 1989.

Irenaeus. *Against Heresies.* Peabody, MA: Hendrickson, 1995.

Jenson, Robert W. *Systematic Theology: The Works of God,* vol. 2. New York: Oxford University Press, 1999.

Johnson, Alan F. "Revelation." In *The Expositor's Bible Commentary,* vol. 12, edited by Frank E. Gaebelein, 397–603. Grand Rapids: Zondervan, 1981.

Johnson, Elliott E. "Covenants in Traditional Dispensationalism." In *Three Central Issues in Contemporary Dispensationalism,* edited by Herbert W. Bateman IV, 121- 155. Grand Rapids: Kregel, 1999.

Jüngel, Eberhard. *God as the Mystery of the World.* Translated by Darrell L. Guder. Grand Rapids: Eerdmans, 1983.

Kaiser, Walter C. *The Promise-Plan of God: The Biblical Theology of the Old and New Testaments.* Grand Rapids: Zondervan, 2008.

Kaiser, Walter C., and Moisés Silva. *An Introduction to Biblical Hermeneutics: The Search for Meaning.* Grand Rapids: Zondervan, 1994.

Karlberg, Mark W. *Covenant Theology in Reformed Perspective.* Eugene, OR: Wipf and Stock, 2000.

Keathley, Kenneth. *Salvation and Sovereignty: A Molinist Approach.* Nashville: Broadman and Holman, 2010.

Keil, C. F., and F. Delitzsch. *Commentary on the Old Testament,* vol. 1. Peabody, MA: Hendrickson, 2006.

Keller, Timothy. *The Reason for God: Belief in an Age of Skepticism.* New York: Dutton, 2008.

Kendall, R. T. *Calvin and English Calvinism to 1649.* Milton Keynes, UK: Paternoster, 1997.

Kent, Homer A. "Philippians." In *The Expositor's Bible Commentary,* vol. 11, edited by Frank E. Gaebelein, 93–159. Grand Rapids: Zondervan, 1978.

Kerr, William Nigel. "Virtue, Virtues." In *Evangelical Dictionary of Theology,* edited by Walter A. Elwell, 1146. Grand Rapids: Baker, 1984.

King, Max R. *The Cross and the Parousia of Christ: The Two Dimensions of One Age-Changing Eschaton.* Warren, OH: Parkman Road Church of Christ, 1997.

Kistemaker, Simon J. *1 Corinthians.* New Testament Commentary. Grand Rapids: Baker, 1993.

———. *James and I-III John.* New Testament Commentary. Grand Rapids: Baker, 1986.

———. *Peter and Jude.* New Testament Commentary. Grand Rapids: Baker, 1987.

———. *Revelation.* New Testament Commentary. Grand Rapids: Baker, 2001.

Kolb, Robert. "Lutheran View: God's Baptismal Act as Regenerative." In *Understanding Four Views on Baptism,* edited by John H. Armstrong, 91–109. Grand Rapids: Zondervan, 2007.

Kromminga, C. G. "Repentance." In *Evangelical Dictionary of Theology,* edited by Walter A. Elwell, 936–937. Grand Rapids: Baker, 1984.

Kruse, Colin G. *John.* The Tyndale New Testament Commentaries. Grand Rapids: Eerdmans, 2004.

Kubo, Sakae. "I John 3:9: Absolute or Habitual?" *Andrews University Seminary Studies* 7 (1969) 47–56.

Ladd, George Eldon. *A Commentary on the Revelation of John.* Grand Rapids: Eerdmans, 1972.

———. "Historic Premillennialism." In *The Meaning of the Millennium: Four Views*, edited by Robert G. Clouse, 17–40. Downers Grove, IL: InterVarsity Press, 1977.

———. "Israel and the Church." *Evangelical Quarterly* 36, no. 4 (October-December 1964) 206–213.

———. *A Theology of the New Testament*, revised edition. Grand Rapids: Eerdmans, 1993.

Laney, J. Carl. *John.* Moody Gospel Commentary. Chicago: Moody, 1992.

Leith, John H. *Basic Christian Doctrine.* Louisville: Westminster/John Knox, 1993.

Lewis, Gordon R., and Bruce A. Demarest. Integrative Theology. 3 volumes Grand Rapids: Zondervan, 1987–1994.

Lightner, Robert P. "Angels, Satan, and Demons: Invisible Beings that Inhabit the Spiritual World." In *Understanding Christian Theology,* edited by Charles R. Swindoll and Roy B. Zuck, 537–640. Nashville: Thomas Nelson, 2003.

———. "Hell." In *Evangelical Dictionary of Theology,* edited by Walter A. Elwell, 506. Grand Rapids: Baker, 1984.

———. *Sin, the Savior, and Salvation: The Theology of Everlasting Life.* Grand Rapids: Kregel, 1991.

Lincoln, Andrew T. *Ephesians.* Word Biblical Commentary. Nashville: Word, 1990.

Lindbeck, George. "What of the Future? A Christian Response." In *Christianity in Jewish Terms,* edited by Tikva Frymer-Kensky et al., 357–365. Boulder, CO: Westview, 2000.

Litton, E. A. *Introduction to Dogmatic Theology.* 3rd ed. London: Robert Scott, 1912.

Lloyd-Jones, D. Martyn. *Spiritual Depression: Its Causes and Cure.* Grand Rapids: Eerdmans, 1965.

Long, Gary D. *Definite Atonement.* Nutley, NJ: Presbyterian and Reformed, 1976.

Longenecker, Richard N. "The Acts of the Apostles." In *The Expositor's Bible Commentary,* vol. 9, edited by Frank E. Gaebelein, 205–573. Grand Rapids: Zondervan, 1981.

Lunde, J. M. "Repentance." In *New Dictionary of Biblical Theology,* edited by T. Desmond Alexander and Brian S. Rosner, 726–727. Downers Grove, IL: InterVarsity Press, 2000.

Luther, Martin. *Commentary on Galatians,* edited by John Prince Fallowes, translated by Erasmus Middleton. Grand Rapids: Kregel, 1979.

MacArthur, John F. *The Gospel According to Jesus.* Grand Rapids: Zondervan, 1988.

Mare, W. Harold. "1 Corinthian." In *The Expositors' Bible Commentary,* vol. 10, edited by Frank E. Gaebelein, 173–297. Grand Rapids: Zondervan, 1976.

Marshall, Bruce D. "Are There Angels?" In *Why Are We Here?,* edited by Ronald F. Thiemann and William C. Placher, 69–83. Harrisburg, PA: Trinity Press International, 1998.

Marshall, I. Howard. *Kept by the Power of God: A Study of Perseverance and Falling Away.* London: Epworth, 1969.

Martin, Walter. *Kingdom of the Cults,* revised edition. Minneapolis: Bethany House, 1997.

McGlasson, Paul C. *Invitation to Dogmatic Theology: A Canonical Approach.* Grand Rapids: Brazos, 2006.

McGrath, Alister E. *Christian Theology: An Introduction.* 2nd ed. Oxford, UK: Blackwell, 1997.

McRoberts, Kerry D. "The Holy Trinity." In *Systematic Theology,* revised edition, edited by Stanley M. Horton, 145–177. Springfield, MO: Logion Press, 1995.

Merrill, Eugene H. *Everlasting Dominion: A Theology of the Old Testament.* Nashville: Broadman and Holman, 2006.

Meyer, Jason C. *The End of the Law: Mosaic Covenant in Pauline Theology.* Nashville: Broadman and Holman, 2009.

Michel, Otto. "μεταμέλομαι." In *Theological Dictionary of the New Testament*, vol. 4, edited by Gerhard Kittel and Gerhard Friedrich, translated by Geoffrey W. Bromiley, 626–629. Grand Rapids: Eerdmans, 1967.

Migloire, Daniel L. *Faith Seeking Understanding: An Introduction to Christian Theology.* 2nd ed. Grand Rapids: Eerdmans, 2004.

Miley, John. *Systematic Theology*, vol. 1. New York: Hunt & Eaton, 1893.

———. *Systematic Theology*, vol. 2. Peabody, MA: Hendrickson, 1989.

Milne, Bruce. *Know the Truth: A Handbook of Christian Belief.* 3rd ed. Downers Grove, IL: InterVarsity Press, 2009.

Moo, Douglas J. "The Case for the Posttribulation Rapture Position." In *Three Views on the Rapture: Pre-, Mid-, or Post-Tribulation,* edited by Gleason L. Archer, 169–211. Grand Rapids: Zondervan, 1996.

———. *James.* Tyndale New Testament Commentaries. Grand Rapids: Eerdmans, 1985.

———. "'Law,' 'Works of the Law,' and Legalism in Paul." *Westminster Theological Journal* 45 (1983) 73–100.

———. "The Law of Christ as the Fulfillment of the Law of Moses: A Modified Lutheran View." In *Five Views on Law and Gospel,* edited by Wayne G. Strickland, 317–376. Grand Rapids: Zondervan, 1999.

Moore, Russell D. "Natural Theology." In *A Theology for the Church,* revised edition, edited by Daniel L. Akin, 67–101. Nashville: Broadman and Holman, 2014.

Morgan, Christopher W., with Robert A. Peterson. *Christian Theology: The Biblical Story and our Faith.* Nashville: Broadman and Holman, 2020.

Morris, Leon. "Church Government." In *Evangelical Dictionary of Theology,* edited by Walter A. Elwell, 238–241. Grand Rapids: Baker, 1984.

———. *The Epistle to the Romans.* Grand Rapids: Eerdmans, 1988.

———. *1 Corinthians.* The Tyndale New Testament Commentaries. Grand Rapids: Eerdmans, 1985.

———. "Hebrews." In *The Expositor's Bible Commentary,* vol. 12, edited by Frank E. Gaebelein, 1–158. (Grand Rapids: Zondervan, 1981.

———. *Revelation.* The Tyndale New Testament Commentaries. Grand Rapids: Eerdmans, 1987.

Moule, C. F. D. *Worship in the New Testament.* London: Lutterworth, 1961.

Mounce, William D. *The Analytical Lexicon to the Greek New Testament.* Grand Rapids: Zondervan, 1993.

Mueller, John Theodore. *Christian Dogmatics: A Handbook of Doctrinal Theology.* St. Louis: Concordia, 1934.

Mullen, Bradford A. "Sanctification." In *Evangelical Dictionary of Biblical Theology,* edited by Walter A. Elwell, 708–713. Grand Rapids: Baker, 1996.

Muller, Richard A. *Calvin and the Reformed Tradition: On the Work of Christ and the Order of Salvation.* Grand Rapids: Baker, 2012.

Murray, John. *Collected Writings of John Murray,* 4 volumes. Edinburgh: Banner of Truth, 1976–1982.

———. *The Covenant of Grace: A Biblico-Theological Study.* Phillipsburg, NJ: Presbyterian and Reformed, 1953.

———. *The Imputation of Adam's Sin.* Phillipsburg, NJ: Presbyterian and Reformed, 1959.

———. *Principles of Conduct: Aspects of Biblical Ethics.* Grand Rapids: Eerdmans, 1957.

———. *Redemption—Accomplished and Applied.* Grand Rapids: Eerdmans, 1955.

Nelson, William B. "Sheol." In *Evangelical Dictionary of Biblical Theology*, edited by Walter A. Elwell, 735. Grand Rapids: Baker, 1996.

Nettles, Thomas J. "Baptist View: Baptism as a Symbol of Christ's Saving Work." In *Understanding Four Views on Baptism*, edited by John H. Armstrong, 25–41. Grand Rapids: Zondervan, 2007.

*New Scofield Reference Bible*. Oxford: Oxford University Press, 1967.

Niehaus, Jeffrey J. "An Argument Against Theologically Constructed Covenants." *Journal of the Evangelical Theological Society* 50/2 (June 2007) 259–273.

Olson, Roger E. "A Baptist Response [to the Reformed view]." In *The Lord's Supper: Five Views*, edited by Gordon T. Smith, 87–88. Downers Grove, IL: InterVarsity Press, 2008.

———. *The Mosaic of Christian Belief: Twenty Centuries of Unity and Diversity*. Downers Grove, IL: InterVarsity Press, 2002.

Osborne, Grant R. "A Classical Arminian View." In *Four Views on the Warning Passages in Hebrews*, edited by Herbert W. Bateman IV, 86–128. Grand Rapids: Kregel, 2007.

———. *The Hermeneutical Spiral: A Comprehensive Introduction to Biblical Interpretation*. Downers Grove, IL: InterVarsity Press, 1991.

Osterhaven, M. E. "Covenant Theology." In *Evangelical Dictionary of Theology*, edited by Walter A. Elwell, 279–280. Grand Rapids: Baker, 1984.

Ott, Ludwig. *Fundamentals of Catholic Dogma*, edited by James Canon Bastible, translated by Patrick Lynch. St. Louis: Herder, 1955.

Owen, John. *The Doctrine of Justification by Faith*. Grand Rapids: Reformation Heritage Books, 2006.

Packer, J. I. "The Atonement in the Life of the Christian." In *The Glory of the Atonement: Biblical, Theological and Practical Perspectives*, edited by Charles E. Hill and Frank A. James III, 409–425. Downers Grove, IL: InterVarsity Press, 2004.

———. "Regeneration." In *Evangelical Dictionary of Theology*, edited by Walter A. Elwell, 924–926. Grand Rapids: Baker, 1984.

Pentecost, J. Dwight. "Daniel." In *The Bible Knowledge Commentary: Old Testament*, edited by John F. Walvoord and Roy B. Zuck, 1323–1375. Colorado Springs, CO: Cook, 2000.

Phillips, Timothy R. "Hell." In *Evangelical Dictionary of Biblical Theology*, edited by Walter A. Elwell, 338–340. Grand Rapids: Baker, 1996.

Pinnock, Clark H. "The Conditional View." In *Four Views on Hell*, edited by William Crockett, 133–166. Grand Rapids: Zondervan, 1996.

———. "Divine Election as Corporate, Open, and Vocational." In *Perspectives on Election: Five Views*, edited by Chad Owen Brand, 276–314. Nashville: Broadman and Holman, 2006.

———. *A Wideness in God's Mercy: The Finality of Jesus Christ in a World of Religions*. Grand Rapids: Zondervan, 1992.

Piper, John. "Are There Two Wills in God? Divine Election and God's Desire for All to Be Saved." In *The Grace of God, the Bondage of the Will*, vol. 1, edited by Thomas R. Schreiner and Bruce A. Ware, 107–131. Grand Rapids: Baker, 1995.

Pratt, Richard L. "Reformed View: Baptism as a Sacrament of the Covenant." In *Understanding Four Views on Baptism*, edited by John H. Armstrong, 59–72. Grand Rapids: Zondervan, 2007.

Rahner, Karl. *Theological Investigations*, vol. 5. New York: Crossroad, 1966.

———. *The Trinity*. New York: Seabury Press, 1974.

Rashdall, Hastings. *The Idea of Atonement in Christian Theology*. London: Macmillan, 1920.

Reichenbach, Bruce. "God Limits His Power." In *Predestination and Free Will: Four Views of Divine Sovereignty and Human Freedom*, edited by David Basinger and Randall Basinger, 99–124. Downers Grove, IL: InterVarsity Press, 1986.

Reisinger, Ernest C. *Lord and Christ: The Implications of Lordship for Faith and Life*. Phillipsburg, NJ: Presbyterian and Reformed, 1994.

Reymond, Robert L. *A New Systematic Theology of the Christian Faith*, 2nd ed. Nashville: Thomas Nelson, 1998.

Ridderbos, Herman N. *Paul: An Outline of His Theology*. Translated by John Richard De Witt. Grand Rapids: Eerdmans, 1975.

Robertson, O. Palmer. *The Christ of the Covenants*. Phillipsburg, NJ: Presbyterian and Reformed, 1980.

Robinson, John A. T. *In the End, God...: A Study of the Christian Doctrine of the Last Things*. London: James Clarke, 1950.

Ryrie, Charles C. *Basic Theology: A Popular Systematic Guide to Understanding Biblical Truth*. Chicago: Moody, 1999.

———. *Dispensationalism*, revised and expanded. Chicago: Moody, 1995.

———. *So Great Salvation: What It Means to Believe in Jesus Christ*. Chicago: Moody Press, 1997.

Sailhamer, John H. "Genesis." In *The Expositor's Bible Commentary*, vol. 2, edited by Frank E. Gaebelein, 1–284. Grand Rapids: Zondervan, 1990.

Sanders, E. P. *Paul and Palestinian Judaism: A Comparison of Patterns of Religion*. Minneapolis: Fortress Press, 1977.

Sanders, John. "Inclusivism." In *What About Those Who Have Never Heard?: Three Views on the Destiny of the Unevangelized*, edited by John Sanders, 21–55. Downers Grove, IL: InterVarsity Press, 1995.

———. *No Other Name: An Investigation into the Destiny of the Unevangelized*. Eugene, OR: Wipf and Stock, 2001.

Saucy, Robert L. *The Case for Progressive Dispensationalism: The Interface Between Dispensational and Non-Dispensational Theology*. Grand Rapids: Zondervan, 1993.

———. *The Church in God's Program*. Chicago: Moody, 1972.

———. "Israel and the Church: A Case for Discontinuity." In *Continuity and Discontinuity: Perspectives on the Relationship Between the Old and New Testaments*, edited by John S. Feinberg, 239–259. Westchester, IL: Crossway, 1988.

———. "An Open But Cautious View." In *Are Miraculous Gifts for Today? Four Views*, edited by Wayne A. Grudem, 95–148. Grand Rapids: Zondervan, 1996.

Scacewater, Todd. "Galatians 2:11–21 and the Interpretive Context of 'Works of the Law.'" *Journal of the Evangelical Theological Society* 56/2 (June 2013) 307–323.

Scaer, David P. "Lutheran View: Finding the Right Word." In *Understanding Four Views on the Lord's Supper*, edited by John H. Armstrong, 87–101. Grand Rapids: Zondervan, 2007.

Schaefer, Glenn E. "Love." In *Evangelical Dictionary of Biblical Theology*, edited by Walter A. Elwell, 494–495. Grand Rapids: Baker, 1996.

Schleiermacher, Friedrich. *The Christian Faith*, edited by H. R. Mackintosh and J. S. Stewart. London: T & T Clark, 1999.

Schnabel, Eckhard. *40 Questions About the End Times*. Grand Rapids: Kregel, 2011.

Schreiner, Thomas R. "The Commands of God." In *Central Themes in Biblical Theology: Mapping Unity in Diversity,* edited by Scott J. Hafemann and Paul R. House, 66–101. Grand Rapids: Baker, 2007.

———. "Does Romans 9 Teach Individual Election Unto Salvation?" In *The Grace of God, The Bondage of the Will,* vol. 1, edited by Thomas R. Schreiner and Bruce A. Ware, 89–106. Grand Rapids: Baker, 1995.

———. *40 Questions About Christians and Biblical Law.* Grand Rapids: Kregel, 2010.

———. *The King in His Beauty: A Biblical Theology of the Old and New Testaments.* Grand Rapids: Baker, 2013.

———. *New Testament Theology: Magnifying God in Christ.* Grand Rapids: Baker, 2008.

———. "Penal Substitution View." In *The Nature of the Atonement: Four Views,* edited by James Beilby and Paul R. Eddy, 67–98. Downers Grove, IL: InterVarsity Press, 2006.

———. *Romans.* Baker Exegetical Commentary on the New Testament. Grand Rapids: Baker, 1998.

———. *Run to Win the Prize: Perseverance in the New Testament.* Wheaton, IL: Crossway, 2010.

Schreiner, Thomas R., and Ardel B. Caneday. *The Race Set Before Us: A Biblical Theology of Perseverance and Assurance.* Downers Grove, IL: InterVarsity Press, 2001.

Schweitzer, Albert. *The Mysticism of Paul the Apostle.* London: A. & C. Black, 1931.

———. *The Quest of the Historical Jesus: A Critical Study of Its Progress from Reimarus to Wrede.* New York: Macmillan, 1964.

*Scofield Reference Bible.* New York: Oxford, 1909.

Seifrid, Mark A. *Christ, our Righteousness: Paul's Theology of Justification.* Downers Grove, IL: InterVarsity Press, 2000.

———. "Righteousness, Justice and Justification." In *New Dictionary of Biblical Theology,* edited by T. Desmond Alexander and Brian S. Rosner, 740–745. Downers Grove, IL: InterVarsity Press, 2000.

———. "Romans 7: The Voice of the Law, the Cry of Lament, and the Shout of Thanksgiving." In *Perspectives on Our Struggle with Sin: Three Views on Romans 7,* edited Terry L. Wilder, 111–165. Nashville: Broadman and Holman, 2011.

Shank, Robert. *Life in the Son: A Study of the Doctrine of Perseverance.* Bloomington, MN: Bethany House, 1989.

Shedd, W. G. T. *Dogmatic Theology.* 3rd ed, edited by Alan W. Gomes. Phillipsburg, NJ: Presbyterian and Reformed, 2003.

Shepherd, Norman. *The Call of Grace: How the Covenant Illuminates Salvation and Evangelism.* Phillipsburg, NJ: Presbyterian and Reformed, 2000.

Sherlock, Charles. *The Doctrine of Humanity.* Downers Grove, IL: InterVarsity, 1996.

Showers, Renald E. *There Really is a Difference!: A Comparison of Covenant and Dispensational Theology.* Bellmawr, NJ: The Friends of Israel Gospel Ministry, 1990.

Silva, Moisés. *Interpreting Galatians: Explorations in Exegetical Method.* 2nd ed. Grand Rapids: Baker, 2001.

Smalley, Stephen S. *1, 2, 3 John.* Word Biblical Commentary, revised edition. Nashville: Thomas Nelson, 2007.

Smart, Ninian, and Steven Konstantine. *Christian Systematic Theology in a World Context.* Minneapolis: Fortress, 1991.

Smith, Morton H. *Systematic Theology.* 2 volumes. Greenville, SC: Greenville Seminary Press, 1994.

Smith, S. M. "Kenosis, Kenotic Theology." In *Evangelical Dictionary of Theology*, edited by Walter A. Elwell, 600–602. Grand Rapids: Baker, 1984.

Snaith, Norman. "The Image of God." *Expository Times* 86/1 (October 1974) 24.

Spong, John. *A New Christianity for the New World: Why Traditional Faith is Dying and How A New Faith is Being Born*. New York: HarperCollins, 2001.

Sprinkle, Joe M. "Law." In *Evangelical Dictionary of Biblical Theology*, edited by Walter A. Elwell, 467–471. Grand Rapids: Baker, 1996.

Stählin, Gustav. "ἁμαρτάνω." In *Theological Dictionary of the New Testament*, vol. 1, edited by Gerhard Kittel, translated by Geoffrey W. Bromiley, 267–316. Grand Rapids: Eerdmans, 1964.

Stanley, Charles. *Eternal Security: Can You Be Sure?* Nashville: Thomas Nelson, 1990.

Stein, Robert H. *A Basic Guide to Interpreting the Bible: Playing by the Rules*. Grand Rapids: Baker, 1994.

Stott, John R. W. *Basic Christianity*. 3rd ed. Grand Rapids: Eerdmans, 2008.

———. *The Cross of Christ*. Downers Grove, IL: InterVarsity Press, 1986.

———. *The Letters of John*. Tyndale New Testament Commentaries. Grand Rapids: Eerdmans, 1988.

Strimple, Robert B. "Amillennialism." In *Three Views on the Millennium and Beyond*, edited by Darrell L. Bock, 81–129. Grand Rapids: Zondervan, 1999.

Strong, Augustus H. *Systematic Theology*. Valley Forge, PA: Judson Press, 1907.

Sungenis, Robert A. *Not by Faith Alone: A Biblical Evidence for the Catholic Doctrine of Justification*. Goleta, CA: Queenship, 1997.

Swartz, Herbert L. "Faith." In *Evangelical Dictionary of Biblical Theology*, edited by Walter A. Elwell, 236–239. Grand Rapids: Baker, 1996.

Taylor, L. Roy. "Presbyterianism." In *Who Runs the Church? Four Views on Church Government*, edited by Steven B. Cowan, 73–98. Grand Rapids: Zondervan, 2004.

Taylor, S. S. "Faith, Faithfulness." In *New Dictionary of Biblical Theology*, edited by T. Desmond Alexander and Brian S. Rosner, 487–493. Downers Grove, IL: InterVarsity Press, 2000.

Tenney, Merrill C. "The Gospel of John." In *The Expositor's Bible Commentary*, vol. 9, edited by Frank E. Gaebelein, 1–203. Grand Rapids: Zondervan, 1981.

Thiessen, Henry Clarence. *Lectures in Systematic Theology*. Revised by Vernon D. Doerksen. Grand Rapids: Eerdmans, 1979.

Thomas Aquinas. *Summa Theologica*. Translated by Fathers of the English Dominican Province. Notre Dame, IN: Christian Classics, 1981.

Thomas, Robert L. "1 Thessalonians." In *The Expositor's Bible Commentary*, vol. 11, edited by Frank E. Gaebelein, 227–298. Grand Rapids: Zondervan, 1978.

———. *Revelation 1–7: An Exegetical Commentary*. Chicago: Moody, 1992.

———. *Revelation 8–22: An Exegetical Commentary*. Chicago: Moody, 1995.

Thorsen, Don. *The Wesleyan Quadrilateral*. Lexington, KY: Emeth Press, 2005.

Tidball, D. J. "Church." In *New Dictionary of Biblical Theology*, edited by T. Desmond Alexander and Brian S. Rosner, 407–411. Downers Grove, IL: InterVarsity Press, 2000.

Tiessen, Terrance. *Providence and Prayer*. Downers Grove, IL: InterVarsity Press, 2000.

Till, Howard J. Van. "The Fully Gifted Creation ('Theistic Evolution')." In *Three Views on Creation and Evolution*, edited by J. P. Moreland and John Mark Reynolds, 159–218. Grand Rapids: Zondervan, 1999.

Tillich, Paul. *Systematic Theology*, vol. 3. Chicago: University of Chicago Press, 1963.

Toon, Peter. "Episcopalianism." In *Who Runs the Church? Four Views on Church Government,* edited Steven B. Cowan, 21–41. Grand Rapids: Zondervan, 2004.

Trench, Richard C. *Synonyms of the New Testament.* 9th ed. Grand Rapids: Eerdmans, 1953.

Turretin, Francis. *Institutes of Elenctic Theology.* 3 volumes, edited by James T. Dennison, translated by George Musgrave Giger. Phillipsburg, NJ: Presbyterian and Reformed, 1992–1997.

Vaughan, Curtis. "Colossians." In *The Expositor's Bible Commentary,* vol. 11, edited by Frank E. Gaebelein, 161–226. Grand Rapids: Zondervan, 1978.

Venema, Cornelis P. *Accepted and Renewed in Christ: The "Twofold Grace of God" and the Interpretation of Calvin's Theology.* Göttingen: Vandenhoeck and Ruprecht, 2007.

Wallace, Daniel B. *Greek Grammar Beyond the Basics: An Exegetical Syntax of the New Testament.* Grand Rapids: Zondervan, 1996.

Walvoord, John F. *The Holy Spirit: A Comprehensive Study on the Person and Work of the Holy Spirit.* Grand Rapids: Zondervan, 1965.

———. "The Literal View." In *Four Views on Hell,* edited by William Crockett, 9–28. Grand Rapids: Zondervan, 1996.

Ware, Bruce A. "Divine Election to Salvation: Unconditional, Individual, and Infralapsarian." In *Perspectives on Election: Five Views,* edited by Chad Owen Brand, 1–58. Nashville: Broadman and Holman, 2006.

———. *Father, Son, and the Holy Spirit: Relationships, Roles, and Relevance.* Wheaton, IL: Crossway, 2005.

Warfield, B. B. *Counterfeit Miracles.* New York: Charles Scribners, 1918.

———. "Trinity." In *The International Standard Bible Encyclopaedia,* vol. 5, edited by James Orr, 3012–3022. Grand Rapids: Eerdmans, 1930.

Watson, Thomas. *A Body of Divinity.* Edinburgh: Banner of Truth, 1890.

Weaver, J. Denny. *The Nonviolent Atonement.* Grand Rapids: Eerdmans, 2001.

Weber, Otto. *Foundations of Dogmatics.* 2 volumes, translated by Darrell L. Guder. Grand Rapids: Eerdmans, 1981–1983.

Welch, Edward T. *Blame It On The Brain?: Distinguishing Chemical Imbalances, Brain Disorders, and Disobedience.* Phillipsburg, NJ: Presbyterian and Reformed, 1998.

Wellum, Stephen J. "Baptism and the Relationship between the Covenants." In *Believer's Baptism: Sign of the New Covenant in Christ,* edited by Thomas R. Schreiner and Shawn D. Wright, 97–161. Nashville: Broadman and Holman, 2006.

Wenham, Gordon J. *Genesis 1–15,* vol. 1. Word Biblical Commentary. Nashville: Word, 1987.

Whisenant, Edgar C. *88 Reasons Why the Rapture is in 1988.* Nashville: World Bible Society, 1988.

White, R. E. O. "Baptize, Baptism." In *Evangelical Dictionary of Biblical Theology,* edited by Walter A. Elwell, 50–53. Grand Rapids: Baker, 1996.

Wiley, H. Orton. *Christian Theology.* 3 volumes. Kansas City, MO: Beacon Hill, 1952.

Williams, J. Rodman. *Renewal Theology: Systematic Theology from a Charismatic Perspective.* 3 volumes. Grand Rapids: Zondervan, 1988–1992.

Wood, Laurence W. "The Wesleyan View." In *Christian Spirituality: Five Views of Sanctification,* edited by Donald L. Alexander, 95–118. Downers Grove, IL: InterVarsity Press, 1988

Wright, N. T. *The Climax of the Covenant: Christ and the Law in Pauline Theology.* Minneapolis: Fortress, 1992.

———. *Justification: God's Plan and Paul's Vision.* Downers Grove, IL: InterVarsity Press, 2009.

———. "The Law in Romans 2." In *Paul and the Mosaic Law,* edited by James D. G. Dunn, 131–150. Grand Rapids: Eerdmans, 2001.

———. *What Saint Paul Really Said: Was Paul of Tarsus the Real Founder of Christianity?* Grand Rapids: Eerdmans, 1997.

Youngblood, Ronald F. "1, 2 Samuel." In *The Expositor's Bible Commentary,* vol. 3, edited by Frank E. Gaebelein, 551–1104. Grand Rapids: Zondervan, 1992.

Zaspel, Fred G. *The Theology of B. B. Warfield: A Systematic Summary.* Wheaton, IL: Crossway, 2010.

# Index of Names

# Index of Scripture

## Romans

## 1 Corinthians

## Deuterocanonical Works

### 2 Maccabees

# Index of Subjects